GERMAN BOY

GERMAN BOY

A Refugee's Story

WOLFGANG W. E. SAMUEL

With a foreword by

Stephen E. Ambrose

University Press of Mississippi
Jackson

Willie Morris Books in Memoir and Biography

www.upress.state.ms.us

08 07 06 05 04 03 02 01 00   4 3 2 1
∞
Library of Congress Cataloging-in-Publication Data
Samuel, Wolfgang W. E.
German boy : a refugee's story / Wolfgang W. E.
Samuel ; with a foreword by Stephen E. Ambrose.
p.   cm. (Willie Morris books in memoir and
biography)
ISBN 1-57806-274-8 (alk. paper)
1. Samuel, Wolfgang W. E.—Childhood and
youth.   2. World War, 1939–1945—
Germany.   3. World War, 1939–1945—
Refugees.   4. Germany (East)—Social
conditions.   I. Title.
D811.5 .S2478   2000
940.54'8143'092—dc21
00-024662

British Library Cataloging-in-Publication
Data available

In memory of Hedy

CONTENTS

Maps

FOREWORD

In early June 1998, the National Archives in Washington hosted a one-day conference on the fiftieth anniversary of the Berlin airlift, with speakers ranging from elderly men who had been in the Truman administration to young scholars just beginning their careers. The high point came at the end of the day, when eight men gathered on the podium. Seven of them had been pilots, the men who took the cargo planes into and out of Berlin on a three-minute basis, day and night, for over a year. The eighth man was listed as retired U.S. Air Force Colonel Wolfgang Samuel, but he looked to be ten years younger than the other men and surely could not have been a pilot in 1948. Each pilot spoke, telling stories that were funny, sad, and gripping, stories that left you weak with admiration.

Finally it was Colonel Samuel's turn. He told us that at the time he had been a thirteen-year-old boy living near the Fassberg airfield, which was one of four bases used by the U.S. Air Force in the airlift. He had watched the planes take off and land on an assembly-line basis (it was one of the greatest feats of flying history). He spoke of how his mother had traded her body for food for her children; when the Americans came, she didn't have to do that anymore, and young Wolfgang and his sister had enough to eat for the first time in years. He told us that he had come to the States in 1951, had attended college, and then had joined the air force. He looked down the row of pilots with him on the podium, and said with the greatest admiration, "You guys were my heroes. I wanted to be like you when I grew up." Colonel

Samuel told this brief story with such simplicity of language and openness of spirit that the entire audience was in tears.

I sought him out at the reception at the German embassy that evening and asked for more. When he said that he had written a memoir, I asked if I could take a look. He sent it on. I was not impressed by the title or by the table of contents, which revealed that this autobiography was going to cover only the period of January 1945 to January 1951, from Samuel's tenth birthday to his fifteenth. That didn't seem to me a very interesting part of someone's life, and surely, I thought, could not be worth over five hundred single-spaced pages (the size of the original manuscript). Still, I wanted to know more about the airlift and Samuel's unusual perspective on it, so I took the manuscript along on my next plane ride. Once I started reading, I couldn't stop. I read in the cab going to the hotel. I read in my hotel room until it was time for the dinner and speech. I read when I got back to my room, at breakfast the next morning, in the cab going back to the airport, at the airport, during the flight, and when I got home. I read the whole thing in less than a day, and I'm writing this the following morning indulging the full flush of my enthusiasm because I can think of no reason to restrain it.

A number of remarkable elements are woven into the fabric of this auto-biography. Most notable is Wolfgang's honesty about what he saw, said, felt, and thought. He is an attractive, sympathetic, and active character, full of determination and grit, with big eyes, a wonderful imagination, and a fun-loving spirit. A boy's boy. But he lived in the most awful poverty, almost never adequately fed or sheltered, owning one shirt, one pair of pants, and wooden shoes. And not only was he poor and hungry; he was also being bombed at night and shelled during the day. He was a refugee caught up in one of the biggest and bloodiest mass migrations in history, the flight of the German people from the Red Army. The year 1945 was the worst in the world's history. That year Wolfgang turned ten, and he was at the epicenter of the catastrophe. His story begins just before his birthday in early February 1945, and recounts the stages in his family's journey, beginning with the flight from eastern Germany, near Dresden, to Berlin, by train. For a few weeks that March, Wolfgang lived in Berlin, where he made four and more trips each night to the air-raid shelter. Then his family went on farther west, traveling by horse-drawn wagon in a convoy of German soldiers, described in scenes that are reminiscent of Napoleon retreating from Moscow.

At the center of this story about a German boy is his mother, a woman of strength, character, and wit. She is remarkable in so many ways. Having grown up a poor farm girl, she has moved up in life and has married an officer. When we meet her, she is depicted as someone who loves to party and is uninterested in politics or the progress of the war or in anything serious. She is a good mother, although she does at times exhibit a bad temper and can be physically cruel in punishing Wolfgang. Her husband, who has flaunted his disloyalty in her face and whom she intends to divorce when the war ends, is away in the Luftwaffe. This young woman of thirty had to take the responsibility of holding the family (including grandparents) together while escaping the Russians. That she did it is astonishing; how she did it is mesmerizing.

The story of a mother and her son may be in some ways familiar territory, but this voyage is unique. After leaving Berlin because of the incessant bombing, they joined a refugee column headed west, but they didn't get far enough and were sealed in on the Soviet side of the zonal boundaries. The view through an eleven-year-old boy's eyes of the general tightening of Communist control over East Germany in 1945–46 is fascinating and instructive. Wolfgang was hungry to learn, and the author is especially good in recounting how the Communists set up the school system and how bad it was. In a harrowing escape, including crossing the border on foot in the midst of a severe snowstorm, the family reached Fassberg, in the British zone, where they lived as refugees. Eventually Wolfgang's mother married a U.S. Air Force sergeant, and he lived in the American zone. He tells us in each case how the system looked to a boy—what it was like to be growing up under Russian rule, British rule, and American rule. He also relates, in vivid detail, what the Berlin airlift was like from his point of view.

I think *German Boy* has all the qualities of greatness, including a strong narrative, the depiction of high drama in ordinary people's lives, memorable characters—some of whom are evil and some of whom perform extraordinary acts of kindness—and two strong-willed and courageous central figures, mother and son, caught up in a cataclysm but enduring, surviving, prevailing. I love the book.

Stephen E. Ambrose

PREFACE AND ACKNOWLEDGMENTS

I wanted to write this story for many years, but either the demands of my adult life interfered or, more likely, I simply wasn't ready to recall events I had covered up so well for such a long time. With the deaths of my mother and father, however, I came to a time in my life when I felt I should face up to what I had tried to forget. Acknowledging an obligation to my children, I elected to pass on this story of lives lived in time of war and lives terminated too soon. I also felt an obligation to those who suffered and died before my eyes. They have traveled with me through life as ever-present companions—innocent women and children whose lives were wasted by an evil empire.

German Boy records events I experienced as a young boy in Germany at the conclusion of World War II and in the years immediately thereafter. It is the story of the German tragedy as seen through the eyes of a boy who, in the years that followed the destruction of the Nazi regime, was forced to come to grips with a world that continued to reward all that is ignoble in man. This is a story about people living under extreme circumstances, about women and children and the horrible consequences war visited upon them. Over time, I was able to gain understanding and perspective enabling me to comprehend the sacrifices my own mother had to make to save the lives of her two children. So this is her story, too, and telling it is my way of acknowledging my eternal debt to her.

In recalling the darkness and despair of those years, I remember quite clearly flickers of light—acts of compassion and kindness offered by strangers and by friends, sometimes at the risk of their own freedom, even their lives. Although kindness and compassion were not widespread in the Germany of the 1940s, they nevertheless continued to exist in the hearts of some in spite of unyielding pressures to the contrary; some selfless people chose to listen to their hearts rather than closing their eyes and turning their heads. Without their help, my family would have perished along with all the others. And so it is their story as well.

I have been asked how I could remember details, including conversations, with such vividness and exactitude. The answer is simple. I carried these pictures of life and death in the vault of my memory, unchanged by time, until I was ready to write them down. For much of my life I tried to forget what I had seen, smelled, felt, and heard in those days of horror. Once I sat down and started to write, it was as if I were stepping back in time and reliving it all. I was there again. The pain was real. The smells came back, and were at times overpowering. The pictures in my mind's eye were vivid and clear, the conversations true and urgent; everything tumbled out as if it were on videotape. The dialogue, of course, was frequently much more extensive at the time it took place than what is recorded here, and it is impossible to replay exactly words spoken such a long time ago. However, the essential nature of each conversation is true and accurate.

Today, I have mostly come to terms with the past, although I can't forget what happened. In writing this story, I struggled with the difficulties of recreating those days of death and chaos, of lost hopes and shattered innocence. It is, after all, so much easier to forget what was and to cover it up with the fullness of the present. As the Danish philosopher Søren Kierkegaard said, "It is perfectly true, as philosophers say, that life must be understood backward. But they forget the other proposition, that it must be lived forward." *German Boy* is the story of one man who chose to look backward in the hope of providing a small stepping-stone in our never-ending human struggle to live forward.

I thank Charles and Shelley, my children, for their gentle prodding to get me to sit down and write this story; Joan, my dear wife, friend, and confidant, for her unflagging support; Craig Gill, my editor, for his thoughtful guidance and direction; and Stephen Ambrose, without whose encouragement and enthusiasm this story would probably never have been published. Finally, I thank my country, the United States of America, for the opportunities it provided to an immigrant boy who expected so little and received so much.

Wolfgang W. E. Samuel
Colonel, U.S. Air Force (Retired)
Fairfax Station, Virginia

GERMAN BOY

Chapter 1

JANUARY **1945**

I ran across the plowed field instead of following the smooth dirt path along the Bober River. I was afraid that someone might be lurking in the dense, dark bushes lining the steep riverbank. Besides, running across the field would get me home more quickly. My hands were stiff and hurting from the unrelenting winter cold. I wasn't sure, though, if I would feel any more secure once I got home. I knew the Russians would arrive any day now. Maybe we would just wait for them. I was more afraid of the Russians than of anyone hiding in the bushes along the river.

It was nearly the end of January and next week would be my tenth birthday. Yesterday, I couldn't wait for that important day to arrive. Tonight, it didn't seem to matter much anymore. "I'm nine years old, almost ten," I chanted loudly as I leapt across the field from one frozen clod of earth to the next. "I'm almost grown up." My voice sounded croaky and brittle. I knew how to skip across a plowed field without falling. I had done it many times on my way home from school, skipping from the top of one clod to another. But never at night. The field was dusted with a fresh coat of snow, which, along with the intermittent moonlight, helped to outline the frozen rows of sod plowed in perfectly straight lines by a Russian prisoner of war working for the farmer down the road.

The moon, although frequently obscured by rapidly scudding clouds, provided a cold, bright, bluish light which allowed me to clearly see my surroundings. When the clouds opened up and the moon shone through, its light illuminated the landscape out to the far horizon. The night had an eerie, fairy-tale quality about it, of hidden beauty and mystery laced with my own fears. I felt as if I were caught in one of Grimm's fairy tales; only the witch and her *Pfefferkuchen* house were missing. But the night was real, I was scared, and I was getting colder every minute. I stumbled on a clod of dirt and nearly fell. I recovered and continued my run across the field. There was little wind, but a chill ran through my body, nearly throwing me off balance. I should have dressed more warmly and taken my gloves when I left home earlier in the evening.

I forced myself to think of something other than the bitter cold. I thought about what I had read in the newspaper, about what happened to German women when they were captured by Russian soldiers. Awful things. I didn't know what rape was, but it had to be terrible the way they wrote about it in the newspaper and spoke of it on the radio. I didn't want my mother to be raped. She was all I had to hold on to, besides Ingrid, my sister. I felt a dull ache rise within me, as if a cold hand were squeezing my insides. Maybe I was hungry. That had to be it. It was my empty stomach that gave me that odd feeling. I couldn't remember when I had last eaten. Maybe it wasn't hunger I felt. Maybe I was afraid of dying.

I stumbled again, and fell flat on my stomach. I was trying to concentrate on my running, but I was so cold. I got up quickly, brushing off the snow and dirt. I had hurt my left knee and scraped my hands. There was some blood. I started running again, this time focusing intently on each step I took.

I had mixed feelings about death. Death had seemed noble when I read about it in my father's old poetry books and in fairy tales. Last summer though, when the fathers of many of my friends died in faraway places, death became real. It wasn't noble anymore. I was afraid for my mother, my sister, and myself. I didn't know where my father was, or whether he was still alive. He was somewhere in Holland or France, I thought, with the Luftwaffe. No one else in my family lived anywhere near us. I finally reached the highway, the Naumburger Chaussee. I felt better after crossing the field, away from the river and its dark bushes. I never was afraid to walk that way during the day. Then why was I scared to walk there in the dark?

Of course, there were the prisoners who had escaped from Stalag Luft III, the prisoner-of-war camp at the Sagan *Flugplatz*. I had heard the adults talking about a great escape from the camp the previous March. The next day several Hitler Youths came and got me and my friends to help them search for the escaped prisoners. The prisoners were English and American airmen whose airplanes had been shot down in raids over Germany. I didn't know if anyone had ever found them or if they were still hiding nearby. The Hitler Youths made us play war in the bushes by the river, rushing us in groups from one clump of bushes to the next, while we were supposed to be looking. My friends and I didn't want to find any of those men, and we didn't.

I continued walking briskly east along the Naumburger Chaussee. I slapped my arms around my body trying to warm myself, and I blew into my stiff hands. It didn't help. My fingers would barely bend. I started to run again. I wore my coveted Hitler Youth trousers, which Mutti had been able to buy for me by telling the saleswoman that I had been accepted into the *Jungvolk* early. I desperately needed long trousers for the winter, so Mutti lied a little about my age, and the saleswoman chose to believe her. I tied the trousers just above my ankles to make them blouse out. Wearing the trousers would be a sure sign to my friends that I was older, which I very much wanted to be. But as much as I liked my new trousers, they were too thin to protect me from the night's bitter cold. No traffic moved on the road. No one was walking, driving a horse-drawn sleigh, or riding a bicycle. I was alone. My teeth began to chatter uncontrollably.

Earlier in the evening my mother had asked me to walk her friend, a wounded army lieutenant, to the train station. She had met him at an army hospital where she entertained wounded soldiers by tap dancing for them. The lieutenant hardly spoke a word as we walked to the station. Why should he? I was just a boy. But I knew the shortest way to the station; that's why I was showing him. The lieutenant had come early that afternoon. It was the first time I had met him. He sat beside my mother on the couch in the living room, and I caught a few words of their conversation. He spoke of Russian tanks being dangerously close to Sagan and tried to convince her to take Ingrid and me and leave Sagan right away. "You should leave today," he said to her. "My parents in Berlin will be happy to have you stay with them." The tone of his voice was urgent.

"It can't be as bad as you say," Mutti replied with a nervous laugh. "When and if the time comes, we will be notified by the authorities and they will evacuate us. I will wait and see what happens."

"Hedy, the official authorization to evacuate Sagan will be given too late.

5

Those orders are always given too late, because the Führer doesn't want to admit we are losing, that it's all over. When the evacuation orders are finally issued, few people will be able to get out. You and the children must go now! It's your only chance, Hedy. I know what I'm talking about. Listen to me, please!" It hadn't been enough to change her mind.

What was Mutti waiting for? Unless she listened to someone soon, it would be too late. But my mother didn't listen to anyone, least of all me. She was headstrong and could be stubborn. I felt so afraid of the future. I didn't like feeling helpless, being little, being tied to a mother who didn't want to understand what was happening around her. I was impatient to grow up, to make decisions for myself, not to be trapped in my nine-year-old body. My mother lived in her fantasy world, refusing to read the newspaper or listen to the radio. All my mother ever seemed to care about were her parties and tap dancing for the wounded soldiers.

On the way to the train station, the lieutenant had walked like a soldier, I thought, fast, with long, deliberate strides. He was lean and tall, his cheeks hollow, and his skin appeared grey, as if he had known pain or hunger, or both. I had a hard time staying ahead of him, which is where I thought I should be since I was the guide. His grey army uniform looked new and fit him well. He wore no overcoat, just his tunic, with a wide, black leather belt around his waist and a pistol strapped to the belt under his left arm. Probably a Luger, its holster was so large. My father had a pistol just like it. The lieutenant wore an oval, silver badge on the left breast pocket of his tunic—the *Verwundetenabzeichen*. The badge depicted a steel helmet over crossed swords rimmed with oak leaves. I knew what that badge meant; he had been wounded in combat, badly wounded. In one of the buttonholes of his tunic, he wore the ribbon for the Iron Cross second class, and another Iron Cross was pinned above the silver *Verwundetenabzeichen*, the Iron Cross first class. He wore still another badge on his tunic's breast pocket, but I couldn't make it out, and I didn't want to stare or ask him about it. The silver epaulets on his shoulders glistened when the moonlight reflected off them. He wore a simple ski cap, like those worn by common soldiers, and his boots were of sturdy leather, laced high, with leggings around his ankles. His bloused pants were tucked into his leggings. I really liked how he looked.

We passed a group of marching and singing Hitler Youths. It seemed strange for them to be out on a cold, bleak evening like this. Didn't they know that the Russians were nearly here with us in Sagan? I didn't know how the war had started, but for as long as I could remember people had been dying and airplanes crashing. There were fewer and fewer men in the streets every year. Many of my friends' fathers were dead or missing, mostly in Russia. In the newspaper they always called it a *Heldentod*, a hero's death, when a soldier was killed. He had fallen for the Führer and the *Vaterland*, the papers said. I knew that they were just dead, no matter what they called it, just dead. Only last week one of my friends began to cry right in the middle of a game we were playing and ran home. I knew why he cried. The war was not good, and now it was coming to an end. It seemed to me that the whole world was the enemy of my country and that they wanted to kill us all. Even us children. Why? I am a German boy. I am not bad.

As we neared the train station, we saw more people walking, their heads bowed. They didn't want to be seen, and they didn't want to see anyone else. Grey, colorless people without faces. They looked cold and afraid. The train station was of solid nineteenth-century brick construction with grey stucco walls blackened from the soot of countless passing trains. On the sidewall facing us in black block letters on a white background was written *Räder rollen für den Sieg*—"wheels turn for victory." I repeated the thought to myself, trying to understand it.

The lieutenant stopped and turned to face me. He removed the grey leather glove from his right hand to shake mine. His hand felt warm and strong. "Thank you for taking me this far, Wolfgang," he said firmly. "I am grateful that you walked all this way to the train station with me on such a cold night. I must see if I can find my train now. You run home as fast as you can, and stop for no one." He let go of my hand.

"I promise I will go straight home," I replied. He turned toward the station, saluting me as he went. On the way home I was startled to see two antitank guns near the bridge across the Bober River where we had crossed earlier. I was sure the guns had not been there on our way to the station. I knew these guns from pictures—88s. The guns had their long, white barrels pointed at the bridge in case a Russian T-34 tank should suddenly come thundering across. I knew why the 88s were there. When I listened to the news on the radio, the announcer frequently spoke of *Panzer Spitzen* penetrating German lines. I figured out that this meant that Russian T-34 tanks had broken through and were driving around behind our lines, causing panic and destruction. The lieutenant was right—we should leave Sagan as quickly as possible. The soldiers near the guns looked relaxed. Some smoked cigarettes. Maybe that was the way soldiers looked. It was their job to destroy tanks, or be killed by them. While I didn't like that thought, it didn't seem to bother the soldiers. One soldier patrolled beside the guns with a rifle slung over his shoulder. His thick winter jacket and helmet were white, too. He had a grey woolen scarf wrapped across his mouth to keep out the cold, and the hood of his jacket was partially pulled over his white helmet. Was he even a little afraid? I wondered.

I finally reached Nord Strasse. Our apartment house, number three, was two minutes further down the road. Nord Strasse was short and ended in an open field. They never finished paving the street after the war began in September 1939. The workmen were there one day, and then they never returned. I often played in the sandpile and among the granite paving stones the men left behind. My frozen fingers bent with great difficulty. I barely got the key out from under the doormat. I couldn't get it into the lock. The key fell out of my hand as I fumbled around. I rang the doorbell and the *Flüchtling* (refugee) woman who lived with us let me in. I ran past her down the corridor into the living room and threw myself on the white fur rug, putting my hands between my thighs for warmth. My hands hurt so badly that I wanted to scream, but I couldn't. The refugee family was in my room next door, and they would hear me if I cried. I felt tears running down my cheeks, into my mouth. I bit into the fur as the pain tore at my hands. When the refugee woman had opened the door for me, she held a not-yet two-year-old girl in her arms; a boy of four stood by her side. She looked happy. She must have felt safe. "Do you mind that we are using your room?" she asked as I ran past her.

"No, of course not," I replied hastily, but I did mind a little bit. Then I was ashamed for being selfish. Why should I mind? They had come from the east, somewhere near Königsberg, and this was their second stop since they had first been evacuated last October. A woman who identified herself to Mutti as a member of an organization responsible for the housing and feeding of Flüchtlinge from the east had brought the family by and told her that they would be staying with us until they were sent farther west. The woman didn't say when that would be.

My hands warmed up, and the tears stopped running. My teeth stopped chattering, too. I lay still on the fur, enjoying the absence of pain. I had frozen my hands many times before when I had snowball fights with my friends and my gloves got wet and I didn't stop in time. This time it had been much worse. As I got off the fur, I realized that Mutti and Ingrid were not home. They were probably with Frau Hennig. One of our downstairs neighbors, Frau Hennig had a daughter, Gudrun, sixteen. Ingrid liked Gudrun. Frau Hennig was pudgy and always had a smile on her face. Her husband was an engineer and worked on the Sagan *Flugplatz*. I liked Frau Hennig, but no more than I did other adults. Adults were all the same when it came to children. They bossed us around or acted like we didn't exist. Except for Oma (Grandmother) and Opa (Grandfather) Samuel, of course. They didn't boss me around. They loved me, and I could do anything I wanted to with them, or with Oma anyway. Sometimes I was mean to Oma, and I always felt guilty afterwards. I wondered if Oma and Opa Samuel were safe.

The impressions of the past hours stormed in on me all at once. I knew I had to talk to Mutti again, and try to persuade her to leave Sagan. I would tell her about the guns. Maybe that would convince her. The Russians would arrive soon, maybe even tonight. I knew the army didn't put up guns to protect bridges unless they thought something might happen. For once, I wished my father was with us.

I walked over to my father's desk and sat down in his comfortable chair. It was a beautiful mahogany desk. He was proud of it. The door on the right was locked. That's where he kept the books he didn't want me to read. I knew where the key was, though, and I opened the center drawer to take it out. I was surprised to see a broken record lying there. The halves lay in the middle of the drawer. I picked up the two pieces and held them together so that I could read the label. It was "Lilly Marlen," sung by Lale Andersen, the Swedish movie star with the deep voice, almost as deep as a man's. I loved the melody of that soldier's ballad. I had heard it many times on the radio and at parties Mutti gave. A soldier Mutti knew had come last year and given her the record. The record had broken in his rucksack, I remembered now, on his long train trip from France to Sagan. He wanted Mutti to have the record anyway, to let her know that he thought of her. I put the broken record back into the drawer.

As I sat behind my father's desk, tired, hungry, and beset by fears, I suddenly realized that this was the only home I had ever known and that soon I might have to leave it behind. My eyes fell upon the dark-green tile oven just inside the door. All of us prized its soothing warmth on a cold winter afternoon. Ingrid and I liked to stand up against its glazed sides, pressing our hands against the hot tiles. I loaded the oven with pressed brown-coal briquettes every morning, using the remaining embers from the night before to start the fire. After I cleaned and reloaded the oven, it became very hot by noon, warming the entire room comfortably. We kept the oven going until early evening, and around eight o'clock I added a last briquette to ensure that I had some hot embers remaining by morning. After that the oven slowly cooled until at dawn it was cold, as was the room. I was careful about how many bricks of coal I burned each day, because our coal ration had to last us through the winter.

To the left of the oven stood a large and comfortable couch, and beside it a table and a modern multifrequency radio. On Sundays I sneaked into the room and turned on the radio very low, pressing my ear against the speaker to listen to the news, to the commentary about the war, and to the half-hour fairy tale in the afternoon. In the early years of the war, there were always special announcements of military victories coming over the radio. Now, the commentary was mostly about the horrible things Russian soldiers did to women and children. The broadcaster also frequently mentioned American bombings and the churches and cultural treasures the Americans destroyed. I needed to ask my Opa Samuel about the meaning of "cultural treasures" when I saw him again. In recent months the radio announcer had frequently spoken of our forces straightening their front lines, especially on the eastern front. The front lines, though, were always moving back toward Germany.

An ornately carved mahogany dining table stood in the middle of the room. When Mutti had guests for dinner, she made me dress up in my sailor suit, or in a shirt and tie, which was even worse. Then I had to walk up to the table and stand behind my chair. I could sit only after I had asked for permission. I also had to eat properly with knife and fork. Table manners were important to Mutti, and I was never to say a word while I sat at the table. Sometimes I really wanted to say something, because I thought I knew more than the adults I listened to. After all, I read the newspaper and listened to the radio, too.

Next to the radio was a double window looking out over the countryside toward the east. We had double windows in our apartment to keep them from frosting up in the winter. From there I could see a weathered barn in a meadow. Along the ridge beyond the barn, I often saw Ju-52 trimotor transports flying low toward the north after having taken off from the Sagan *Flugplatz* just south of us. Sometimes I saw other planes, too, even Stukas, the famous single-engine dive bombers. When I saw a war movie about them, I decided I wanted to be a Stuka pilot when I grew up.

The walls of our living and dining room were decorated with two oil paintings. One was a still life of flowers, while the other was a mountain scene with a bull elk bellowing in the foreground by an open meadow. Two other hangings always intrigued me. One was a silver relief of a stag's head mounted on a black piece of wood. To me it really looked beautiful with its silver horns thrusting out into space. The other, smaller, relief was a profile of Adolf Hitler's head, also in silver. Opa and Oma Samuel had given the first relief to Mutti and my father as a wedding anniversary present. I thought maybe my father had bought the other one, because I know Opa Samuel never would have. Opa didn't like the Führer or the party. I remembered going to church with Opa Samuel on Christmas Eve when he suddenly came to visit us. Mutti and Ingrid didn't go with us because it was so cold. Opa chose a seat near a pillar upstairs in the church. The church was cold and we kept our coats on. When the pastor prayed for the Führer and the party, Opa grabbed my hand firmly, pulling me out of the pew. We left. I asked Opa, "Why?"

He replied, with anger in his voice, "That idiot pastor doesn't know what he is talking about, Wolfgang. His dear Führer is killing all of us, and he prays for him." Opa cursed at the pastor and at the Führer, but quickly apologized for doing so. Opa was rarely angry, and he never cursed. We walked the rest of the way home in silence. Opa had come hoping to persuade Mutti to accompany him to Schlawe, where he and Oma Samuel lived in their house near the beaches of the Baltic Sea. "The war will be over soon," he told her, "and you and the children will be safer with me. I may be old. I can still protect you and the children." She had laughed at Opa. He left the next day.

At times, when Mutti gave her parties, after I had helped clear the dinner dishes the guests would sit around the table talking of war and politics, smoking and drinking wine. The parties would last until early the next morning, when I always cleaned the room. The room then stank of cigarette smoke, and there were many wine glasses and empty bottles. I sampled one or another bottle at times, but wine never tasted good to me. At one party in 1943, one of the guests was a tall Luftwaffe colonel. I found him interesting because he wore a silver badge depicting a biplane on the left breast pocket of his tunic. I knew the badge meant he had been a pilot in the

Great War. Maybe he had flown with Richthofen, or Bölke, or Immelmann. I had read about those great German flyers in one of my father's books, and I was awed at the thought of being near someone who might have flown with those heroes of the air. I really wanted to ask the colonel what airplanes he had flown in the Great War and with whom, but I was never able to. I could listen, though. After dinner, when they drank wine and lit their cigarettes, the colonel talked about the war. "The war was lost," he said, "when that idiot Hitler declared war on the United States of America." Mutti and the other guests didn't want to believe what he was saying.

"We are winning the war," one of them said.

"No, we are not winning the war," the colonel replied. He leaned his head back and blew cigarette smoke toward the ceiling. "I've been to America," he said. "I know how big that land is and what it can do. For every airplane we build, they will build a hundred. They will utterly destroy Germany by the time this war is over." At the time, my father was home on military leave from Holland. I saw him nod his head in agreement with the colonel, but he said nothing. Then my mother closed the door, and I couldn't hear anymore. I never forgot that Luftwaffe colonel and what he said about the Americans and what they would do to Germany.

Across the hallway from the dining room was the kitchen, making it easy to serve dinner guests. Mutti had soon discovered my willingness to do things for her, and before I knew it I was washing and drying dishes. Initially, I liked doing dishes because it gave me responsibility for something new I could accomplish by myself. I wanted to help my mother, as well as to learn new things. I built myself a perfect trap. Mutti was all too willing to let me take over the kitchen work she didn't care to do. By now, most manual jobs around the house were mine. I didn't mind helping, but sometimes Mutti seemed to think she had an obligation to keep me working rather than letting me go play. At those times she took all the fun out of my helping her. I had some good times with Mutti in the kitchen, baking cookies; I also had some bad times. Once she tried to force me to eat oatmeal oversweetened with saccharin. She had added a generous portion of the pills to the oatmeal. Since she didn't like milk, she never tasted the oatmeal. I tried eating it. I couldn't. It made me gag.

"Eat that oatmeal," screamed Mutti. I tried again. It was so sickeningly sweet that I threw up. Mutti flew into a rage and went to the broom closet to get the rug beater. She first threatened to beat me if I didn't eat. Then she beat me across my back and over my head screaming, "Eat! Take that spoon and eat! Eat! Will you eat now!"

I turned to her in desperation, begging, "Please, Mutti, taste just a little and you'll know why I can't eat it. I don't want to make you angry. I love you, Mutti. Please, stop beating me—please." I thought she was going to kill me. Suddenly she stopped in midswing. She took my spoon and tasted the oatmeal. The expression on her face changed from rage to disgust. I think she was sorry that she had lost her temper and hadn't tasted the oatmeal first. Ingrid hadn't said a word the entire time. She just sat there looking at me with her blue eyes. I noticed how beautiful Ingrid's golden hair was, and I felt lucky to have such a pretty sister. That didn't prevent me from cutting off one of her locks a few days later and hiding the severed strand behind the tile oven in our room. Of course, Mutti found the hair and this time locked me in the broom closet for punishment.

Ingrid's and my room, the *Kinderzimmer*, was now occupied by the *Flüchtlinge* from East Prussia. Over my bed hung an oriental tapestry depicting a forest scene and a herd of elk. When the morning sun shone on the tapestry, it came to life, and I would imagine at times escaping into its lush and thick forest. On the other side of the room was a couch, and Ingrid's bed was right behind that couch, near the tile oven. An ordinary table stood in the middle of the room, coming in handy on rainy days when Ingrid and I spread out our games on it. Double doors led onto a balcony which we rarely used. In summer Mutti grew geraniums there. I thought they stank, so I never went on the balcony.

Across from the *Kinderzimmer* was the broom closet. If I did something to displease Mutti, she either hit me with the rug beater or put me in the closet, or both. I really didn't mind the broom closet. I much preferred the closet to a beating. For every wrongdoing—and I often didn't know what I had done—Mutti would beat me. She didn't care where she hit me. I would try to shield my head with my hands, only to finally drop them when my fingers could stand the pain no longer. When she tired of beating me, or couldn't remember anymore why she was doing it, she would push me into the broom closet. As I got older, I began to run away when I saw her getting the rug beater. I would stay outside, fearing to go home until the dark of night forced me inside. Usually she had calmed down by then. If these scenes happened early in the morning, then I wouldn't eat all day, unless it was the season when carrots or rutabagas ripened in the fields. At times my

January 1945

playmates felt sorry for me and took me home with them. Their mothers would usually give me a piece of bread to eat. But my friends' mothers scolded them for bringing me home. They didn't care for sharing rationed food with other people's children.

The master bedroom was at the end of the hall and was dominated by a massive double bed. I never went into the elegantly curved *Schrank* that held Mutti's and my father's wardrobes, a lady's vanity, and two nightstands. We also had a basement storage room which held the usual cardboard boxes and things. I cut the corrugated boxes into strips to fit around my head, and stuck colored chicken feathers into them to make an Indian headdress. I liked to play the Indian and whoop and dance, as I knew Indians did from reading my James Fenimore Cooper and Karl May books. It was forbidden for us to play cowboys and Indians anymore, or to have books about America, because we were at war with America. But nobody could keep me from reading my Karl May books. Someday, I thought, when there was no longer a war, I would go to America.

Footsteps and laughter in the hall jarred me out of my thoughts. Mutti and Ingrid walked into the room, both smiling and laughing loudly. How could they be so happy, when Russian tanks could be here even that night?

January 1945

Chapter 2

FLIGHT FROM SAGAN

I rose from my chair and slowly walked toward Mutti. She stopped laughing as I approached. Her expression changed to something between
annoyed curiosity and a frown. It was the expression she put on her
face when she was about to scold me. It didn't matter. I had her attention.
Just as I opened my mouth to speak, there was a loud, insistent knock at the
front door and the simultaneous ringing of the doorbell. It was ten o'clock
at night. No one was expected at such a late hour. I bolted for the door to
look through the peephole. To my astonishment I saw the lieutenant whom
I had taken to the train station earlier in the evening. Lieutenant Schmitt
kept on pounding on the door and ringing the bell.

"Who is it?" Mutti asked.

"It's Lieutenant Schmitt," I replied in a loud whisper. Mutti hurried to
the door and opened it. For once she seemed both troubled and perplexed.
Without stopping to say *Guten Abend* or giving an explanation, Lieutenant
Schmitt took Mutti by her arm and led her straight into the living room,
leaving Ingrid and me standing in the corridor.

"Hedy, you and the children must leave tonight. There is a train scheduled to arrive at about two o'clock this morning. You must be on it. It goes
to Berlin. You can stay with my parents. Sagan is lost. It will fall to the
Russians any time now."

"No," Mutti cried out, "I won't leave! I don't know why I should. What you say can't be true. And what they are saying about the Russians is probably propaganda. I can't leave my home from one minute to the next, just because you say so." When I heard her defiant response, my spirits sank. I was tired, hungry, and afraid, and I knew the lieutenant was right. Lieutenant Schmitt refused to accept my mother's objections.

"Hedy," he said, with resolve in his voice, as if he were her brother or her husband, "you have to understand that this is your last chance to get out. You must leave immediately. Now! Think of the children." He paused. "They are evacuating Liegnitz, only a few kilometers east of here. That means Sagan is going to be next. When that happens you won't have any choices about where to go. This is your last opportunity to get out of here. You must take it. You must! Please, think of Wolfgang and Ingrid, Hedy. Russian tanks have broken through our lines everywhere. They could be at your front door tonight."

There was a long silence. Then I heard a loud sigh, like a cry of desperation coming from deep inside my mother's chest. In a tear-choked voice, she called out, "Wolfgang, get the suitcases from the basement. And hurry." Suddenly I no longer felt hunger, fear, or despair. I felt elated. I grabbed the basement key from the rack in the hall.

I heard her ask Lieutenant Schmitt, "What do I take with me? I don't know what to take."

I didn't wait to hear his answer. I rushed outside and down to the basement. I slid down the bannister as I had done so many times in happier days—it was the fastest way down. Climbing upstairs, loaded down with three suitcases, I couldn't take my usual two stairs at a time. I felt happy, though. We were leaving. We were actually leaving. We would be safe after all. Lieutenant Schmitt watched closely as Mutti packed and spoke only when she tried to put something other than what he considered essential into the suitcases.

"No, Hedy," he would say, "you won't need that." Ingrid sat quietly on the bed in Mutti's bedroom watching her pack. I really loved my sister. I had loved her since the day she was born. We packed in thirty minutes. Mutti removed some pictures from our photo albums and pushed them into a pocket on the inside of the lid of the largest suitcase. I still wore my new Hitler Youth pants. Mutti helped me put on a sweater, a jacket, and my light-brown camel hair overcoat, and she helped Ingrid into her coat and matching cap. She wore her new boots. I had no boots, only shoes which were too small and hurt my toes. As we stood close together in the hallway, ready to leave, Mutti took one last look around. I could read the pain in my mother's eyes as clearly as if she had cried out. She didn't want to leave her beautiful world behind. She had been able to make the difficult decision only because Lieutenant Schmitt had left her no other choice. She had waited until the last minute, and the last minute had arrived. I knew that, without Lieutenant Schmitt's persistence, we wouldn't be leaving Sagan.

My father had tried earlier in 1944 to convince Mutti to move from Sagan. He had even made arrangements for movers to take our furniture to a house near an air base in the west of Germany, in the Lüneburg Heath. He failed to convince Mutti. She laughed at his letters, which she left lying around. I read them. She was having lots of fun that last year and nothing was going to take her away from that. She went to parties and played tennis with people she thought were important. She learned to tap dance and entertained wounded soldiers at the numerous military hospitals in the area. She was having a great time. Officers picked her up in their staff cars in the afternoons and returned her late at night after she had finished her dance routines. My mother looked beautiful in her costume, like a dancer in the movies, I thought. She didn't mind dancing for me in the living room before she left for the evening. She received many presents for her performances. What she liked best, though, was the attention men paid to her and the applause; she told me so. She didn't even open most of the presents, and had me store them in the attic. She didn't want to leave that world behind. I knew that, and Lieutenant Schmitt didn't.

Mutti knocked on the *Kinderzimmer* door, and the refugee woman opened the door immediately, as if she had been waiting for that knock. She had her baby girl in her arms. Mutti looked at the woman with a mixture of sadness and pity in her eyes. She said softly, "I must tell you that we are leaving to stay with friends in Berlin. Please, make yourself comfortable. Use the bedroom or any other room anyway you like. Take anything you need with you when you leave." The woman looked stunned, not wanting to comprehend what Mutti was saying.

"Oh, no. You have such a beautiful home," she protested. "I couldn't take anything from you."

Mutti said more firmly, "You are welcome to everything. It'll just go to the Russians if you don't take it." The woman said nothing more, pressing her baby closer to her bosom. She looked at Ingrid and me with big, lost, fearful eyes. For a moment I thought she was going to cry.

Lieutenant Schmitt reminded Mutti, "Hedy, it is time to go. We must hurry to catch our train. Children, go quietly down the stairs. Make as little noise as possible." Ingrid and I went down the stairs as quietly as we could. I knew that Frau Hein, a party member who lived across from Frau Hennig on the first floor, had probably heard us coming down the stairs and was watching through her peephole as we passed. She always looked old to me, like my grandmother Samuel, although she probably wasn't. Her hair was streaked with grey, and she combed it back into a bun. Her clothes were dark, and she walked with a slight stoop, always looking at the ground as if she had lost something. The way she dressed and walked made her look old. While she didn't miss much of what went on in our apartment house, she never got anyone into trouble.

We crept past her apartment. I didn't see her eye at the peephole. Just inside the house door lay a pile of ice skates, mine amongst them. I knew it would be a long time before I skated again. We exited into the cold night. It was snowing lightly, and for a brief moment the bracing cold felt refreshing. Only for a moment. The moon was partly hidden behind a thin layer of clouds. It was dark and light at the same time, and the freshly fallen snow appeared to have an iridescence of its own, seeming to light our way. Carrying my suitcase and keeping up with the fast pace set by Lieutenant Schmitt soon made me warm. Ingrid stumbled along beside me with her hands in her muff. We walked the same path I had taken earlier in the evening.

Frau Hein came back to mind. Her youngest son, Eberhard, was fifteen years old and an enthusiastic Hitler Youth. Eberhard was fun to play with when he chose to play with us younger children. He was good at organizing games, and we listened to him because he wore a uniform. Last summer he really made Mutti angry when he stood outside on his balcony in his Hitler Youth uniform, his right arm stretched out and his left hand clasping his belt buckle, in the traditional Hitler pose. For several afternoons he gave loud speeches in a nearly perfect imitation of the Führer. He shouted into space from his balcony, moving his head from side to side. He flicked his hair back with a rapid toss of his head, just like the Führer did. Mutti finally couldn't stand it any longer and shouted at Eberhard from our balcony, "Stop that nonsense, Eberhard. You are driving me crazy with your incessant screaming." Later that afternoon I heard Eberhard give his speeches from his room, standing at the open window, in the same Hitler pose as before. He shouted without letup until late into the afternoon, day after day. Mutti closed our windows in resignation and let Eberhard be.

Frau Hein's husband was an invalid, wounded in the Great War. She had two sons older than Eberhard. One was in the army and the other was in the Waffen-SS. Herr Hein was a heavy smoker. He smoked his monthly ration of cigarettes the first two weeks of every month. Then Eberhard had to go to the movie theater on the weekend and pick up cigarette butts discarded by theater-goers before and after the movie. Herr Hein would take the tobacco from the cigarette butts and make cigarettes from the scraps others had thrown away. I liked going with Eberhard. While he looked for cigarette butts, I looked at the movie posters. Most movies were for adults. Sometimes there were movies for children, too. I had seen *Snow White and the Seven Dwarfs* and *Hansel and Gretel* and a movie about Frederick the Great and the Battle of Leuthen. There were so many soldiers killed in that battle, Prussians and Austrians; I didn't like watching it. Soldiers were people, too.

Stumbling over ice in the darkness, I snapped out of my daydreams. Ingrid held me by the arm and looked up at me with worried eyes. "Are you tired, Wolfgang?" she whispered.

"No, no," I whispered back, even though I was. "I just didn't see the ice in the dark."

"Is the suitcase heavy?"

"Yes, it is heavy." I shifted the suitcase from one hand to the other.

"Can I help you carry the suitcase?"

"No," I replied, surprised at her sudden interest in me. "Just keep your hands in your muff and tell me if you see ice on the path." She broke into a slight run trying to keep up with me and then settled down, looking intently for ice.

Lieutenant Schmitt carried one suitcase, the heavy one; Mutti carried a third, smaller case; mine was the smallest. I overheard Lieutenant Schmitt say to Mutti, "When I got to the train station, I found out my troop train was delayed until morning. And then I saw a full passenger train heading west toward Berlin or Dresden. When I inquired of one of the attendants where the train was going, he told me Liegnitz was being evacuated and the train was heading for Dresden. He added that other trains would go to Berlin because Dresden couldn't handle any more. He thought the next train

Flight from Sagan

would arrive at two o'clock in the morning and would definitely go to Berlin. I asked him if it would stop in Sagan, and he assured me that it would, to pick up authorized passengers. I decided I had a God-given chance that would never come again. It was high time to get you and the children out. So, I came back to get you, Hedy. My parents will be surprised to see you, but they will put you up for as long as you need to stay. I got through to them on the phone and told them that you might be coming."

The moon was obscured by clouds again, and it was snowing lightly. A lone snowflake landed on the tip of my nose. It tickled. I couldn't do anything about it, with my suitcase in one hand and Ingrid holding onto the other. Ingrid's fur muff was held around her neck by a twisted cord which attached to each end of the muff, so she wouldn't lose it. She had one hand stuck deep into her muff, nearly up to her elbow. Mutti wore her grey fur coat and a matching muff. A hat sat at a jaunty angle on her fashionably combed-up hair. The boxy-looking hat was in fashion, and it looked nice on her, I thought. It did remind me of a hat worn by General Ziethen, one of my favorite cavalry generals, who had ridden for Frederick the Great. I liked Frederick the Great. My grandfather Samuel had told me many stories about him. Of course I couldn't tell Mutti that; she wouldn't like the comparison.

When we got to the bridge across the Bober River, I snapped out of my dream-like state and noticed that the antitank guns were gone. I could detect no trace of them ever having been there. We walked past several old villas. There was a park between two of the villas. In times past it had been graced by a statue of Bismarck. Only the concrete base remained. A steel screw which had held the statue projected from the concrete like a finger pointing into emptiness. Bismarck's statue had been removed, along with many of Sagan's church bells, and melted down to support the war. Beautiful things turned into bombs and bullets. A few isolated flakes of snow continued to fall. I hoped we'd get to the train station soon. I didn't think I could carry the suitcase much longer. My fingers were so numb I couldn't feel them anymore, and I couldn't feel my toes in my tight shoes either.

The train station smelled of steam and coal, of sweat and urine. It was much warmer than the outside, not because the station was heated, but because of all the people standing and scurrying about. Many soldiers walked around or stood about in groups with their rifles leaning against their packs or slung over their shoulders. One soldier who crossed in front of me looked exactly like a war poster I remembered. He wore a dirty, winter camouflage jacket, and had a Schmeisser submachine gun slung across his chest. A thick bandage around his head was bloodstained. He hurried by, the nails in his boots making a loud, authoritative sound. His helmet, painted white and scuffed, was hooked to his belt, and clanked against his mess tin as he hurried by. I noticed many other soldiers in the station with bandaged limbs or heads. When I first saw them, I thought they were old men, but, looking at them more closely, I discovered that they were not old, just exhausted.

Lieutenant Schmitt found a sheltered place for us behind a pillar, and we moved our suitcases there, hidden from the roving eyes of officials and passing military police. Ingrid and I sat on our suitcases, both of us thankful for the opportunity to rest. I asked Ingrid if I could use her muff for a few minutes to warm my fingers. She willingly gave it to me. The muff was a bit small for me. It was warm. I gave it back to her quickly, because she had nothing to keep her own hands warm. Mutti and Lieutenant Schmitt discussed how best to approach the man behind the ticket window. They waited until the line was fairly long, and then he nudged Mutti's arm.

"Go and get into line now," he said. "Just act as if you are passing through after stopping off for an emergency. Remember, you are from Liegnitz, and if he wants more information just give him the same street name and number as yours here in Sagan. How is he to know the difference? Look tired." I thought that advice was funny. We all were tired. Mutti walked across the mostly cracked ceramic tiles of the entrance hall. The tiles were yellow with a blue design. The floor was dirty from too many soldiers' boots and too few people to clean up after them. I noticed that Mutti wore her warm, fleece-lined boots. I was glad. It reminded me that my feet were cold. Ingrid's feet were probably cold, too. I watched her banging her feet together as she sat on a suitcase. I told her to stomp her feet to get warm. I showed her how. She thought it was a game, and her spirits lifted right away. We kept on jumping up and down and laughing out loud. Some of the soldiers noticed and smiled at us. We smiled back at them. Ingrid was thirsty and wanted a drink.

Lieutenant Schmitt watched Mutti as she joined the slowly moving line at the ticket window. Impulsively I ran over to her. She motioned me away, but I wouldn't go. I grabbed her leather-gloved hand and held on tightly. Then I ran back to our place and got Ingrid, too. We both stood next to

Mutti as she reached the ticket window. I moved up so I could hear what was being said. The man at the counter looked like any railroad man, pale and old. He wore a blue linen uniform with a gold wheel with wings sewn to the collar of his jacket. He looked at Mutti with tired eyes. He was neither friendly nor unfriendly, and he asked where Mutti wanted to go. She told him exactly what Lieutenant Schmitt had told her to say, that we were *Flüchtlinge* from Liegnitz and had had to stop for an emergency on our way to Berlin.

"There is no evacuation for people from Sagan," he admonished her, as if he hadn't heard a word she had said to him. He appeared to lower his face just a little as he spoke, looking at Mutti over the top of his wire-rimmed glasses. They were little, round glasses, and they looked funny on him. "You will be duly notified by designated evacuation personnel when to evacuate," he said. Mutti ignored what he said, just as he had ignored what she had said, repeating that we were from Liegnitz and that sickness had forced us to get off the train earlier in the day to seek medical attention in Sagan and that we had lost our tickets. Suddenly he asked her to fill out a short form declaring our place of residence in Liegnitz, our names, dates and places of birth, and where we were going. When Mutti had completed the form, he issued her three one-way tickets to Berlin. He told her when the train for Berlin was expected—"one-thirty in the morning, or so; who can tell these days?" Then he took her money for a one-way ticket for one adult and two children and turned to the next person in line. I wondered why we had to pay if we were *Flüchtlinge*.

As I stood in line close to Mutti, with Ingrid at my side, I felt for a moment that it was just like all the other times I had passed through the station with my grandfather Samuel when he had bought our tickets to Schlawe. I knew I was not going on vacation, and maybe we were never coming back. It was the end of the war. The Russians were coming. But the ticket seller and everyone else did their work as if it were just another day. Didn't they want to go somewhere else, too? Away from Sagan? I hope you get to go to Berlin, old man, or someplace safe, I thought to myself. I looked up at the ticket seller as we turned to leave and said out loud, "*Auf Wieder-sehen.*" He heard me, briefly nodded his head toward me, and then turned to sell tickets to the next person in line.

Mutti took my hand as we walked back to our suitcases. I liked that. Her hand was firm, reassuring, and warm. She brushed my hair out of my eyes and said, "Wolfgang, you look tired. Go sit down for a while and rest." I felt good all at once. Mutti knew I was there, she saw me, she loved me, she cared for me. Ingrid and I sat on the suitcases for about ten minutes, leaning against each other. Then we took our suitcases and passed through the checkpoint. A gate attendant punched our tickets, and we slowly walked to track number two. Our train was expected in an hour. Lieutenant Schmitt advised us to position ourselves halfway down the platform so we would be in a good position to get into a coach once the train arrived. A cold, gusty wind blew down the tracks, driving snow and coal dust before it. We huddled together on the platform, sitting on our suitcases. Mutti's fur coat gave me some warmth when I pressed against her, but my feet were cold, so I jumped up and ran around to get warm. Two o'clock passed. No one knew why the train was late. Hours passed. I slept sitting on my suitcase, waking when I was about to fall off. We repositioned our suitcases next to a small building on the platform to get out of the wind. We hadn't had anything to eat or drink for a long, long time. I sank into a dream-like state; at times I couldn't tell whether I was dreaming or awake.

Lieutenant Schmitt left us around five o'clock in the morning. "Hedy," he said, "I must go now. My train is here. You have my parents' address in Berlin, and I gave you a map of how to get there from the station. You have all that?" Mutti nodded her head. She looked tired. "It's a long walk from the Zoo Station. Once you get there, you and the children can get some rest." Mutti put her arms around him, and he held her close. She looked up at him and whispered, "Thank you, Hans. Take care of yourself."

I remembered the Zoo Station well from my many vacation trips to see my grandparents. I remembered those warm and loving days in Schlawe with my grandfather and grandmother Samuel. I hoped they were safe. Twice each year, for as long as I could remember, I had visited Oma and Opa Samuel. To them I was their *lieber kleiner Junge*, their dear little boy. The word "dear" was always in their vocabulary when they mentioned my name. Their love was warm and comfortable, like the cozy embrace of my feather-bed on a cold winter's night. At home, Mutti was always busy—when she was not sleeping late—sending me off on long errands, or thinking up onerous tasks for me to do. Rarely did she thank me for what I had done, and she never told me she loved me. Never. She took out her frustrations with life on me, and frequently that culminated in a beating with the rug beater or banishment for hours to the darkness of the broom closet. Although we had a beautiful home, I felt there wasn't much love in it. Not for me anyway.

Whenever Opa Samuel came to take me to Schlawe, I felt an immediate change come over myself, something similar to the fascinating transformation of a caterpillar into a butterfly. I felt a surge of self-confidence, making me feel almost physically light and unconstrained. Opa gave me wings. He made me feel free—free to grow up, to be a boy, to ask any question that came to my mind. I wanted to be near him, and I could tell he wanted to be near me. When Opa and I would leave to catch the train for Schlawe, I would feel as if I had just escaped a prison my mother had built for me.

In the home of my grandparents Samuel, I felt important, because to them I was important. I was not just an errand boy, someone to wash the dishes and beat the rugs. There was no broom closet, no rug beater. They did not respond to my inquisitive mind and constant questions by setting boundaries, and a scolding word was never uttered. For every question I raised, they provided a reasonable answer, or another question leading to another answer. They were both wonderful teachers. I loved to talk to them about the many questions I had that arose from reading my books, listening to the radio, or reading the newspaper. There were so many things I didn't understand, especially about the awful war. They listened to my questions patiently and helped me in my search for answers. They talked to me as if I were a real person with a mind of my own, a person who could learn from them. Oma and Opa Samuel provided the freedom and guidance I needed to grow up straight and strong and helped me to understand the troubled world I lived in. Mostly they provided the love I so desperately needed. They gave me a sense of security, a sense of personal belonging and value, which in turn gave me the self-confidence I needed to deal with the problems of my boyhood.

Opa always arrived in Sagan on the first or second day of my summer or fall school vacations. When Opa Samuel arrived, our rituals were nearly always the same. First, he would give me a hug, and then tell me how anxious Oma was to see me again, and how she was already cooking and baking my favorite dishes and cakes in anticipation of my arrival. Then he would shake his head over how much I had grown since the last time. A smile would come to his face when he stroked my hair off my forehead. I could feel the pleasure he felt when he touched me, as if I were something precious to him. I knew Mutti was glad to be rid of me for a while, and I was happy

Flight from Sagan

to be away from her. She and I never spoke of our feelings. At times I felt we were burdens to each other, and I wished it were different.

Leaving our apartment the day after his arrival, Opa would take my hand firmly in his and off we would march to the train station. His hand was strong yet gentle. We would take the train from Sagan to Berlin, and then from Berlin through Stettin to Schlawe. Sometimes we'd stop in Stettin to visit Oma's brother, who was a director on the railroad. At other times we would stop in Berlin to go to the zoo, or visit with one of Oma's sisters whose daughter attended the university there. To me it seemed to take forever for Opa to finish with his visits. Eventually, we would be on the last train. That last train was always my favorite. One such train ride was a particular pleasure. We were on that last train bound for Schlawe. Opa and I had our tickets checked by the conductor before we got to the stop just before Schlawe. The conductor nodded his head toward Opa and said, "You are getting off in Köslin, *Ja?*"

Opa nodded his head. I almost blurted out that we weren't getting off in Köslin, we were going to Schlawe. A stern look from my grandfather kept my lips sealed. After the conductor left, I walked up to Opa. I knelt on the floor in front of him, put my elbows on his knees and my face into my open hands, and looked him straight in the eyes. We looked at each other for some time.

"We are not getting off in Köslin, Opa, we are getting off in Schlawe," I finally said to him, "don't you know that?" I could see the twinkle in his eyes.

Then he said, "Never mind, my dear boy. I want you to promise me to do something special for your grandmother."

"Yes, Opa," I replied instantly, "anything to make Oma happy," and I jumped to my feet.

"Well," he said slowly, "Oma knows you are a fast runner. She asked me if on the way back I would test you to see just how fast you can run." Hearing that pleased me immensely. I jumped onto the seat next to him, rocking back and forth on my knees.

"Yes, Opa, tell me, what must I do?"

"When we get off the train in Schlawe, we'll walk to the gate where the attendant checks our passes. As soon as we get there, I'll say, 'Run.' And when I do, you run as fast as you can to the corner of the *Finanzamt* where I work. Don't stop, no matter what you may hear behind you. Do you understand what I just told you? It's important that you do exactly as I say, so I can time you properly."

"Yes, Opa. I know what I have to do. I promise Oma will be proud of me and I will be very fast. I have grown and my legs are longer. I can run much faster now than last year."

"We'll see what you can do in just a few minutes," Opa cautioned me, a smile crossing his face. The conductor who had reminded Opa that we were getting off in Köslin didn't come back again. We passed through Köslin. Then we finally arrived in Schlawe. Opa and I sat for a few minutes before he rose, picked up his scuffed briefcase, and said, "Now is a good time for us to go." As we walked down the aisle toward the exit, I began to wonder why Opa wanted me to start running at the ticket booth. I would do what he told me to do. Opa got out of the car first, holding on to a handle by the door. I carefully stepped down the two stairs to the platform. We joined the other passengers heading for the exit. Maybe Schlawe was the end of the line for this train. It could have been, because it seemed everyone was getting off. The passengers patiently stood in line to get through the checkpoint where an old man in a blue railroad uniform was checking and collecting tickets. We were in the middle of the line. The stationmaster carefully checked each ticket to ensure that it had been properly validated. As Opa stepped forward to surrender our tickets for inspection, he whispered, "Run." I was ready. I raced off toward the *Finanzamt* as fast as I could. Soon, behind me, I heard shouting. Looking back over my shoulder, I saw the stationmaster gesticulating with his hands and Opa striding toward me with long steps.

Opa saw me turn my head and shouted, "Keep running, Wolfgang," and I did. I stopped at the corner of the *Finanzamt*. Opa soon caught up with me. "Good boy," he commended me. "You were exceedingly fast, and your Oma will be proud of you."

"Did you time me, Opa?"

He gave me a time which he said was very fast for a boy of eight. We walked on toward home, he in his green loden coat and floppy hat and carrying his scuffed leather briefcase under his right arm, and I in shorts, a short-sleeved shirt, a light jacket, brown socks, and sandals.

"Opa, was I fast?" I asked him again, just to make sure.

"Yes, dear Wolfgang, you were fast," he repeated, "and I'll tell Oma as soon as we arrive home. She will be proud of you, and maybe she will have something special for you to eat as a reward. Maybe *Streuselkuchen*. Would you like that?"

"Hmm, that sounds good, Opa. I can taste it already." Then I remembered the conductor on the train saying that we were getting off in Koeslin. I also recalled the commotion at the checkpoint as we were leaving the station.

"Opa, did we have tickets to Schlawe?" I held onto his hand and looked up at him.

He turned toward me, bent down slightly, and looked me in the eyes. "No, Wolfgang, we didn't have tickets to Schlawe. I didn't have enough money with me. I only had enough to take us to Köslin. I figured that the conductor at the gate would be busy checking tickets and couldn't possibly run after us once he discovered we hadn't paid our full fare."

"Opa, that is cheating," I chided him.

"Maybe, Wolfgang. You must know how to help yourself in life. In this situation, if we had been perfectly honest, they would have kept us at the station and tried to figure out what to do with us. Now, all of us are happy. We will be at Oma's pretty soon, and they don't have to worry about what to do with us because we were two marks short of our train fare. And you were very fast, *mein lieber Junge*. I'll report that to Oma as soon as we get to the house." He laughed loudly. My grandfather had a happy laugh, and always a twinkle in his eyes. I squeezed his hand tightly as we walked silently the rest of the way. Opa was a great storyteller. As I got older, I figured out that when he was telling stories he was also trying to teach me. Opa would never talk about the Great War, and he never spoke of the Führer. He got a peculiar look in his eyes when people spoke glowingly about the Führer. I also noticed that he never said *"Heil Hitler,"* the "German greeting," as the party people referred to it. Coming into a store in Sagan, I was expected to say *"Heil Hitler"* rather than "Good morning" or "Good day." It became habit with me. I said *"Heilitler,"* slurring the greeting, because I didn't really know what it meant. Somehow, I always felt embarrassed saying it.

I once said *"Heilitler"* in Opa's presence in Schlawe. When we came out of the store, he held me by my shoulders, looked me in the eyes, and said, "We don't use that greeting here, Wolfgang. We say 'Guten Morgen' or 'Guten Tag' or 'Guten Abend.' Never that for a greeting. Do you understand me?" I never used that greeting in his presence again, and avoided it elsewhere if I could.

Flight from Sagan

When we finally arrived at the house, Oma was ready and waiting. She allowed me to hug her briefly, and then she was back in the kitchen getting something for me to eat. My favorites were the crepes she made using the rich milk from their goat. Early in the war Opa had built a shed. Over time he had added chickens, rabbits, and now a goat, to provide a steady supply of meat, eggs, and milk. Oma, a farm girl, didn't believe that anyone could be healthy without a daily glass of milk. Since I didn't care much for warm milk, I had convinced her to serve my milk in the form of pancakes on which she liberally spread her homemade jellies. She talked me into trying a tasty concoction of hers. I later found out that it was goat milk with a raw egg and sugar stirred into it. Since it tasted so good and it made Oma happy, I continued to drink it once a week, deciding not to recall where it came from.

My grandparents' house was full of mysteries, I thought. They lived on the upper floor, which they had turned into a self-contained apartment. The lower floor, which I really liked because of its modern windows and sliding doors, was rented to an army captain and his wife. One of the rooms at the top of the stairs was Oma's room, and Opa was not allowed to go into it. It was called the Green Room, and was completely decorated in green velvet—furniture, walls, and drapes. Oma always pulled the heavy drapes to keep out the sun.

"The sun bleaches everything," she told me, "and furniture has to last a lifetime." Oma would let me go into her private room. I would open the drapes just enough to get some light so I could read. Oma left me in there alone as long as I promised to be careful and not to get into everything. I was always careful. I also got into everything. There were photographs of Oma's family all over the room, standing on dressers and bureaus and hung on the walls, mostly of her brothers in gaudy cavalry uniforms. Oma had a large family, eight brothers and sisters, and at one time or another the boys had all served in the kaiser's army. One brother, Martin, was a *Schwarzer Husar*. He wore a tall, furry, black military hat, such as Napoleon's soldiers had once worn, with a tall black plume. In his left hand he gripped a sheathed, slightly curved cavalry saber with its point resting on the floor in front of him. He looked fearsome, the Black Hussar. I liked Martin right away and spent a long time looking at his picture. His mustache reached from one side of his face to the other. I thought it was magnificent. Oma told me that he had died on their farm unexpectedly of some unknown disease. "People were always dying from something," she said.

I asked Oma's permission to go into the Green Room mostly on rainy days when I felt inspired to learn more about my family's past. She rarely came to check on me. I spent much time revisiting her postcard collection and examining the foreign stamps on many of the cards. Whenever I could, I peeled some of the stamps off. I started a small stamp collection which I carefully hid from Oma, because I was afraid she wouldn't like me taking the stamps off her postcards.

The upstairs of Oma and Opa's house had a wide corridor, off which lay the individual rooms—a bathroom, the kitchen with its large wood-fired stove, and then the bedroom where Oma and Opa slept, in separate beds. On the other side of the hall was a smaller bedroom where I slept and a family room. There Opa smoked his pipe and told me stories after dinner. Their basement was filled with good smells and with many secrets, too. Tools and lumber filled one room. In another, Opa stored coal and potatoes for winter, and in a third he kept his secrets. I sneaked into that room once when he forgot to lock it. Many shelves were filled with jars of fruit and vegetables preserved by Oma, all from their garden. Much more interesting, though, were the many glass "balloons," as Opa called them, sitting in neat rows on the concrete floor. Some were full, some empty. Others were half full, and some balloons had foam on top of the liquid inside. I stood there amazed. When Opa came home that evening I told him what I had discovered in the basement. He listened attentively, then took my hand, and we walked down to the cellar.

"These, Wolfgang," he said, pointing to several glass balloons, "are apple and plum juice which I ferment to make cider, and even stronger stuff." He smiled when he said that. He took a Bakelite cup, tapped one of the glass balloons, and handed me the filled cup. I brought it gingerly to my lips. As soon as the liquid touched my tongue, I spit it out.

"Opa," I shouted, "this is awful-tasting stuff! It tastes like yeast! How can you drink this?"

"Oh, you can," he said. "But it's not really for you. Maybe when you're older you will want to drink some of it."

"Never!" I proclaimed with certainty, making a face to show my disdain for his brew. He laughed loudly.

"The reason I lock the room is to keep you from getting hurt," he said.

Flight from Sagan

"When juice is fermenting, pressure builds up inside the containers. Sometimes all it takes is just a minor disturbance and one of them could explode. Then glass would be flying all over the room. I don't want you to get hurt, my dear boy. That's why I lock the room. I have no secrets from you." He again locked the door when we left and hung the key on the key rack in the upstairs bathroom.

Pleasant memories of Schlawe floated through my mind as I sat freezing on my suitcase on platform number two in the Sagan train station. A sudden chill shook my body violently. I was not in Schlawe. Not with my grandparents. Not in a safe, warm place. It was only a trick of my mind that had taken me there. I saw Ingrid and Mutti sitting next to me on the large suitcase, huddling close together for warmth. I rose to walk around. My body felt stiff. The train for Berlin still had not arrived.

Chapter 3

THE TRAIN

The stationmaster's hut was set in the middle of the weathered concrete platform. I looked at my reflection in its tiny window. I was just a little taller than most of my classmates. Once blond like Ingrid's, my hair was now brown, and was covered with a thin layer of snow. I brushed the snow away. The boy looking back at me from the window didn't look like me at all. He looked so normal—not cold, hungry, and tired as I was.

Looking down the platform, I decided to run back and forth, from one end to the other and back again, to warm up. My shoes sounded loud on the cold concrete. When I passed Mutti on my way back, she beckoned for me to stop. "I don't like you doing that," she said with a frown on her face. "You might get separated from us. Stay put and quit running around. Do you hear me?"

"Yes, Mutti. I won't run anymore," I replied. Instead, I jumped up and down. I didn't know if I was getting warmer, but at least I was busy. When I sat down on my suitcase, the cold reasserted itself. On the open platform there was no way to stay warm. We spent the entire night on platform number two waiting for the train from Liegnitz. The morning light seemed dim and grey, only slowly pushing back the shadows of night. I could imagine the sun somewhere up beyond the grey layer of clouds. A warm, round, golden sun. A dreary winter sky emitted snow showers now and then, as if deliberately wanting to add to our misery. Many more people had joined us since our arrival just after midnight. They arrived in ones and twos all night long, silently, not wanting to be noticed. Like us, they waited for the west-bound train, waited to get away from something dreadful. I looked at the round platform clock sitting on its decorative cast-iron post. It was ten-thirty. The old clock still worked. It had to be very old, maybe from before the turn of the century. Most things still worked in spite of the war.

I was hungry, very hungry. There simply was no food, and it made no sense for me to complain to Mutti. I knew she couldn't do anything about it. None of us had thought to bring along bread, or cookies, or anything to eat. We were in such a hurry to get away, to keep from missing the train, that we forgot about food. No train. No food. No train. A chant formed in my head. We could, of course, buy a meal in the station restaurant using our ration cards. If we did that, we took the chance of missing the train if it arrived while we were eating. Time passed, agonizing minute by agonizing minute. My eyes remained riveted on the old clock. Its hands moved exceed-ingly slowly, I thought. Every minute the big hand jumped forward. In be-tween, time seemed to stand still. I waited for that long hand to jump and jump again. Noon. Then afternoon. The platform filled with even more silent people, all waiting for a train which was over twelve hours late. I had no idea where they had all come from or why they wanted to go to Berlin. Like us, they were waiting patiently. I stayed close to Mutti so we wouldn't lose our place on the crowded platform. Everybody tried through unobtru-sive movements to obtain a position along the tracks so as to have the best possible opportunity to get on the train once it arrived. The assembled mass of people was in ceaseless motion.

My thoughts moved slowly, as if the cold had frozen them, too. At two o'clock in the afternoon, well over twenty-four hours since any of us had slept, I fell into a stupor, unable to fight my fatigue any longer, barely able to stand on my feet. I had to concentrate hard to even remember where I was, and at times I couldn't remember anything about why we were here. All I wanted to do was sleep and get warm. I blew into my hands for the hundredth time, vainly trying to warm my fingers. My breath rose in front of my face like a little cloud of steam. Occasionally it snowed. The wind seemed to have died down. When I looked up at the clock, it was three o'clock. I had slept standing up, drifting in and out of consciousness.

Suddenly I felt something icy cold touch my lips. When I came to my

The Train

senses, I realized that what was touching my lips was not cold, but hot. Hot food. Mutti held a soldier's aluminum mess tin to my mouth and urged me to drink the soup. She had gotten hot chicken soup from a Wehrmacht field kitchen set up at the far end of the platform to serve soldiers in the station and others coming through on troop trains. I grasped the warm aluminum mess tin with my cold hands and for just a second savored the warmth flowing from the tin into my hands. I lifted it slowly to my mouth to drink the soup. Real chicken meat floated in the soup, skin, too. I remembered for just a brief moment that I didn't like chicken and I even thought about refusing the soup, hesitating momentarily. Then, with one long, big gulp I drank all of the soup, including the chicken meat and the skin. The soup felt like fire going down inside of me, and my strength and spirits soon revived.

People crowded near the platform's edge, shifting their positions whenever a whisper came through like a wave slowly hitting the beach. When the whisper passed, the crowd settled down again, waiting for the train. No one wanted to lose a position on the platform, and the few latecomers had to find a place at either end of the crowd or simply stand in the middle of the platform behind those at the edge near the rails, figuring that once the train arrived, in the confusion, they would somehow be able to push their way through and board the train. Four o'clock. Five o'clock. Seventeen hours on the platform.

I huddled with Mutti and Ingrid for a few minutes, pressing against Mutti's fur coat. It was getting dark again, and chilling wind gusts sporadically swept across the platform. I worried about how all these people would fit on one train. Just because we had arrived first didn't mean we would be able to get on. We could be left behind. But maybe it would be a long train and I was worrying needlessly. I sat down on my suitcase again, exhausted. With my fingers, I forced my eyes wide open, trying to stay awake. I wrapped my arms tightly around myself, pulling my head down into my coat. I forgot about Mutti and Ingrid. My thoughts wandered to our apartment house. To the past summer. To our attic. At one end of the attic was a window. I had come up to take a look from up high. A Ju-52 transport from Sagan *Flugplatz* came flying by low and gave me an idea. I got my old teddy bear and an umbrella. I would jump from the window using the umbrella as my parachute. As I stood by the window and looked down, it didn't seem all that far—just three floors. No need to do a test with Teddy first. When I looked again, I noticed that I would land on a gravel walk and not on the grass. I decided to do the test after all. I tied Teddy to the umbrella shaft with twine and let go. Teddy plunged to the ground like a rock.

I hit the hard, cold concrete of the station platform. I had fallen off my suitcase. Mutti didn't notice. She held Ingrid in her arms. At six o'clock in the evening, it was dark again. Only a few dim lights illuminated the platform. We had been there for eighteen hours. There was no change in the weather—the same low cloud cover, a few snowflakes falling. I had always liked winter, a time for snow forts and snowball fights, skiing and sledding, a time of Christmas trees and cookie smells, but I didn't like it anymore. Winter seemed like a cold blanket preparing to smother us all, to rob us of our breath and our lives. I touched my throat. For a moment I felt no sensation, and panic welled up inside me. Then I felt the touch of my cold fingers and I relaxed again. I couldn't tell what was real and what was imaginary anymore.

The crowd became restless again, and I heard mention of the word "train." People began lifting and repositioning their suitcases. I didn't see how they could know where the train was or if it was coming. They seemed to sense its arrival. And there it was. Around the bend lunged the shadowy outline of a low-slung, black locomotive, pulling behind it a long string of cars. A white plume of steam marked the train's approach. The steam, emerging from the locomotive's short stack, immediately enveloped the cars behind before slowly dissipating in the cold night air. The approaching locomotive overwhelmed us with the thundering noise of its iron wheels crushing the cold tracks and the hiss of escaping steam from its boiler. The wall of sound increased in intensity until I heard nothing else. As the locomotive rushed past with loudly screeching brakes, it wrapped itself in a mantle of steam. Coal particles flung from its stack stung my eyes, and the smell of coal penetrated my nostrils. The sudden heat from the locomotive's boiler felt pleasant against my face. Just as quickly as the locomotive had made its way down the platform, its sudden warmth was gone again. The locomotive came to a full stop at a place far beyond where the three of us stood. The screech of brakes and the sound of iron wheels clackety-clacking across the gaps between the rails was incessant. The brakes screeched for one final time, then the train came to a shuddering halt. There was momentary silence.

Mutti, who had risen off her suitcase and set Ingrid on her feet, grabbed one of our suitcases and lifted it up, then put it down, then up again, down again. I didn't know why she did that, because we didn't yet know where the train would come to a stop. As the train rolled past us, my heart sank. Every coach appeared to be full. People stood in the aisles. Some cars had open windows, and people leaned out of the windows looking at us, as people do who are on the inside looking at those on the outside. Even before the train had stopped completely, the waiting mass of people was surging for the doors. No one got off the train. People shoved, shouted, and pushed. Seeing the turmoil around us, I became afraid that we three would be left behind. All doors to the coaches were mobbed instantly. We were positioned near the middle of a coach, at the furthest possible point from the doors at either end.

"Stay put," Mutti shouted, as she ran to find a place for us to board. She disappeared in the crowd, pulling Ingrid behind her. I stood there alone next to our suitcases. The crowd had exploded into a mass of desperate humanity, all wanting to claw their way to safety. I thought I heard Mutti's voice calling me. I looked for her on the platform. I couldn't see her. Then a strong male voice called from further up the train, "Wolfgang, Wolfgang, Wolfgang . . . over here." I looked hard and saw a man waving at me from two cars up. Mutti was beside him; she was on the train. I could barely make out her face among the people who were trying to climb into the car through the window.

"Push the suitcases through the window, Wolfgang," the man shouted. Mutti gestured with her hands. I carried our three suitcases to the car directly across from me. People ran by me screaming, bumping into me from both directions, nearly knocking me down. A man leaning out of the window had followed the exchange between Mutti and me. He reached down, saying, "Give me the suitcase, boy." I could handle our two smaller suitcases easily. The man grabbed each suitcase by its handle as I held it up for him. Our largest suitcase, though, was heavy and difficult for me to lift high enough so he could pull it through the window. I struggled to get the suitcase onto my right shoulder, to lift it so that he could reach it. Finally he got his hand on the grip, but still had a difficult time pulling the suitcase through the window. It took a while. I heard a faint whistle. The train shook slightly as the locomotive strained to pull the cars slowly away from the still-crowded platform. I shoved once more, the stranger pulled, and finally the suitcase disappeared through the window.

The train was moving. People were frantically searching for a way to get

The Train

on. All around me there were loud shouts, occasional screams, and whimpers born of desperation. When I pushed the suitcases onto the train, Mutti couldn't see me very well. As the train picked up speed and I stepped back from the car, she spotted me. I saw panic in her face, I thought. I walked alongside the slowly moving train looking for a door. All doors I could see were choked with desperate, struggling people. I began to comprehend that I might be left behind, that I might remain on the platform watching my mother and sister leave, that I might never see them again. These were random thoughts flitting through my head, eliciting no emotion. It was as if I were somebody else entirely, not the boy on the platform. Everything seemed to be happening slowly, precisely. Time had slowed down, like the hands on that platform clock. I was acutely aware of my surroundings, yet I felt apart, as if I had suddenly become an observer of the scene rather than a participant. A sense of pleasant relief overcame me momentarily. Perhaps I was dreaming, and the train hadn't arrived after all. Surely I would wake up at any moment and find myself sitting on my suitcase, Mutti and Ingrid beside me.

The train began to move faster, and the wheels went clack-clack, clickety-clack as they passed over the gaps in the rails. The locomotive hooted loudly. The sounds yanked me back to my frantic reality. I was not asleep. I was not dreaming. I was on platform number two in Sagan beside the moving train that carried my mother and my sister. After we had waited nearly twenty-four hours, enduring the bitter cold, the train had arrived, and it was leaving the station—without me. I could not find a way to get on. Panic rose like a chilling icicle within me. I ran alongside the ever-faster-moving train, barely able to stay even with the car into which I had pushed our suitcases. I searched for Mutti's face. I couldn't see her. Then a loud, animal-like scream penetrated my consciousness. It came from ahead. It was my mother. I knew she couldn't do anything to help me. But her scream was oddly comforting. I knew then that she loved me. I was sorry for the things that had happened between us. Tears burned my cheeks as I ran without seeing.

"W-O-L-F-G-A-N-G, W-O-L-F-G-A-N-G, W-O-L-F-G-A-N-G . . ." Her pleading scream echoed over and over down the platform. I could see her face clearly now. She leaned out of the open window, her hands gripping the edge of the frame. At the sound of her pitiful screams, people stopped. From the way they looked, I knew I was right—I was going to be left behind.

My body kept on moving, and I kept looking at Mutti's face as if somehow she could will me on board. I picked up my pace alongside the train even more, trying to reach her window before it was too late. The train, too, picked up speed rapidly. I couldn't keep up. People dropped away from the doors. Others inside slammed the swinging doors shut—bang, bang, bang. Mutti seemed to be trying to jump out the window, but people were holding on to her. Her mouth was open, her arms flailing helplessly before her. I ran beside the train as fast as I could with my eyes riveted on her face. I was so afraid that I was losing my mother.

I sensed the end of the platform approaching. I looked up at an open window passing me by. I saw people standing by the window, watching. I heard the clack-clack of the wheels, the sound quickening. I wanted to die, for it to be over. I raised my hands over my head, and, in a plea to no one in particular, born of the desperation of a young boy losing his mother, I shouted into the noise of the passing train, "Please, somebody help me, please help me." I had no expectation of an answer.

Then I felt myself lifted off the platform and slammed against the side of the railroad car as it thundered across switches and tracks and into the night. I felt hands holding me by my coat, my pants, my head, my arms, my legs. Slowly and firmly, invisible hands cradled my body and pulled me through the open window into the safety and warmth of the railroad car. I fell to the floor. The train was going fast, the station far behind us. My rescuers tried to help me off the floor. I was overcome by such paralyzing fright that my knees buckled. I simply could not stand. I remained lying on the floor of the car, which was gently rocking from side to side as it sped down the tracks. I still couldn't believe what had happened, much less understand it. I stared at my rescuers, wanting to thank them, but I was unable to speak. I wanted to cry out loud, but no sound came from my throat. All I could do was stare. People looked down at me, the boy they had saved, and their eyes were kind and gentle.

A woman sitting in the compartment near where I lay came over and gently lifted me to my feet. She put her left arm around me and walked me into her compartment, to a seat by the window. When I was calmer, I explained to her that I didn't know where my mother was, or my sister. The woman took my hand in hers and put an arm around me, positioning me on her lap. She talked to me in soothing tones. I didn't comprehend anything she said; I only knew that I was safe, and that she was kind. Her gentle tone calmed me, and I lay back and let her hold me. I was so tired I could not think. I heard her say several times, "Your mother and sister are fine, my child. Just relax, everything is just fine." I sat on her lap looking out the window into the pitch-black night. The compartment was warm; it felt good to be warm again. I no longer shivered from cold nor fear. The woman continued to talk soothingly, pointing at shapes in the passing darkness. I didn't comprehend what she was saying, but her voice was gentle and soothing. I felt safe with her and fell asleep.

The train came to an abrupt halt, the locomotive's brakes screeching loudly, our car shaking from the impact of one carriage crushing into another. When I opened my eyes, I didn't immediately know where I was. The woman holding me said, "While you were sleeping, your mother came by. She and your sister are three cars ahead of us. They are both fine. There is no room for you, so you just stay here with me. Everything is all right now. I'll look after you until we get to Berlin." She was a total stranger, yet she treated me as if I were her child. I wondered who she was. She had on a dark-red wool dress with large buttons down the front covered with the same material. She wore a black patent-leather belt and new black shoes, I noticed later on, with elegant heels. A print silk scarf was tied around her neck. She was nicely dressed, just like Mutti when she dressed up.

The train moved slowly. At times it stopped again, and we sat in the dark with only dim night-lights illuminating our compartment. One of the men in our compartment said, "We are stopping because of an air raid on Berlin. They won't go in while a raid is in progress. I've come into Berlin before at night and the same thing always happens. The engineers wait until the all-clear is given before they move into the city."

I looked around the compartment. Every seat was occupied, and men and women stood between the seats holding onto ceiling straps. The lady who had been so kind to me was the best dressed of them all. The others wore mostly black or grey suits or dresses, and their coats were thick and bulky. I was surprised at how many men were in the compartment dressed in civilian clothes. Who were they? Where did they come from? Why were they not in uniform? Most German men I knew who were healthy had been drafted. Even my barber in Sagan had been drafted in 1944, and he had been in the Great War and looked old to me. I looked out the window into the blackness. Occasionally I saw a railroad signal flash by. I watched the reflections of the people in the window glass. Most seemed to be sleeping. One man ate a thick salami sandwich. I kept watching him, and the more I watched the more I could smell the sandwich. My stomach growled. When I looked away, at other faces, my hunger subsided.

No one spoke. The compartment was warm with so many people in it. I didn't mind the warmth, because I remembered how cold it had been when I was standing on the platform in Sagan. I kept looking at the reflections of the people in the window. They were there, yet they didn't seem real; they didn't look back at me. They seemed like puppets. I dozed off again. "We are near Berlin," said the woman, and I awoke. People sat on suitcases in the aisle outside our compartment. The train stopped again, and I heard people say there was another air raid in progress. I made out loud, sharp, booming sounds, and objects began falling on the roof of our coach.

"What is that sound?" I asked the woman holding me.

The same man answered who had talked knowledgeably before about why the train had stopped. "Those are antiaircraft guns. What you hear on the roof is shrapnel. Nothing to worry about unless you are standing outside and one of those pieces hits you in the head."

Finally, the guns stopped firing and the train began to move again, slowly. We passed through the Berlin outskirts and a number of outlying stations. Antiaircraft guns with their barrels pointing nearly vertically at the sky stood on several platforms. None were firing. The English bombers must have gone. I looked for evidence of the bombing. I saw nothing. Trains moved on other tracks. Slowly, very slowly, our train pulled into the Zoo Station and came to a halt. I realized how safe and secure I felt on the train with the kind woman watching over me and making sure I was comfortable. I felt as if I had been running for days, from something unknown and horrible. I became anxious. The people slowly started to get off. I needed to find Mutti and Ingrid. I needed to touch them. They were my family, all the family I had, and I needed to be near them.

The woman in the red dress rose and pulled her coat from the overhead rack. I jumped up and held her coat for her. She looked tired. She smiled gratefully for my assistance and quickly got into her coat, pulling the wide belt tightly around her.

"*Auf Wiedersehen*, my little friend," she said. "Your mother will be here looking for you as soon as enough people are off the train to allow her to move around. Just wait until she comes for you." She gave me a pat on my cheek with her fingers, and I noticed for the first time that she had long fingernails painted dark red. Then she turned, picked up her black leather purse, pulled a suitcase off the overhead rack, and was gone. I felt lonely and abandoned without her. I didn't even know her name. The train emptied slowly. I stayed put as the woman in the red dress had told me to do. The platform was illuminated and there was a dusting of snow on the tracks, though not as much as we had had in Sagan. Mutti's face peeked into my compartment through the aisle window. She had a happy smile on her tired face.

"Come, Wolfgang," she said, motioning for me to come out to her. "We must leave quickly. The train will depart in just a few more minutes." We located our three suitcases. Mutti took two, I took the smallest. Ingrid hung on to me as we trekked down the long platform, down the many stairs, until we finally came into a hall where the ticket windows were. Only a few people were in the hall at two o'clock in the morning. Ingrid and I sat down on the large suitcase while Mutti reviewed the directions Lieutenant Schmitt had given her.

"It is a long walk from here, children," Mutti said. We set off into the heart of Berlin. As I walked beside my mother in the strange city, I felt deeply grateful to be with her. I tried to forget that I had almost been left behind in Sagan. I still didn't know how I got on the train. Things had turned out all right. I felt safe being near her. We were together and we had a place to go to, and that was all that mattered.

Chapter 4

161 SCHÖNHAUSER ALLEE, BERLIN

e walked out of the Zoo Station—a young mother of thirty years, a five-year-old girl and a nine-year-old boy—following Lieutenant Schmitt's directions into the heart of the city. In the dark I didn't see any evidence of destruction from the English and American bombing raids. We came to a wide, tree-lined boulevard and the entrance to an underground passage. Carrying our three suitcases, we carefully descended the steep steps. Once below ground we found the passage lit by both overhead lights and lighting from several store windows. I stopped in front of one of the windows to rest my arm from the weight of my suitcase. Fashionable brown and blue ladies' shoes were on display. I found it incredible to see such beautiful shoes in a shop window in January 1945. I had not seen shops in several years with anything but pictures or replicas of merchandise in their window displays. "Can you buy these shoes, Mutti, or are they just to look at?" I asked her.

"I guess you can buy them if you have the right ration card, or if you know someone," she replied, exhaustion coloring her voice. "They probably say they don't have the right size once you go into the store and you want to buy a pair."

We struggled up the many stairs on the other side of the long underground passage, and, as we emerged from the display of bright lights and fantasy merchandise, we were engulfed by the absolute darkness of Berlin's city streets. Our footsteps echoed down the empty streets, and I tried to walk more quietly. I don't know why I felt I had to be quiet in a city that had been bombed only hours earlier. In the dark the empty streets seemed inhospitable. I had no idea where we were going. Ingrid held onto one of Mutti's two suitcases. We walked and stumbled, too tired to complain, carrying our heavy loads. Occasionally Mutti stopped at corners trying to make out the street signs. After many stops and shifting of suitcases from one hand to the other, Mutti said loudly, pronouncing each word carefully and distinctly, "Schönhauser Allee, that's it. Children, we've found the street we're looking for."

She again compared Lieutenant Schmitt's hand-drawn map to the street sign and announced with confident finality that it was the right street. It was four o'clock in the morning. We had been walking through Berlin for two hours.

"Look for 161, children," she said. Small, enameled number shields were mounted on the walls next to each house entrance. Since there were no streetlights, the house numbers were nearly impossible to read unless Mutti or I walked up to them. Finally we stopped in front of a five-story house. It was number 161. Mutti found the name Schmitt on the nameplates in the entryway. She pushed the bell button.

"They don't know for sure we are coming," Mutti said. A dim light came on in the stairwell, went out again, came on again, went out again, came on again. The light was on a timer and the Schmitts lived on the top floor. The door finally opened, and there stood a sleepy-eyed, rotund little man with a friendly face and a smile so wide it reminded me of the clown in the circus. He held out his hand immediately to greet Mutti and motioned for us to come in.

"You must be Hedy," he said with approval in his voice. "And these are your two children, Ingrid and Wolfgang." He gave each of us his hand. "Our son, Hans, phoned yesterday and told us about you." Even in my sleepy state, I noticed the word "telephone." Only important people had telephones in Germany. I wondered who he was. He didn't look important. But then I didn't know what important people looked like. Herr Schmitt ushered us upstairs to the fifth floor, a laborious, long climb with our suitcases. It seemed as if the contents of my suitcase had finally turned to lead. I could only lift it one stair at a time. I had no strength left in my arms. For five flights of stairs—up one stair and rest, up another stair and rest—on and on and on I climbed. Mutti, Ingrid, and Herr Schmitt arrived upstairs long before I did. The light in the stairwell only stayed on for fifteen seconds at a time. I pushed the light button at every level. The light soon went out again, and I proceeded noisily up the stairs in the dark. At the top floor, the apartment door stood wide open. Smiling broadly at me, a plump lady rushed forward to help. She took my suitcase, lifted it with ease, and carried it the final few steps into the apartment. Frau Schmitt closed the door behind us. It was January 25, 1945.

The smell of old drapes, old clothes, and old furniture entered my nose. Oma's Green Room. Was I at Oma's? I was confused. My eyes wouldn't stay open any longer. I was so tired that I found it difficult to remain standing. I had to sit down somewhere, anywhere, before I fell down. I saw my suitcase next to the wall. I sat on it. When I awoke again, I found myself enveloped in a clean-smelling, soft and warm featherbed. The pillow was big and scrunched-up on both sides of my head. I didn't know how I had gotten into that bed. My last thought before falling asleep again was of lying in a puffy white cloud floating high up in the blue sky over Sagan. I sensed someone near me. Over me. Shadows. Friendly shadows. Smiling shadows. I opened my eyes, and there were three faces looking at me. Ingrid knelt by my side, staring me in the face as if she were watching someone slowly rise from the dead.

"He is awake," she shouted gleefully. "His eyes are open." On the other side of the bed, Mutti was bending over me, with the plump, friendly woman from last night standing by her side.

"*Guten Abend*, Wolfgang," said Mutti in mock seriousness, holding my face in her hands. "Did you sleep well?" I rubbed the sleep from my eyes and sat up.

"Yes, I slept well. I am not tired anymore. I feel fine."

"Wolfgang," Mutti said, sitting down beside me, "you slept for fourteen hours without moving a muscle. You never moved once, I believe. I came in to check on you often. You just lay there sleeping like a little angel." She laughed. There were no worry lines in her face. She, too, looked rested. "While you slept we had two alarms and one raid. We went to the basement. I left you in your bed because you needed sleep so badly and you were sleeping so tight that even when I shook you, you didn't wake up. They have never been bombed in this area before; why should they be bombed now?"

161 Schönhauser Allee, Berlin

She ran her hand over my hair. "I know I took a chance. God knows I wanted to do the right thing for you. You needed your sleep."

I got out of bed, and Mutti showed me the toilet and the wash basin. It was an old-fashioned toilet. The water tank hung near the ceiling, and an elongated porcelain handle on a long chain dangled from it. When I pulled on the handle, the water rushed down fast, and I knew if I was slow in getting off the bowl my behind would get wet. Mutti brought me warm water in a kettle and poured it into the basin. I washed my hands and face. After dressing, I combed my hair and went into the hall, following the smell of food and the sound of voices. They were in the dining room. I joined them around a large, oval mahogany table to eat my breakfast. Or maybe it was dinner. I didn't know what to call it after getting up in the evening. Slices of fresh, sweet-smelling rye bread lay in a basket. A boiled egg with a knitted cap to keep it warm sat in its cup. There was a cake of real butter, jam, and a steaming cup of coffee. Not real coffee, of course, ersatz coffee, which was all right for children to drink. I ate every slice of bread in the lovely little basket. Ingrid and Mutti sat near me and watched.

The Schmitts' apartment was quite large compared to ours in Sagan. They had two large bedrooms, a living room, and a separate dining room. The hall was wide and long. The ceilings were much higher than ours in Sagan and were ornately decorated. The kitchen and the bathroom, however, were small and plain, as if they didn't much matter. To me, the Schmitts' apartment smelled old. Maybe it was the furniture or the curtains. The windows looking out onto the street were hung with long, lacy drapes and thick, reddish-brown velvet curtains which could be pulled across each window to keep out the light. Frau Schmitt busied herself with cleaning and cooking. Mutti stayed close to her. They talked a lot. Ingrid kept near the two women, who fussed over her blond hair and her pretty blue eyes. Ingrid liked all the attention, and soon became almost permanently attached to Frau Schmitt. Herr Schmitt liked Ingrid, too, squeezing and hugging her and bouncing her on his knees. He held her on his lap and told her stories, or played *hoppe-hoppe-reiter* with her.

My tenth birthday was on the second of February. At one time, I had looked forward to turning ten with great anticipation. Now it wasn't important anymore. I had no friends in Berlin with whom to share my special day. Mutti and Frau Schmitt baked a cake with one candle stuck in the middle. The candle stood for ten years, Mutti said. There was no party such as I used to give for my friends in Sagan. I missed my friends. I missed running and playing with them. I hadn't even said good-bye to them. Herr Schmitt let me accompany him on his daily trips to the tobacconist, the grocer, the butcher, and the post office. These outings gave me a chance to look at my new world in the light of day. I could tell he liked having me near him. Maybe I reminded him of his own boy, Hans, when he was my age. I was awed by the destruction. Not too far from the Schmitts' were entire streets with every house burned; only barren walls remained standing. Some inside walls still had plaster on them, some even wallpaper. Mostly I saw only bare brick walls with gaping holes. The holes had once been doors leading to rooms sheltering girls and boys like Ingrid and me. Where were the people who had once lived there? I didn't ask the question. I didn't want to hear his answer.

One apartment house, five stories tall, caught my attention as we walked by. I counted the floors from the ground up. The ground floor was filled with debris from the collapsed floors above. On the fifth floor, however, I could see a kitchen—a cabinet with dishes in it, a sink, a stove, a table with four chairs around it, and a picture on one wall. A checkered red-and-white oilcloth covered the table. The tablecloth must have been tacked to the table or it would have blown away in the wind long ago. I could see the stacks of plates and cups through the unbroken glass front of the cabinet. Kitchen utensils hung on the wall under the picture. On one of the walls was a closed door. On the other side of the door there was nothing. The kitchen stood there on the fifth floor as if waiting for a family of four to walk in and pull out the chairs stowed neatly under the table and sit down for dinner. I knew there would never be a family sitting around that table again, only their ghosts. Everything around the kitchen had collapsed except for two walls and the floor. The kitchen sat there unchanged day after day. Every time Herr Schmitt and I walked past the gutted building, I would look up at the kitchen. After several days I thought I knew the two children, the mother, and the father who had sat at the table. I could picture them eating dinner and talking to one another. I could not get them out of my mind. Where were they?

Because of the bad February weather there weren't as many daylight bombing raids. "Once the weather clears, the Americans will come back day after day and bomb what's left of Berlin into ruins like this," Herr Schmitt said, pointing to the burned-out houses around us. "The Americans don't fly at night," he continued. "The English only fly at night. The English drop their bombs anywhere. They don't need to see anything for that. The Americans bomb specific areas of the city. For them to do that they must be able to see the ground. Soon it won't matter who bombs what. There won't be anything left of Berlin but ruins. You don't want to stay with us too long, Wolfgang. It will get much worse in the coming weeks." For once, Herr Schmitt wasn't smiling.

The streetcars ran soon again after the English night raids ended. Sometimes in the mornings we could not go into the streets because Russian prisoners of war were still at work defusing or exploding bombs which had not detonated when they were dropped the night before. "Some of the bombs are just kaput," Herr Schmitt explained. He was my new friend and he was good about telling me things without my asking. He seemed to read my mind. "Others have timers and they don't explode for hours, even days after a raid. The Russian prisoners clear those bombs. Sometimes the bombs explode while the prisoners are working on them." We passed a group of Russian prisoners working their way through rubble in a newly bombed building. They wore long, brown Russian army coats and funny-looking winter hats with dangling earflaps. They stood close together and did not look our way. I couldn't see their faces.

When Mutti, Ingrid, the Schmitts, and I went into the shelter at night, sometimes more than once, people quietly shuffled down the stairs without haste. No one ran. We sat silently in the narrow basement shelter pushed against each other shoulder to shoulder, listening to the thump and ripple of the exploding bombs, trying to judge how close they might be and if they were coming toward us. Sitting in the shelter late one night, half asleep, I listened to the antiaircraft artillery and the ripple of exploding bombs and thought about the daylight bombing raids on the town of Sorau I had witnessed in 1944.

On a clear, beautiful April day, the air raid sirens in our housing area had gone off. An unusual occurrence. The helmeted wardens, all women, came running out of the apartment buildings to chase anybody still outside into the houses and down into the basement bomb shelters. That day, hearing the sirens, I quickly hid behind a bush, and the air raid warden didn't see me. The raid seemed exciting, and I knew I wouldn't be able to see much from the basement shelter. What could they bomb in Sagan? I thought. We were surrounded by open fields, and the *Flugplatz* was several kilometers away to the south. Then I heard a sound I had never heard before; it resembled the sound of a huge swarm of bees heading straight for me, although I knew it wasn't bees. As the unfamiliar sound grew stronger, I strained to see something in the clear, blue sky. Then I saw what looked like a thin, dark cloud in the west. The cloud had a faintly shimmering quality to it. It grew larger, the sound louder. Seconds passed. Now I was sure the ominous sound came from the dark cloud. Then I saw that it wasn't a cloud at all. It was a formation of bombers, the sun reflecting brightly off their canopies and their many whirling propellers.

The propellers gave the mass of airplanes a glittering, shimmering quality, like the ripples of fast-flowing water in a stream reflecting bright sunlight. The sound made by their hundreds of engines churning through the cloudless spring sky was a deep, penetrating hummmm, hummmm, hummmm . . . With every minute the bombers got closer and the sound became stronger. The windows in our house began to vibrate. The bombers seemed to be heading on a straight line from west to east. On their present course, I decided, they would pass right in front of me, several thousand meters above me. The humming sound preceded the huge formation by several minutes. I began to make out individual aircraft. It looked to be about two hundred airplanes, maybe more. I had never seen so many airplanes at one time. I knew they were B-17s, judging from their four engines, their clean bodies and high tails.

I had thought all airplanes flew in small formations or as a bomber stream as the English and the Luftwaffe did. The American airplanes flew instead in one huge formation, close together. I was fascinated by the sight of the spectacle. What was it like to be part of a huge formation of bombers deep over enemy territory? I wanted to fly one of those bombers one day. I wanted to be one of the unknown men high up in the sky. Forgetting that they were there to bomb my country, I felt no hatred toward them. Instead, I felt admiration and a deep sense of kinship with the unknown flyers passing above. I saw the bombers clearly; they were making a slow, ponderous turn to the north, over the nearby town of Sorau. I didn't see the bombs fall, and I heard no explosions. After the bombers had passed out of sight, a huge, black, mushroom-like cloud rose into the sky from the direction of Sorau. Since there was no wind, the black cloud hung in the sky for the rest of the day, until it slowly dissolved and drifted away to the northeast. Two days later I heard two women talking in our stairwell about the attack and how the people of Sorau had run for the cemetery when the attack started because they thought the cemetery was a safe place to go. Many did not live in houses with shelters, and, of those who ran for safety to the cemetery, most were killed.

When a second attack against Sorau occurred six weeks later, our air raid warden was more alert than she had been the first time, and she personally herded me into the shelter. After the first raid, the warden had found me and given me a harsh reprimand. "Don't you know that you could be hurt, even killed, if you stay out in the open?" she shrieked at me. "The next time you better be in that basement," she threatened, shaking her right index finger at me, "or I will report you." I didn't mind her screaming at me. It was worth her shouted insults to have seen the American bombers.

Our air raid shelter in Sagan covered one-fourth of the area under our apartment building. According to the air raid warden, that part of the building had steel plates in the ceiling to protect us from bombs. I didn't believe her. I wondered how they could have known in 1937, when the apartments were built, that there would be air attacks. Maybe someone was already planning war in 1937? Two shelter windows covered with perforated steel screens looked west toward Sorau. The screens were designed to prevent bomb debris from entering our shelter. I pressed myself against one of the windows and tried to focus my vision through the holes in the screen. I saw the American planes passing over Sorau on their second raid. There was little smoke after the bombs dropped, and, instead of turning north, the B-17s kept flying east. Behind and above them I noticed a single aircraft following the formation, higher than the others, more compact, less graceful. I wondered about that airplane. I never forgot the American bombers over Sorau, flying unchecked through the blue skies of my homeland. I knew the flyers were from the land of the Mohicans, and I was in awe of them. I wondered what the men from America looked like.

The all-clear signal was finally given, and we shuffled back upstairs to our fifth-floor apartment in the center of Berlin. Herr and Frau Schmitt looked exhausted when we got there. It was a long climb from the basement, and it was the third time that night we had gone to the shelter. No one complained. After every raid there was a noticeable sense of relief. It hadn't been our turn. Everyone knew that our turn would come. It was just a question of time. At least once each night we went to the basement to sit out an air raid. Some raid warnings were false alarms, at least for me.

The siren on top of our apartment building began to assume an identity: it was an evil being tearing me out of the depths of sleep at any hour of the night. I began to fear its penetrating wail. Sometimes I was confused when it went off, and it would take a while for me to come to my senses and understand what was happening and what I had to do. At other times, I bolted from bed before I was fully awake—almost as if I were not in control of my body—pulled on my pants, grabbed my coat, and joined the people walking down the stairs to the shelter before I understood what I was doing. I dreaded the siren more than the bombs. The siren played a terrifying game with me. I began to imagine hearing it when it wasn't wailing. I would jump out of bed and pull on my clothes before realizing that no one else in the apartment was moving. I would stand there in the darkness, my heart pounding with the sound of the siren in my head. Finally awaking fully, I would grasp the situation, and the sound would slowly leave my head. I became afraid of the night with its terrors. Mutti tried to calm me whenever she could, but she wasn't always there to do so.

On February 16, I sat on the floor in the living room, half listening to the radio announcer and playing train with empty matchboxes. I heard the announcer report on two days and nights of nearly continuous air raids by English and American bombers against the city of Dresden. At first I listened only out of habit, because bombings were routine and nothing unusual. Berlin was always mentioned. As I listened more closely to what the announcer was saying, I realized that the Dresden raids were much more destructive than anything I had experienced in Berlin. The raids apparently had destroyed the entire city of Dresden and burned to death nearly everyone in it. I was glad that it wasn't Mutti, Ingrid, and I who burned to death in that fiery hell, and then I felt guilty for thinking such thoughts. I knew we had to get out of Berlin or the same would happen to us. I wondered if the men who bombed Dresden had also bombed Sorau. I knew I wanted to fly airplanes when I grew up, but I didn't want to kill children and their mothers.

The same afternoon I found Mutti and Frau Schmitt sitting by the radio listening intently. It was unusual to see Mutti paying attention to the news. She had one ear pressed against the loudspeaker so as not to miss a word the announcer was saying. I only caught fragments of the announcements, since I had entered near the end of the news. Mutti turned the radio off, and for once her usually expressive face showed nothing. As I walked up to her, she said in a monotone, "The Russians have taken Sagan, Wolfgang. Don't go away yet, my dear boy." She reached for my hand. "I must tell you something else here in front of Frau Schmitt." She paused briefly. "You must promise to be strong."

"I will be strong, Mutti," I responded, wondering what was so important, and if being strong meant that I couldn't cry.

"Lieutenant Schmitt called this morning. I spoke to him after he had spoken to Frau Schmitt. He said the people from Sagan were evacuated just ahead of the Russians."

"Yes, Mutti."

"They were loaded on trains just like the one we took to Berlin. Many of the trains from Sagan went to Dresden. The trains still stood in Dresden when the town was bombed. They are all dead, Wolfgang; those people are all dead." The tears ran down her cheeks, into her mouth, and dropped on her skirt in a steady stream. Frau Schmitt cried, too. "I almost killed you and Ingrid by not paying attention to what was going on around us. If it weren't for Lieutenant Schmitt, we wouldn't be alive today."

I put my arms around my mother and held her tight. After a long time, she pulled me close to her and kissed me on both cheeks. I felt sad for her. That afternoon I rummaged through drawers in the Schmitts' kitchen until I found what I was looking for. A map. It was a tiny map in the back of a pocket-sized appointment book from the year 1942. It showed most of Europe in red under German occupation with a swastika over the occupied countries. Looking at the map, I realized for the first time that we had not come far even though it had seemed that way. Berlin was only about 150 kilometers from Sagan, the width of a pencil on the map. Then I knew it would be only days, or a few weeks at most, before the Russians reached Berlin.

Chapter 5

A TOWN CALLED
STRASBURG

On Monday, March 5, 1945, Mutti decided it was time for us to leave Berlin. We'd been at the Schmitts' since January 25, nearly six weeks. Leaving Berlin was fine with me. I was getting bored—I had no school, no friends to play with, no books to read. Only ruins and the never-ending bombing raids. "We are leaving tomorrow," Mutti said. Just like that. Herr Schmitt, standing nearby when she made her announcement, readily agreed with her.

"Yes," he replied, "the weather will improve as we get into spring, and the Americans will surely take advantage of that and increase their raids." He laughed, as if he had said something funny. "It is time for you and the children to leave Berlin, Hedy."

"We'll go to my mother's in Strasburg."

I was totally surprised when Mutti announced our destination. Strasburg was a smallish, poverty-stricken farm town about 150 kilometers north of Berlin where my grandparents Grapentin lived, and where I had been born. I had visited Oma and Opa Grapentin infrequently in the past years, because Mutti never really liked going there, back to the poverty she had escaped. And when I did visit, I stayed only a few days until my grandfather Samuel came to get me. He was born in a village near Strasburg. They didn't even have a real bathroom in Strasburg, I recalled with distaste, only a cold and drafty outhouse near the pigsty, with newspaper for toilet paper.

I grabbed Mutti by the arm. "Mutti," I pleaded, knowing she wouldn't listen, "we should be going somewhere in the west like Dad asked you to do last year."

She wasn't interested in my suggestion. Her decision was final. She immediately began to pack our few possessions. Then she sat down with Herr Schmitt to work out a plan of departure. We were leaving, even if we had to walk to Strasburg, that was clear to me. In March 1945, traveling anywhere by train from Berlin was only possible with official authorization, as Herr Schmitt had told me on one of our many walks through the city. Mutti, however, thought she could just walk up to the train station, buy a ticket, and take a train to Strasburg. Herr Schmitt, who didn't seem to be the least surprised by anything, told Mutti with a mighty laugh, "That is out of the question, Hedy. You can't just walk to the station anymore and expect to find a train. Even if there is one, you can't get on it without some kind of document authorizing your trip. The carefree days are gone, Hedy. This is March 1945. Not much of Germany is left to travel in."

Looking her straight in the eyes he said, "I think I have a solution. Once there was a time when I was active in the SA [Hitler's brownshirted storm troopers]. You remember the SA, don't you? I still have my uniform." He paused. Mutti continued packing. "Some would even consider me to have been a man of fairly high rank. I have been out of favor for a long time and have not gone to any of their meetings since 1940. Haven't worn my uniform since then either. I hope it still fits." He patted his ample stomach with his right hand and said, "As you can see, Hedy, I have not lost weight, so we should be all right. My old uniform with its badges, ribbons, and armbands looks impressive enough to do what we need to do. In that uniform, even in Berlin, I should be able to persuade the ticket agents to let you get on any train they have running to anywhere." Then he added, "Berliners can get nasty when they see anyone in SA uniform these days. They never liked Hitler to start with, and they like him even less today. I'll put on the uniform one more time just for you, Hedy." Now I understood why Herr Schmitt had a telephone.

Mutti and Herr Schmitt walked to the nearest train station that afternoon and discovered that a train to Strasburg was scheduled the next day. In the morning all three of us dressed for travel. Herr Schmitt was resplendent in his SA uniform, including a pistol which he wore on his brown belt. He wore a red armband around his left sleeve with a black swastika set in a circle of white. He looked much like the German newspaper caricatures I had seen of Winston Churchill—big and fat, that is—only Herr Schmitt didn't have a cigar in his mouth and Herr Churchill surely would never be seen in that uniform. His brown hat was round and boxy with a short, stubby brown bill. His pants looked like cavalry pants, with leather sewn in the seat, and he wore brown riding boots and matching gloves.

Frau Schmitt wished us a cheerful *auf Wiedersehen*, waving her hand after us as we slowly moved down the familiar stairway. Only when we were out of her sight did I hear the door close behind her. Herr Schmitt walked ahead of us with a firm stride. People seemed to avoid him when they walked by, going as far as they could to one side or the other. No one looked him in the eyes, and no one greeted him. We followed behind with our three suitcases—not out of respect, but because it was difficult for us to keep up with him. I knew Herr Schmitt was pleased to be able to help his son's friend. Although he was careful in how he spoke to me, I had the clear impression that he no longer cared for the Führer nor for the party he had once served. I liked the old man. I knew I would miss him. At the station, Herr Schmitt walked Mutti directly to the front of the ticket line. I felt funny about that. I guessed that was the way he had to act. He couldn't be polite and stand in line, because that would make him look ridiculous. Party people didn't stand in line. Mutti got her tickets to Strasburg without question. Herr Schmitt escorted us to the platform. The station agent punched our tickets, respectfully standing aside as Herr Schmitt walked us to the center of the platform. The train was already there. He helped us into a compartment. We briefly stepped outside again to shake hands.

"I hope we see each other again in better days to come, dear Hedy," he said in parting, winking at me with one eye. "Until then, I wish you luck." He saluted Mutti and then he turned smartly and strode away. We watched him walking briskly down the platform until he passed out of sight. The train was composed of old, pre–World War I carriages. Ours was a third-class compartment with hard wooden benches. Every compartment was accessed through its own outside door, leaving little space for walking around between the two facing benches. People quickly showed their annoyance with me when I tried to walk from one side of the carriage to the other and stumbled over their feet. Mutti admonished me to "sit still like a good boy." Since there were others in the compartment, she didn't miss the opportunity to demonstrate how obedient I was and how well I listened to her directions without back talk. So I mostly sat on the bench, shifting my weight from one side to the other as best I could to alleviate the numbness in my bottom.

As the train drew away from Berlin, the countryside began to look more peaceful. There were no signs of war. At four in the afternoon we arrived in Strasburg, after having stopped at every station between there and Berlin. Strasburg looked just the way I remembered it. The late afternoon sunshine felt pleasantly warm. I grabbed my suitcase, and we started the long walk to my grandparents' house. The street from the *Bahnhof* to the *Marktplatz* was lined with shade-spreading horse chestnut trees. There were no burned-out buildings, no ruins, no bombs exploding, no guns guarding bridges. Children were playing in the streets. Maybe war would never come to a peaceful country town like Strasburg. We crossed between two cemeteries. On our right, the old cemetery, no longer used and with few gravestones evident, was shadowed by huge beech trees. On our left, in contrast, a new, well-kept cemetery revealed a profusion of gravestones and family tombs. Once we passed between the two cemeteries, open spaces gave way to shops and apartment houses.

We rested frequently, finally arriving at the *Marktplatz*. The square, like most of the old streets in Strasburg, was paved with cobblestones. To me, Strasburg had always looked like a town where Till Eulenspiegel, a famous thirteenth-century prankster, might have turned his tricks. The place was old, dusty, poor, and neglected. Oma and Opa, who didn't know we were coming, rented a one-bedroom apartment without running water. Most everybody was poor in Strasburg, living as they had a hundred or more years ago. We passed the *Kaufhaus*, a department store with surprisingly attractive and ample window displays. We entered a narrow, cobblestoned street just off the *Marktplatz*, and I recognized it as the street my grandparents lived on. The household water and effluent were dumped directly into the street, running downhill between houses to an open field beyond. A persistent putrid smell filled the air. Why did we have to come to Strasburg when we could be somewhere nice? I knew the answer. Mutti was stubborn. She wouldn't do anything my father suggested. Several boys played stick hockey in the street with a dirty tennis ball and walking canes. Their clothes were old hand-me-downs with many patches. The boys paused briefly to look me over and then continued batting the ball back and forth, screaming loudly at each other. They looked tough. I hoped we wouldn't stay too long in Strasburg.

We came to a grey, one-story house with crumbling plaster walls. The windows of the house were almost at sidewalk level, which meant that the rooms inside were partially below ground level, probably damp and uncomfortable. The entry led to a narrow, unlit hallway with a low ceiling. The unpainted floorboards showed signs of rot and creaked loudly when we stepped on them. A door to the right opened to the Zoske apartment, according to a simple nameplate mounted in the middle of the door. Behind the door to the left was my grandparents' apartment. There was no nameplate. The doors were low and narrow, built for the smaller people of an earlier century. My mother opened the door without knocking and peeked inside.

"Hallo, Mutti," she said loudly. Oma Grapentin stood behind the wood-burning kitchen stove, and, judging from the noise of pots and pans, she was badly startled by our sudden arrival. My mother walked across the family room into the kitchen and hugged Oma. Oma begged Ingrid and me to enter, drying her hands on her apron as she spoke. Oma looked just as I remembered her, with her warm smile coming right from her heart. I knew she was poor, but she was my grandmother and she was nice. Her greying hair was pulled back in a bun. I remembered seeing her comb it in the mornings; before she put it up, her hair reached down to her knees when she stood. Her skin was white and soft, with only her hands showing the effects of years of manual labor. Her finger joints were swollen just like my Oma Samuel's, and her fingernails were broken. Oma hurried off for a moment and quickly returned. She had to put her false teeth into her mouth. She wore a simple, grey linen dress and a blue apron without frills covering her from her bosom to the hem of her dress. The apron was tied in back, and a loop held it up around her neck. On her feet she wore grey, frequently darned socks. Oma hurried back to her stove to tend to the gravy for the evening meal. Mutti joined her in the kitchen. Ingrid planted herself between Oma and Mutti, stuck her left ring and middle fingers in her mouth (as she had done for as long as I had known her), and stood there sucking them.

I sat down on a couch in the family room and looked around my new home. There was the customary oven. Unlike our oven in Sagan, it had a door on one side, chest high. The space behind the door was used to warm food or mittens. The rest of the room was simply furnished: two couches, a large unfinished table showing years of wear, four equally worn chairs, and a rocking chair for Oma. A *Volksempfänger* sat on a table near the oven, a doily protruding from under it. The simple radio permitted listening to German stations only, except for the BBC, which was usually jammed. I walked over to the bedroom, the only other room besides the kitchen. Two steps led up to the door with its lace-covered windowpanes. When I opened the door I saw two tiny windows facing the street at sidewalk level—the same windows I had noticed as we entered the house. Feeble light came through the heavily curtained windows, which Oma and Opa probably never opened. The room smelled musty, and the dark brown of the furniture made the place look even darker than it already was.

I heard Opa Grapentin open the outside door and park his bicycle in the hall. He was coming home from work at the sugar refinery. The handles scraped the wall as the bike settled into place. Opa, over six feet tall, was surprised to see me. He stooped as he entered the room to keep from hitting his head. He was totally bald and had a huge Kaiser Wilhelm mustache with long handlebars. I jumped into his arms. Carefully he lifted me up with his powerful hands, not wanting to smash my head into the low ceiling. His eyes were bright blue and shining with excitement. He put me down again and went over to Oma to give her a squeeze. Then he greeted Mutti. "Hedwig, how are you?" he said. I knew she hated to be called Hedwig. "Lots of lipstick and powder on your face again, huh? You know people around here are going to talk when they see you with this big-city stuff on your face. You ought to get rid of it while you're here." Oma had never worn makeup. Opa hugged his youngest daughter. A frown spread across my mother's face. Opa didn't notice. He hugged Ingrid and then proceeded to wash his hands in a chipped porcelain basin which sat on a worn chair in the kitchen. Next to the wash basin, on a wooden bench, stood two dented tin buckets of water. The water was for all purposes—cooking, washing, drinking. A ladle hung from the rim of one bucket. The water came from a hand pump in the backyard. I had forgotten that many people still lived without running water, without sinks, and without gas or electric stoves.

Oma was not nearly as tall as Opa, perhaps five feet at most, but tall for an old woman, I thought. Oma Samuel wasn't even five feet tall, I was sure of that. Oma Grapentin had blue eyes just like Opa. Mutti had told me that Oma's hair had once been blonde. When she was young, Oma must have looked like one of those BDM girls I had seen in a poster with their blue eyes and blonde hair, dressed in black athletic shorts and a white athletic shirt. The *Bund Deutscher Mädel*, BDM, was for girls what the Hitler Youth was for boys. They were the only authorized youth organizations in Germany.

Ingrid and I washed our hands in the same water Opa had used. We sat down for dinner around the table in the family room, Opa on the sofa against the wall. Oma served white gravy, her specialty, and a heaping bowl of boiled potatoes. We peeled the potatoes ourselves at the table as we ate. Mutti peeled Ingrid's. I watched Opa use his fork to cut his potatoes into pieces and pour a generous helping of the gravy over them. I did the same. The gravy tasted fine. Mutti and Ingrid didn't eat much. After dinner Oma and Mutti cleared the table, and I helped Opa feed Max.

Max was really a she-pig. In my mind she was a he, because her name was Max. Max was close to three hundred pounds. Oma had boiled a pot of red potatoes for Max. "Red potatoes are pig potatoes," Oma told me. When I tasted them, they seemed just as good as white potatoes. Opa took the potatoes and poured off the water. With a special tool he chopped the steaming potatoes into pieces, adding chopped grain, and poured the mixture into Max's trough. Max knew it was feeding time and squealed loudly in anticipation of his dinner. Her dinner. Max, like her predecessor, was destined to be food for the coming year. Opa smoked the hams, bacon, and sausages in a room in the attic. The rest of the meat he put in brown earthen jars, and packed it in salt for preservation. After feeding Max, Opa washed up. Then he lit his pipe and lay down on the sofa, letting out a loud sigh. He soon seemed to get tired, and placed his pipe on the table and closed his eyes. Ingrid climbed on top of him and stroked his bald head. She ran her hands over his head and squealed with delight. I hadn't heard Ingrid laugh in a long time. I fell asleep watching her and found myself the next morning covered with a blanket and undressed to my underwear, sleeping on one of the two couches in the family room. Opa was ready to go to work at the sugar refinery when I awoke. He was finishing his breakfast of rye bread thickly spread with lard. He had an enamel mug of ersatz coffee before him. He was a teamster at the refinery near the *Bahnhof* with his own team of powerful draft horses. Opa had been around horses most of his life. He liked horses, I could tell from the way he talked about them. He spoke of them as if they were people. Opa left early in the morning and came home at five-thirty in the evening. On Saturdays, he worked until noon.

While we were in Berlin, Mutti had applied for ration cards. She was issued a certificate from the *Prenzlauer Berg Stadtverwaltung*, the city council, certifying that we were *Flüchtlinge*, refugees, and authorizing us to receive ration cards. Without ration cards, we could not obtain food in any store in Germany. Our cards provided for bread, sugar, flour, meat, milk, and other basic foods. As in Sagan, the cards had to be registered at the grocery store of our choice, and it was the only store where we could buy our rations for that month. My thoughts of ration cards brought back memories of Sagan. For some reason, although we lived outside the town limits, Mutti always registered our cards with stores in town. The grocery store of Mutti's choice was Jacobs Kolonialwaren Geschäft. The milk store, bakery, and butcher shop she chose were also in town. Jacobs was twice the distance it would have been to a smaller nearby grocery store. Mutti wouldn't allow me to shop there, because the store didn't have the food selection she required. Maybe Mutti knew what she was doing, but she wasn't the one who went shopping most of the time.

One week the previous summer I ended up going to the store every day, twice on some days. When I wasn't doing that, Mutti made me vacuum the rugs and the sofas, sweep the floor, wash the dishes, or just sit near her in case she needed help. The weather was beautiful, and I wanted to be outside playing with my friends. All week long she never had a nice word for me. I began to feel sorry for myself and wanted to hurt her—not to harm her, but to have something happen that would make her appreciate the things I did for her. Every time I went to town on another of her many errands, I prayed to God to let me die. That would hurt her for sure, I thought. Then she would be sorry.

One Sunday my friends wanted to go to the Bober River. We played there on a small beach where the river came around a bend. To my surprise, Mutti let me go. I ran off quickly so she couldn't change her mind. The river was high, and the water was flowing fast, eddying around the bend, forming little whirlpools. Other people were enjoying the cool, refreshing water on a beautiful summer day. I waded straight into the river up to my hips. Almost immediately I felt the water pulling me toward the middle of the river. I tried to walk back to shore. To my astonishment, I couldn't. I felt a powerful force holding me back as I turned against the flow. And I couldn't move my feet without being pulled farther into the river. As much as I tried, I couldn't overcome the unexpected undertow. I stood still as the water swirled around me, trying to tear my feet out from under me. I felt scared, but not panicked. I asked a girl nearby to hold my hand. She gave me a funny look, then held out her hand for me to hold on to. I asked her please to pull me out. Instead, she let go. The undertow dragged me down immediately, sweeping me under the water and out into the middle of the river. I couldn't swim.

The swiftly running water thrust me down. I thrashed with my arms and kicked with my legs as hard as I could to get my head above water. I screamed, *"Hilfe, Hilfe!"* Then I was under again, out of air, fighting to get my head above water for one last time. Mustering my remaining strength, I forced my head up once more. Then my strength was gone, and I swallowed water. Below, all I saw was swirling green water and rising air bubbles. I knew I was drowning. Then, suddenly, strong arms grabbed me from underneath. Holding me under his left arm, the man swam to shore using his right. When the water was shallow, he stood up and set me on my feet. "Are you all right?" he asked.

"Yes, I am fine," I sputtered, coughing water from my lungs.

"Bend over," he said. "Let's get the water out of you." He patted me forcefully on the back. I coughed for a long time until the water was out and I could breathe normally. I thanked him and stood there on the beach not knowing what I should do next. I was in deep shock from the suddenness and near finality of the experience. The man walked back to his girlfriend and the blanket they were sharing. He was probably a soldier back from the *Front* on home leave. I realized that only chance had saved my life. If the soldier hadn't been lying in the sun with his girlfriend, I would have drowned. I became aware of the girl who had let go of my hand. She still stood in the river, staring at me with an expressionless look. I slowly walked home. I never again asked God to let me die.

I stopped daydreaming. We were not in Sagan. The Bober River was far away. We had ration cards, and in Strasburg I no longer had to do the shopping.

With Mutti's cooking skills, the Grapentin diet became more varied. It seemed that Oma Grapentin knew how to cook five meals, and did so over and over again, if we let her do the cooking. Oma's meals all included potatoes—salt potatoes, peeled when raw and cooked in salt water, potatoes boiled in their jackets and peeled at the table, potatoes fried in margarine or lard, mashed potatoes, and, finally, sweet-and-sour potatoes, which really were salt or mashed potatoes in a sweet-and-sour gravy. Oma knew how to make only one kind of gravy, a flour-based, white gravy. With vinegar and sugar added, it became a sweet-and-sour gravy.

We ate salt herring whenever it was available, which was frequently, and pork sausages and ham from their own pig. Sometimes Oma got beef or chicken at the butcher's. Beef was expensive, so she usually bought mixed ground beef and pork and made *Königsberger Klopse*, hamburgers in gravy. Vegetables were available in season either from the store or from Opa's garden near the sugar refinery on the *Schlammberg*. Opa was assigned a small piece of land on a hill created from the dirt washed off sugar beets as they were delivered to the refinery from the fields. Over the years this mound of dirt amounted to a sizable hill called the *Schlammberg*. On Opa's patch of land, he planted potatoes, tomatoes, cucumbers, cabbage, kohlrabi, onions, rutabagas, and carrots. Potatoes, rutabagas, and carrots were the most important crops, because they could be stored to last through the winter. After Opa harvested his potatoes, he stored them, along with carrots and rutabagas, in a shallow silo. He covered the vegetables first with a thin layer of straw, then a layer of dirt, then a second layer of straw and more dirt to keep them warm and dry through the winter. Unless it was a really severe winter, the straw and dirt blanket kept the potatoes and carrots from freezing.

The daily life of my grandparents Grapentin differed from that of my grandparents Samuel. Oma and Opa Grapentin rented a tiny apartment, which was old and without conveniences. They had nearly no possessions. And yet, they seemed to have few wants and were happy. The simplicity of their life, heightened by the contrast with that of my other grandparents and with my own home in Sagan, led me to think about what was important if one was to be happy. My mother and father were not happy, and we had once had all the things my grandparents didn't have. Why were they happy when they were so poor? The small plot of land on the *Schlammberg* was my grandparents' only private possession of any substance. On the *Schlammberg* they did things for themselves. It didn't seem to be work to them when they toiled there. I sensed pride radiating from my grandparents whenever they spoke of the *Schlammberg*. They loved that little patch of land.

Although I knew that Mutti had an older sister and a younger brother, I didn't really know them. Uncle Ernst was in the Wehrmacht, assigned to the artillery in the fortified town of Brest on the Atlantic coast of France.

No one had heard from Ernst in a long time. Marie lived in Strasburg with her three children—Vera was the oldest at fifteen, Kaete, the second girl, was thirteen, and Heinz was my age. At first sight Heinz and I disliked each other. He told his friends that I was from Berlin, a big-city kid. His friends didn't like big-city kids and immediately threatened to beat me up. I had never been in a fight in my life. I didn't even know if I was strong enough or had the courage to defend myself. It bothered me that I didn't know if I had courage. I thought I did. But that was like thinking I wasn't afraid of big dogs when there weren't any around. I knew I would find out soon enough.

The boys on my street asked me to join their stick hockey game. I soon discovered that it was a ruse, an opportunity to beat up on the big-city kid. Over and over again they whacked me across the legs when the ball should have been played. I was playing with my grandfather's cane. Once I figured out that whacking me across the legs was no accident, I quickly got back at the legs of my tormentors until their watching mothers came running over, screaming at me that I was a city ruffian, and chased me off.

The streets on our side of the *Marktplatz* led to a cross street at the bottom of the hill which turned north after a few hundred meters, eventually running into the main east-west road to the town of Woldegk. A minor dirt road ran between houses into open fields. The dirt road was closed off by a tank barrier. I became uneasy at seeing the barrier. If they had built tank barriers, they must be expecting Russian tanks. My sense of security diminished with the sight of the barrier. From its top, though, I gained a great view of the surrounding area, and I discovered to my surprise that the town had a medieval wall.

On the *Marktplatz* stood a two-story building with yellow stucco walls. Its offices were occupied by the *Bürgermeister*, the police, and the many party functionaries. In front of the building stood a flagpole with the *Hakenkreuzfahne*, the Nazi swastika flag, flying from it. Next to it grew an oak tree, chest high. I knew that every German town and village had such a tree planted in a prominent place. It was the *Tausendjährige Eiche*—an oak to show the destiny of the Third Reich, which was to last for a thousand years. When my grandfather Samuel had told me about the tree one year while I was visiting him, he had laughed loudly and said, "What fools they are." I didn't know what he meant. Russian prisoners of war were building a platform next to the flagpole.

A Town Called Strasburg

The *Marienkirche* towered on the northeast corner of the *Marktplatz*. Built of cobblestones and red brick, it and the town wall were the oldest structures in Strasburg. The *Marienkirche* was the church my mother and father had been married in, and where I had been baptized. Strasburg's main street ran east and west, coming from the town of Pasewalk in the east and leading to the town of Woldegk in the west and known locally as the Pasewalker Chaussee and the Woldegker Chaussee. The road skirted the *Marktplatz* and was frequently used by Wehrmacht traffic. I crossed the *Marktplatz* heading north on Bahnhof Strasse, the way Opa Grapentin rode to work every morning on his bicycle. I passed small stores and apartment houses. Two stores caught my attention. They appeared to be permanently closed, their windows dirty. I peered through the glass in the door of one. Inside were empty shelves and barren counters. In Germany a dirty window was truly rare except maybe in a cow barn. I went on my way, puzzled.

Farther down the street was the post office, near the two cemeteries. Built of red brick with a red tile roof, it was one of the more modern and prominent buildings in town. Its architecture copied a style once favored by merchants in the old salt town of Lüneburg and in coastal cities such as Hamburg, Lübeck, and Rostock. The face of the building narrowed in stairstep fashion until it came almost to a point at the apex. Had it been one of the old merchant buildings, there would have been a winch or some sort of lifting device installed at this point. The entry was framed by a gothic-style facade, and above it in German script was a wrought-iron sign which read *Postamt*.

Just beyond the post office, I noticed yet another cemetery, very small with broken and toppled gravestones. Weeds grew everywhere. Its poor condition prompted me to enter through a rusty gate. I tried to read the inscriptions. It was difficult. Nearly every stone was badly defaced. Then I found one stone on which I could make out a name—my own, Samuel. I couldn't read anything else. I deciphered another name, Jacobsohn. Every cemetery I had ever seen was well taken care of. Why not this one? I left the cemetery troubled, wondering. Just beyond it lay the larger old and new town cemeteries, which were neat and clean. Why not this one?

As I continued walking down Bahnhof Strasse between the two cemeteries, I suddenly noticed a number of men and women in blue work uniforms digging a deep trench. Their guards were Volkssturm men wearing rumpled, old uniforms, with old-fashioned long rifles slung over their shoulders. The workers were silent as they dug; the only sounds came from their spades and pickaxes penetrating the once-sacred earth. The trench they dug went right through the middle of the old cemetery. Bones and skulls were thrown aside as the workers came to them. Some bones still had bits of clothing on them. One skull landed right in front of my feet. I was startled by the hollow sound the bouncing skull made as it came to rest before me, eye cavities staring emptily up at me. The skull seemed to have a full set of teeth. Around me I could hear the sounds of shovels and pickaxes striking the ground, of dirt as it thudded into an ever-growing barrier, and of skulls being tossed aside. No one spoke. The workers didn't look at each other. Whoever they were, they made me feel afraid, even though they appeared to be ordinary men and women, just looking tired and gaunt. How could anyone disgrace a cemetery like this? I thought. I was appalled. I was taught to respect the dead. I had to talk to Opa Grapentin about this. The trench led right across the sidewalk and into the street. Only one lane was left open for traffic. I felt sick to my stomach at the sight of what was happening here.

I walked back toward the *Marktplatz*. As I entered the square, I noticed immediately that the platform the Russian prisoners had been working on was finished. They were in the process of raising a beam into position. I watched as they worked. They moved slowly. It took several of them to do simple tasks. The beam was slowly placed into a hole dug next to the platform. An arm at the top of the beam reached out, and a heavy rope ran down from it through several pulleys. One end of the rope ended in a noose. It was a gallows. This was 1945, I thought. We didn't use gallows anymore. I was confused by all I had seen on my walk through Strasburg. When we first arrived, Strasburg had looked like a peaceful country town. Now, Strasburg scared me.

It was dinnertime when I got home, and Opa was already there. I hurriedly washed my hands. The five of us sat around the table in our usual places. Opa helped himself first from a steaming bowl of potatoes. Then he proceeded to peel the hot "earth apples," as Oma frequently called them. To me "potato" was just a word. "Earth apple" sounded as if it belonged in a poem. Opa put a generous helping of salt on the rim of his plate. His plate was chipped like all the others. Mutti would never have kept a chipped plate in our cupboard in Sagan. Opa dipped his potatoes one by one into the heap of salt before biting off half or more. When I tried to imitate Opa, Mutti gave me a stern look. I ate my potatoes with knife and fork. When Opa was finished eating, he wiped his hands on his trousers, pushed his plate away, and rested his elbows on the table, hands folded before him.

Each evening after dinner, Opa lay down on the couch, and soon his loud snoring announced that he had fallen into a deep sleep. He usually didn't get to sleep long, because Ingrid quickly climbed on top of him, either lying down at his side or sitting astride his chest. Ingrid liked to stroke Opa's bald head with her hands. Sometimes she took a piece of firewood from the bin and gently tapped him on the head with it.

"Don't let Ingrid do that, Father," Mutti warned him one evening.

"The little one just wants to play, Hedwig," Opa said, brushing her off. His eyes were closed as he spoke. "She means no harm. You are too strict with the children anyway. She is such a sweet little girl." Then, Ingrid hit Opa over the head with the piece of firewood. The blow cut his skin and a rivulet of blood ran down his bald pate. I nearly laughed out loud when I saw how he shot up from the couch, dumping Ingrid on her back. I ran outside in the yard so I could laugh without being seen or heard. After that experience Opa never humored Ingrid again.

This evening, though, I needed to talk to Opa before he went to sleep. When Mutti and Oma were busy washing dishes and before Opa had a chance to lie down, I reached over and touched his hand. He looked surprised. He had just lit his pipe and was enjoying the first puff of fragrant smoke after a long day of manual labor.

"Opa, I am confused about a lot of things I saw today."

"Yes, Wolfgang," he replied with a tired smile, taking his pipe out of his mouth. "What is it that you saw that would trouble a young boy enough to keep his old grandfather from enjoying a bowl of tobacco?" His comment made me hesitate, but I went on.

"In the old cemetery, people are digging a ditch. The diggers throw the bones aside as if they didn't matter. Someone even threw a skull right at my feet. I don't know why anyone wants to dishonor the dead. It's awful. Why are they doing that?" He appeared uncertain how to answer and hesitated. The silence was interrupted by the clatter of dishes and pans from the kitchen. When he spoke he did so slowly, puffing on his pipe, watching smoke rings drift lazily toward the ceiling.

"Wolfgang, the Russian armies are east of the Oder River. There are some people who think they could break through our lines and advance as far as Strasburg. As a precaution they are building a trench to stop any tanks that might get this far." He paused, puffing on his pipe to keep it from going out. "Don't worry," he continued as if speaking to himself, "it will not happen. The Oder is a wide river. The Russians will never get across. You are quite safe here. I am sorry about the cemetery." He paused, tamping his pipe, then he laid it aside. "I am sorry about everything, Wolfgang," he said softly. Then he lay down on the couch and closed his eyes.

Opa hadn't said anything about the bones of the dead, or why they were being treated with such disrespect. I didn't speak to him about the unkempt cemetery either, or about the gallows and the empty shops with the dirty windows. After his comment about the Oder River I decided not to ask any more questions. I knew my Opa Grapentin was good with horses, but maybe he didn't know much about the world. Why did he think the Oder was so wide that the Russians couldn't cross it? I knew how narrow the river was, because I had crossed it frequently when I went to visit my grandparents Samuel. I knew the Oder would not stop the Russians. They had crossed much wider rivers in Russia. I knew that our peace and quiet wasn't real and soon would come to an end.

Mutti roused me from my thoughts. "To bed with you," she said, playfully scooping up Ingrid. Ingrid and I slept with Mutti in the bedroom. Opa slept on one couch in the family room while Oma slept on the other; they always got up early anyway. After the evening chores, Oma liked to sit in her rocking chair by the oven, knitting. Sometimes she would nod off, I thought, yet never stop knitting. I would be sure she was asleep and watch her closely. Yet her hands would still be knitting. She denied ever having gone to sleep when I asked her about it. "It just looks that way," she said, smiling. "I don't ever fall asleep, Wolfgang."

The following day Oma asked me if I would like to go shopping with her. She held my hand as if I were still a little boy. I let her because I sensed it made her feel good. Touching was good. We passed one of the empty stores with the dirty windows. "Oma," I said, "tell me why this store is empty. And why are its windows dirty and not washed?" She gave me a sideways glance, continuing to pull me away from the store. "Oma," I persisted, "why don't you want to stop and answer me?" My voice was rising. People were looking. "I want to know."

We walked on more slowly. After a long pause, she looked down at the concrete walk and said in a low voice, almost a whisper, "The people who owned that store were Jews. I don't know why they were taken away three years ago. We never saw them again. The store has been empty ever since. They must have done something wrong or they wouldn't have taken them away, would they?" Oma looked at me with her pale blue eyes, troubled now. She wasn't smiling.

"Why take people away because they are Jewish?" I continued to question her. "Weren't they Germans like you and me? Who took them away and where did they take them, Oma?" She didn't answer. Instead she gripped my hand harder, pulling me along. Oma, always kind and gentle, had a serious look on her face for the first time since I had known her. I was sorry for causing her pain. I could tell she didn't want to be near that store or talk about it. She was afraid.

The days in Strasburg were exceptionally sunny and warm for early April. Ingrid turned six on the seventh. I was sitting outside by the front door on a stone cemented into the sidewalk next to our door. A young man with a dull expression in his eyes, his mouth open, his lower lip hanging and drooling, came stumbling toward me. He moved his head from side to side, back and forth, just like I had seen horses do on my uncle Alfred's farm. His winter coat was tattered and his sweater was full of holes. When he became aware of me, he stopped, his body leaning forward, his arms hanging. Then he moved into something like a trot, stretched his hands out toward me, and simply said, *"Brot. Brot."* Smelling unclean, he stood before me.

"Wait," I said, feeling pity for him, "I get you some *Brot*." I gave him two slices of bread thickly spread with lard. He nodded his head in thanks several times before he stumbled on, eating his bread as he went. I went inside to talk to Oma.

"Who is that man begging for bread?" I asked her.

"Oh, he is our town idiot."

"Where does he live?"

"In a shack down the street near the old town wall with his mother. He is lucky to be alive," Oma whispered, not interrupting her knitting.

"What do you mean, he is lucky to be alive, Oma?" I blurted out.

"You ask so many questions, Wolfgang," Oma chastised me. "I don't really know myself. One day last year he disappeared for several weeks. We thought they had taken him somewhere where they put people to sleep who are not right in the head. He came back. They castrated him instead, so he can't have children. He was lucky." I went back out into the street and sat

A Town Called Strasburg

down on my stone near the door. Castrated. I didn't know what the word meant. Put people to sleep who are not right in the head? Who did those things to people who needed our help? And why?

On Thursday, April 12, Opa Grapentin came home in uniform. He had been drafted into the Volkssturm. An old man of fifty-nine. Why would they try to make a soldier out of my grandfather? When I asked him, he gave me no answer. He took off his jacket, his face haggard, his eyes unsmiling, and sat down at the table. Over dinner, between bites of potatoes, Opa explained what happened to Mutti and Oma.

"About noon they came by and asked for my name. Grapentin, I said. They went down a list of names and then said, 'Oh, here he is,' and scratched my name off their list. 'Herr Grapentin,' one of them said, 'you are now a member of the Volkssturm. You are relieved of your duties at the refinery. Go and draw your uniform and weapon.' He told me where I was to go. I stabled my horses and went there. They gave me an old rifle, like the one I had in 1914. When I told them I knew how to use it, they said, 'Good, you don't need any further training then.' They immediately assigned me to guard Russian prisoners of war at the refinery. The regular guards have been withdrawn for duty at the Oder front." I knew Opa had been a real soldier once. He fought in the battles around Verdun in France in 1916. There he was poisoned by gas. Now he had to go to war again. It wasn't right. I nearly cried as I looked at my grandfather.

On April 13, the radio announcer spoke of the death of the American president, Roosevelt. He forecast, in a voice filled with euphoria, that the death of that evil man was a significant event and a major turning point of the war. "Victory in the end will be ours," he prophesied.

I overheard boys talking about a trench system being dug east of town. I got there just in time to see a group of Volkssturm soldiers being instructed in the use of the *Panzerfaust*. About twenty-five meters from where they stood, someone had erected steel plates to serve as targets. I walked up to the group of old men and stood next to a wounded Wehrmacht soldier, unfit for duty at the front but healthy enough to teach the old men the basics of firing the *Panzerfaust*.

"It's a simple weapon, dear sirs," the instructor said to the old men looking at him with wide eyes. "You aim, squeeze the trigger slowly, and fire." He hit the steel plate squarely with his *Panzerfaust*. I didn't know he was actually going to shoot the thing, and it startled me badly when the weapon suddenly went off right next to me. A hole burned through the steel plate where it hit. I learned from his demonstration not to stand behind a rocket when it is fired. Then the old men fired several *Panzerfaust*, some hitting their targets, most not. That completed their training, and the old men and the instructor walked off to receive their weapons. I stayed to inspect the new trenches which extended north and south of the Pasewalker Chaussee where it entered Strasburg, near the lake.

That evening it drizzled, then it turned cold. The rain soon stopped, the clouds broke, and I could see stars as I looked up at the sky before going inside for dinner. We were eating later than usual because of Opa getting home late. Tonight Oma had made something special, knockwurst. The wurst tasted of sawdust, and I shoved mine to the side of my plate, hoping Opa would ask for it. Opa Grapentin talked about his day and about the slow, phlegmatic Russian prisoners he was guarding. He spoke of them every evening.

On Monday evening, April 16, the radio announcer spoke of massive Russian attacks against the German lines along the Oder River. The announcer confidently reported that, with the exception of minor bridgeheads, which were in the process of being eliminated by counterattacking German troops, the attacks had been repulsed, with heavy losses to the Russians in men and matériel. I had heard words like that before in Sagan, and I knew the opposite was probably true.

At the dinner table on Wednesday evening, Opa acted agitated. He poked around in his potatoes with his fork and then he blurted out, "My Russian prisoners broke into our potato silo on the *Schlammberg*."

"How did that happen?" Oma asked quietly, as she cut up her potatoes with her fork and mixed them with the white gravy.

"As I marched them past the *Schlammberg* on our return to camp, they suddenly broke away from me and headed straight for our silo. They tore it open and stuffed potatoes into their pockets; some started eating them right there on the spot."

"They were probably hungry," Oma interjected. "What did you do?"

"I had to maintain order. When they didn't listen to me, I grabbed a stick and ran over to our silo and hit them over their backs until they left our potatoes alone."

"Why did you do that, Wilhelm?" Oma said, her voice quivering. She put down her fork and wiped tears from her eyes with her apron. Oma rose from the table and went into the bedroom, crying.

"What could I do?" Opa continued. "We need our potatoes until the new crop comes in, or we won't have enough with you and the children here."

"Couldn't you let them have the few potatoes they took without beating them, Father?" Mutti spoke up.

"Yes, I could have," Opa answered. "My temper got the best of me. I am sorry I hit them. I know they don't get much food." We finished dinner in a somber mood. Mutti cleared the table. Opa, instead of relaxing on his couch as he usually did, went outside and cleaned the pigsty.

The following day, April 19, a somber radio announcer—so confident of German successes against the attacking Russians three days earlier—spoke of heroic resistance by encircled German troops in East Prussia. He spoke of Allied bombing raids causing severe damage to churches, hospitals, and cultural treasures, and he mentioned finally that Soviet troops, in their attempts to encircle Berlin, had been able to expand their bridgeheads over the Oder against stubborn German resistance. That night our dinner was potatoes and salt herring. Each of us had half a herring, except Ingrid, who had rice with cinnamon sugar. As Opa talked, I heard a faint and most unusual sound. It was high-pitched, persistent, penetrating, and totally unfamiliar. At first I thought it was an angry bee buzzing my head. "Do you hear that sound, Opa?" I asked.

"What sound?" he replied, showing his displeasure at being interrupted in mid-sentence. He continued eating and talking about the Russian prisoners. Then, in a rush, the noise rose to an overpowering crescendo, heading straight for us. I looked at Opa; the potato stuck on his fork was stopped halfway between the plate and his mouth, which was wide open. The sound grew louder, demanding our full attention. Whatever it was seemed about to crash into our house. I pulled my head down between my shoulders. Mutti, Oma, Opa, and Ingrid sat rigid, shocked into silence, engulfed and mesmerized by the strange, ever-increasing sound. It reached a painful crescendo, passing directly over us, rattling dishes in the cupboard, shaking pictures on the walls, passing through my body like an invisible knife, then quickly receding into the night. I knew instantly that it was an aircraft, a Russian aircraft that had dived at us out of the night sky and passed only meters over our house, at chimney height. The sound of its two engines was brutal and raw. For the briefest of moments, I thought I could hear the pounding of the laboring pistons and the turning propellers clawing their way through the heavy night air. Into my head sprang a vision of a leather-helmeted, begoggled pilot, straining to see through the dark night, hunched forward over his control column, grasping it tightly in his sweating hands, guiding his aircraft in a death-defying dash over the darkened town beneath him. Then the sound of the engines receded into the night.

'Four explosions followed in quick succession, shaking our house. All five of us jumped up from the table. Mutti grabbed Ingrid and ran outside, with me close behind. We were joined by others in the street. I could make out flames from a fire raging somewhere in the street behind ours. I ran over to the street where the bombs had exploded. A building was burning brightly, and people were running in and out of it trying to save their possessions. I watched women carrying furniture, dishes, and fine crystal into the street. Several men were in the house and in the courtyard fighting the fire with buckets of water, passing them from one to another. Others furiously pumped water from a hand pump. Unlike Berlin, Strasburg had no organized fire brigade. The horses that pulled the ancient fire wagon had long ago been drafted into the Wehrmacht. I went closer to get a better view. The old town wall was at the back of the courtyard. I climbed on it. To my surprise I found that one of the bombs had hit the wall near where I stood but had done little damage; there was only a bowl-like indentation. The damage to the house was not extensive. The high flames had come from burning straw in a barn behind the house. As the fire came under control, the women who had brought their precious possessions into the street be-came more concerned about losing them to the crowd which had assembled to gawk. They posted guards while they carried their treasures back into the house.

Early the next morning, I returned to the neighborhood near the bombed house. I searched along the sides of buildings and soon found what I was looking for—shrapnel from the exploding bombs. Splinters lay along the housefronts that had been exposed to the bomb blast. Most fragments were one to two inches long and twisted, with sharp, jagged edges. I knew that if one of the fragments had hit me, it would have torn a hole in my body. I was certain that I had heard four explosions. I wandered about looking for the fourth bomb crater. I knew the house had been hit by two bombs. I returned to the old city wall where I had found the first crater last night.

Not far from it I saw another in a garden, also a shallow crater. The bombs couldn't have been large, not like those the Americans and the English dropped on Berlin. I sat on the old town wall basking in the morning sunshine, looking at the craters. I heard larks singing in the fields beyond. It would be a beautiful day. It was April 20, 1945.

Chapter 6

A BRAVE
GERMAN SOLDIER

Frau Zoske, Oma's next-door neighbor, was a mousy-looking woman, no more than five feet tall, with rotting blackened teeth, who rarely left her apartment. Her husband was in the Wehrmacht and had been declared missing the year before somewhere in Russia. Her second son, Horst, at fifteen, was in the Hitler Youth; he proudly wore his uniform when he went to his weekly meetings and on most other days of the week, too. His brown uniform shirt was adorned with the customary Hitler Youth patches and insignia. He wore black corduroy shorts held up around his thin waist by a wide, black leather belt on which he wore a Hitler Youth knife—short and stubby, with a diamond-shaped, enameled swastika emblem embedded in its black Bakelite handle. Around his neck he wore a black scarf, rolled under his shirt collar and held together by a leather fastener, a *Knoten*, with a triangular section of the scarf showing in back.

"This uniform belongs to my older brother, he is in the SS now," Horst said to me proudly. "It's difficult to get a winter and summer uniform anymore. I guess I am lucky, I have both." Horst paused briefly, looked at me intently, and then asked, "How old are you?"

"I'm ten," I replied with pride in my voice. Horst walked around me as if he were sizing up a prize horse. "Are you in the *Jungvolk?*" he asked.

"I don't know what you are talking about," I replied.

"You're ten years old, and the law says you have to join the *Jungvolk* when you are ten. You should know that you don't get into the real Hitler Youth until you are fourteen. We prepare you for entry into the real HJ"—he pronounced it HaYot—"when you are older and you've passed our tests. I'll take you to our office tomorrow and you can register there." I didn't know what to think. Just like that, Horst was signing me up for the *Jungvolk*. At two o'clock the next day, April 21, Horst knocked on our door to escort me to the Hitler Youth office. I followed reluctantly. We walked to the *Marktplatz*, Horst in his uniform, I in shorts, short-sleeved shirt, and sandals. Halfway across the *Marktplatz* I stopped and asked Horst what the gallows in front of the party offices was about.

"Oh, that? *Ja*, that is for Wehrmacht deserters, for spies and others who have committed treason against the Führer and the *Vaterland*. They'll be hung right there"—he pointed to the top of the gallows—"if we catch them. With their bodies hanging there, others will think twice before they run away from the enemy like cowards." He continued toward the Hitler Youth office. We walked down Bahnhof Strasse toward the *Postamt*. Horst pointed to a shop on our left, one of the two shops with dirty windows. "There is our office. Go in and register." I hesitated. He explained, "That is an old Jew shop we are using temporarily for our office. That's why the windows are so dirty. It hasn't been used in a long time. Go on in. Don't be afraid."

I kept stalling. "What is a Jew?" I asked Horst. "It is a religion, isn't it?"

He looked at me as if I had asked a stupid question. "You don't know what Jews are?" he said, planting himself in front of me with his hands on his hips. "They are our worst enemies. The Führer said so himself. Go on"—he motioned with his left hand impatiently—"go in there and register. You have much to learn." I slowly approached the shop. I could see several Hitler Youths standing behind the counter to the right of the door. Some were in full uniform. Others wore only their uniform shirts open at the neck without the scarf. I timidly opened the door and stepped inside. No one seemed to pay attention to me. I stood by the door undecided about what to do next. The dimly lit room was illuminated with one fly-specked lightbulb dangling from the flaking ceiling. Daylight filtered through the dirty store windows. As I stood in the shadows by the door someone shouted for me to step forward. I walked toward the shouting boy.

"How old are you?" he screamed into my face. I was terrified of him.

"Ten," I said in a whisper. "I am ten years old."

"When did you turn ten?" He continued shouting loudly.

A Brave German Soldier

"The second of February." I knew I was in deep trouble. It was April. He came around the counter and stopped in front of me with anger lighting up his eyes.

"You little swine," he said in a lowered tone of voice. "Why didn't you come and register in February when you turned ten? Don't you like the Hitler Youth? Maybe this little swine doesn't like us." He was shouting again, laughing loudly, and mimicking surprise by throwing his arms up in the air. My tormentor turned to face his fellow Hitler Youths behind the counter. No one responded to his act. Others were yelling at a pair of unfortunates like me whom I had not seen as I entered.

As he turned back toward me, I quickly said, "I am a *Flüchtling*. I couldn't register in February. I wasn't here."

"Fill out this form," he said in an almost civil tone of voice, handing me a stubby, dull pencil and a form. I was glad he had stopped calling me a swine, and was no longer screaming at me. I sat down in a chair behind a small table. The Hitler Youth remained standing. The form asked the usual questions—name, place of birth, date of birth, religion, address, mother's and father's names, places and dates of birth, religion, and occupation. I handed the completed form to the waiting Hitler Youth. Studying it for a while, he looked at me for a long time, and then he said, "Be here next Saturday, April 28, at four in the afternoon for your first meeting." I nodded my head and rose to leave. As I got to the door and was about to reach for the handle I muttered an embarrassed *"Heilitler,"* slurring the words as I always had in the past when I used the embarrassing greeting. I thought I was expected to render it in a place like this, though my grandfather Samuel had told me never to use it again.

A fist smashed into the right side of my head, downward across my face. I fell to my knees on the dirty wooden floor. My nose bled profusely. Blood dripped onto the raw, unpainted floorboards. I was both stunned and confused. I got back on my feet and looked around frantically, trying to figure out who had hit me, and raised my arms in front of my face to defend myself against further blows. I was close to tears, but I didn't cry. I couldn't let them see me cry, and I wanted out of this awful place. I wanted my mother. Several Hitler Youths gathered around me, shouting and screaming. They had not heard me give the German greeting loudly enough and with sufficient respect for the Führer.

"Maybe you want to try all over again," suggested one of them. "Maybe

A Brave German Soldier

you are a Jewish swine after all," my interrogator shouted more loudly, "with a name like Samuel." He said my name slowly—SA-MU-EL—enunciating every syllable clearly, loudly, as if it were distasteful for him to even speak my name. "Maybe we should have you taken away like the people who once had this store," he said, laughing loudly. "Now, show us a proper *Gruss*." They laughed. Blood still dripped from my nose, some fell on my shirt. I raised my right hand and shouted, *"Heil Hitler."* Ten or more times I shouted the German greeting. I was finally allowed to leave when they got bored with me.

"Out with you," one of them shouted, and I bolted out the open door. Once outside, I ran away from them as quickly as I could. I didn't want to go back ever again. I didn't want to have anything to do with those ugly boys. Blood was crusted on my face, and bloodstains were over the front of my shirt. I peeled the blood off my face where it had dried. I decided to hide my shirt at home and tell no one what had happened. Maybe the Russians would arrive before the first Hitler Youth meeting, I hoped in a wish for revenge, and I would never have to go back. Horst was nowhere to be seen. When I got home, I ran into my mother. She saw that I had a bloody nose and bloodstains on my shirt.

"What happened to you, Wolfgang?" she asked in a matter-of-fact voice. Then, without waiting for an answer, she added, "Take the shirt off and put it in cold water to get the blood out." I didn't tell her what had happened, and I knew she didn't really care to hear about it, either. The experience had been so ugly that I couldn't put it into words, and I wasn't sure if I could keep from crying if I told her.

"I had a fight," I said. "It doesn't hurt." That satisfied her. Mutti thought fighting was part of growing up, and in this neighborhood I, the big-city kid, was a favorite target anyway, and she knew that. I suspected she thought it was all right for me to get into a fight; in her opinion, it built character. I hated fights, but could do nothing about my situation. Unless I wanted to stay home all the time, I needed to be prepared for a fight whenever I walked the streets of Strasburg. The attacks from the local bullies were sudden and without provocation. Two or three, never just one, would come charging out of a doorway where they had hidden themselves from view, and all would start punching me in the face at the same time. When they tired of punching, they would run off as fast as they could to brag to their friends.

At first I was passive. I ignored the beatings and told myself that they

A Brave German Soldier

didn't hurt much. I just stood there and put my hands up to my face to fend off the blows. My behavior only encouraged the bullies and made them feel they were strong and powerful. Soon, as I finally figured out, every boy in the neighborhood thought he had to prove himself by beating up the big-city kid. Even my cousin Heinz sneered at me disdainfully. I was ashamed of myself. I had no courage after all. That's when I decided I had to do something about it. The next group of boys that attacked me was too large to properly defend myself against, and my response was haphazard and timid at best. The few punches I threw, most of them missing, were not recognized as fighting back. As they ran away screaming victoriously, which they always did after beating up on me, one small-statured boy lingered and came back a second time, wanting to get in one last punch. I knocked him flat on his back with a blow as powerful as I could muster, straight into his face. His surprise was total. Fear showed in his eyes as I stood over him. He ran off howling, humiliated, his right hand covering his bleeding nose and cut lip.

I stood there expecting the others to return and beat me up again in retaliation for what I had done. They didn't come back. They shook their fists at me and yelled obscenities. I felt good about myself. I looked at the knuckle on my right hand, which I had cut on the boy's front teeth, and sucked the blood off my wound. Maybe I wasn't a coward. Maybe I had had the strength all along to defend myself. After this encounter, I began to work out a plan for coping with the bullies. I thought about Winnetou and Old Shatterhand—two of my heroes from Karl May books I had read the previous summer. Winnetou was a fictional Indian chief, and Old Shatterhand, a German traveling in the American West, was his blood brother. They had to anticipate constant ambushes as they traveled in the wilds of North America. They survived by being vigilant and fighting more intelligently than their opponents. Strasburg was my wild America, I decided, the place in which I had to survive. So I made a plan. I wanted them to fear me so I would have peace and could go wherever I pleased.

Once I had my plan, the difficult part was putting it into action. I knew where to find my tormentors, but when I did, fear took hold of me. I wanted to turn and run away. If I ran, I knew they would catch me and beat me up. If I attacked instead, I tried to reason with myself, I would confuse them and maybe be able to whip them. So, taking my heart in my hand, I surprised them in their doorways and beat them with such fury that they forgot to fight back and ran. My plan worked the first time I tried it. Soon I had

A Brave German Soldier

whipped enough boys so that they left me alone, unless there were a lot of them. I learned two important lessons. First, there is no respect for weakness. Second, I found to my surprise that fear that built up inside of me before a fight gave me increased strength once I got into it. I didn't know why, but it worked that way. I found it interesting to learn such things about myself. Given a choice I would rather not have fought. But what could I do? This was my world. I had to survive in it.

Early Tuesday afternoon, April 24, while I still smarted from my bloody sign-up with the local Hitler Youth chapter, every boy in our area was rousted from his home and into the street by Hitler Youths. A uniformed Hitler Youth shouted, "Quiet. Everyone listen. You will form into groups of twenty. We will march east out of town where American bombers have dropped propaganda leaflets. You will pick up the leaflets. You will not read them. Your leader will tell you what to do with the leaflets if you find any. Understood? Now, let's go and form up."

A Hitler Youth shouted for those nearest him to form up. He counted off twenty of us, and we lined up according to height. Then he had us count off. "One, two, three, four . . . numbers six, eleven, and sixteen line up here in front of me, next to number one. Everybody else follow behind your man," he shouted. We shuffled around and lined up. "Stand still," he commanded. "Hands on your sides. Forward, march." We stumbled up the street toward the *Marktplatz* in a column of four. We marched past the gallows and then east out of town in the direction of Pasewalk. We joined up with other groups. All at once there were a hundred or more of us marching out of Strasburg. Women stood in their doorways, wiping their hands on their aprons—women were always wiping their hands on their aprons, it seemed to me—and watching. Wondering. Most of them wore head scarfs, and, if they had lost a family member in the war, their dresses were black, or they wore a black armband.

Our leader thought I was slouching, not looking like a good Hitler Youth. "Stand up straight," he shouted. "Get in step and move your ass smartly or I'll kick your butt."

I straightened up and tried to look like he wanted me to, paying attention to good marching form to keep him away from me. He passed on, yelling at others. We marched for an hour or more. Once we were out of town, we weren't really marching anymore, just loping along. The sun beat down on us from a milky white sky. We were hot and sweating profusely. Many of us were dressed much too warmly for the unseasonably hot weather. There was no rest. Our leader became tired, too, and didn't shout anymore. We turned off the main road onto a *Feldweg*, a rutted dirt path used by local farmers to get to their fields. The grass was thick and high in the middle and to the left and right of the two paths worn by countless wagon wheels. It was difficult to walk down the lane four abreast. So we strung out to fit onto the *Feldweg*. We came to a stumbling halt on our own without any commands being shouted. I was too tired and sweaty to wonder why. We started to sit down.

"Stand up," someone shouted, and others down the line echoed the command. We stood there in the midday heat. I watched our leader running to an assembly point where he and other group leaders received instructions. Each group leader soon returned. "Listen now," he shouted as he tried to catch his breath. "You will spread out in two lines so that when you stretch your arms you will just barely touch the fingers of the person on your right and on your left. Do it now." We scrambled to get into rank and file, double arm lengths apart. The same thing was happening in the groups next to us. When we stopped shuffling around, our group leader told us, "When the command is given, we will all step off at the same time and carefully search the field for leaflets. Pick them up. Don't read them. Turn them in to me." He must have seen a sign because he turned to us, raised his right hand, and pointed straight ahead, shouting, "Forward. Eyes to the ground."

I didn't know what I was looking for. I searched the ground in front of me, occasionally glancing at my neighbors, who seemed equally puzzled. Then I saw a cardboard roll, about one inch wide, around which was wrapped something silvery. Everyone started finding these rolls and running to our group leader for instructions. Our disintegrating line came to a ragged halt. As I looked to the left and right, it seemed everyone else was holding the same thing I was. Some boys held long, silvery aluminum strips. The word came down not to pick them up. It was *Düppel*, someone said, used by the Americans against German radars. What was radar? I had never heard of radar. I peeled back the covering of one of the spools I had picked up and discovered that I could pull out a long strip of aluminum foil which had not opened properly when it was dropped from the American bombers. We got rid of the aluminum strips and started moving forward again.

Then I saw a pink leaflet. I picked it up and glanced at it. It proclaimed in black block letters that the war was nearly over and that Hitler's days were numbered. It promised that no harm would come to us if we stayed off the roads and in our homes. I quickly turned the leaflet over and acted as if I had not read it. Others started finding leaflets, too, and soon everyone seemed to have found at least one or two. Then we were directed to return to the *Feldweg* from which we had started our search. I wore my long Hitler Youth pants. My pockets had holes in them by now. I stuffed one of the leaflets into my pocket, and it quickly slipped down my pants leg. Since the pants were tied off at the bottom the leaflet couldn't fall out. I turned in the remaining leaflets, and we started our long march back to Strasburg. It was dusk when I finally got home.

During the return march, I wondered why we had come out to pick up leaflets. There was no one in the fields except an occasional farmer. The first rain would have soaked the leaflets and made them unreadable. I was sure that everyone who found more than one leaflet probably kept one to take home to his family. I knew the war was coming to an end; I didn't need an American leaflet to tell me that. But we couldn't talk about what was happening. Everyone instead talked about *Wunderwaffen*, weapons which would destroy Germany's enemies and at the last minute save the Third Reich. Once I got home, I took Opa Grapentin and Mutti aside and pulled out my illegal find. They read the leaflet, and Opa kept it, cautioning me not to say anything to anyone. That evening I saw the American leaflets openly passed around by people up and down our street.

By April 28, the day of my first official Hitler Youth meeting, I had decided that I would not attend. Four days had passed since the leaflet-gathering episode. I found an opportunity to sit down alone with Mutti. I was deeply troubled about our situation. The news on the radio spoke of a great battle being waged around Berlin. That meant the Russians were actually in Berlin. I didn't want to believe it, yet I knew it was true. I also knew they would be in Strasburg soon. I took Mutti by the hand and pulled her down next to me on the sofa.

"Mutti," I pleaded, "you've got to listen to me, please."

"I will listen," she said with a thin smile on her face, "to what my smart boy has to tell me." It was not a good beginning for our talk. She was treating me like a baby.

"The Russians are in Berlin, Mutti, do you know that? I heard it on the radio. They will be in Strasburg any day. If we don't leave soon, it will be too late for us. I am afraid of what the Russians might do to us once they get here. We have to get out now, Mutti, or we will be stuck here like we almost got stuck in Sagan."

"Opa doesn't think the Russians will get here, Wolfgang," she replied in a colorless tone of voice, not looking me in the eyes.

"Mutti," I said in desperation, "Opa doesn't understand. He thinks this is the Great War again, when it isn't. The Russians will be here soon. You *must* know that, too. Don't you? You read the American leaflet."

My mother sat there for a minute, not moving, looking nowhere in particular. Her smile faded from her face. Then she said in a low monotone, almost as if she weren't speaking to me, "When we first came to Strasburg, two letters were waiting for me from your father. He thought that we would come to Oma's if we were able to get out of Sagan. Your father is now at a *Flugplatz* called Fassberg in the Lüneburg Heath. It's somewhere near Hannover. He had a house assigned to him for our use. He wrote that he wanted us to come right away. I could not get myself to go. Now it is too late. We can't go to Fassberg anymore." I was stunned by what she said.

"Why didn't you take us to Fassberg when the trains were still running, Mutti?" I said to her accusingly, looking up at her ashen face. I continued to stare at her in disbelief. How could she have done such a thing? Why? I suddenly felt abandoned by the only person left to me.

"You know your father and I do not get along, Wolfgang," she said tiredly. "You are too young to understand all the details, but, as I told you once in Sagan, as soon as the war is over I will divorce your father. I can't live with him ever again."

"Mutti," I protested, "this is different. He wants us safe, and he has a house for us. Let's go today. Maybe it's not too late."

"Wolfgang," she said, in the same monotone she had used throughout our conversation, "you may be right in what you are saying. This is April 28 and there is no way out of Strasburg anymore. We can't get to your father's even if I wanted to. I've checked. This time I waited too long. I am sorry, my boy. I know we have to leave Strasburg, no matter what Opa says. You are right about that." Fear of the future mixed with disappointment in my mother overwhelmed me. I could feel the tears rolling down my cheeks. She had betrayed us for no good reason. I had no one to hold on to anymore. I missed my grandfather Samuel.

"As you know, I have an army friend who is a dentist at the field hospital here in town," she continued. "The hospital is in the school near my sister

Marie's house." She paused. "He will help us." I didn't know how her friend was going to help us. All I could think of was what she had done to us. I wanted to run away and hide somewhere from her and everyone else. I hated war. I hated all the people who hurt people. I wiped the tears off my face. I knew the war wasn't Mutti's fault. It struck me suddenly that I was really afraid for my mother. I was afraid of what the Russian soldiers would do to her.

"I am not feeling well," Mutti said. I looked at her closely, and noticed for the first time that her face was pale. I felt guilty over my thoughts about her. She looked frail and small, as if she were trying to disappear into herself. Why hadn't I noticed before that she was ill?

"I think I'll lie down," she whispered, leaving me sitting on the couch with my feelings of guilt. That evening we again ate our usual meal of potatoes seasoned with salt. Mutti stayed in bed with a fever, shivering violently. Oma fixed *Kamillentee* for her and applied poultices to her forehead and chest to draw out the fever. Ingrid ate boiled rice with cinnamon sugar. Mutti's friend, the army dentist, brought a mess tin of boiled rice every night after the evening meal. The rice was intended for Oma, because Oma still had sore gums from the new set of false teeth he had made for her. Usually Ingrid got to eat the rice, because Oma claimed that she didn't like rice, and instead preferred eating potatoes dipped in salt with the rest of us. Opa spent most of his evenings away guarding the Russian prisoners at the sugar refinery. Tonight he was home for dinner. We sat in our usual places. Mutti remained in bed.

Opa Grapentin got up from the table and turned on the *Volksempfänger*. He tuned through the single-frequency band until he got to the station he was looking for. He turned the volume low. An ominous sound emanated from the radio. It was a rhythmic boom from a drum repeated four times in succession with the last boom higher in pitch than the others—boom, boom, boom, BOOM, boom, boom, boom, BOOM. It went on continuously. It was the BBC—the forbidden English radio station. Usually the broadcast was jammed with noise or squealing sounds and I couldn't understand very well what was being said. Tonight the station was clear and there was no jamming.

"Opa," I began haltingly, apprehensive about what he was doing. He motioned with his hand for me to be silent. The boom, boom, boom, BOOM went on for some time. Then an announcer came on the air and

A Brave German Soldier

reported in an even, unemotional tone of voice about happenings on the front in the west. As he described heavy German army losses, I learned for the first time that English and American troops were across the Rhein River deep inside Germany and that the Americans had linked up with Russian troops on the Elbe River. I was even more surprised by my grandfather's action of tuning in the BBC in my presence. I realized he had been listening to the BBC for a long time and had tried not to alarm us about the seriousness of the war situation. It was no longer any good to hide the truth. He felt we should share in it now, and turning to me he said, "Wolfgang, the Russians have crossed the Oder River. Berlin is lost."

Love for him welled up inside of me. My dear Opa wanted to protect us. He knew he shouldn't protect us from the truth any longer. He rose from his sofa and put on his worn army tunic. He wore no rank. On the lower sleeves of his overcoat he wore a band with the inscription VOLKSSTURM. Opa looked taller and more gaunt than ever before. His Kaiser Wilhelm mustache with its long handlebars sticking out on each side of his white face gave him the look of someone from another time. I knew this was not my grandfather's time, not his war. Opa struggled into his shapeless overcoat and put on his army cap. His cheeks were shiny. He looked tired, old, and apprehensive. He put his belt on over his overcoat. Leather cartridge cases were attached to the belt. When he finished dressing, he slung his old rifle over his right shoulder, put his left arm around Oma, and hugged her briefly. Then he said, *"Auf Wiedersehen."* He stooped low and went out the door. My Opa is not a soldier anymore! I felt like shouting. Let my Opa go! He needs to be with us here at home! But there was no one to scream to, no one to plead with.

The army dentist came later that evening bringing his mess kit of boiled rice. Mutti got out of bed, dressed, and put on her makeup before she went out to see him. I peeped through the windowpanes in the bedroom door and watched her and the dentist sitting on the couch. He was holding her hands and speaking softly. I could not make out his words. From the set of his body, though, I knew that whatever he was telling her was important. He seemed tense, without the friendly smile that was usually on his boyish-looking face. I opened the door slightly, carefully, so I could hear. He held Mutti's hands in his own and looked her in the eyes. I heard him say, "Now remember, Hedy, if you hear a knock on your door and you find an empty mess tin hanging from the handle, tonight or any other time, that means

A Brave German Soldier

we are leaving. We are a field hospital, and when we leave the Russians will only be a few kilometers behind us. You must go then. There will be no time to waste. Don't think about it, just take the children and go. The mess kit is the only way I have to send you a message. If I can't come myself, one of my orderlies will. Don't ask questions of him, just go. It will be your last chance."

Mutti nodded her head ever so slightly. He kissed her on the lips and held her tight for a moment. I felt embarrassed and closed the door, but I kept on watching. He let her go, held her hands for another moment, and then turned abruptly and left. I went back to bed quickly so Mutti would not discover I had been listening. I dozed off and woke when I felt Mutti shaking me, calling my name.

"Wolfgang, get up and get dressed. Put on your warm clothing. Help Ingrid dress. We are leaving." Her words were both terrifying and exhilarating. I had wanted to get out of Strasburg ever since we had arrived, and we were finally leaving. I also knew the Russians couldn't be far from town. On a table near the door in the family room sat an empty Wehrmacht mess tin.

Mutti was still sick, I could see that. Her face was ashen, as if there were no blood left within her, except for an unnatural red over her cheekbones. Her eyes had dark, almost black shadows around them, and they seemed to have sunk deeply into her head. A bright fire appeared to be burning in her brown eyes with an intensity that I had never seen before. Maybe it was the fever. When she thought no one was looking, I saw her standing with her arms wrapped around herself, shivering. That didn't keep her from doing what she felt had to be done. She was sick, yet full of purposeful action.

I dressed quickly and helped Ingrid into her dress, long stockings, and shoes. I tied her shoelaces. Her shoes still looked new, probably because Ingrid didn't play in the streets as I did. She wore a button-down sweater over a warm, dark-green dress with a pretty white collar. I helped her into her overcoat, placing her green cap on her head, the cap Mutti had sewn for her only days earlier. Her entire head was covered except for her face. I tied the strings under her neck. Ingrid sat quietly, letting me help her get dressed. Then she sat in Oma Grapentin's rocking chair near the tile oven, watching. She held her doll in her right hand, and over her left hand she had her muff. Mutti had an objective, that was plain to me as I watched her move around the room. Her usual flightiness and lack of interest in the outside world were replaced by an intense focus. She packed our things into the same three suitcases with which we had traveled from Sagan to Berlin and then on to Strasburg. She packed Oma's clothes into a fourth cardboard suitcase.

"How are we going to carry four suitcases?" she asked Oma. Oma suggested using a handcart. Mutti sat down, holding her head, overcome by a dizzy spell. She got up, holding her stomach, and went outside. She came back ten minutes later, not looking much better than before. Oma had retrieved a hand wagon from the shed in the backyard and pulled it into the corridor. Mutti took a quick look at the wagon and said, "We have to repack. Three suitcases is all that will fit." She started repacking our four suitcases into three.

"I don't need much," Oma said. "Only one dress and I'll wear my new winter coat."

"No," Mutti said, "I won't hear of it. Let me see your things." They climbed the two stairs to the bedroom where I sat on the bed, trying to stay out of the way. Looking in the *Schrank* and the dresser, Mutti took several additional things which she thought Oma would need. "Put on your best and sturdiest shoes," she told Oma.

"I only have one pair of shoes, Hedwig, and that's what I'll wear," Oma said firmly. I marveled at Oma. She did what Mutti told her, putting up no fuss about leaving her home. Opa must have talked to her. Oma, Ingrid, and I were ready to go. Mutti wore the hat she had worn when we left Sagan and a short, black skirt. She looked fashionable in her white silk blouse, silk stockings, and winter boots, as if we were going for a Sunday walk in the park. I was puzzled about her choice of clothing. She pulled a tailored, black velvet jacket over her blouse, and then she slipped into her fur coat. Although my mother obviously was still sick, probably with the flu, she looked pretty to me, all dressed up with her makeup on.

"Hedwig, no, not that coat. Not at a time like this," protested Oma.

Mutti turned around quickly, her eyes blazing. She looked Oma straight in the eyes and said, "Mother, our only chance of escape is to be picked up by an army truck heading west to the American lines. Do you think anyone is going to stop and pick up a frumpy-looking woman with two children and an old woman by her side? No. They'll stop for a pretty, well-dressed woman, if they stop at all. I am trying to look my very best. If we are lucky, someone will have a heart and will take a look at me—and stop for us." Oma turned away, chastened, and busied herself loading the suitcases onto the handcart.

A Brave German Soldier

Mutti put on her black leather gloves, and she, too, was finished dressing. I knew that underneath her fine clothing and makeup she was still ill.

"We are ready. Come, children, let's go," Mutti said resolutely. And with that, she grabbed her purse and stepped out into the hall, leaving behind her the humble place that was my grandparents' home. Oma could not tear herself away that quickly. I saw tears well up in her eyes. I knew Oma had never been anywhere else in her life. She had never left Strasburg. Yet she was going with her daughter Hedwig into the unknown, leaving her husband and her home behind. I felt sorry for her. We pulled our wagon through the front entrance into the street.

The door to Frau Zoske's apartment opened. Frau Zoske, suitcase in hand, stood in the doorway fully dressed, with her two boys, Horst and Günter, at her side. She gestured feebly toward Mutti, saying in a timid voice, "Hallo. Can we go with you? I have been watching you and I know that you know something, and we want to go along with you if you will have us. Please, let us come. We won't be any trouble." Frau Zoske was dressed as if she were going shopping. Her two boys stood behind her, fearful eyes dominating their pale faces.

"We have no time to waste," I heard Mutti say. "Come on. Let's go." Then, hesitating, she turned to the oldest boy, Horst, and said, "All those Hitler Youth things have to go. Get rid of them. Right now." The young teenager looked shaken. I knew how proud he was of the uniform he was wearing. He didn't want to understand Mutti's directions. His mother did.

"Come inside," she said to Horst. When they came out again, five minutes later, all vestiges of Horst's Hitler Youth pins, badges, and other distinctive items were gone from his clothes. He no longer wore his Hitler Youth shirt. Mutti motioned for us to hurry and join her on the street. A fine, cold rain was falling. Seven of us assembled in front of our tiny house. Our street was empty. It was just after midnight, the early morning hours of April 29, 1945. When I looked up the street toward the *Marktplatz*, I could see occasional dim lights and motion. From a distance it looked as if many vehicles were moving along the street, all going west, toward Woldegk. A low rumble emanated from the direction of the *Marktplatz*, an incessant monotone of sound coming from man, machine, and beast as they passed. Mutti walked up the street with Oma at her side. Horst and I pulled the cart. Ingrid, Günter, and Frau Zoske followed. As we approached the *Marktplatz*, the rumble of steel-rimmed wagon wheels pounding against hard cobblestones became louder and more distinctive. The sound of horseshoes striking stone, drivers yelling, truck engines revving, and gears shifting and grinding filled the night air—the sounds of a fleeing army, an army in retreat. I was scared as I looked at the chaotic scene. Strangely, I also felt anticipation and a glimmer of foolish hope that everything would turn out all right after all.

I saw Mutti standing by the side of the road, a woman in a fur coat with an elegant fur hat perched on her fashionably up-combed hair, waving her leather gloved hand at passing vehicles, wanting them to stop. Mutti turned toward us and told us to stay back. She moved a bit further up the sidewalk, separating herself from the rest of us, continuing to wave and call out to the passing traffic, "Hallo, please take us along. Hallo, somebody be so kind, please, stop and take us along. My husband is in the Luftwaffe and I need help with my two children. Please, hallo, somebody help us and take us . . ." She stood there alone in the cold drizzle by the side of the road, waving her arm incessantly at the mass of passing vehicles, pleading for help for her family. The usually empty and quiet *Marktplatz* was filled with the pandemonium of organized chaos. There was little light except from the occasional army truck or car whose headlights were covered with black electrical tape, leaving only small slits open to throw the narrowest beam of light on the road ahead. Some trucks were gasoline powered and others had been converted to charcoal burners, the gasses providing the means of propulsion. Those trucks smelled bad and were dirty. Most of the passing vehicles, though, were horse-drawn wagons.

Everything the Wehrmacht still possessed was mixed together, passing before my eyes. Men, horses, wagons, and trucks came from the east, heading west. Mixed in with the trucks and horse-drawn wagons were occasional antiaircraft guns. The vehicles were closely spaced and seemed to be pushing each other through town. As they passed I heard only the sounds of flight—an occasional shout when something went wrong, horses' hooves striking stone, wagon wheels clattering across uneven stones, engines revving, and the sound of nailed boots hurriedly passing. Mutti, undaunted by the chaos around her, waved at the passing vehicles, calling out to whoever cared to listen.

"Please stop and take us with you. Please, please, help us," I heard her say over and over again. Once, looking up at a soldier slowly driving his truck past who had apparently looked down and into her eyes, she pleaded, "Don't you have a wife and children?" The driver said nothing and looked

A Brave German Soldier

away quickly. He drove past the lone woman reaching for his heart. That sick woman, my mother, elegantly dressed, stood there untiringly, waving her hand, pleading for our lives. To me she looked like some lone figure out of a movie that was running before my eyes. Everything seemed unreal. But I could see, hear, and smell it all happening.

Wagons passed. Drivers occasionally cursed at their horses, using whips to urge them on. I looked up at the drivers, but they never looked down at me. In contrast to the near-panicky, disorganized mixture of vehicles that had passed us so far, a disciplined army unit came into view. They, too, had horse-drawn wagons, closely spaced like all the others, but the soldiers driving the wagons looked different. I saw no fear or panic in their moves or in their eyes. It was a unit of *Feldgendarmerie*, military police—the men other soldiers referred to in jest as *Kettenhunde* (chained dogs), because of the shields they wore around their necks. They rolled past us in a seemingly endless column of horses and wagons. Soldiers on motorcycles, some with sidecars attached, went up and down the column giving instructions to drivers. Suddenly, one of the drivers reined in his horses and brought his wagon to a full stop squarely in front of Mutti. She stood on the broken concrete sidewalk waving her hand, pleading for help, not realizing that someone had actually stopped.

"*Gnädige Frau*," the driver shouted loudly, trying to penetrate the word-swallowing noise of the road, "please give me the pleasure of your company and join me up here on my bench." My mother's hand stopped in midmotion, revealing for the briefest time her astonishment at what was happening. Quickly she regained her composure.

"I have children and my mother, can we all come?" she shouted.

"*Ja*," the soldier responded, "but, please, hurry."

First the wagon behind and then the entire column had come to a reluctant stop. A driver cursed. What had brought them to a halt? The soldier wrapped his reins around the wagon brake and jumped off his wagon. He grabbed our handcart and pulled it to the back of his huge army wagon and, with expert hands, using a piece of rope he pulled out from under his wagon, tied our cart to the back. Then he grabbed Ingrid and me and heaved us into the back of his covered wagon.

"The others have to go, too!" Mutti insisted, pointing at Oma, Frau Zoske, Horst, and Günter.

"They'll have to walk," the soldier said crisply. Then, turning to Mutti, he said, "Would you please give me the honor of your company and join me on my bench?"

Mutti responded with a smile in her voice, "*Ja*, I'll be happy to join you."

Behind us, the driver of the next wagon continued to shout foul curses. "Why are you picking up these *verfluchten Flüchtlinge*, bringing us to an unnecessary halt? Get going, you *Arschloch*. Move out, you *Scheisskopf*. I can't believe what this crazy man is doing," he screamed angrily. His cursing went on and on. The soldier remained unperturbed until he had Mutti settled on the wagon bench. Then he jumped off his wagon, and, in long, deliberate strides, he approached the impatient driver.

Looking the man straight in the eyes, he said coldly, "Do you have a family? If they were standing by the side of the road, would you want someone to stop and pick them up? Or would you want them to fall into Ivan's hands?" Without waiting for a response, the soldier walked back to his wagon, climbed aboard, unwrapped the reins from the brake handle, and released it. The horses moved forward without urging. The column began to move again. From my perch in the back of the wagon, I could see Mutti sitting up front. She looked even more beautiful to me now. She had done the impossible. She had worked a miracle.

Ingrid curled up with her back pushed against a cardboard box. She looked like she was going to sleep, or at least she was shutting out the world around her by closing her eyes. The noise of the steel-rimmed wagon wheels passing over the uneven cobblestone pavement and the clip-clop of horseshoes was tranquil music to my ears. I began to doze off happily in my newly found security. In our wagon. We were going west, away from the Russians, toward the American lines.

I was awakened by unfamiliar noises. I didn't know immediately where I was. Then I saw Mutti's silhouette next to the driver, and I remembered. How could we have been so lucky? How could Mutti have thought up such a plan and made it happen? She was extraordinary, I thought. I saw Ingrid next to me sleeping comfortably. Her breathing was regular. I found a more comfortable position for myself amongst the boxes. I saw Oma Grapentin, Frau Zoske, Horst, and Guenter walking behind our overloaded handcart, making sure that the cart did not overturn as it bounced over the cobblestoned road. We were moving fast, much faster than we could have done walking and pulling a cart. As I stared at Mutti sitting in front of me, I recalled happier times, times when she would gather Ingrid and me into her bed and, with her arms around us, tell us about her childhood. We loved to hear those stories and asked her to tell them over and over again.

Mutti had grown up in a tiny row house in Neuensund, a village about ten kilometers north of Strasburg. The house was owned by the estate on which my grandfather Grapentin worked as a farmhand. Marie and Ernst, Mutti's older sister and younger brother, were good little children, as Mutti described them. Ernst was almost always sickly. Marie, the oldest, was Opa's favorite. Hedwig, in contrast to her brother and sister, was always getting herself into trouble. Now, as I thought of my mother, I tried to imagine her as a young farm girl tending geese in a sun-drenched meadow near the church behind their house. I had trouble reconciling the picture of that girl with the one of the woman who only moments earlier had stood by the side of the road in a fur coat, wearing rouge and lipstick, flagging down an army wagon.

Hedwig had left school at the end of eight years and found a position at the estate in Neuensund as a cleaning girl. It was a sought-after position, she told us. Wearing a black dress with a lacy, white apron, she found herself in another world—a world she wanted to be part of, but not as a servant. She also knew by then that she did not want to stay in Neuensund for the rest of her life. Shortly after she started working in the manor house, she was hired as a housekeeper for an elderly lady in Berlin. In the city, Hedy, as she was calling herself, had her own room, and in return for food and a small monthly salary, she cooked the meals for the aristocratic old lady and cleaned the apartment. From her mistress, Mutti learned the mysteries of make-up, how to apply it to her face so that she would look prettier. And she learned table manners—how to set a table, serve food, and use silverware properly while eating.

Life in the cosmopolitan city of Berlin served as an explosive education for Hedy. She improved herself in ways she had never before imagined, grasping instinctively at those things which would take her out of and away from the circumstances of her birth. The story Ingrid and I liked best was the one about Mutti meeting a dashing cavalry soldier. At a time when unemployment in Germany was rampant, soldiers represented job security and were considered good catches for girls looking for husbands. Mutti laughed when she told us that. She went dancing one evening with several of her girlfriends in Pasewalk, a town with a cavalry garrison. She wore her prettiest dress. It was springtime, and, as the girls had expected, there were several soldiers in the dance hall. The soldiers wasted no time asking the young girls to dance. Mutti had a wonderful time dancing. The soldier she danced with for most of the night was to be our father, Willi Samuel. It was 1933 and Mutti was nineteen years old.

Willi was Mutti's first boyfriend. He talked her into staying late that night and smuggled her into his room in his *Kaserne* in Pasewalk. Although Mutti thought this was exciting, she dreaded what her father would do if he found out. She and her new boyfriend saw each other often after that first meeting. When Hedy went to Berlin, the young cavalry soldier transferred to a new posting near Berlin. In Berlin they exchanged rings and got engaged secretly. Soon thereafter Willi took Hedy to Schlawe to introduce her to his parents. I was born in February 1935. Mutti told us she almost died in childbirth because the old country doctor left some of the burst placenta inside her. My parents had not been able to get married earlier because Willi could not get permission from his superiors. They finally were married in October 1935, eight months after my birth.

As I rode along in the jolting army wagon, a new picture of my mother began to evolve in my mind. In the darkness of the wagon, I discovered that I could relate to the girl who was my mother. Maybe, I thought, she could even become my friend. The person I remembered from Sagan, the person who screamed at me, beat me, and locked me into the broom closet was beginning to fade from memory.

Chapter 7

THE FACE OF DEATH

A
s we drove through the darkness, a cold mist masking the wagons
ahead and behind, I drifted in and out of sleep. I heard Mutti ask
our driver if he couldn't get Oma on our wagon. He handed her
the reins and crawled into the back where Ingrid and I lay. He motioned for
Oma to climb up. She came running, and he grasped her hands and pulled
her up. He rearranged some boxes to make room for her to sit. Oma took
off her shoes and rubbed her feet. Then our driver jumped off the wagon
and found room on the wagon directly behind us for Frau Zoske and her two
boys. I drifted off to sleep again. When I awoke, dawn was breaking. I saw
Mutti sitting next to our driver, bent far over, asleep. The wagon came to
an abrupt halt. Mutti sat up straight, shaken awake by our sudden stop. She
turned around, looking for Ingrid and me. She waved her hand, smiled, and
bade us *"Guten Morgen."*

Behind us, the column of wagons reached as far back as I could see. Many
more were ahead of us. Much further up the meandering road I could see
refugee wagons, army trucks, some armored vehicles, and artillery slowly
moving through the town of Woldegk. The road ran directly into the middle
of town and out the other side. There was no way to go around. Horses and
wagons, trucks, tanks, and artillery were trapped on the road in Woldegk,
making their way through town only as fast as the slowest vehicle would
allow. I jumped off our wagon and walked alongside until Mutti told me,

with firmness in her voice, to get back on and to stay on. Clambering back up, I felt privileged to have a wagon to climb into. In the far distance to the west, on the other side of town, I could see black smoke rising.

Our pace through Woldegk continued to be agonizingly slow. Stop and go, stop and go. I saw the same kind of tank barriers in Woldegk's side streets that I had seen earlier in Strasburg. In the midst of the pandemonium, I noticed people going in and out of a bakery buying their Sunday morning *Brötchen* as if nothing unusual was happening. My stomach growled loudly. I wondered when we would eat. Women, children, and old men pushing heavily loaded bicycles or pulling overloaded handcarts trudged alongside us, heading west. As we neared the western edge of Woldegk, I suddenly heard unfamiliar noises, like explosions. I also heard the revving and whining of engines far ahead of us. I couldn't see anything. We rounded a curve and emerged from the last housing area into open country. To our right, I could see two arms of an old windmill sticking out above a hill. The mill itself was hidden from view. Our wagons moved at a faster pace. As we crested a hill, I could clearly see that the road ahead was crowded with the wagons of *Flüchtlinge* and various Wehrmacht vehicles, in some places two abreast.

I perceived a sudden change in the people around me, as if a cloud had pushed itself in front of the sun, throwing its dark shadow across those below. I could smell the change in the air the same way I could smell bread near a bakery. I didn't know precisely what it was that was suddenly different. Maybe it was the way our driver sat on his bench with his head cocked toward the sky, urging the horses to move out faster. Maybe it was the way the driver behind us looked, with his eyes constantly darting from the sky to his horses and back to the sky. I suddenly felt constrained, as though I couldn't breathe; I wanted to jump off the wagon and run out into the fields and be free. Instead, I sat still, gripping the side of our wagon until my hands hurt. The movements of soldiers walking past us appeared rigid and square, not fluid and relaxed. Instead of holding their weapons with accustomed ease, they gripped them tightly. Their eyes, too, were directed upward at the sky. The soldiers moved in groups, like flocks of birds trying to hide from a hawk. Mutti cautioned Ingrid and me to lie down and close our eyes, but I couldn't do either.

Our driver pulled the reins of the horses hard to the right. I could see him with the leather reins wrapped around his hands, lifting them up high as he pulled them back and over. The two horses swerved sharply off the road, pulling the wagon over to the shoulder and up against a tree. Before the horses had come to a full stop, the driver dropped the reins and flew through the air, jumping into the grassy ditch alongside the road. I heard him screaming at the top of his lungs, but I didn't understand him. I saw Mutti jump off the wagon, too, directly into the ditch. I grabbed Ingrid by the arm and pulled her toward the back of the wagon. I finally understood what the driver had been shouting as he ran alongside the wagon toward us—"*Kinder*, get out; hurry up, get out of the wagon."

Ingrid and I jumped off the back of the wagon into his strong arms and ran to seek shelter behind the trunks of large, old chestnut trees. Ingrid went with our soldier. I ran in the opposite direction and threw myself behind a tree. I still didn't know what it was I was hiding from. A *Sturmgeschütz*, an infantry assault gun, ran into the side of the ditch just one tree behind me. I saw soldiers, weapons in hand, frantically jump off the back of the tank and scramble over its side, seeking shelter in the ditch. I didn't know where Mutti had gone or Frau Zoske and her boys or Oma. My full attention was occupied by the roar of powerful engines coming from the direction of town.

From the ditch, cowering behind the old tree, I looked up at the sky. I saw two aircraft bearing down on us. They looked black and terrifying as they leveled off at treetop level and immediately opened fire with their cannons and machine guns. The strafing planes looked like demons from hell with the shimmer of their whirling propellers before them. As they leveled out of a slight bank heading straight toward me, I saw red-and-yellow tongues flickering from their black wings, tongues that seemed both to reach for us and to slow down the planes' forward motion. In spite of the incredible speed of the unfolding attack, the scene slowed down for me as if each frame of the picture I saw had its own distinct identity. When the planes made their pass over our column, I understood the morning's mystery of black smoke and the strange sounds and explosions. I lay there exposed in the ditch, frozen with fear. Helpless. My world was exploding around me. Still I could not keep from looking. The cannon shells stitched their way across the road and into the field, into people and animals. The bullets ran up to the tank, into trucks and horse-drawn wagons, leaving behind screams and twisted, burning metal, splintered wood, and torn flesh. Disemboweled horses lay on the road screaming horribly as life ran out of their thrashing

The Face of Death

bodies. Men, women, children, and animals died side by side on the road and in the fields. Death had no favorites.

I followed the two planes with my eyes until they disappeared over the crest of a hill. They were so low that for a moment I thought one of them was going to crash into the field as its left wing dipped toward the ground, nearly making contact. I heard the roar of still more aircraft engines approaching and then the staccato sounds of guns as successive flights of aircraft passed overhead. As I tried to claw myself deeper into the ground, I could feel my body vibrate from the raw and punishing sounds of their engines. The planes flew off to the right, behind the windmill. Then they turned slowly over Woldegk, gaining altitude in their turn, and dove down toward us to attack again. Down our disintegrating column they flew, with the red-and-yellow tongues reaching out of their wings to kill, and kill, and kill again. Then they flew off across the fields toward the north, and the roar of their engines diminished and died away as suddenly as it had come upon us. All that remained behind was the silence of death—crackling flames, exploding ammunition, and the occasional sob or whimper of human or animal. A cemetery-like quiet settled upon the scene.

The attacking fighters hadn't looked like any I had seen before in my books or in the air. They looked almost like German Me-109s, and at first I thought that was what they were. But their noses were more pointed, and I could see the red stars painted on their sides when they passed in front of me. There was no Luftwaffe over Woldegk on April 29, 1945. I could see our horses munching serenely on green shoots of fresh grass at the base of the tree behind which Ingrid had hidden herself. Was she alive? I couldn't see her. I stood up to get a better look and stopped in shock. The carnage around me was awful. At the edge of the road, just one wagon length away, stood the *Sturmgeschütz*. It had a short, stubby gun, no turret like a real tank, and it was open from the top. It didn't seem damaged, but I had seen the cannon shells walk across it and then into the ditch and into the field. Those of the crew who had sought shelter from the attacking fighters in the shallow roadside depression and behind the trees lining the road lay there dead. All five. I knew they had been killed by the first two fighters. Some of the soldiers lying there looked peaceful, as if resting, their Schmeisser submachine guns beside them. The arms of other soldiers stuck up in the air as if reaching for something. I saw blood on their uniforms. I saw their torn bodies. I wanted to vomit, but I couldn't. I had nothing in my stomach.

The Face of Death

I just stood there retching dryly, with my eyes riveted on the dead tank crew meters away from me.

"Ingrid," I called out. I saw her come out from behind her tree, excitedly claiming that a bullet had ricocheted off her cap and that the cap had saved her life. Soon Mutti joined us, and we three stood there looking at the dead horses and the many dead bodies of men, women, children, and soldiers. Our driver was alive, and he and others immediately tried to get our column moving again.

In the roadside ditch ahead of us lay several dead horses. Broken civilian wagons lay beside the horses with their contents strewn about the side of the road by the exploding shells. I looked in the direction in which the planes had disappeared. For the first time I noticed the many civilians lying in the fields. They lay there alone, or two, or three, or four together. I looked intently at some of them, hoping they were just resting, still alive. None of them moved. They were all dead. Only ten meters from where I stood, a woman knelt over an infant in a clothes hamper, a basket woven of split willow branches. The woman looked as if she were soothing her baby. She seemed to be leaning on the hamper, holding on to its handles. She didn't move.

"Mutti, why is the woman so still? I have looked at her for a while now and she doesn't move. Why?"

Mutti turned toward me with a stunned look in her eyes and put her arm around me. In an unsteady voice she simply said, "She is dead, Wolfgang."

"And the baby, Mutti?"

"The baby, too, is dead."

I looked again at the dead woman and her baby. I saw no wounds. No black stains discolored her clothing. The kneeling woman wore a black wool skirt and a white, short-sleeved sweater with a black, shiny belt around her waist. She was young, and her hair was pulled back in the traditional bun country women wore. Her face was white. She didn't look like a farm girl. What had driven her out into the fields? Where had she come from? What had she been running from? Maybe she had been killed in an earlier attack in the morning. I only knew that she and her baby were dead, and their images burned themselves into my mind.

On the left side of the road, the carnage was worse. Most of the dead were soldiers. A military car sitting in the field still burned fiercely. The driver had tried to avoid the attack by taking a ninety-degree turn off the road, over the roadside ditch and into the field. They all lay facedown beside their car. Flames flickered off their charred, burning uniforms. The car doors stood wide open on both sides. They must have tried to jump out of the car as they saw the planes coming. It was too late for them. Trucks lined the left side of the road, many of them still smoldering. Some soldiers lay alongside their trucks, others were hanging out of their cabs in contorted positions. Still others had died in the fields trying to escape the merciless guns of the Russian planes.

"Back on the wagon," our soldier ordered, motioning with his right hand for us to climb on. "We must get out of here as quickly as possible."

I took a last look at the unlucky tank crew. The face of the nearest dead soldier was turned toward me, and his eyes looked straight through me— blue eyes which saw nothing anymore. His hair was blond, combed straight back, and his face was white and peaceful in death. I could see no wound on him either, yet he was dead, just as the others were whose torn bodies lay beside him. His left hand reached into the air, holding nothing. His uniform blouse was open at the collar, its sleeves partially rolled up, and his Schmeisser lay by his right hand. His pants were tucked into his *Knobel-becher* boots. I could see the Iron Cross pinned to his tunic, another ribbon for a second Iron Cross pulled through a buttonhole, a bronze *Verwundeten-abzeichen*, and a tanker's badge. His decorations and badges told me he had seen much combat before he died on the road out of Woldegk. Why did he die at the end of this awful war, next to a boy he never knew? "*Auf Wiedersehen*, soldier," I said out loud, and waved at the man who could no longer see.

Our cart with the suitcases strapped to it was still upright, tied to the back of our wagon. A fat *Oberfeldwebel*, master sergeant, directed the assembly of our column from a motorcycle sidecar. I crawled up behind our soldier.

"Who is that man?" I asked him.

"That man," he said, with respect in his voice, "is our *Spies*, our first sergeant." The motorcycle approached, and when it was almost even with us the *Oberfeldwebel* motioned with his left hand. His driver stopped the cycle alongside our wagon. He looked up at Mutti, but said nothing.

He looked at our soldier and said, "Get moving as quickly as you can. Bear left up the road. Hurry." Then he drove on. Mutti moved back into the wagon with Ingrid and me. Frau Zoske and her two boys reappeared suddenly behind our wagon. I had completely forgotten about them. Our soldier was joined by another soldier up front, and the two skillfully directed the horses through the burning, splintered, and torn trucks and wagons littering the road. Ingrid was excitedly babbling to Mutti about the bullet that had bounced off her cap. Something had hit the tree she was hiding behind, right above her head, and made her head vibrate. She had shown me where she hid during the attack, and I could see a tear in the tree trunk where a bullet had entered. Of all of us, Ingrid probably came the closest to dying on the road out of Woldegk.

Our column slowly reassembled, moving out of the debris littering the road. The trucks and tanks which had been ahead of us in Woldegk were gone. Either they had driven on, or they were burning wrecks alongside the road. Soon there was no more debris, and we pulled away from the place of horror and death. The images of the tank crew dead in the roadside ditch, of the burning staff car with the two dead soldiers in their smoldering uniforms, and of the dead woman bending over her dead baby in the basket would not leave me. The scenes were like black-and-white photographs seared into my mind. Almost everything was black and white in the land of death, except for the green grass the horses had eaten alongside the road, the blue eyes of the dead soldier, and the red star on the Russian planes. Death seemed to make nearly everything look black and white.

We moved at a fairly rapid pace, as fast as horses could go pulling a heavy load on a cobblestone road. Our soldier walked beside the wagon, holding the reins loosely. I jumped off the wagon and walked at his side. The other soldier had left. There didn't seem to be anyone else on the road except our wagons and several motorcycles. I couldn't tell for sure how many of us there were, because I could never really see the entire column at one time. Probably about seventy wagons, I counted. I did not know if we had lost any of our wagons or soldiers in the attack.

Judging from the position of the sun, I thought it must be close to noon. The sun had finally broken through the overcast and turned a bleak morning into a bright, sunny spring day. I was warm and hungry, starving, in fact, but there was no food and I didn't ask for any. I knew our family hadn't taken any food along when we left Strasburg because our departure had been so hasty. It was the same way we had left Sagan—at the last minute. I had no idea when soldiers ate. I thought of Oma. Where was she? I hadn't seen her since the start of the air attack. Fear for her safety surged through my

The Face of Death

body. I looked for Mutti and found her in the back of our wagon, her empty eyes seeming to look at nothing. Maybe she was tired, maybe sad.

"Mutti, where is Oma?" I yelled, petrified with fear that something awful had happened to my grandmother. She motioned for me to come closer. I climbed into the wagon.

"Didn't you know? A nice soldier took her with him. She is in one of the wagons up ahead of us. Don't worry. Oma is just fine." I must have sighed loudly with relief, because Mutti smiled. I jumped off the wagon and rejoined our driver up front. Our column snaked its way through the verdant spring countryside heading northwest. We turned off the main road onto an unpaved, rutted *Feldweg*. It seemed easier going for the horses through the soft, smooth dirt than over cobblestones. All day long we traveled over different *Feld-* and *Waldwege*, through fields, meadows, and forests. In early evening we approached a village.

"We'll rest here," our soldier said to me. He looked tired, his face covered with stubble. I was relieved. Maybe we could get something to drink, even some food. The wagons spread out all over the village. Our wagon stopped at what appeared to be the central gathering point for our company. I saw the *Spies* conferring with others under a horse chestnut about to break into bloom. His motorcycle, with its sidecar and his driver, were nearby. Soldiers were loosening harnesses, watering horses at a nearby trough, or putting feed bags filled with oats around their horses' heads.

I smelled food, a whiff of something that smelled so good I had difficulty keeping myself from drooling. During the day I had been able to control my hunger. I knew there was no food, so there was no need to think about it. The killing near Woldegk had completely occupied my mind. But with the smell of food intruding, my hunger took full possession of my body. I couldn't think of anything else. I saw under the chestnut tree what the soldiers called a *Gulaschkanone*, an old-fashioned mobile field kitchen. The contraption's long smokestack gave it the look of a cannon—if I used my imagination—and I guessed that was how it got its name. The cooks had arrived in the village ahead of us.

Our wagon had stopped near a nice-looking farmhouse. The driver led Mutti, Ingrid, and me to an upstairs apartment, which the woman of the house kindly made available for our use. I heard footsteps behind me as we ascended the stairs. It was Oma. She smiled, her new teeth making her face look younger than I remembered.

The Face of Death

The apartment had one bedroom with two beds and a couch, a small kitchen, which we didn't need, and a bathroom with running cold water. We washed up and then immediately went downstairs to join the soldiers for dinner. Frau Zoske and her two boys were waiting for us. Our soldier took us over to the *Gulaschkanone*, where he introduced us to the cook who promptly served us. He then introduced us to a group of soldiers, and we sat down with them for dinner. With much laughter, they discussed their recent experiences. Miraculously, none of our wagons had been hit, nor had anyone been killed or wounded. After the soldiers had been served a second time, I went back for another helping. The cook, a large man with a white apron protecting his uniform and the sleeves of his shirt rolled up above his elbows, saw me standing nearby with my mess kit.

"Come here, my boy," he called out good-naturedly, "you have much growing to do. Have some more of this tasty, strengthening bean soup." He refilled my aluminum mess tin with his huge ladle. It was wonderful-smelling soup. Pieces of pork fat floated on top. It took all the constraint I possessed to walk slowly to a place under the chestnut tree, where I sat down alone to eat. I let the pieces of pork fat slowly dissolve on my tongue before I swallowed. I went back for a third helping, and the jovial cook was pleased to give me another ladle of his soup.

"This is wonderful soup. The best I've ever eaten," I said to him, looking up into his beaming, sweaty face.

He gave me an appreciative smile. Then he said loudly, so everyone nearby could hear, "It's about time someone appreciates my fine cooking. None of these old fools do." The soldiers laughed along with the cook and made some teasing remarks about his cooking skills. For the moment we were at ease, young and old, happy to be alive. I ate my third helping of soup slowly, savoring the flavor of the beans and pork fat. As we rose to go upstairs to our quarters, our soldier told us that we would leave at four o'clock in the morning, maybe earlier.

"Do not take your clothes off while you sleep because you never know what might happen during the night. We might have to leave suddenly. Ivan is close behind us," he said with undisguised concern in his voice. Mutti thanked him for his advice. The cook stayed outside cleaning his *Gulaschkanone*, getting ready to move out. I didn't know where Frau Zoske, Horst, and Günter were staying for the night; they were somewhere in the house. Frau Zoske seemed to be keeping to herself. I wondered if perhaps she was having

The Face of Death

second thoughts about her rash decision to join us in our flight from Strasburg. I felt as if we had been on the road for days, although actually it had only been one night and one day since we fled Strasburg. This was our second night. Mutti seemed to be much better. Her fever was gone, and her cheeks were no longer red. The black shadows around her eyes had also disappeared. What mattered most was that we were together. I washed my face and my hands in refreshing cold water and fell asleep the second I lay down. I did not dream. I was shaken awake by Oma.

"Get up, Wolfgang," she said gently. "We must leave quickly. It is two o'clock. Russian tanks are in the village." I sprang to my feet as Mutti and Oma rushed around the room collecting our few things.

A soldier stood in the doorway and sternly said, "You must come this minute or we will have to leave you behind." We grabbed our coats and rushed down the narrow stairway behind the departing soldier, who carried Ingrid in his arms. The stairway echoed loudly from his hobnailed boots pounding the wooden steps as he descended two stairs at a time. Mutti, Oma, and I frantically scrambled after him. When we got outside, we saw our wagon already pulling away. We ran after it, throwing our things into the back on the run, clambering up from behind, helping each other. Ingrid smiled at me as the soldier handed her up to Mutti.

I didn't know where Frau Zoske and her two boys were. I thought that someone must have warned them. We wouldn't leave them behind. Our wagon moved into the black of night, silent except for the noise of wheels crunching through dirt, horses straining in their harnesses, their hooves sounding as if someone were pounding stakes into the ground, and soldiers gently urging them on to greater effort. I crawled up front between Mutti and our soldier. He moved aside and made room for me on the bench. He was a tall, strong man, gentle with his horses and kind to us. He was always in full uniform, his hat on his head, his tunic buttoned and clean.

As our wagon moved onto the road, joining up with other wagons, our soldier turned to me in a fatherly manner, put his right arm around my shoulders, and said, "These are battle-tested horses, my boy. They know when we need all they can give. We've been together for a long time, and we know each other well. They won't let us down. Don't worry. We won't let Ivan catch us. Everything will be all right." He paused. Then he said reassuringly, "We've been in tighter spots than this before." His arm was strong, and I felt safe being close to him. The horses leaned into their har-

The Face of Death

nesses and pulled with all their might. It took only gentle commands or a slight movement of the reins to get the two massive animals to perform.

"The taller, greyish mare on the left is the intellectual," the soldier continued, chuckling as he spoke. "She is the one who makes the decisions— she initiates a turn, she decides how hard they will pull. She is a bit shell-shocked from artillery fire, so you have to be careful around her and not make unexpected noises. The gelding to her right is a charlatan. He'll wait until I am between the two of them, such as when I adjust their harnesses, and then he'll try to put the squeeze on me. Or he tries to hit me with his head or his tail, or better yet, stomp on my foot if I am not careful about where I stand around him. He, too, is a real hard worker. They are used to each other, and I like them equally well. They are my family." A quiet, private smile crossed his face.

Our column moved laboriously through the black night. I was surprised at how little noise we made. The wagons merged from their various overnight locations in the village into one long, straining column, silent except for the sounds of horses and wagon wheels. It was an eerie feeling to be part of a ghost-like company of men and animals escaping through the sheltering cover of night. At one point, I heard Oma let out a gasp. I quickly went back to see if she needed help. I leaned forward on my hands and knees, almost touching Oma's face with my nose in the pitch black of the wagon's interior. "What is it, Oma?" I asked. "Did you hurt yourself?"

She answered slowly, as if speaking to herself. "In all that hurry I forgot to put my teeth back into my mouth." She placed her right hand over her mouth as she spoke, as if to confirm that her teeth were, in fact, not there. I could barely discern the movement of her hand. "I left them at the house in the water glass in the bathroom. Yes, that's what I did," she mumbled to herself. I couldn't see Oma's face clearly; she sounded embarrassed. I crawled back up front to tell Mutti about Oma's teeth.

"We can't go back, you know that," our driver said matter-of-factly. He kept looking straight ahead into the night. "Ivan's tanks caught up with us as we were sleeping. They arrived sooner than we expected. They were on the other side of the village when I pulled out of the farmyard, only a few houses away from us. I don't know how many there were. Even one is dangerous. We don't have the weapons to oppose them. It's best to get away from them as quickly as possible. *Ja,* I am sorry for your old mother losing her

The Face of Death

teeth"—and he briefly turned his head to look at Mutti—"but it's a lot better than losing her life."

I didn't see any need to return to Oma to tell her that we couldn't go back. She knew that. I found a comfortable place behind Mutti and the driver which allowed me to look between the two of them and see outside our wagon. The driver continued talking—maybe to calm the horses, maybe to reassure us. "The first sergeant, the fat fellow, you know who I mean. The one who stopped by our wagon yesterday on the motorcycle after Ivan's fighters had worked us over." He looked at Mutti when he said that. "Well, he took several *Panzerfaust* with him in his motorcycle, and he and several others went back to the other side of the village to stop the tanks, if need be. We needed time to get everyone out of the village. It's a slow process getting a company of soldiers back on the road. He is an old hand in this tank-killing business, but he doesn't want to die on the last day of the war anymore than the rest of us. Somebody had to go and delay them or we might all have been lost." He paused and said, "Had Ivan caught us in the village asleep it would have been a massacre. Thank God that our guards were able to warn us just in the nick of time." Not until that moment did I understand how dangerous our situation had been.

Oma was still talking to herself. "My new teeth," she moaned. "They were the new teeth Hedwig's dentist friend made for me in Strasburg just before we left. I never had beautiful teeth like that before. They still hurt my gums, that's why I took them out of my mouth. Oh, why did I take them out of my mouth? Now I don't have any teeth at all." I felt sorry for my grandmother. She continued to moan softly, talking to herself aloud in a low, singsong tone of voice, mourning the loss of her beautiful, precious new teeth.

As our wagon train came through a pine forest, I heard a motorcycle approaching from behind. It was our *Oberfeldwebel*, the *Spies*, and his driver. Several other motorcycles followed. The *Oberfeldwebel* stopped about four or five wagons ahead of us. As he dismounted from his sidecar, he held up his right hand and the wagon train slowly came to a halt. By the time we stopped, our wagon was only a few meters from where he stood. I couldn't see the end of the column because of the darkness, nor could I see how many wagons were ahead of us. Some soldiers went over to the *Spies*. He wore a garrison hat with a shiny bill, such as officers wore, and an overcoat, just as he had when I first saw him outside of Woldegk. The wide black belt

The Face of Death

around his ample middle had a pistol holster attached to it, a Walther pistol. He wore black riding boots, different from the high-top raw leather boots our soldier had, and he wore a grey leather glove on his left hand. The *Spies* looked well groomed, not as I had imagined a frontline soldier would look. He pulled out a map and studied it briefly, using a hand-actuated flashlight. He seemed to be giving directions to the soldiers who formed a circle around him. He stopped what he was doing momentarily and got out a box of ciga-rettes from under his overcoat and flicked the box open with his thumb. I saw the glint of silvery paper. He took one cigarette from the box, offered another to his driver, then expertly closed the lid with one hand and put the box back into his coat pocket. He lit the cigarette, took a long drag, and let the smoke slowly curl out of his mouth into the cool night air.

The *Spies* held the cigarette in his right hand and motioned with his left. Other soldiers joined the group. He kept on smoking, slowly and deliber-ately. The circle of soldiers continued to grow around him. The men stood at a respectful distance. When he resumed talking, he spoke loudly. I tried not to miss a word of what he said. He spoke in firm, directive sentences as if he were used to giving orders and having them obeyed. The soldiers said nothing. When the *Spies* finished giving directions, there was momentary silence. "Are there questions before we move out?" he asked, looking around the group.

Someone said, "What about Ivan?"

The *Spies* let out a short, tense laugh, put his right foot on the fender of the motorcycle sidecar, and rested his right forearm on his knee. I could see the muzzle of a Schmeisser submachine gun protruding from the sidecar, and his driver had a Schmeisser strapped across his back. The *Spies* looked down at the ground. He pushed his hat back on his head with the thumb of his right hand. "*Ja*, you want to know about Ivan and his tanks," he said. "Well, we drove up close to them, hidden by a hedgerow. We could hear their engines idling. There were three of them parked close together strad-dling the eastern entrance to the village. T-34s. They had no infantry. If they had, we couldn't have done much except commit suicide." The soldiers listened intently. The *Spies* changed his position.

"Their hatches were open. A tanker leaned out of one hatch smoking a *papyrossi*, looking east, the way they had come. There were flares going up behind them, and he was looking at the flares. Three others stood in front of another tank, talking and pointing into the village. We were on a narrow

The Face of Death

Feldweg that merged into the road about where the tanks stood. They obviously had not heard us coming, nor could they see us because of the hedge. They acted as if they didn't expect to see anyone. The seven of us took our *Panzerfaust*, and then we shot them. One of them blew up, its turret blowing off the tank so forcefully it nearly fell on us. We must have set off the ammunition or some other stuff."

He paused, looking at the ground. Then he straightened up. "We have some breathing room between us and Ivan—not much. There had to be more than just those three. And infantry, too. Others must have heard and seen what we did to them. So let's move out smartly." He dropped his cigarette butt and ground it into the dirt with the heel of his boot. "Get moving," he said loudly, and he dismissed the group of soldiers around him with a wave of his hand. He remounted his motorcycle sidecar, and he and Gefreiter Krause drove off, swallowed by the darkness of night. Our soldier hurried back and sat down next to Mutti. I slipped off the bench and cowered behind them. The wagon began to move again.

"Did you hear what the *Spies* said?" he asked Mutti.

"No," she replied. I said nothing.

"The fat one is fabulous," he continued. "He always reconnoiters the area well ahead of us and behind us, and he knows where to go. He is really good at keeping Ivan off our backs. I knew he could do it." I sensed our driver's relief, and it made me feel better, too. As we neared the far edge of the forest we were passing through, I heard unfamiliar noises. Breaking out of the trees I saw a battery of German artillery getting ready to fire. The guns were in staked-out positions with several soldiers surrounding each gun. The soldiers wore what looked like earmuffs. The guns were lined up in a long row behind the pine trees, up and over a hillside. I couldn't tell how many there were. As we passed them, they started firing, one after the other, right down the line. Again, and again, and again.

The guns fired continuously. *Womp, womp, womp, womp, womp* . . . I saw flames shooting from the ends of the gun barrels and smoke coming out of the breaches as the guns were reloaded. At times I imagined I could see a shell leaving the barrel. The stench of burnt gunpowder wafted over us. I held my nose. The guns fired and reloaded, fired and reloaded, without letup. Our horses showed no reaction to the artillery fire, but kept on pulling steadily, putting one foot in front of the other—shlup, shlup, shlup, shlup—as their hooves dug into the soft, sandy soil of the *Waldweg*. Soon

The Face of Death

we were out of sight of the guns, passing over a hill and into another pine forest. The sound of the firing guns became muffled, then faded.

The *Waldweg*, which had taken us around a lake, soon joined up with a road lined with stately horse chestnuts. We passed to the left of groups of refugees with heavily loaded wagons. The women sat up front on the wagon benches and the children cowered behind the women. The men, some with whips in their hands, walked beside the horses, guiding them and urging them on. Most of the men wore coats of animal skins with the leather side out and the fur inside. Several military trucks passed us, going too fast, nearly scraping the trunks of trees as they went by on the narrow, crowded road. The long barrel of an 88 mm antitank gun pointed at us momentarily as the truck pulling it passed. Open fields lay to our left and right, flat land to the left and hilly on our right. I could see red lights behind us illuminating the skyline.

"What are those lights?" I asked our driver, pointing in their direction.

"Those are not lights, my boy, those are fires," he said. "Burning villages. Probably the village we left two hours ago is one of them. Ivan is all around us." The reddish light from the burning villages reflected off the scattered, low-hanging clouds, bathing the landscape in a soft, eerie light. Suddenly I shuddered violently. I felt cold and naked. Then an unusual, persistent sound penetrated my consciousness, seeming to come from directly overhead. The sound was made by the engine of a small plane. I turned to our driver.

"Is it German?" I did not really believe there were any more German airplanes flying anywhere.

"Oh, that's an old friend," the driver responded, with the slightest touch of irony in his voice. "It's a Russian plane. He comes out every night just before they are going to attack. He carries a small bomb or two to harass us. Never really hits anything. He is supposed to panic us, we think. Keep us from going to sleep. Scare us. Psychology, boy, psychology. We don't pay him any mind. We shoot at him if we can see him. Sometimes he makes a mistake and is silhouetted against the moon, but usually we can't see him in the dark and we just ignore him. You can see for yourself; our friend is here and Ivan is attacking. *Ja?*"

I didn't know what he meant by psychology. I knew the Russian was probably supposed to scare them, just as he said. He said they didn't get scared, though. "I am scared," I said, "but not by him." I pointed at the sky.

The Face of Death

"By this night and everything that's happening around us. Everything seems so strange and threatening."

Our soldier patted me on the shoulder. "This is nothing for children," he said, "but have faith, we will make it out of here." *Womp, womp.*

"He finally dropped his two bombs, boy. Now he can go home," our driver said, chuckling to himself. The change was brutally sudden. At first I didn't know what the new sound was; then I instinctively knew it had to be artillery—not German artillery firing at the Russians, but Russian artillery firing at us. Some of the projectiles made a horrible shrieking sound as they passed overhead and exploded in the village beyond, in the fields around us, and alongside the road. The shells whooshed and sometimes whistled, and then exploded with a loud crash. Fire, smoke, and flying dirt marked the spots where they exploded. I cowered behind Mutti and our soldier. Ingrid lay next to me, and Oma sat further back in the wagon, her face hidden in the shadows. The night was no longer dark as it had been when we passed through the forests. Now it was brightly lit, not only from the burning villages behind but from the burning village ahead and from the exploding artillery shells and the fires they started. Shells exploded directly behind us, throwing debris against our wagon. The Russian shells and rockets crashed down in random patterns, sending up high geysers of dirt. Horses whinnied, and panic moved through the mixed train of army wagons and *Flüchtlinge*. To the east I could see red star flares shooting into the night sky.

Our column kept moving, wagon after wagon. We passed a rudimentary tank barrier consisting of stacked logs pulled through narrow gates on either side of the road. A farmer with a team of horses was in the process of pulling the logs into place and closing the road to all traffic. I saw the farmer clearly silhouetted against the backdrop of the burning villages to the east. He was fighting his horses, which were rearing frantically on their hind legs in panic from the artillery shells exploding around them. They were not battle-hardened army horses. Several artillery rounds exploded near the barrier, terrifying the farmer and his horses even more. Then I saw our *Oberfeldwebel*, and from the motions of his hands I could tell that he wanted the farmer to stop what he was doing and leave. The farmer seemed indecisive and held on to the rearing horses. The *Spies* then took the reins from the farmer's hands while the farmer ran over and unhooked a log from behind the horses. Just as another artillery shell burst nearby, the *Oberfeldwebel* let the horses go. Relieved of their constraints, they galloped wildly off into the fields.

The Face of Death

On the road, movement came to a halt. The road led directly through the village, which was burning fiercely from the rocket and artillery attack. Some of the refugees turned their wagons into the fields trying to get around the village; most waited for the flames to die down. Our column became mixed with those of the *Flüchtlinge*. Our soldiers tried to disengage from the stalled mass of horse-drawn wagons by driving through the roadside ditches to get around obstacles. Our once-orderly column scattered. A soldier drove up to our wagon on a motorcycle and gave new directions. "Take the next *Feldweg* to the right," the soldier shouted. "It goes around the village," and he drove on to give the same message to others further behind us. Suddenly our wagon lurched wildly to one side and came to a halt. We were stuck in a shallow depression.

Our soldier and several others tried to free our wagon. The horses strained in vain. The wagon wouldn't move. The rest of our column reassembled further up on the *Feldweg*, pulled away, and disappeared over the ridge to the right of the village. On the ridge I saw another of our wagons abandoned by the side of the *Feldweg*. Its horses and driver were gone. As hard as the soldiers tried, our wagon wouldn't budge. Then I heard our soldier say matter-of-factly to Mutti, "It's no use. The right front wheel has to be changed if we want to get this wagon out of here. I don't know if we can do it."

A surge of fear raced through me as I realized that the wagon which had given me such a sense of security was doomed. Maybe all of us were doomed, finally to be caught by the advancing Russian tanks. We sat there alone in the open field. The village houses burned intensely, like large harvest bonfires, lighting up the scene. Looking from our broken-down wagon at the fiery scene before me, I felt vulnerable. Doomed. Death seemed to be reaching for me personally, and I knew I didn't want to die. If it wasn't one of the exploding artillery shells, I thought, then it would be the Russian tanks that would soon be amongst us. I realized how much security I had derived from the presence of our soldiers. They were gone. They had left us behind. In the eerie half-light of the burning village and the exploding rockets and artillery shells, I became convinced that my family had finally reached the end of its own road.

Mutti sat quietly on our wagon's bench. I crawled closer to her and looked over her shoulder at the road ahead. In the light of the burning village, I saw a Volkssturm soldier, looking much like my Opa Grapentin,

The Face of Death

with a rifle slung over his shoulder. He stood there in the middle of the road, starkly outlined by the burning houses around him—a grotesque figure, like Don Quixote looking at the windmills, I thought. The old soldier had a suitcase in his right hand. He just stood there looking east. He put his suitcase down, opened it, took out a few items, and put them in his pockets. Then he continued to stand by his open suitcase in the middle of the road, staring into the night.

"I hope you live, old man," I whispered under my breath.

"What did you say, Wolfgang?" Mutti asked.

"Nothing, Mutti, nothing."

The tragic figure of the old Volkssturm soldier standing in the road heightened my premonition of our own coming disaster. Our horses were still in front of our wagon, and I could hear our driver talking with other soldiers. I thought the Russians would soon arrive and we would be trapped in a broken-down army wagon by the side of the road. I looked at Mutti, and this time I didn't derive a sense of security from her presence. Not even Mutti would be able to get our family out of the unfolding disaster. Panic rose within me, choking me at the throat; I knew no one could help us now, only God. Oh God, I am so afraid. The thought flashed through my mind that I had seldom gone to church, and I felt guilty asking God for help. I lay down inside the dark wagon so no one could see me, folded my hands, and prayed.

"Please, dear God, please, help us out of here. No one else can help except you. Please, dear God, help us." Tears streamed down my face. I felt self-conscious about the fear that had overtaken me and ashamed for crying, although no one saw me. I wiped away my tears and crawled toward Mutti. "Mutti. Mutti," I whispered. She turned her head toward me. Her face looked lined and tired. "Mutti, I am so afraid. Is the dear God going to help us?" I looked at her steady, tired eyes, seeking reassurance.

My mother reached over, put her hand on my cheek, and said slowly and calmly, "Wolfgang, the dear God is always with us. He will help us and show us the way as He has in the past. I know you are afraid, my dear son, but the dear God is with us. We will get out of this." I don't know why, but I believed her. Her touch was calming and her eyes were steady and firm, full of love and caring. The intense fear that choked me fell away as I felt the touch of her hand, and her steady voice stabilized my disintegrating self. I sat back, looking at my beautiful, brave mother. I felt suddenly calm and unafraid. How could I have been so afraid, I thought, when she was right there? Why did I doubt her when she had always taken care of us before? The artillery fire stopped. The Russian plane was gone. Except for the occasional shouts of distressed *Flüchtlinge* on the road below, it was quiet. The soldiers who had tried to free our wagon came over to Mutti and told her to get out.

"What's on this wagon, anyway?" I heard one soldier ask our driver.

"Records and the unit history, typewriters and headquarter's supplies," he answered.

"Paper," said the other soldier with disgust in his voice. "Leave it. Take your horses over to that supply wagon up there on the hillside. Try to pull it out. We were going to abandon it, but it's of more use to us than this *Scheiss-papier*."

Our soldier and two others unlimbered the horses and led them across the field, up the hill to the supply wagon at the side of the *Feldweg*. They backed the two horses into the wagon and hooked them up. We carried our three suitcases to our new wagon and heaved them into the back. We had abandoned our handcart in the last village where we were surprised by the Russian tanks. Our soldier urged the horses on, and with a concerted effort they pulled the mired supply wagon out of the sand. We were moving again, although we were quite a distance behind the others. The horses strained mightily to pull our new wagon through the soft, sandy soil up and over the hill.

We were alone. One wagon, two horses, and five people. The other soldiers had left on their motorcycles once the wagon had been pulled out of the sand. Below us, flames still flickered in some of the village houses. Refugee wagons and several army trucks attempted to enter the burning village. As our wagon crested the ridge, the horses broke into a trot. With no one in front of us to slow our progress, we moved rapidly, and soon saw the last wagon of our reconstituted column ahead of us. We were the last one now, but we were back with our people. What I had thought was a trap had opened and released us. God had answered my prayers and rewarded Mutti's faith, I thought. The horses pulled steadily. For them, there was no good or bad day; they just did what they were told.

I hunkered down in my new surroundings, trying to get acquainted with the wagon. I found I was sitting on a box of cans. Food cans. I wished they were filled with meat and potatoes. I could see boxes stacked around and

The Face of Death

beneath me and compressed chunks of hay for the horses. Occasionally, motorcycles drove up and down our column, some continuing on behind us for a distance before they turned back again. One motorcycle stopped long enough for its rider to give our driver new directions. As morning came I could see that we were approaching a village. Outside it, our column halted, shaded by the thickly leafed trees lining the road. The soldiers dismounted, and groups of them formed, smoking handmade cigarettes. Many used newspaper to wrap the tobacco because they had run out of cigarette paper. As the blue cigarette smoke rose from the groups of soldiers, I could hear occasional laughter. There was a general feeling of peace and relaxation.

I felt relaxed, too, after our narrow escape. There was no sound of guns anymore, no men or women screaming, no sobs from frightened children, no noisy tanks clanking down the road or airplanes overhead. It was a moment of perfect tranquility. Only the calming sound of a horse pounding the ground with one of its hooves and the squeak of shifting leather harness disturbed the momentary silence. Then the moment passed. The soldiers put out their cigarettes, carefully removing the remaining tobacco from the cigarette butts and putting it back into their pouches or tobacco boxes. They crowded around our *Spies*. When our soldier returned, he said that the *Spies* had met last night with their commander, who was leading another group of them through the Mecklenburg lake district. Their reinforced company had split before coming through Strasburg, he explained, because they thought their chances of getting through to the Amies, as he called Americans, would be better if they moved west in two smaller groups rather than in one long column. It was the first time that I had heard what their specific objective was.

"Our captain told the *Spies* to be careful in the village ahead," our soldier whispered to Mutti. "We could have problems getting through it. SS. Fanatics, who want to fight to the end. We'll see what happens." He nodded his head, and with a tug on the reins urged the horses to move out. Our column entered the village, which had a large commons covered by luscious green grass and was surrounded by stately horse chestnuts. The village appeared to have been abandoned in great haste.

The Face of Death

Chapter 8

SURRENDER

Our wagons rumbled into the abandoned village, parking on and around the grassy commons in the village center. The horses immediately started to feed on the succulent grass. The commons was a long rectangle edged by huge horse-chestnut trees, which had begun to bloom. The old trees and the solidly built, neatly kept farmhouses and shops facing the commons gave the village a welcoming, friendly look. Yet there was not one person in the village other than us. No wagons to be seen near any of the farmhouses. No horses or cows in the stalls of the adjacent barns. No one sneaking a furtive peek from behind a curtained window. No children gawking at the soldiers. Weathered oak beams surrounding squares of red brick made the houses look especially attractive. Steep roofs of red clay tiles graced many of the houses, and some of the older roofs were overgrown with the dark green moss of old age. Two *Gasthauses* with beer gardens invited passersby to enjoy their hospitality. There was no one there to serve. Our soldier pulled up in front of a barn just off the commons. I was glad to be able to stretch, walk, and run again. He unlimbered the horses and tied them to iron rings attached to a stone water trough. He spread hay before them and then left. Mutti led us into the barn. Frau Zoske and her two boys followed. We spread straw near the barn door so we could sit. We could see the commons and observe anything that might be happening there.

"Relax and stay together," Mutti told us. "I will try to find out what the situation is." As soon as she left, Horst, Guenter, and I jumped to our feet and ran out of the barn to explore the village. It felt good to run. We quickly discovered that the commons contained an arsenal of weaponry. Stacks of hundreds of hand grenades with wooden handles sat in front of several houses. Also, numbers of boxes with smaller, fist-sized grenades, looking like blue iron eggs, lay all over the place. I picked up one of the hand grenades with a wooden handle, and swung it back as if I were going to throw it.

"Put that grenade down!" a soldier shouted authoritatively. I stopped in midswing and laid down the hand grenade, carefully. A number of aban-doned military staff cars sat in front of two farmhouses. The houses must have served as an army headquarters until the occupants left in a great hurry, probably when the Russians attacked last night and we were forced to run for our lives. The Russian attack seemed to have halted for the moment. The insignia on the cars were army, not SS. The car doors stood wide open. Maybe they had run out of gas. Triangular banners mounted on the fenders of two of the cars signified that they had once belonged to high-ranking officers. We looked into some of the farmhouses through their curtained windows. Massive oak furniture graced the rooms which looked out toward the street. Everything was in place—furniture, dishes, vases, ornate table-cloths. Nothing was disturbed.

On the commons, some of our soldiers had donned steel helmets and had guns slung over their shoulders or in their hands. I had not seen our soldiers wear steel helmets or carry weapons before. Others had set up machine guns at each corner of the commons with bands of ammunition feeding out of steel boxes into the guns. I noticed that most of the soldiers carried subma-chine guns instead of rifles. Some even carried Russian submachine guns, the ones with the round magazines rather than the straight magazine of the Schmeisser. More and more soldiers entered the commons. Armed. Instead of drivers of horse wagons, they now looked like combat soldiers.

Mutti stood near several of the armed soldiers. She waved her hand for me to come over. When I got there, she took my hand and we walked to the barn. She asked us to gather around. "Listen closely. Our soldiers just informed me that the SS troops are determined to fight the Russians to the end. The SS are stopping all troops coming through the village and are attempting to force everyone to join them. The SS is threatening to execute anyone who refuses. Our *Oberfeldwebel* is meeting with the SS commander.

If the SS insist that our soldiers join them to fight the Russians"—Mutti paused briefly—"then they intend to fight the SS and make good their escape to the American lines. There are about one hundred and sixty of them. They don't know how many SS there are. Our soldier told me that if they have to fight, we are to stay here in the village. It would be too dangerous to accompany them. They will abandon their wagons, and he said that we should take one and try to leave on our own." Mutti paused, looking at the ground as if there were something written for her in the hard-packed dirt floor of the barn. Then she continued, speaking more slowly.

"I told our soldier that we would go with them wherever they went. We, too, would abandon the little we had and would try not to be a burden on them as they fought their way through the SS. We will not stay here. Of course, I was speaking for myself and my children, and for my mother. You may want to stay here." Mutti looked at Frau Zoske. "If you like, you may accompany us. The choice is strictly yours, Frau Zoske. I only know that we have come this far with our soldiers and they have taken good care of us. We will be better off going with them regardless of what they do."

Frau Zoske rose slowly. She brushed off some straw that clung to her brown coat. Then she said almost too loudly, looking at the ground, "We will not accompany you, Frau Samuel. The boys and I are tired. I don't know if we did the right thing anyway when we left Strasburg with you. How will my husband find me when he returns and I am not there? No, we will stay here with the SS. I was disloyal to the Führer and to my husband when I left Strasburg. I should not have gone with you. It was a mistake. We will stay with the loyal SS in this village, like good Germans."

Mutti listened to Frau Zoske until she finished and then replied just as deliberately, "You do what you think is best for your family, Frau Zoske. My family will go with our soldiers. Staying here would mean that everything that we have gone through up to now would have been in vain. Should you change your mind, you can always rejoin us." Mutti motioned to Ingrid and me to join her and Oma. We walked to our wagon. Frau Zoske and her two boys went to their wagon, removed their suitcase, and returned to the barn.

In the square I saw the first sergeant's motorcycle. He was back. I told Mutti. We hurriedly walked toward his cycle. As we entered the square, we saw that our soldiers were smiling. They were taking their helmets off and slapping each other on the back. One soldier came up to Mutti, drew her aside and said, "The SS will not try to stop us from leaving, we think. We

Surrender

were too many for them and they saw that we were prepared to use our weapons." He laughed. Mutti and the soldier stepped to the side, away from Ingrid, Oma, and me.

"Our 'fat one' told the SS major we had come all the way from Rumania and that no one was going to stop his men from going on. Not even the SS. The SS had no jurisdiction over us, he told them. We are combat troops and we are ready to fight them or anybody else who gets in our way. The SS major then spoke to our *Spies* about loyalty to the Führer." The soldier laughed derisively. "Then the meeting was over and the *Spies* just got up from the table and walked away." The soldier laughed again. "He didn't even salute when he left. We won. The war is almost over for us."

The soldier took off his helmet and sat down with others near us. The cook with his *Gulaschkanone* had miraculously reappeared and prepared another of his great-tasting soups with lots of meat and pork fat. Everyone ate hungrily. There was no more talk of our being left behind. Our soldier joined us after dinner. He carried a thin red book of poetry by Schiller. "I don't know what will happen tomorrow," he said to Mutti, "but I want you to have this book of poems." He looked at the red book with gentle, watery eyes. "It has been my constant companion throughout this idiotic war. All the way into Russia and back again. At times, when things really looked bad and I thought I would despair, I read a poem. I would read the poem slowly until I was totally absorbed in its message and regained my equilibrium. The poetry reaffirmed my belief in the nobility of man and that beyond this madness lay another, better world." He paused briefly. "This book of poetry helped me survive, helped me remain a civilized man in spite of all the horror I was forced to witness. I know these poems by heart, and they have served me well through the years." He held out the red book to Mutti. "Please, take this as a gift. You have brought light into our life the few hours you spent with us. When I become a prisoner of war they will surely take my beloved book away from me. It is better you have it."

Mutti was visibly overcome by the soldier's grace. Her eyes barely held back the tears. She sat there quietly. Then she said, "Thank you very much for everything you and your comrades have done for me and my family and my friends. You made us one of you, and no one can do more than that." The soldier seemed embarrassed. "Thank you for stopping your wagon in Strasburg to pick up a desperate family. That took courage. We cannot ever thank you enough for what you did that night. I will take good care of your book, and it will always remind me of what a compassionate and brave man did for my children one dark and terrible night in April 1945." Our soldier rose to his feet. He looked at Mutti, and then, with his head bowed, he slowly walked away.

After everyone finished eating, we went to the barn. Our soldier soon came by and said, "We'll move out at dusk. Get some rest if you can. I will wake you in time." Then he took Mutti aside and spoke to her for some time in a low voice. I couldn't understand what he was saying. Then I heard Mutti reply, "No, we cannot do that. If they cannot go, then we won't go. We will stay together." Our soldier nodded his head and walked off toward the commons.

"They want to leave Frau Zoske and her boys behind," Mutti whispered when she sat down next to me. "I told him no. Frau Zoske has been bab-bling dumb things to some of the soldiers about how wonderful the Führer is and about the bravery of SS soldiers. She told them that her oldest son was in the SS. The soldiers got angry with her and don't want her around anymore." Mutti rose and found a place to lie down. I relaxed and stared up at the roof of the barn. I could hear pigeons cooing. There was no more shooting, no planes overhead. We seemed to be on a small island of tranquil-ity while all around us the war was coming to a fiery end. What was this terrible war all about? What had happened to the German Wehrmacht? Our soldiers didn't want to fight anymore unless someone like the SS got in their way. I didn't understand any of it. I drifted off to sleep. In my sleep I found myself on the train platform in Sagan. It was cold and the wind was blowing and Mutti was on the train calling out to me. "Wolfgang, Wolfgang, Wolf-gang. . . ," but my feet wouldn't move and no sound came out of my mouth when I tried to speak, and the train was pulling out of the station and leaving me behind. Suddenly I was falling into an endless black hole. I screamed for my mother, and again no sound came out of my mouth—I knew I was going to die once I hit the bottom of the black chasm. Then I awoke.

"Are you all right, Wolfgang?" Mutti asked. Her arm was around me as she knelt by my side. "You sat up straight, your eyes were wide open, and you opened your mouth as if you were screaming. My dear boy. This is hard on you, I know. Go back to sleep and try to get some rest." She gave me a kiss on the forehead, straightened my hair with her hand, and lay down

Surrender

beside me in the straw. I felt better. I was not dead, and my mother was near me.

"Wake up!" our soldier shouted. We jumped up almost simultaneously, brushed off the straw, and quickly mounted our wagon—Mutti up front, Ingrid, Oma, and I in back. Oma had at last reconciled herself to the loss of her false teeth. It was helpful that the food we received was mostly soup and bread, soft enough for her to chew. With a sly smile crossing her lips, she said she could even eat the bread crust. "I just keep it in my mouth a little longer."

As our wagon train pulled out of the empty village, I saw Frau Zoske with her suitcase and her two boys running after us. She caught up with the wagon they had traveled in, and the three of them climbed into the back while it was moving. Our two horses yanked and pulled their familiar load and eased themselves into the column that formed as we left the village whose name I didn't know. I never saw any of the SS. Our wagons drove through the night over rutted farm roads, our direction changing constantly as new information came in from the soldiers out ahead of us scouting roads on their motorcycles. By morning we again traveled a cobblestone road heading northwest. The sun came out. I saw several simple wooden crosses topped by steel helmets in a roadside ditch. The crosses were handmade from young trees and tied together with wire. I could see the abbreviated rank of the dead soldiers, the years of birth and death. They were privates and very young, in their teens. They had died the day before.

Our wagon train stopped in front of an army field hospital. Wounded soldiers sat on chairs in front of the wooden barracks, the more seriously wounded in wheelchairs, enjoying the warm, summer-like sunshine. Many men were wounded in several places. I saw bandages on their arms and legs, around their chests and heads. Uniformed nurses stood near the most severely wounded soldiers trying to make them comfortable. Mutti got off the wagon and quickly ran inside one of the hospital barracks. In a few minutes she reemerged accompanied by two doctors. They waved good-bye to her. Mutti climbed back onto our wagon with a handful of aspirin, salves, and bandages.

"We'll need these in the future," she said. "This is all they could spare. They haven't received any shipments of medicine in some time, and they have to keep what they have for their patients. They know the Russians are coming soon. They have no transport to move the wounded. The nurses and the doctors decided to stay." Mutti's eyes took on an empty, distant look when she said that. After several bumpy kilometers, our wagons rumbled into the town of Wismar to merge with other army units traveling on foot and by bicycle, car, armored vehicle, truck, and horse-drawn wagon.

"There is no easy way around this town," our soldier said. "We really didn't want to come through Wismar, because every town is crowded, a fat target for *Tiefflieger*, just like Woldegk. We are close to the English and American lines, and we have to be prepared to surrender if we should suddenly come upon them." Our driver seemed ill at ease for the first time since I'd been with him. I could feel that he was worried about what lay ahead.

"We've been together too long to split up now," he continued. "We have decided to surrender as a combat unit with our heads held high." All at once he busied himself with things having to do with the horses. The horses seemed to be getting along just fine. I thought I saw a tear in our soldier's eye. Maybe I was wrong about that. Soldiers didn't cry unless they hurt a lot. Wismar was a madhouse. In parks and on side streets, soldiers were getting rid of weapons and unnecessary items of uniform. I saw a company of soldiers equipped with bicycles take off their camouflage uniforms. Some put on civilian clothing. They were abandoning their bicycles, so I impulsively ran over and took one and rode it back to our wagon. I walked behind our wagon for several minutes with my prized bicycle. I couldn't ride the bicycle because there were too many people on the sidewalk and too many vehicles crowding the road. I soon realized I would be left behind in the mass of people and vehicles if I didn't climb back on our wagon. I laid the bicycle down in the middle of the sidewalk. By the time I climbed on our wagon, someone had taken it.

Slowly our wagons wound their way through Wismar and out of the congestion of the town. As the last houses dropped away behind us, we were again surrounded by open fields, hedgerows, and forest. Other roads joined ours at the west end of Wismar, and our train of wagons, staying together only with difficulty, became mixed in with remnants of other Wehrmacht units. No one seemed to be afraid of being attacked by *Tiefflieger*. "We are too close to the Amies, so the Russians won't try anything here," our driver pointed out. "And we are just a few in a long line of surrendering units, so there is no sense for the Amies to attack us. The war is over, my boy," he said, smiling. "You made it. You will be safe."

It was a marvelous first day of May, sunny and warm, unusual for that

Surrender

time of year. A few puffy white clouds drifted lazily in the blue sky. The closer our wagons came to the American and British lines—no one yet knew exactly which—the more army units pulled off to the side of the road to abandon their equipment. Our *Oberfeldwebel* came by on his motorcycle and instructed his men to discard their steel helmets, weapons, and ammunition and to follow the other wagons off the highway onto a narrow *Feldweg* leading toward a village. When every wagon was off the road, the *Spies* ordered the unit to halt so he could make sure that any stragglers had caught up. Once he had made certain his full command was assembled and ready to proceed, he had a large white flag and an equally large American flag, both on long poles, mounted on the left and right front of the lead wagon. Then, seated in his motorcycle sidecar, he assumed a position at the head of our unit and led us into surrender.

A thin skirmish line of American troops was deployed at the edge of the village. The American soldiers stood about ten meters apart from each other for as far as I could see on each side of the *Feldweg*. There was a roadblock directly ahead of us where their line crossed the *Feldweg*. A Sherman tank sat there with its barrel pointing at us. Several smaller American military cars, jeeps, were parked on each side of the *Feldweg*, also with white stars painted on their car hoods and doors. Some of the cars were manned by soldiers behind mounted machine guns. Several American soldiers stood around, casually smoking cigarettes, watching us approach, their weapons held as if they didn't anticipate needing them.

Our *Oberfeldwebel* at the head of our column rode up to the roadblock. Seventy horse-drawn army wagons followed behind. I saw the *Oberfeldwebel* climb out of his sidecar and salute an American lieutenant. The American returned his salute. Then our *Oberfeldwebel* took off his leather belt, wrapped it around his pistol, and handed belt and pistol to the American officer. The two soldiers talked. I could see our *Oberfeldwebel* point back at his wagon train. Then he gave the command to move out. Mounds of rifles, submachine guns, machine guns, and pistols lay near the roadblock, as well as heaps of *Panzerfaust*, hand grenades, and helmets. It seemed all so simple the way the war was ending for us.

The American soldiers, with a few English soldiers amongst them, didn't look hostile. They wore brown uniforms, with their pants bloused at the bottoms and tucked into brown, high-top boots. Most wore short, grey jackets over brown woolen shirts. Their helmets sat on their heads at an angle with the chin straps dangling. Their faces were mostly smooth shaven, and they looked well fed, in contrast to our soldiers, whose faces were gaunt and unshaven. Around their waists the Americans wore web belts with canteens, pistols, and grenades hanging from them. They carried submachine guns. The English were easy to tell apart from the Americans because of their flat helmets and their sleeveless brown leather jackets. Carrying rifles, they looked stiff and soldierly compared to the relaxed Americans.

Was the war really over for all of us? I looked up at the blue sky and felt the welcoming warmth of the sun. I looked at the village and the green fields. The soldiers, German, English, and American, looked out of place. This small island of sun-brushed green fields and exhilarating bird sounds seemed to be a place of peace. Our wagon train wound its way into the village, which was much larger than it had first appeared. We proceeded to a soccer field in the center of the village, and the drivers parked their wagons in four long, neat rows. Nearly seventy wagons had made it from Strasburg, from Rumania, and from Russia. As our wagon pulled into its place, our soldier turned to the four of us and said, "This is the end of my six-year journey. *Auf Wiedersehen, Kinder. Auf Wiedersehen, Oma.* You, dear lady"— he held the reins out for Mutti—"take this wagon and these horses. The wagon is loaded with rations and feed which will keep your family and the horses fed for some time. It is yours now. They are strong horses. Drive out of here immediately after I leave, or the mob you see out there will plunder this wagon and take the horses away from you. Give the horses one unit of pressed hay each day and a few oats and plenty of water, of course."

There were no American or English troops at the soccer field. Our soldier got a frantic look in his eyes and asked Mutti, "You don't have any civilian clothes in your suitcases I could wear, do you?" Mutti shook her head. He folded his hands and let them hang between his legs, his head bowed. Then he straightened up resolutely, took off his watch, handed it to Mutti, and said, "I won't need that either where I am going." Mutti took the watch. He jumped off the wagon. "*Auf Wiedersehen* and much luck," he shouted, giving us a last wave with his hand. He walked away toward the assembly point without looking back. He was now a prisoner of war. I was sad to see our soldier leave. I felt unprotected without him and without the presence of the others. There was no time to daydream, though, or to feel sorry for myself. Several scraggly-looking men started to move across the soccer field toward our wagon, eyeing it as a target of plunder. It was time for us to move out.

Surrender

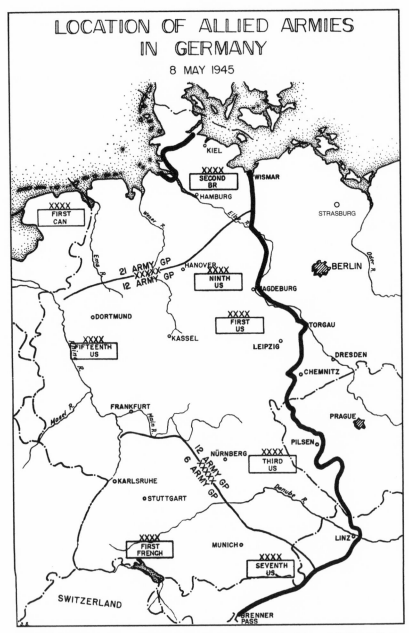

Location of Allied armies in Germany on May 8, 1945. *The American Military Occupation of Germany 1945–1953*, Headquarters, United States Army, Europe, 1953, 3.

Chapter 9

THE AMERICANS

utti handled the reins of our horses expertly. *"Hue-hot,"* she cried loudly, urging the horses to move out. The horses responded, and the wagon moved forward effortlessly. I sat on the driver's seat between Mutti and Oma. Ingrid sat in the wagon's interior in a place she had fashioned for herself. As Mutti moved our wagon away from the threat of the looters, both she and I looked for a place to go. Simultaneously we saw what looked like a manor house on a hill near the edge of the soccer field. With a smile Mutti directed the horses toward our impromptu destination. Once we got close to the building, we discovered it wasn't a manor house, but a military hospital. A red cross was painted on the side. It had probably been a school once, and had been turned into a field hospital. Mutti stopped the horses, tied down the reins, and, turning toward me, said, "Wolfgang, find Frau Zoske and her boys. Also, see if you can find more feed for the horses. We'll need all the feed we can get our hands on. I will go into the hospital and see if I can get more medicines."

While Mutti gave me directions, the hospital door opened and out stepped a German officer in full Luftwaffe uniform. He wore his sidearm. From the rank insignia on his tunic, I determined that he was a colonel in the medical corps. He wore his military garrison hat, and it struck me as curious that on a warm spring day his left hand was sheathed in a grey glove of fine leather, clutching his other glove. Wasn't the war over? Didn't our soldiers just surrender to the Americans? And yet here stood a German officer, impeccably dressed in full military uniform with a pistol strapped to his side. Mutti noticed the stunned expression on my face and, looking around, saw the officer standing in the hospital doorway. Was she shocked as I had been? No, my mother wasn't that easily shocked. I continued to look into her revealing eyes and saw only a slight moment of uncertainty. The officer took off his hat with his un-gloved right hand and put it under his left arm. A long, blond hank of hair fell across his face. He brushed it back. The entire scene was unreal, I thought. He walked slowly and deliberately, coming down the steps toward us, his black riding boots glistening in the early afternoon sunshine. He stopped in front of Mutti and bowed slightly from the waist up. To me he seemed pompous. I watched him intently. Suspiciously.

"I am a medical doctor and the commanding officer of this military field hospital," he announced to Mutti. "No one has come yet to accept my surrender. That is why I am still in full uniform. I am ready to surrender my weapon and my command to the English or the Americans. Now I have a better idea, if it is agreeable with you. Do you have a man with you?" he asked.

"No," said Mutti without hesitation.

"You need a man with you to protect you," he continued self-assuredly. "Just look at that rabble down below plundering those army wagons. They will stop at nothing if they want something. There is no law here to enforce order. Why don't I change into civilian clothes and accompany you? I assume you intend to continue heading west?" Mutti nodded her head. "If anyone asks we can say we are refugees from the east and I am your husband. If you agree to my proposal then it will only take me a few minutes to change."

"Yes, your proposal sounds fine to me," Mutti replied. Without hesitation the doctor strode off and disappeared into the hospital. Although I disliked the man, I changed my mind about him somewhat. His proposal made sense. It would be useful for us to have a man along.

Remembering Mutti's earlier directions, I jumped off the wagon and ran down the hill to where I saw Frau Zoske walking aimlessly amongst the abandoned wagons with Horst and Günter. The mob was still busy ransacking the wagons. I sent her and the boys to our wagon. Then I climbed on one of the abandoned wagons to see if I could find additional fodder. It had not taken the plundering mob long to strip most of the wagons of everything of value. Finding nothing in the first wagon, I climbed on another. While looking through that one, I was joined by a group of unkempt-looking men, their clothes reeking of sweat and urine. They threw things over the side as they methodically worked their way toward me. Suddenly, one of them punched me in the ribs with his elbow. It hurt. He was unshaven, and strands of long black hair hung in his gaunt face. He shouted at me in Polish. I didn't understand him. Judging from his hostile look and the threatening stance he assumed, I was certain he wanted me out of his way. Without thinking, I blurted out, "Don't do that again or I'll get some German soldiers to arrest you."

He looked at me in amused astonishment and then broke into loud laughter. "Yes, you go and get some German soldiers, you little Nazi," he shouted in heavily accented German. "There are no more German soldiers. Don't you know that?" He grabbed me by the throat. His fingers dug deeply into my neck. I couldn't breathe. "Get out of my way before I throw you off this wagon," he shouted into my face. His breath was foul. "Do you understand?" I clawed at his hand, trying to get him to loosen his grip. I gasped for air as he let go, pushing me against the sloped side of the wagon. I fell. I jumped over the side and ran toward our wagon as fast as I could. I finally grasped our situation. We were on our own, and we had better know how to protect ourselves. When we passed the American lines, we also passed into no-man's-land. Only the strongest ruled here, those who were physically strong and who could protect themselves somehow. There were no police, no American or English soldiers. The law was the law of the moment, enforced by a gun, if necessary, and if one was lucky enough to have one.

I continued my flight from the looters, looking back once to make sure no one was following me. No one was. They were busy amassing plunder and didn't care about a boy running away from them. I slowed down. Walking up the hillside, I took a shortcut through a clump of trees. In the deep grass at the foot of a tree, I saw a leather gun holster and belt. I picked it up, opened the holster, and removed the gun. It was a 9 mm Luger. The pistol had a full clip of ammunition in its handle. In a pocket of the holster was a spare clip. I removed the spare ammunition clip and discarded the holster. I hid the gun and the clip under my shirt and slowly walked to our wagon, hoping Mutti would not see me.

"Wolfgang," Mutti called my name. I froze in my steps, thinking I had been discovered. "Did you find feed for the horses?" she shouted. I still didn't see her. Looking under the wagon, I saw her legs on the other side. She must have heard me coming, she couldn't have seen me.

"No, Mutti," I answered hastily, "there wasn't any feed left. The wagons have been stripped clean by the looters."

"We will make it somehow," she responded, still not seeing me. I hurriedly hid the gun and the ammunition clip between two boxes on the back of our wagon—not a good hiding place, but the best I could do. I knew for sure that Mutti wouldn't let me keep a gun. After my encounter with the looters down below, I felt we needed a gun for protection. Finding the gun was a stroke of luck, I thought. I had every intention of using it if that became necessary. In the meantime, Frau Zoske and her boys had made themselves comfortable in the wagon. Mutti climbed on the driver's seat, and I joined Ingrid in back, as far away from Frau Zoske as possible. I didn't like her. While Mutti sat waiting for the doctor, she decided to take a last look around the wagon. I jumped off the wagon with her and watched her from a distance as she did her walk-around. I was hoping she wouldn't find the gun, but I soon heard a gasp. She came running toward me holding the gun at arm's length in front of her. "Did you put this gun in the wagon?" she asked me, fright plainly audible in her voice.

"No," I said, too startled to admit the truth. I knew I could not explain it to her.

"Look at this, Wolfgang," she said. "Someone stuck this gun in our wagon while we were busy so they could come back in the dark and attack us." I was sorry to cause her pain. I was even more sorry that I had been so careless in hiding the gun. I still believed we would need it, and I felt defenseless without it. The doctor came bounding out the front door of the hospital. He looked different in his civilian clothes, without his uniform and his paraphernalia of rank and privilege. Much less imposing. He brought nothing with him except a small military medical bag. Mutti showed him the gun, telling him where she had found it and what she thought it was intended for. He looked at the gun impassively, took it from her hand, and threw it into the trees. He climbed onto the wagon and took the reins. Mutti followed and sat beside him, to his right.

"This looks more natural," he said. He moved the reins slightly, causing the horses to move out. I could tell right away that he knew about horses. With his knowledge of the area, we were soon out of the village. It was midafternoon and we were heading west. I remembered our soldier telling us earlier in the day to keep moving west toward Luebeck and not to stop until we got there. "It will be best for us if we go as far as we can today, driving right through the night if possible," the doctor said, smiling at Mutti. "With a little luck we can make it to Lübeck by early tomorrow morning."

The road was chaotic, littered with abandoned Wehrmacht equipment—wagons with no horses, trucks without drivers, guns standing at odd angles pointing at nothing, and here and there a lone armored vehicle. A huge Royal Tiger tank, a *Königstiger*, stood aslant in the middle of the road; we barely squeezed by. It was hard for me to believe that such a large tank could actually be useful. It looked both unwieldy and unconquerable, like a mobile fortress. It sat abandoned with its huge gun pointing westward, straight down the road we were traveling. After we passed the tank, our progress became fairly swift. As we came upon an abandoned truck with its tailgate down, a man yelled, "That truck is full of food. I just got off it, and there are boxes of pudding powder and sugar and flour. Get it while there still is some left." The man continued walking to his own wagon, where a woman wrapped in a black shawl sat on the driver's bench while several children crawled around behind.

"Stop," Mutti said to the doctor, "so we can load up on some of the food." The doctor paid no attention to her.

"We must go as fast and as far as we can today without stopping. We must get to Luebeck by tonight, tomorrow at the latest," he mumbled, "if we can possibly do it." I jumped off our wagon to see what food there was in the truck, but I couldn't get on it; the truck bed sat too high off the ground for a boy my size to climb onto. It was frustrating. I became angry at the doctor for taking over our wagon and not stopping. I made a last attempt to claw myself onto the truck. I just couldn't lift my foot high enough to reach the first step of the dangling tailgate. Meanwhile, our wagon was pulling ever farther away. I was forced to abandon my search for food.

I had almost caught up with them again when I noticed a partially burned white silk parachute on the side of the road. I thought of Mutti and how she liked silk. I knew she could make several blouses from the material. I rushed over to pick up the chute. The dead pilot was still attached, lying face down, his head ensconced in a brown leather cap. He wore a brown leather fleece-lined jacket. I thought he was an American. I ran to catch up with our wagon. We continued to encounter large quantities of abandoned weapons and military equipment, as if an army had just walked away from it. Rifles, machine guns, mortars, submachine guns, trucks of various sizes in camouflage paint, and hundreds of boxes of ammunition lay everywhere. At a crossroads, we encountered the first sizable group of people we had seen since leaving the hospital—a makeshift camp for German prisoners of war. All were SS soldiers in their distinctive, mottled green camouflage uniforms. Mutti jumped off the wagon and ran toward the prison enclosure, waving at the prisoners. One came over to speak to her. They talked for a while. Soon she came back, walking slowly. She motioned with her hand that it was all right to move on again.

"The soldier said it would be wise for us to get off the road or we will probably be stopped and interned," she said. "He thought we were lucky to get this far without running into a patrol." The doctor took the next side road.

"It will also get us where we want to go," he said. "I know the area well. This country road is just fine." Our wagon soon entered another area filled with abandoned German army equipment. Hand grenades and land mines lay on the road. We had to be careful not to drive over one and cause it to explode.

"Let's get out of here and take this *Feldweg*," the doctor proposed. "By staying in the fields, we should encounter fewer abandoned weapons, especially mines. We should also be able to avoid any roving military patrols, since they are more likely to stay on the main roads." Mutti said nothing. We moved off the road onto a rutted *Feldweg*. I worried about our horses. They hadn't rested for a long time and hadn't been properly fed and watered that day. They bravely kept moving onward at a pace slower than usual. Their muzzles were covered with foam. Their heads lowered as if they were fatigued. The sun was no longer visible behind the low clouds on the horizon.

I heard loud engine noises. I recognized that sound immediately—tanks. Two American Sherman tanks, throwing clods of damp earth into the air with their rubberized tracks, came around a hedgerow, heading straight for us. Infantry rode on the tanks. They were armed with the same type of snubnosed submachine guns I had noticed on the American soldiers earlier in the day. The soldiers did not look friendly. One tank stopped in front of us, the other behind us.

The Americans

"Wer seit ihr?" asked one of the American soldiers in fluent and accentless German.

"Wir sind Flüchtlinge," said the doctor, "and this is my wife and my children."

"Why are you here?" the German-speaking soldier persisted.

"We took a shortcut around the village because the road is blocked with abandoned trucks and loose ammunition. We want to go to Lübeck to join our relatives."

The American soldier looked skeptical, but he wasn't inclined to waste any more time on us. "Turn here toward that village in the distance," he said, gesturing toward the village with his left hand and pointing his submachine gun at us with his right. "There is an internment camp in that village where you must remain until authorized to leave. You must get off the roads tonight or you could get shot." The two tanks roared off. The doctor turned the horses toward the village. We followed the *Feldweg* leading to the village as the German-speaking American soldier had ordered us to do. We were careful to avoid mines and loose ammunition lying about. American soldiers armed with carbines and submachine guns stood along the village road in groups. They looked at our wagon with amused expressions and pointed to what appeared to be the largest farm in the village. We followed their directions. The soldiers looked relaxed in their demeanor, like the ones we had surrendered to earlier in the day. Many of them were constantly chewing, the way cows chewed cud, I thought. I wondered what was in their mouths—tobacco?

The farmyard we drove into was surrounded by a whitewashed stone wall one meter high and capped with red clay roofing tiles. It was our internment camp, as the Americans called it. The doctor drove our wagon up to the side of a two-story barn. The barn's wooden walls at the upper level looked a weathered grey, almost black in places. At the lower level the walls were built of red brick, set in squares between weathered oak beams. The barn served now as a prison for captured SS troops. Its door was bolted shut. As soon as we stopped, Mutti jumped off the wagon and tended to the horses. She, too, had noticed their exhaustion. The doctor remained seated on the wagon bench, appearing dejected, at a loss as to what to do next. The situation had turned out differently from what he had planned.

"Give me a hand," Mutti said firmly to the doctor, and he slowly climbed off the wagon to help. She instructed him on what he was to do. He seemed reluctant and inept, although he was no stranger to horses. His fingers were long and thin, without callouses. He obviously had never done any real physical work and was uncomfortable doing it at the direction of a woman. After Mutti loosened the harnesses on both horses, she fed them a bundle of compressed hay. I used the two tin buckets which hung underneath our wagon to get water for the horses from a hand pump in the farmyard. Thankfully Mutti remembered that we hadn't eaten for a long time either.

"Wolfgang," she called out, "see what we have in the wagon to eat." It was getting late in the day. There remained just enough light for me to take a quick inventory of the food in the wagon. I found boxes with cans of bread, meat, and beans. Most of the cans seemed to be meat. They were the usual brown Wehrmacht cans with the contents stenciled in black letters on the top of the lid. I told Mutti what we had, and she asked for two cans of meat and one can of bread.

Many Italians, former prisoners of war, were camped in front of the farm's pig barn. The pig barn stood at a right angle to our barn, only ten meters or less away. Three fires burned brightly in front of the pig barn. Over one of the fires the Italians were roasting a whole pig. Mutti asked them for some utensils. They were friendly and helpful and assisted her in heating our meat over their open fire. While she cooked, they told her how happy they were that the war was over and that they would soon be going home to Italy. They laughed constantly and sang melodious Italian songs. I had heard no songs and little laughter over the past weeks. I dozed off sitting in the dirt watching the Italians roast their pig.

Oma awakened me when it was time to eat. Mutti distributed the food— first to Oma, then to Frau Zoske, Horst, and Günter, then to Ingrid and me. She served the doctor and herself last. The doctor took his food silently and climbed back on the wagon bench. The rest of us sat on stones by the side of the barn. The meat was pork, and it tasted delicious to me. My serving contained a large amount of fat, which I liked. I was ravenous and cleaned my mess tin quickly. I could have eaten a second portion. But there wasn't any more, so there was no sense in asking Mutti for another helping. The doctor sat on his bench and picked through his food. I guess he hadn't been away from fine food long enough to have experienced hunger. He might not even know what hunger is, I thought. I wished I could have his portion of food. When Mutti was momentarily distracted, he got off the wagon and went around the barn, soon returning with an empty mess tin. Mutti rose from her stone and went to the spot where the doctor had been.

Returning angrily, she walked up to him, shouting in his face, "It is obvious that there are people in this camp who are going hungry tonight because they don't have enough food. Look around you. But you are too good for what I served. And you went scurrying around the corner of the barn while you thought I wasn't looking and buried your meat in the dirt. I found it. You are no longer welcome with us. You may stay until you find another place to sleep. I want you out of here by tomorrow. You disgust me, *Herr Doktor*." She turned away from him and went for a walk. I could tell that Mutti was really angry at this man. The doctor said nothing. He climbed back up on the wagon and sat on the driver's bench, acting as if he were going to sleep. Without our noticing, it had clouded over and a slight drizzle had begun to fall. We lay down to sleep in and under the wagon on straw given to us by the happy Italian soldiers, who were still singing their songs of Italy. We slept comfortably that night.

The next morning at sunrise, we turned our two horses out into the meadows behind the barn. The Italians, who had partied until late and kept their fires burning through most of the night, were quiet and sleeping on loose straw strewn around the dead fires. Roosters crowed loudly and persistently, cows mooed, and pigs squealed in the pig barn where someone was feeding them. There were no lavatory facilities of any kind available to us, so we went into the alfalfa field next to the barn, as did a hundred or more other internees—old men, women, and children. We used the alfalfa to clean ourselves. As the morning progressed, an American soldier had several of the Italians dig a latrine at the edge of the field. The latrine consisted of a long trench and cross bars made from young trees freshly cut near the farm pond and nailed to supporting poles on either end of the slit latrine. The idea was to sit on the cross bar and do your business. For privacy, a board fence was erected on the farm side of the trench. I quickly noticed that men did not use the trench when they knew women were using it. I wanted to avoid the trench, but the forest was too far away, so I mostly used the trench like everyone else.

At eight o'clock in the morning, the doctor walked away from our wagon without saying a word, returning half an hour later. He took his medical kit and in passing said to Mutti, "I will not be back." He had used us when he needed us. He didn't need us anymore. We had used him, too, of course.

The Americans

The doctor headed toward the main building, and I saw him entering the front door. Our wagon sat in front of a barn which formed the east side of the internment camp. The residential building, with its linden trees, was on the west side. The long, low-slung building on the south side housed the farm's pigs, and to the north stood another two-story barn for horses and cows. On the other side of our barn, which probably served mainly as a hay and straw barn, was the farm pond. Open fields and meadows lay beyond the pond. In the middle of the barnyard was a single hand pump, where we and everybody else pumped water for ourselves and the horses. We washed our clothes in two tin buckets which we had found hanging under our wagon. We cooked in them, drank out of them, and bathed in them. Those two buckets were the only large containers we possessed. At one end of the pig barn was a huge manure heap, and another heap was next to the cow and horse barn. They attracted more flies than we could swallow. At the main entrance to our camp, an American soldier stood guard with a submachine gun slung over his shoulder.

A small village firehouse was located across from the entrance. A Sherman tank was parked adjacent to it, its gun barrel pointing straight at me as I looked at it. The American tank crew lived in the firehouse. The fire engine, which must have been very small judging from the size of the house, was nowhere to be seen. The American tank crew looked bored; I could tell from the way they paced the floor or just lay around sleeping. Every morning and afternoon an American truck drove up in front of the firehouse, dropped off four jerry cans of water, picked up four empty cans, and then roared away in a cloud of gasoline fumes and dust. Occasionally I saw English soldiers in the village. The Americans and the English didn't speak to one another.

The American soldier standing guard at the gate scowled at me. I sat by the wall watching the American tank crew across the street. The guard continued to look at me as if I were something ugly and offensive. Suddenly he called out to me. I didn't understand what he was saying. Then he motioned for me to come over to him, pointing his snub-nosed submachine gun at my belly while he beckoned with his left hand. I walked toward him slowly. He didn't look friendly. He pointed at my belt and motioned for me to take it off. I handed it to him. He looked at me with open hatred in his eyes as he took my belt, and with his gun he motioned for me to leave. Tears sprang involuntarily to my eyes. I was stunned that an American soldier could rob me of my only belt. It was a shiny, black-lacquer army ceremonial belt with an army belt buckle which carried the inscription GOTT MIT UNS. One of our German soldiers had given it to me out of pity, because I had forgotten to put on my belt in our hurried flight from Strasburg. My pants kept falling down. The German soldier said when he gave me the belt, "It's a parade belt. I'll never be going on a parade again and won't need it. You take it, boy. It will look good on you." The belt was gone. My only belt had become a war trophy for an American soldier.

I remembered there were some leather tent straps in the wagon. I took two of the straps, and, by joining one to the other, I fashioned another crude belt for myself. I noticed the barn was being emptied of its SS prisoners. The prisoners were loaded onto American trucks, which then drove off in the direction of Lübeck. A stout, swarthy American soldier approached, smiling. He wore a tanker's uniform with brown combat boots laced high, pants bloused over the boots, a light-brown web belt with a shiny brass buckle, a brown army shirt open at the throat, and a short, beige wind-breaker-like jacket. He wore his helmet as all the other soldiers did, straps dangling under his chin. He carried his submachine gun upside down, slung over his right shoulder and under his arm. He was just the opposite of the soldier guarding the gate. Still smiling broadly, he stretched his hand out toward me and offered me something wrapped in yellow paper. I took it. Noticing that I didn't know what to do, he took a piece for himself, unwrapped it, and shoved it into his mouth. Then he started chewing vigorously. I did the same thing. I pushed the long, flat thing into my mouth. Strangely enough it didn't break into pieces. It bent like rubber, and when I chewed, it turned into a rubber ball. Whatever it was, it tasted strangely refreshing.

"C-h-e-w-i-n-g g-u-m," the American soldier said slowly into my face. I knew then what the American soldiers had been chewing. Why would I want to chew anything other than the food I ate? I didn't understand the logic of it. I spoke no English so I couldn't ask the friendly American why anybody needed to chew a stick of rubber. I chewed and smiled, which seemed to make the American soldier happy. Soon the chewing gum lost its flavor and my jaws got tired, so I spit it out. The soldier shook his head in disappointment. He didn't give up on me, and continued to go through motions indicating I should keep on chewing the gum and not spit it out. Finally, he took the gum he was chewing out of his mouth and stuck it behind his left ear. I laughed. When he removed his helmet, I could see he had pitch-black hair. He wiped sweat off his forehead, laughing along with me, and put his helmet back on. He then gave me another stick of gum. I put it in my pocket this time, smiled at him, and said, *"Danke schön."* I was happy to have met a nice American soldier.

The soldier then turned away from me, indicating with the sweep of his left hand that we could use the barn. Mutti and I went into the barn right away and found a place for ourselves to the left of the door. The barn stank from mounds of feces left behind by the SS soldiers. Oma, Mutti, and I cleaned our area and found pressed bales of straw on the other side of the barn. We used some of the straw to make beds for ourselves and our horses. Mutti and I then went to the meadow and retrieved the animals. We put them into their harnesses with great difficulty. The horses were huge and the harnesses were heavy. I learned to watch the gelding carefully, as he tried to step on me with his hind legs or whip me with his tail, just as our German soldier had told me he would. The other horse was much milder and did not try to punish me. Mutti and I maneuvered the wagon into the barn and parked it in front of our living area so we could watch it at all times. After that we took the horses back to the meadow and let them loose to graze. Other *Flüchtlinge*, real farmers, had also moved into the barn and put their horses in the meadow just as we had. Soon the barn was cleaned and fully occupied. Other wagons were parked down the middle of the barn aisle across from their owners. Frau Zoske, Horst, and Günter sat stoically on a pressed bale of straw and watched Mutti and me work, doing nothing to help us arrange our place. Finally Mutti said to Frau Zoske, "Please make a place for yourself and for your boys next to ours."

Frau Zoske had been moody and uncommunicative since she had re-joined us at the hospital. Suddenly, while Mutti was helping her spread straw for their sleeping places, she started to scream, accusing Mutti of luring her away from her home in Strasburg and then neglecting her and her boys. "You rode on the wagon like a lady while we had to walk behind like ser-vants," she screamed. Mutti stood and listened, her face impassive and con-trolled. I couldn't read from her facial expression what she was thinking, but she must have felt bad. I felt sorry for my mother. She didn't deserve the spiteful attack. Frau Zoske continued screaming at the top of her lungs, gesticulating wildly with her hands and becoming progressively less coher-ent. She began to foam at the mouth. She fell to the barn floor on her back, onto the newly spread straw, and continued to scream at the top of her lungs with her arms flailing and her body rolling around. Her eyes looked like those of a cornered animal, large and white, shifting constantly. Other refugees looked at her for a moment, then ignored her.

Mutti attempted to calm Frau Zoske with no success. Whenever she came near, Frau Zoske renewed her frantic screaming, berating Mutti when she caught her breath. Mutti left her alone. Eventually Frau Zoske exhausted herself and lay on her back quietly, her mouth covered with foam, staring at the roof of the barn. She made no attempt to clean herself. After a long time, she rose, wiped the foam from her mouth with her coat sleeve, summoned her two totally confused sons, and walked off with them to an empty place behind us. There she sat and stared in front of herself with vacant eyes. Horst and Günter gathered straw to make beds for themselves. Frau Zoske did not move from her position for a long time.

Mutti called to me, "Wolfgang, climb up on the wagon and hand down some food to me. Some of each, and about half of each. Do you understand what I said?"

"Why, Mutti?" I protested. "This is ours, you don't have to give any food to her."

"Yes, I do," Mutti replied firmly in a voice which did not tolerate dissent. "And now be a good boy and get up there and do what I told you." Mutti took several armloads of cans to Frau Zoske, who continued to stare into space. My survival instincts had matured during our odyssey from Sagan to a barn thirty kilometers east of Luebeck. Times were going to be hard, and I was determined to play my part, whatever it would be, to help keep my family alive. I knew we had to have shelter and food first; everything else was secondary. We would also have to be watchful for our safety, and not get careless with the precious few possessions we had. Mutti was too good-hearted, I believed; she had given away too much to Frau Zoske.

The weather remained exceptionally nice—mostly dry, sunny, and warm. The Italian prisoners of war departed, just like the SS had a few days earlier. They, too, were loaded into American trucks which left in the direction of Luebeck. I missed having the Italians around, because they were so friendly toward us children. I missed their singing, their laughter, and the open fires. Every morning they had gone into the pig barn and killed a pig which they roasted for their dinner. They never offered us food, but I liked to listen to them sing.

Horst and Günter Zoske were embarrassed by their mother's behavior. They didn't understand her outburst any more than I did. The Americans stopped guarding the entrance to our compound. It appeared that, once the German prisoners of war and the Italians were moved out, the Americans lost interest in us *Flüchtlinge*. We could have moved on. Maybe no one was allowed on the roads except English and American troops. No one left the camp. Finally, the Polish forced laborers, the last group of people other than us *Flüchtlinge* who were not there of their own free will, left with much noise and celebration. They seemed ecstatically happy to be returning to Poland. The women dressed in whatever finery they still possessed, some wearing lacy shawls around their heads and shoulders. The men had on the same old, worn clothes they had worked in before their liberation. Shouting for joy and singing patriotic songs, the Poles drove out of the village in former German Wehrmacht trucks. They were driving east, not west like the Italians and the German prisoners before them. I couldn't figure out why they were so pleased to be returning to the Russians.

Only *Flüchtlinge* remained in our detention camp, and our lot worsened every day. There was no food to buy anywhere, nor was any food distributed to anyone by the English or the American troops. Water came from the one pump in the barnyard, and the slit trench smelled more putrid each day, even after the Americans put lime into the pit. It was a beautiful month of May. The flies, though, had become a nearly unbearable plague. We could hardly open our mouths without swallowing flies. Big, black-and-blue, shiny flies. The slit trench and the horses in our barn attracted more flies than we could swallow. Mutti claimed that flies were our dessert after every meal. The flies plagued people and animals alike. They didn't differentiate between American and German bodies either. They landed on everyone and in everything.

The Americans continued their bored existence in the firehouse. Every day I watched the soldiers from across the street. I wanted to know more about these men from the land I so admired and had read so much about in my Karl May books. They continued to ignore me. Every morning and afternoon the truck came by, dropping off its jerry cans filled with water. The Americans washed themselves with the water from the jerry cans; they brushed their teeth using the water from the jerry cans; they drank the water from the jerry cans; they ate cold rations from tiny boxes and out of small tin cans.

We had lost contact with the outside world and were ignorant of anything that might have been going on. In the evenings Mutti and some other women gathered near the barn door and sang songs. Soon American soldiers came and sat nearby and listened to them sing. The soldiers brought candy and cigarettes and generously shared them with us. Mutti said they were lonely and homesick. I thought they looked sad. Their eyes looked like the eyes of the German soldiers who had rescued us from the Russians. When they laughed their eyes didn't.

The German inhabitants of the village were invisible most of this time, rarely venturing outside their houses. In contrast, the people who worked on the estate, our internment camp, tried to get back to normalcy as soon as they could, ignoring us *Flüchtlinge* as if we didn't exist. They provided no food for us and no help of any kind. They, too, were Germans, but to them we were nothing. We were like foul air—an invisible, stinking presence. They milked their cows, but gave us no milk even when we begged for it. They had potatoes, carrots, and beets for themselves and the animals, but they shared none with us. After the Italians left, they guarded the pigs jealously to make sure we didn't kill any. They took in the doctor because they didn't have a doctor in the village, and they figured it was a good trade—his skills for their food and shelter. Later on he also acted as their veterinarian, and I saw him castrate young horses.

Inheriting a supply wagon from our German army rescuers had been our good fortune. I remembered the night two weeks earlier when our wagon had broken down before the burning village during the Russian artillery bombardment. If our wagon wheel hadn't broken, we would have had a wagon loaded with office supplies instead of food. And someone had had to abandon the food wagon so that it was there for us. It was all too bizarre to believe something like that could really happen. It had to be God's will. The more I thought about how we came into possession of the food wagon, the more I believed in God and his power. Since all of our food supply was canned, it was safe to eat. Many of the *Flüchtlinge* in our barn had come from as far away as East Prussia and had little, if any, supplies left. They collected the freshly sprouting greens such as nettles along roadsides and fence lines, and cooked them into a spinach-like consistency for food. Mutti shared our food with others when she saw someone who needed help desperately. But none of us knew how long we would have to stay in the barn, and we had to conserve what little food we had. The English and Americans provided no food, no drink, no medicines—even though by now there was ample evidence of spreading epidemics of cholera and typhus.

The Americans

It had been two weeks since Frau Zoske's nervous breakdown. She seemed to have recovered from whatever it was that had caused her mental collapse. She still did not speak to Mutti. I played with the two Zoske boys in the alfalfa field next to our barn. Horst had to excuse himself frequently to run to our smelly latrine. On each occasion he sat there for a long time. I asked his brother, "What's the matter with Horst?"

"I don't know myself," Günter replied, "but he has to go all the time, and only blood comes out." I was shocked to hear that.

"Has he tried to see the doctor?"

"Yes. The doctor said it would be all right in time. He told Horst he couldn't do anything for him because he had no medicines." During the night Horst got worse. I could hear him moaning and running outside to the latrine. Early in the morning, Frau Zoske came to Mutti wringing her hands. "Frau Samuel," she said in a tortured voice, "my boy Horst needs help. He is so sick, and I don't know what to do." Mutti knew about Horst and about his visit to the doctor. She took Frau Zoske by the hand and led her toward the farmhouse. The doctor's only advice was to get Horst to a hospital quickly. The nearest hospital was in Grevesmühlen, about ten kilometers away. Frau Zoske, Horst, and Günter left immediately. The following day only two of them returned. Horst got to the hospital in Grevesmühlen just in time to die. Cholera, they were told. I felt deeply saddened by Horst's sudden death, and a shadow fell over my world. One day he was there and we were playing, and the next day he was dead.

There was little for me to do around the camp, nor did I find playmates. I first explored the farm, then the nearby fields and woods. On one of my excursions, I found several boxes of German machine gun ammunition in a ditch. I took one box into a wooded area, where I extracted the rounds from the belt. It was something to do. I saw several stones nearby, which gave me an idea. By smashing a stone down on a bullet, which I had first placed on another flat stone, I could make it explode. The sound was the same as that of a rifle firing. Soon I could set them off as quickly as I could replace them. Suddenly a young girl appeared next to me. She looked down at what I was doing and said, "There are soldiers coming with rifles at the ready. You better leave quickly." Then she ran away. I got off my knees and walked out of the forest.

I could see a skirmish line of English soldiers coming toward me across the field, ten or twelve of them. When I looked back, I saw an equal number approaching the woods from the opposite direction. I decided not to run but to walk toward them the way I normally would. A young English soldier approached, rifle at the ready. He looked at me suspiciously. He seemed uncertain what to do, so I said *"Guten Tag,"* looking him straight in the eyes and giving him a broad smile. He looked startled when I spoke, and, after hesitating slightly in his measured gait, continued past me. As I crossed a field of young wheat with the fresh shoots reaching to my knees, I stumbled over something. It was a brown leather belt and gun holster holding a small Walther pistol. Herr Schmitt in Berlin had worn such a pistol when he took us to the train station in early March. I discarded the belt and the holster and kept the pistol and the spare clip. I put the pistol in my pocket, keeping my hand over it to make sure its outline was not visible through my pants. I entered our barn through the doors opposite our sleeping area. I seldom entered the barn from this direction, but I wanted to get into the twilight of the barn as quickly as possible so I could hide the pistol. I thought the day might come when my family needed protection.

I went from bright sunlight into the barn's semidarkness, stopping for a moment to accustom my eyes to the sudden change. I heard moaning coming from my left. As my eyes got used to the twilight, I saw a teenage girl in a red dress lying on a bed of straw. I had seen her before, picking nettles for her family's dinner. She was three or four years older than I, tall and lanky. Her moans told of her pain. She held her stomach with one hand, while the back of the other lay across her forehead. She moaned as I had heard Horst moan only a few nights earlier. In a tearful voice she cried out to her family kneeling around her, "I don't want to die. I don't want to die. Please, God, don't let me die. I don't want to die." Over and over she pleaded for God to let her live. There was no help for her, I knew that. She had cholera like Horst, and she was going to die soon. She was one of the East Prussians, coming with her family from so far away, only to die in a barn near Lübeck. Her mother knelt beside her, taking her hands into her own, and the men sat or kneeled around her humble bed of straw with long, sad faces and bowed heads.

My heart seemed about to explode with pain as I listened to her plaintive pleading. I ran further into the darkness of the barn to hide from the girl's moans. I found a wooden pillar and hid the pistol behind it. Then I hid in a dark corner of the barn among bales of straw and cried for the girl in the red dress who I knew was dying. I felt indescribably sad, and the pain of my sadness entered my heart until it hurt. Even in my hideaway, I could hear the girl's voice softly pleading for her life.

After a restless night, I went to her end of the barn first thing in the morning hoping that somehow she had gotten better. It was quiet there. I heard no moans. She lay there in her red dress, her eyes closed, her hands neatly folded over her chest. I could think she was sleeping. I knew better.

The Americans became more visible. Several Sherman tanks drove into the farmyard and positioned themselves around the pond. A truck arrived with a compressor in tow. The soldiers started it up, attached a hose, and began to pump water out of the pond to wash the mud off the tanks. The stream of water produced by the pump was very powerful, and cakes of mud flew off the tank treads when hit by the water. The soldiers were laughing and horsing around. I thought it looked like it would be fun to hold the hose and wash the tanks. Maybe the soldiers would let me. I went over to the soldier who was hosing down a tank. He was short and wiry and looked like the Italian prisoners of war, dark-skinned with curly black hair. I asked him if I could wash the tank for him. At first, he didn't seem to understand what I was saying and ignored me. When I pointed at the hose and the tank he got the message. Laughing, he handed me the hose and walked away.

The instant I took the hose I knew I had made a mistake. The water pressure was so immense that it was difficult for me to hold on and keep the hose pointed at the tank. The American soldiers sitting in the shade of the barn paid no attention to me. They were smoking cigarettes and laughing. I looked to them for help, but they chose not to see me. If I let go, I would have to run from the flailing hose. I knew that if the brass nozzle hit me I was going to be hurt severely. My strength waned quickly. I had to act. I let go of the hose and ran away from its flailing head as fast as I could. The hose flopped all over the ground like a snake gone mad, spraying the soldiers who had paid no attention to my plight. They jumped up, dropping their cigarettes and trying to get away from the hose. The little Italian guy finally shut off the compressor and the "water snake" died.

In the evening we ate our one meal of the day. Mutti would open a can of meat, usually pork. Since it was precooked, all she or Oma had to do was heat it over an open flame. We cooked the meat in one of the water buckets. Ingrid and I always ate everything we were given. Fat, meat, gravy—everything. We were hungry all the time.

Across from the entrance to our camp and past the firehouse stood a prosperous-looking farm. Mutti met the owner while begging for potatoes and eggs. She had lunch with him and his farmhands. He was a single man, Mutti's age. She told me how they sat around a long table in the kitchen. A maid brought a wooden bowl of steaming potato soup and placed it before them. Then everybody took some from the community bowl. A loaf of farm-baked rye bread was passed around, and everybody cut off as much as he or she needed. Then they dunked the bread into their soup. The farmer gave Mutti several eggs, our first fresh food. The day after, Mutti took me to meet the man. He seemed nice and was friendly toward me. He wore black rubber boots smeared with mud. His pants were tucked into the boots, and the brownish, three-button tweed jacket which he wore over a thick sweater made him look heavier than he really was.

One of Mutti's concerns was the welfare of our horses. We were running out of hay and oats. Mutti persuaded the farmer to stable the horses while she found a place for us to stay once we were allowed to leave the camp. In return for keeping the horses, the farmer had their use. To my great surprise, Mutti confided to me that the farmer had proposed marriage to her. She hadn't worn a wedding ring in a long time; still, they had only just met. I was more than astounded by her revelation. "But you are already married," I said to her.

"Well, Wolfgang, I am not really married. As soon as your father and I are together again, I will divorce him. I told you that before. All that does is give me a piece of paper that tells the world what is already true. You know that I cannot live with your father under any circumstances. You also know why. Of course, the farmer doesn't have to know all that."

I tried to recall what it was that had made my parents strangers to each other, why my mother wanted to divorce my father so badly, what had happened to them in Sagan that made her hate him. Why couldn't she just forget about it and try to start anew once she and Dad were together again? Sagan seemed like a place I had left years ago. I recalled how I had once found my father with his secretary, lying between her legs on the couch in my room. Another time when he was home on military leave from Holland, early in the war, I heard Mutti and Dad arguing in their bedroom. Ingrid and I listened at the door. When I heard him threaten to shoot her, I opened the door. I saw him standing at the foot of their bed pointing his pistol at her.

"You are not going to shoot my mother, are you?" I cried out to him, terrified at what I was seeing and hearing. He put his pistol down and looked away—not at me, away.

Then he shouted, "I'll shoot you and the children, too." Mutti grabbed Ingrid and me by the hands and ran with us out of the apartment. We nearly fell down the basement stairs, we were running so fast. We hid behind the trash barrels in the refuse room. My father came looking for us, pistol in hand. He didn't find us. Maybe he didn't want to find us. The three of us stayed in the basement for a long time that night before Mutti took us back upstairs.

Yes, I did remember why Mutti could no longer live with my father. There were those ugly things. I had hoped those memories would just go away. They never just went away; they always came back at a time of their choosing. Mutti couldn't forgive or forget the things my father had done. I couldn't, either.

She seemed amused by the farmer's proposal of marriage. "I didn't tell him no, Wolfgang. I said I would think about it. It made him feel better than my saying no to him. We have a place to stable our horses and that is important. And I may need him for something else in the future. 'No' is such a final word. 'Maybe' is much better. Don't you see?"

"Yes, I see," I said, but I didn't really. I admired how caring she was toward our horses. She could have just left them in the meadow and abandoned them. That thought, I was certain, never entered her mind. She was responsible for the horses, and that meant that she would find them a warm stall when she no longer needed them. On returning from visiting the farm, we were told by an American soldier that we would not be allowed to leave the camp until further notice. For several days the rumor had made the rounds that the Americans and the English were ready to leave and would surrender this area to the Russians. I sensed that the Americans and the English were leaving that night or the next day. That's why they had washed their tanks; that's why they were restricting us to the camp.

That night, as I lay on my straw bed, I was awakened by the rumble of tanks moving through the village. All night long and into the early morning hours, I heard the sounds of tanks and heavy trucks. It was the sound of an army on the move, again a retreating army, and I didn't like being left behind. Then followed a crushing silence. I felt vulnerable and afraid again. I couldn't go back to sleep. I was sorry the Americans were gone.

The Americans

Zones of occupation. *The American Military Occupation of Germany 1945–1953*, Headquarters United States Army, Europe, 1953, 15.

Chapter 10

THE RUSSIANS

A t first light, even before I washed up, I ran down to the village. The fire station was empty. The Americans and their tank were gone. The only evidence of their stay was a broken tank tread in the ditch alongside the road. There was no army now to keep order, and no police. I knew it was again a time to be especially careful. The Russians would come soon. After all our running away from them, they would finally catch up with us. I went to check on my gun. It was still where I had hidden it under the straw by the pillar.

It didn't take the other *Flüchtlinge* long to size up the situation. They retrieved their horses from the meadows that morning, and by noon most families were leaving and heading west toward Lübeck and beyond. Mutti and I reclaimed our horses from the farmer across the street, harnessed them with the usual difficulty, and finally managed to hook them to our wagon. By the time we were ready to leave, we were the last ones, except for Frau Zoske and her youngest son. I wondered what would become of them. What would she decide to do? They would probably walk to Grevesmühlen and try to take a train to Strasburg, if there were trains running. Frau Zoske had to make her own choices now. I was glad we were leaving the internment camp. The stench from the latrine was overpowering. Huge swarms of flies were everywhere. Soon all of us would have been sick or dying from cholera or typhus. I decided to leave my gun behind. We traveled west like the others, but only for two kilometers. Mutti had found an abandoned barracks one village over.

"There may still be some space available for us to move into when we get there," she confided in me. "At least I hope we are not too late." As we passed the western edge of our village, I saw a sign by the side of the road that read SIEVERSHAGEN. I finally knew the name of the village of our internment. In the camp, Mutti had met Llydia, a woman her age. They had spent time together each day. Llydia occasionally arranged to borrow a couple of bicycles, and she and Mutti rode around the immediate area, which is how they came across the barracks in Hanshagen. The lone barracks had housed BDM girls who had abandoned it just days before the war ended, breaking most of the dishes, furniture, and stoves before they left. There seemed to be space for one more family; at least Mutti thought so. It took an hour to cover the two kilometers to Hanshagen. The road was empty of other traffic. Everything was peaceful. We saw no signs of Russians. Once we arrived at the barracks we found the people already there friendly and helpful. Some had come from our barn in Sievershagen. Two sisters from Berlin gave up a room for our use. They had left Berlin a week before the Russians entered the city. They thought they were lucky to have escaped the Russians just in time. Both women were about Mutti's age. Mutti would turn thirty-one on May 31. The older of the two women had a boy my age. She and the boy lived in one room. The younger sister lived with her boyfriend in an adjacent room. We would live next door to both.

Our room was furnished with a plain wooden table, two chairs, a chest of drawers, and two single beds with the usual straw mattresses. The walls were raw pine boards, thin enough to allow us to hear a person whispering in the next room. We didn't care. We had a clean, dry place and real beds to sleep in. That's all that mattered. We unloaded our wagon, and Mutti and I drove it back to the farmer in Sievershagen, this time turning both wagon and horses over to his care. As we were leaving, the farmer said to Mutti, "I am only keeping your horses until you decide what to do with them, Hedy. You can have them back anytime." It was getting dark when we got back to Hanshagen.

The barracks was located on a narrow, tree-lined, dirt road at the west end of the village. Hanshagen had two or three farms and several detached houses—no church, school, store, or any other public building. When we entered the east end of the village, we had passed an abandoned Wehrmacht

The Russians

truck, loaded with pontoons, which had become stuck in the ditch during the last retreat. The abandoned truck and our barracks were the only reminders of war I could see in this remote part of Germany. The village inhabitants shunned us *Flüchtlinge* by turning their backs on us when we walked by their houses, or by closing their doors or windows as we passed, often loudly. We were not welcome. Refugees were not welcome anywhere. Mutti and the two women from Berlin looked in one of the storage rooms and located some boards and plywood, which they then nailed over the lower half of our windows to keep marauding Russian soldiers out. They also tried to find a better lock for the entrance to the barracks. They couldn't find anything. Although they laughed and smiled, I could tell that Mutti and the two women were scared of what the future might hold for them. In the evenings people gathered near the front door of the barracks as they had in the internment camp in Sievershagen. They didn't sing as they did then, and there were no American soldiers handing out candy or cigarettes.

Behind our barracks was a ripening field of winter wheat and a small garden started by the BDM girls. I could see some things sprouting, but none were far enough along to harvest. The boy next door and I talked, and he told me that he had arrived before the BDM girls left. He, his mother, and his aunt had briefly been quartered in the farm next door. As soon as the barracks was abandoned, the farmer's wife had moved them out. It was early June now, the seventh day after the American and English troops had withdrawn. I wandered into the village and sat by the side of the road, watching for anything that might come by. Then, to my great surprise, I saw a strange-looking wagon enter the east end of the village. As the wagon came closer, I could see that it was pulled by one diminutive horse with an unfamiliar harness. I knew I had seen pictures of such harnesses—a wooden yoke running around the horse's neck. Then I recalled my book on Napoleon and the French winter retreat from Moscow in 1812. Pictures in the book showed sleighs and wagons pulled by little horses using the same harness. The man driving the wagon must be a Russian.

I was curious to see what our conqueror looked like. At last he came close enough for me to discern his facial features. He was Mongolian, with the features of the great desert people imprinted on his face. A slight man, he was deeply tanned or maybe brown-skinned by nature. He was smoking a cigarette made from tobacco rolled into a scrap of newspaper. His uniform was like the ones I had seen on Russian prisoners of war, a simple shirt-like tunic over a pair of pants skintight at the lower leg with cloth wrapped around his legs. I couldn't see his feet. His cap was pulled down to just above his eyes, and the earflaps dangled below his chin. He rolled slowly past me in his *Panjewagen*, looking neither left nor right. As quietly as he had entered the village from the east, he disappeared to the west, heading for Schönberg. I ran to the barracks to tell Mutti what I had seen. I had expected T-34 tanks, trucks, and many soldiers, as with the American army that had left a week earlier. Instead, a soldier who wasn't even Russian had come through our village driving a horse and wagon.

I announced the news to anyone who would listen. Mutti didn't act surprised. I thought for just a moment that the pupils of her eyes got larger. Two days after the lone Russian soldier with his horse and wagon came through our village, the Russians arrived in earnest. Late that afternoon a group of officers walked up to our barracks. They were tipsy and laughing, unsteady on their feet. They walked down the street side of the barracks, looking through the cracks between the boards the women had nailed over the windows. Then they walked around the barracks to the back door smoking cigarettes hand rolled in newspaper, with bottles of vodka in their hands.

"Frau," they shouted, laughing loudly, and a chill ran down my spine as I watched them approaching. Gruesome things I had read and heard about Russian soldiers filled my mind. They were different from the American and English soldiers. The Americans had been kind and shared things with us; the English were disciplined and had stayed away. Neither ever threatened harm. The Russians forced themselves into our lives. They opened the front door and came into our room. Mutti sat on the chair behind the table, her face a mask of fear. Oma and Ingrid stood behind her. Although tipsy, they remained friendly, pointing to a travel chess set which had belonged to the German soldier who rescued us in Strasburg. They spoke to Mutti in Russian. We couldn't understand them, but it became clear they wanted to play chess. Mutti arranged the chessmen and played. She was a skilled chess player. I had seen her play before. She lost. Maybe she was afraid to win. Several of the Russian officers played chess with her. She lost each time. While Mutti was playing chess, the others looked around the barracks. They finally left—laughing, drinking, and smoking.

They came back that night and went directly next door to where the two women from Berlin lived. The women screamed only briefly while the Russians laughed and danced Russian dances, one of them playing an accordion.

The Russians

Throughout the night I could hear the women moan, give off occasional cries of pain, and plead with the Russians to stop. Mutti told me to hold my ears and to go to sleep. Oma cried all night, refusing to lie down. Mutti slept with Ingrid and me under the table. She put her arms around us, and we covered ourselves with a fur-lined army coat we had found in our German army wagon. I finally fell asleep. The Russian officers were gone when I awoke in the morning.

The same group of officers came back every night. They always brought with them several bottles of vodka and were usually already drunk by the time they arrived. After the first night they were also accompanied by a uniformed and beautiful blond woman who spoke fluent German. They would first stop in our place and talk to us—to Mutti and Oma, Ingrid and me. The woman would translate into Russian or German every word that was said. Mutti didn't want to play chess with them anymore, but the woman smiled at her and told her that she really should play chess and not anger them. So Mutti played and lost, day after day. Mutti's face had become hard. I could tell she was afraid. The Russians kidded around with Oma and Ingrid, putting their arms around them and hugging them. They spoke of their grandparents, their mothers and sisters. It became a daily, macabre ritual for them to stop with us first before going next door to gang-rape the two women. Every day the Russians came, they would send someone to the farm nearest the barracks and have the farmer bring fresh milk for Ingrid and me. We had to drink the milk while they watched. I hated warm milk fresh from a cow. I drank because I was afraid. Then, after they tired of their games with us, one by one they drifted next door. They sang their Russian ballads and danced to their accordion. They took their turns raping the two women in one of the two rooms, over and over again. After the first night the women didn't scream anymore.

Mutti and I walked to Schönberg. She had heard that the Russians had opened a prisoner-of-war camp there and that every German soldier who had evaded the Americans or the English was put into the camp when he turned himself in or was turned in by someone else. When we arrived in Schönberg, we found that the prisoner-of-war camp was an apartment building around which the Russians had laid barbed wire and posted guards. Mutti approached one of the two guards. They were young soldiers with pink cheeks, dressed in heavy brown overcoats, wearing winter hats which they had pushed up high on their heads because of the heat of the day. They carried submachine guns slung across their chests. Mutti asked the guard if he spoke German. He was not hostile. He didn't answer her question either. Instead, he pointed to the other guard. She bribed the German-speaking guard with her favorite gold bracelet. The guard looked at it, turning the bracelet over in his hand several times, and then said, *"Fünf Minuten,"* and pointed at the building and then at one of the three watches strapped around his left arm. He had several more watches on his right arm. Mutti walked over to the barbed wire. The German prisoners were on the second and third floors, leaning out of windows watching her.

"Has anybody heard anything about Captain Samuel? He is my husband," Mutti shouted, cupping her hands around her mouth. "He was in the Luftwaffe." The soldiers looking out the windows wore the field grey colors of the army. There was no answer. Some shook their heads. Others came and pushed their way forward to see the woman who was calling to them. "Has anyone heard about Ernst Grapentin? My brother. He was a *Soldat* like you. In the artillery. He served in France." Again, there was no reply and some shaking of heads. After waiting a minute, Mutti continued her futile task. "How about Jochen Kolbe?" She paused and looked at the somber faces of the prisoners looking down at her like she was some curiosity. She didn't give up. My mother never gave up easily. *"Leutnant* Hans Schmitt," she shouted with renewed vigor. I could see the tears running down her face. "He was in the army in the east." She paused again, looking in vain for a response from the blank faces staring at her. There was no response and no one shook his head anymore. They just stared at her.

"Peter Frank." Her shout was more like a whimper now. "He was a dentist in an army field hospital. Have you heard of Peter Frank?" She didn't look up. Her head hung low in dejection. She wiped the tears off her face and turned to go. She took my hand and we walked away quickly. It was a long, silent walk back to our barracks. A Russian army truck occasionally came through the village, the sole evidence of Russian occupation. Rarely did I see Russian troops, nor did they freely mingle with the German population. Mostly they stayed in their camps. Only officers seemed to be able to come and go as they pleased. And it was officers who were raping the women next door.

A German man, a stranger, came to the village. I saw him walking down the road toward our barracks. He had a peculiar look about him. It was something in the way he dressed and how he walked and swung his arms.

The Russians

He wore a black beret, the sort usually worn by Frenchmen or Spaniards, I thought. Berets were not commonly worn in Germany, at least not in the parts where I had lived. A thin, unbuttoned summer overcoat flowed behind him in the breeze, and he wore a red scarf around his neck. He smoked his cigarette nervously. When he reached our barracks, he announced in a loud voice that school would start for all school-aged children up to the eighth grade. School was to begin the following Monday morning in the adjacent village. After making his announcement several times, the man left the way he had come—black beret in place, coat flapping, and cigarette smoke rising above his head. I thought about what he had said and decided that my life was pretty boring. School, any kind of school, had to be better than sitting around idly. Mutti agreed.

On Monday morning I was one of the first to arrive at the school. I was excited. I hadn't been to school since January, six months ago. I missed it, and I especially missed the companionship of classmates. I was looking forward both to learning and to meeting new boys my age. A huge, ancient oak tree stood in front of the old schoolhouse. Its once-red bricks were now age-blackened. Soon children began arriving in ones, twos, and threes, and stood waiting, ill at ease, around the tree. There were thirty or more. Around nine o'clock a dour-looking man stepped out of the schoolhouse and picked one boy, escorting him into the building. One by one, the children were taken inside. Time passed, and our group standing around the tree shrank slowly. We said little to each other. My earlier enthusiasm had vanished. The procedure seemed peculiar. It was nearly noon when my turn came. Having been the first to get there, I was the last to be called. Excitement and anticipation had given way to resentment. The man with the sad face gestured for me to follow. I entered a narrow, musty-smelling corridor. It smelled like old schoolhouses where many children have passed through over the years. The floorboards were worn and creaked. Two doors led from the corridor into classrooms. The door to the left was open. There was no one inside that room. I followed the man into the room to the right, where I saw the others patiently sitting in their chairs.

The stranger who had come to our village the previous week sat in a student's chair at the head of the room. He beckoned with his right hand for me to sit in a chair across from him. I squeezed into the chair, not knowing what to expect. Maybe he wanted to know what grade I was in and what I had studied when I last attended school so he could place me with

The Russians

others at the same level. He wore his long, thin, grey summer coat even in the classroom, the same red silk scarf and black beret. No teacher I knew wore his overcoat or a hat of any kind inside a classroom, not to mention a scarf around his neck. Under his beak-like nose was a thin moustache, and a goatee hid his chin. His smile, which seemed too wide, revealed even, stained teeth. In his eyes I saw something that made me cautious.

"Where are you from, son?" he said patronizingly. I resented him calling me "son" since I was not his son, and I didn't like to be patronized. Instinct told me to be careful. I sensed danger.

"Strasburg," I said reluctantly. "That's north of Berlin in the Uckermark."

"Where is your father?"

"I don't know where my father is," I replied honestly.

"Was your father in the Wehrmacht?"

After some reflection, I responded, "No, he was in the Luftwaffe."

"Oh, the Luftwaffe," he repeated, saying the word expansively as if it were something special. "What kind of airplanes did he fly?"

"He was not a pilot," I blurted out, becoming more and more aggravated by his interrogation.

"But what did your father do in the Luftwaffe? He had to do something, don't you agree?"

"I don't know what he did," I replied.

"But you must know." He continued to pressure me. "What rank did he hold? Was he an officer?"

"He was a captain," I replied. That got him interested; I could tell from the look in his eyes and from the way he leaned forward, his beak-like nose almost touching mine. The man was a Communist, I decided, there to interrogate children, not to teach. That explained his strange dress. I refused to answer any more questions. He became angry and took me roughly by my left arm, pulling me out of my chair and outside to the front of the school.

"You and your family will be severely punished unless you answer my questions honestly and correctly," he shouted. "You have something to hide, or you would answer freely like the others have. Make up your mind quickly, boy."

"No," I shouted at him defiantly, "I will not talk to you. You are not a teacher. If you want to know anything about my family come and talk to my mother. I don't know anything." He was still holding my arm. Suddenly

The Russians

he let go, and the instant he did, I ran away as fast as I could, back to our barracks. I realized I had made a mistake when I told him my father had been an officer in the Luftwaffe. I needed to be more careful in the future. Our lives might depend on what I said to people. As soon as I reached the barracks, I told Mutti about what happened at the school. "The Communist is going to make trouble for us," I cautioned her. Mutti was annoyed by what I told her. I didn't think she was angry. "He's coming by tomorrow to speak to you."

"Did he say when he was coming?"

"Tomorrow noon, I think. I wasn't listening to him too closely anymore. I just wanted to get away." The next day the so-called teacher did indeed show up at noon, dressed in the same coat, red scarf, and black beret. He was holding a burning cigarette high above his head, between his right forefinger and middle finger, and gesticulated with that hand as he spoke. He did most of the talking, and Mutti did the listening. He wanted detailed information about my father. After listening to him for some time, Mutti suggested he come back the following day.

"I'll write things down for you, and that way you'll have much more information available than I can remember right now," she proposed. He agreed and promised to be back the following afternoon at three o'clock. After he departed, Mutti took the bicycle she had borrowed from her friend Llydia and rode off to see her in Sievershagen. Mutti returned late that day. "Everything will be all right, Wolfgang," she assured me with a smile. "Don't worry, everything will be all right." At two o'clock in the afternoon the following day, Llydia arrived.

"Are we ready?" Llydia asked Mutti with a conspiratorial smile. Mutti smiled back at her. Both women went to the farmhouse down the road. Mutti returned without Llydia. At three o'clock our expected visitor arrived, accompanied by the man with the sad face. He didn't say anything and merely stood next to and behind the "teacher." Both men walked directly into our room without knocking. The teacher sat down on a chair without being invited to do so and immediately asked Mutti for her notes.

"Frau Samuel, you have your notes for me, *Ja?*" he said in a demanding tone of voice. "Then we can sit down and go over them in detail."

Mutti remained standing. Slowly and deliberately she said, "I don't know who you are and why you are asking me these questions. I don't owe you any answers. Instead, you owe me some answers. Why do you want to know these things about my husband? You told us you were a teacher." Mutti spoke forcefully, and I thought she was acting a bit. The man was clearly taken aback by her unexpectedly belligerent attitude and pointed questions. He rose from his chair to face her. Then Llydia arrived at the barracks entrance with a flourish.

"Where is my good friend Hedy?" she asked loudly of anyone who might be there. "I can't wait to see Hedy again." Llydia had acquired a heavy Russian accent. She wore a black, lacy, heavily fringed shawl around her shoulders. Her head was covered with a colorful babushka, and her peasant dress was a beautiful print, tight at the waist with heavy folds hanging half-way down her legs, covering part of her shiny, black, soft leather boots. Llydia looked exactly like what I believed a Russian woman would look like. Llydia saw Mutti and the two men in our room. In a perplexed voice and using a mixture of Russian and German, she asked, "Are you having visitors, Hedy? I am interrupting? Yes? I can always come back. I just wanted to say hello. I was driving through the village."

"No, no," Mutti answered hastily, "I am not having visitors, Llydia. And I am really glad to see you. You have come just at the right time. I don't know who this man is. He claims to be a teacher. Instead he has been interrogating Wolfgang and me for the past two days. We are afraid of him. We don't know why he is here or what he wants from us. Can you help?" The two men stared at Llydia coldly, their eyes revealing nothing.

Llydia stared back at them with equally cold eyes. Then her perplexity changed to visible rage. Turning to the teacher, her hands pushed into her hips, Llydia bellowed in her heavily accented German, "Do you know who I am?" Not waiting for a reply, she proclaimed, "Of course you don't. I am on the staff of the Russian *Kommandatura* in Grevesmühlen. I am the personal assistant of the *Kommissar*. I feel offended to have my friend Hedy and her son interrogated by a German nobody. That's what you are, aren't you? A German nobody. You are not registered with us, that I know for sure." She paused, stepping closer to the "teacher." "I have never seen you around the *Kommandatura*," she whispered, her face close up against his. "Tell me who you are! Let me see your papers! Are you registered at the *Kommandatura* in Schoenberg? Since you are not registered with us in Grevesmühlen, you must be registered with the *Kommandatura* in Schönberg, *Ja*?" Llydia held out her hand. "Let me see your pass. And it better not be a forgery. You

The Russians

know what will happen to you then." A deep frown settled over Llydia's face. Her right hand made a cutting motion across her throat.

The Communist teacher, or whatever he was, fumbled in his coat pockets as if he were searching for papers. Then he assumed a servile slouch in front of Llydia; he couldn't back away from her since he was up against the wall. He held his hands, tightly knitted together in a prayer-like gesture, in front of his chest, and a torrent of words spewed from his thin mouth. "Dear comrade, I meant absolutely no harm to your friend or her son. To the contrary, I only wanted information to assist her in obtaining better housing and food for her family." His words continued to tumble out of his mouth protesting his innocence and noble intentions.

"You liar," Llydia interjected brusquely. "You have the nerve to come up with such a phony story."

Undaunted, the "teacher" continued, "I am exceedingly sorry to have offended anyone and especially you, comrade. My intentions were honorable and have been totally misinterpreted."

Llydia acted aghast at that comment. Feigning rage, she responded in a measured tone, "Are you accusing me of being a liar, you Fascist swine? Is that what I understand you to say? I have a good mind to arrest you and take you with me for interrogation." Llydia paused and stared at the man, her face again up close to his. Speaking slowly, enunciating each word carefully and nearly whispering, she said to him, "Maybe you are a spy!" The word spy seemed to go through the man like a dagger. His body jerked briefly. He turned his head away from her. His eyes betrayed his rising panic.

"Oh, no, comrade, I am not a spy," he whispered. "I am above all the obedient servant of the victorious Red Army. With your permission we will leave now, my presence here is totally superfluous," he croaked, his voice failing him.

"I should take you in," Llydia mumbled, turning away from him. And then more forcefully she said, "But you disgust me, you pretend-German-Communist. Now that we Russians are here and have liberated the German people from the Fascist yoke, now all of you are good Communists. There aren't any more Fascists anywhere. You make me want to throw up. Just get out of here and don't ever let me see you and your friend around this part of the country again, or you will find out what a real interrogation is like."

The two men needed no further encouragement. They had already inched their way along the wall away from Mutti and Llydia. They proceeded to exit in earnest now, with the leader bowing toward Llydia several times as he backed out the door. Then they turned around and hastily departed, as close to running as they could come without actually doing so. I ran to the street window, jumped on a chair, and looked over the boards, watching them leave. They never looked back or slowed their pace. I watched until they disappeared into the village.

Llydia lit an English cigarette, and both she and Mutti laughed and hugged each other. "You are a natural," Mutti complimented Llydia. "You really did that very well." Neighbors who had overheard every word of the exchange came out of their rooms and joined in the laughter. It had been a long time since anyone had had cause for a good laugh. Mutti and Llydia sat around our table and talked. Llydia's Russian accent had vanished. After she left, I watched Mutti cook dinner in the communal kitchen.

"How did you come up with the idea of having Llydia impersonate a Russian woman?" I asked her.

"Well, when I told Llydia about our problem yesterday, she said she knew how to handle it. It was her idea. People are afraid of authority, you know. You only have to look and act like you have authority and most people will believe you do. Those two sure did. They are opportunists. They obviously want to ingratiate themselves with the Russians and gain favors and privileges by labeling someone a Nazi and turning them in." Mutti stirred the thin gruel she was preparing for us on the one wood-fired stove. The other three stoves were electric and of no use to us. "Llydia and I have decided to go to Grevesmühlen tomorrow to the *Kommandatura* to meet with the Russian *Kommissar*. Llydia speaks fluent German, Russian, and Polish. She comes from Riga, in Latvia. We think," Mutti continued in a soft voice, "that we have to stop the Russians from coming here every night. If we don't do that, they will attack us next, and then the others. We have to put an end to it. We think if we speak to the Russian *Kommandant* directly, maybe he will stop his officers from molesting the women next door. Maybe he can even use a translator like Llydia." She smiled when she said that. "It would be a perfect job for her, don't you think so, Wolfgang?"

I didn't answer immediately. I was surprised at her courage, expecting that she and Llydia might meet the same fate in the *Kommandatura* as the two women next door. We were desperate and scared to our bone marrow. Her plan promised nothing, but it was better to try something than to wait for the Russians to do to Mutti and Oma what they were doing nightly to the two women from Berlin. "Yes, Mutti, you are right to do something," I finally answered. I hope everything turns out well for you and Llydia." I left her standing over the hot stove. Her courage impressed me. I feared for her safety.

The next morning Mutti and Llydia rode their bicycles into Grevesmühlen, about twelve kilometers from Hanshagen. They had no trouble finding the *Kommandatura*, she told Oma and me that evening. "It had a sign posted above its entrance proclaiming *KOMMANDATURA*. We walked directly up to the Russian guard, who carried the usual submachine gun. As we approached him, he started playing with the trigger of the gun. I was getting nervous. Llydia started speaking to him in Russian. He was visibly startled by her and appeared confused about what to do. Llydia suggested he take us to see the *Kommandant* on important business. The more Llydia talked to him the more helpful the soldier became. Finally, he escorted us into the *Kommadatura*, where we soon found ourselves face-to-face with the Russian commander, a major. A short man in his thirties. His face badly scarred by smallpox. He was courteous and immediately insisted that we call him by his first name—Serje."

"Serje promptly called for vodka, onions, bread, and caviar, which his batman, his personal servant, promptly delivered. At Serje's insistence we joined him in several glasses of vodka. I didn't think we had a choice. We sipped ours, he drank his straight down. Llydia told him about the officers who came to the barracks every night and pleaded with him to stop them. She also offered him her services as an interpreter, asking only for safety, a room, and food in return. Serje agreed to Llydia's requests. At his direction the batman immediately requisitioned an apartment for Llydia near the *Kommandatura*. Serje apologized profusely for the behavior of his officers and promised they would not be coming back. Both Llydia and I couldn't believe that we had actually succeeded. We have to see if he keeps his word now."

Mutti told Oma that she planned to return to Grevesmühlen the following day to help Llydia move into her apartment. She also mentioned that the major had invited both of them to dinner and dancing that night. "He said it would be a perfect occasion for Llydia to meet his officers. I shuddered at the thought. But what choice did we have?" Mutti said. "The officers will be the same men I played chess with. The men who rape the women next door night after night. Let's hope that he keeps his word and stops those beasts from coming here again."

Mutti left early the next day to meet with Llydia in Sievershagen. A Russian staff car was to come for Llydia and her things, and Mutti was to go with her if there was room in the car; otherwise, she was going to ride her bicycle to Grevesmühlen. By dinner time Mutti had not returned. I was worried about her safety. I didn't trust Russian soldiers, any of them. The Russian officers who had come nightly to molest the two women next door didn't come that evening. I awoke about one o'clock in the morning. I heard a car pull up in front of the barracks and muffled voices. I always slept lightly, and strange sounds woke me easily. I climbed out of bed and peeked out the window. A car sat out front with the passenger door open. Two Russian soldiers were in the process of carefully removing a bundle from the backseat of the car. When the bundle was finally out of the car, they carried it toward our barracks. Llydia walked next to them, bending down, and she held a hand in hers. Then I saw it wasn't a bundle they were carrying. It was a person wrapped in a quilt. It was my mother.

I ran outside, consumed with fear that my mother was dead. Her face was pale and bloodless, her eyes closed. The Russian soldiers kept moving slowly, carefully. They carried Mutti into our room, put her on her bed, and went outside to wait. She looked dead—dead like the German soldier in the ditch in Woldegk, dead like the woman who knelt over her dead baby in the field outside Woldegk. Dead. Llydia adjusted Mutti's hands and carefully arranged the quilt. Mutti didn't move. Llydia continued to make gentle adjustments to the bed and to Mutti's position. Maybe she wasn't dead? Then Llydia turned to Oma, whose cheeks were wet from tears, and put her arm around her.

"After I moved my belongings to my apartment in Grevesmühlen," Llydia said, "Hedy and I joined the major and his officers for dinner. How could we refuse? Much vodka was drunk at the dinner. One officer played an accordion and others danced Russian dances. Everyone seemed to be having a good time. Then, at some point during the celebration the major, by now drunk, grabbed for Hedy, pushed her under the table, and attempted to rape her. That's what it looked like from where I sat. Hedy tried to scramble away from him and slapped his face as he continued to grab at her. He pulled his pistol and shot at her several times. One of the bullets hit Hedy, going through her neck—in one side and out the other, just barely missing her aorta and the spine. She hasn't bled much. I think she will be all right. But she will need all the help we can give her to recover." Llydia squeezed

The Russians

Oma's hands. I looked down at Mutti's neck and saw what looked like a small red puncture. That was the bullet hole. There was no bleeding. As Llydia started to leave, she said, "I'll be back to check on Hedy every day. The major is sorry and doesn't want this incident known, or he will face a military court."

Oma and I stood by the bed looking down on Mutti. I don't know what Oma felt. I was shocked. I wondered how we were going to keep Mutti alive. The sudden responsibility I felt thrust upon me was terrifying. I fully understood how much it was Mutti who was the captain of our ship. It was Mutti and her plans and ideas which gave us hope and direction. When I looked at the entry wound again, it looked so tiny and innocent. There was no blood. Maybe it would heal quickly. Oma took off her nightgown and slipped into her grey dress. She pulled a chair next to Mutti's bed and sat down to watch over her.

"You go to sleep, Wolfgang," she said. "I will watch Hedwig."

"I can help, Oma," I responded dutifully, but she waved me off.

"Go to bed, my boy, you need your rest. You are still growing. I am old. I don't need much sleep."

I crawled back into bed. Ingrid had remained asleep the entire time, rolled up into a ball under the table, lying on the fur side of the army coat. (She liked to sleep on the floor under the table. She told me it made her feel safe.) The next morning when Mutti briefly woke, I saw her hand move up to her neck, and, before Oma and I could stop her, she felt around her neck and stuck her index finger with its long fingernail directly into the bullet hole. I took her hand and laid it alongside her. She looked at me with bright, shiny eyes, but said nothing. She tried to smile, but didn't seem to have the strength to do so. Her eyes closed again, and she went back to sleep. Llydia came the next day to visit Mutti in a staff car driven by the major's batman. The following day the Russian major came himself to visit Mutti. His batman left behind a bucket of butter and several loaves of Russian bread. We lived off that bucket of butter and that bread for some time. We traded butter for potatoes with others in the barracks, because the butter would soon turn rancid if it wasn't eaten. We had little else. The canned food from the German army wagon had run out. Oma was too old to beg for food; her feet hurt and were swollen around the ankles. That left only me to obtain the food we needed to survive.

I went every day to the villages in our immediate area, begging farmers

The Russians

for vegetables, fruit, berries, and eggs. Especially eggs for Mutti. She ate little. While I never received much from the farmers, it was enough to keep us from starving. Oma fed Mutti the strawberries and red currants I brought home. If I could not beg enough food, I occasionally went into farmers' gardens and stole what I needed. I didn't really consider it stealing, because I needed the food to keep my mother alive. Mutti needed fruit, the only food other than boiled eggs she would eat, and I was determined to do everything I could to keep her alive.

One night, shortly after midnight, a week after Mutti had been shot, the Russian major drove up in his staff car—drunk. Mutti was sleeping. Oma sat next to her keeping her nightly vigil. I slept in the other bed. Oma would lie down with me whenever she decided to come to bed, usually late. "I don't need much sleep, my boy" was her standard answer whenever I expressed concern for her health. Ingrid continued to sleep on her makeshift bed under the table. Our only light was a candle. The major staggered into the room with a bottle of vodka in his hand.

"Where is Hedy?" he shouted in a voice heavy with drink. I could smell his alcoholic breath all the way across the room where I lay in my bed. He terrified me. He began to undress. First he took off his leather boots, then his belt with its pistol, then his pants and tunic. He lifted Mutti's quilt and tried to get into bed with her. Oma pushed him away with both of her hands and stood squarely in front of him.

"Take me if you need a woman," she shouted into his face, "but leave my daughter alone!"

The major kept muttering in Russian and drinking from his open bottle of vodka. Finally, he put down his bottle, staggered toward me, and fell into my bed. I was petrified with fear. I pushed myself against the wall, as far away from him as I could get, hoping he wouldn't know I was there and that he would go to sleep immediately. Then I felt something hard and smooth against my leg and the major's hand on my body. I realized instantly that he was touching me with his hard penis. I threw his hand off me and jumped out of bed, leaping over him to hide under the table with Ingrid. He grunted and went to sleep. Before I woke the next morning, the major's batman had returned, dressed him, and driven him back to his quarters, Oma said.

"I hope he never comes back," I said to Oma. I shuddered when I thought of the experience with him in my bed. I said nothing to Oma about what had happened. After my first scare for Mutti's life, I was too busy and weighed down with my many responsibilities to spend much time worrying about her dying. I probably should have, especially after she also contracted typhus. All I could think about was what I needed to do to keep her alive and to put food on the table. Mutti's temperature rose dangerously. We had no thermometer, but Mutti looked as if she were burning up. She felt hot to the touch.

"Hedwig's fever must be 40 degrees or higher," Oma said. She bathed her with wet, cooling rags all day and all night, and she placed Mutti's left hand in a pan of cold water. Oma did everything she knew to bring down Mutti's temperature. Llydia had not come by for several days. All I could do was wait, hoping that Mutti would improve, beg for food and make sure we had enough to eat. My sister quietly watched the tragedy being played out in front of her. Although she was only six, she tried to help in her own way and spent hours fanning Mutti with a piece of cardboard to help keep her cool and keep the ever-present flies away. The mere touch of a fly on Mutti's arms or face would make her cry out with pain. I thought that as long as Mutti felt anything and was able to respond she was still fighting to stay alive. She passed from sleep to delirium and back to sleep. She had had no real consciousness of where she was and what was happening to her since the fever started. The wound from the bullet appeared to be healing; a scab had formed. The fever could not be related to her wound.

Since the night Mutti was shot, an owl had been calling from an oak tree by the road. "A bad omen," Oma said to me. "It means someone in our family is dying." We looked at Mutti and listened to the owl's call every night, and I prayed to God for help. We three had so little to give to help her recover—only some berries, a few eggs, and some water from the pump in back of the barracks near the latrine. The owl continued to call "come with me" every night at the same time—*Komm mit, komm mit, komm mit, komm mit* . . .

"Don't take my mother, owl," I pleaded as I lay in bed, hoping the bird would hear me. "Don't take my mother, please." It is just a bird, I thought. I knew in my heart that the superstition was probably true—the owl was a messenger of death. It was gruesome having to listen in the pitch black of the night, our room lit only by a lone candle, Mutti lying there fighting for her life. *Komm mit, komm mit, komm mit* . . . the owl cried night after night.

A Russian soldier came by with a German interpreter and ordered us to vacate the barracks within two days. It was to be torn down and reassembled in the Russian camp near Grevesmühlen. I began to sense the by-now familiar feeling of panic. I fought hard to suppress it. We couldn't move Mutti in her condition. I knew that. Even if we could, where could we move her to? Life was getting even more complicated for me, and the burden of maintaining our family felt extremely heavy. Our neighbors moved out quietly one by one. The two women from Berlin found a room with a farmer in the village. The boyfriend of the younger woman had moved when the Russian officers first started making their nightly visits. He had taken the older woman's young boy with him. I was left alone with my sick mother, with Oma and Ingrid to care for, and a barracks that was about to come down around my ears. "Dear God, I must ask you for help again," I prayed that night. "Please forgive me for coming to you so soon again. I don't know what to do and I need help desperately."

For the first time in my life, I could not go to sleep. I lay in bed under the table with Ingrid, listening to Mutti's labored breathing and to Oma shifting occasionally on her hard chair as she wafted a piece of cardboard back and forth over Mutti's emaciated face.

Chapter 11

MESSENGER OF DEATH

The day our barracks was to be torn down had arrived, and I knew we had to move. I planned to go to the farmer up the road and plead for help. Maybe he would let us stay in one of his barns. As I was getting ready to go see him, a car drove up and stopped in front of the barracks. It was Llydia. I ran out to meet her, ecstatic with relief.

"I am sorry I didn't come sooner," Llydia apologized as she gave me a hug, "but the major kept me so busy I just couldn't get away. I heard about the scheduled teardown of your barracks, so I came out to help as soon as I could. How is your dear mother, Wolfgang?" I could not speak. I was choking with emotion at Llydia's sudden appearance. I took her hand and led her inside to Mutti's bedside. Llydia couldn't hide her shock at seeing Mutti, who looked more dead than alive. Her skin was shiny, stretched tautly over her frame. Her fingers were bony, and long nails gave them the appearance of claws. Her face was covered with red fever spots, and her eyes were sunk deeply into black holes. Her cheekbones protruded prominently. Llydia took Mutti's hand in hers, held it for a long time, and then gently placed it back into Oma's. I heard the squeal of trucks braking. Llydia went outside with me. The workers were German prisoners who were to disassemble the barracks. There were two Russian drivers, and another soldier appeared to be the supervisor. Llydia and the Russian supervisor spoke briefly. Then he jumped back into the first truck, and they turned around and drove away.

"I sent them back," Llydia said to Oma once we got back inside. "I told the soldier that it was the commander's wish to delay the teardown of the barracks for a week." Llydia explained to me, "The commander is the major who shot your mother. He wants to help and make up for what he's done, and he doesn't want the word to get out about what happened at his party. So, young man, let's go. I have an idea how to solve your housing problem, Wolfgang." Llydia took my hand. I felt instant relief, as if a heavy weight had been lifted off my chest. Her hand was warm, her grip firm and reassuring. We walked out to her car parked under an oak, the one in which the owl sat at night calling out its gruesome omen. "Get in, little man," Llydia said with a smile in her voice. I crawled into the backseat. Llydia spoke to the driver in Russian. He drove to the nearby farm, into the middle of the cobblestoned yard. Llydia pointed to the front door. The driver swerved around a dung heap and stopped in front of the door. Llydia got out and motioned for me to follow.

"Come, Wolfgang," she said, heading for the rear entrance to the farmhouse, "we have work to do." Llydia knocked forcefully on the kitchen door. After two or three minutes, a stern-looking woman opened the door. She wore the customary dark dress with a grey apron. Her black, grey-streaked hair was pulled back into a bun, giving her an especially severe look. Her face was devoid of makeup. It seemed to me that the woman had probably never smiled in her life. Llydia, in contrast, was dressed in a fashionable tan suit of finely woven material; she looked like a city woman to me. A dark-brown hat with a floppy rim sat on her head at a rakish angle. Her hair was combed upward in the back and on the sides. Llydia wore silk stockings—I wondered where she had gotten them—and practical, brown walking shoes, not her usual boots. Her makeup was bold, not unlike the makeup Mutti had worn before she was shot. Llydia's lipstick was bright red, and rouge highlighted her high cheekbones.

Before the farm woman could speak, Llydia said, "I am the personal representative of the Russian area commander in Grevesmühlen. I demand to see your house." She offered no explanation. The woman obediently took Llydia through the house, with me in tow holding on to Llydia's hand. We completed our walk-through back at the kitchen. Llydia had said nothing. Across from the kitchen was a single bedroom. Llydia entered it. Turning to the farm woman, she said in heavily accented German, "I am requisitioning this room. It is for a family in the barracks. The barracks will be torn down soon."

"My husband is in the field plowing," the woman responded calmly to Llydia's demand. "I must speak to him first."

Llydia interrupted, speaking in Russian first, for effect I presumed, because neither I nor the farm woman could understand Russian, and Llydia knew it. Then she switched to her heavily accented German, saying, "You don't have to speak to anyone. If you don't want to cooperate, I will requisition the entire house and evict you." She looked at the woman directly, her cold eyes promising no relief. Llydia started to leave, then turned around again, facing the farm woman, and said, "The move will take place tomorrow or the day after. Be prepared for it, and cooperate." Llydia rapidly walked out of the room, pulling me after her. We departed in the staff car, leaving a stunned farmer's wife behind.

"All right, now you know where you are going to sleep. I must go and see if I can get your mother into the hospital," Llydia said as she let me off in front of the barracks. My spirits soared. I had thought all of us were supposed to stay in the farmhouse, including Mutti. For Mutti to be taken to a hospital was the best news of the day. "*Auf Wiedersehen*, and don't worry, Wolfgang. Everything will be fine," Llydia shouted from the open car window as she drove off in a cloud of blue gasoline fumes. I watched until the car disappeared around the bend. Then I ran inside and told Oma the good news while she continued to fan Mutti's face to keep her cool and to keep the always-present flies away. That afternoon Llydia returned, accompanied by the Russian major. The two wrapped Mutti in her quilt and carried her to the car. No one spoke. Mutti looked fragile. Her hollow cheeks and prominent cheekbones made her nose stick out of her face as if it didn't belong there. Her eyes were closed. Llydia and the major laid Mutti in the backseat and drove off for the hospital in Grevesmuehlen. The major drove. I knew Mutti was dying. She needed professional medical care, not just someone fanning the flies off her face. I thanked God for what I knew to be his intervention, and I again added a silent apology for only turning to him when I was in need. Before driving off, Llydia told me that I had to move my family to the farmhouse immediately because the teardown crew would begin its work the next morning. The night before, the owl had not called. Maybe it had not been calling for Mutti after all.

Oma, Ingrid, and I carried our few possessions to the farmhouse. When I knocked, the farmer's wife answered, and, without saying a word, she led us to our room. For the first time in many days, Oma was able to tend to herself—wash up and take her hair down. Ingrid followed Oma and me around, making small talk.

"Where will I sleep?" she said to me. "With you on the floor? It is cement." She touched the floor with both of her hands. "It is hard and cold, Wolfgang." Her eyes were large and questioning.

"We all will sleep in the bed," Oma said, smiling at Ingrid's sudden concern about where she was going to sleep. "It is large enough for all three of us." Then, to my surprise, Ingrid said, "I am hungry. I want to eat." And with that she walked into the kitchen, where she made friends with the dour farm woman. Within minutes she had in her hands a piece of bread liberally spread with butter. She sat down on a chair in the kitchen, eating and watching her new found friend doing chores. I was utterly amazed by my sister's behavior. The next day the Russians returned with their crew of German prisoners and began to tear down the barracks, which came apart as if it were an assembly kit. A few long iron bolts had held it together, and once they were removed the walls collapsed. The German prisoners neatly stacked roof and wall sections, as well as the water pump, on the two trucks to the constant shouts of their Russian boss—"*Dowoi, dowoi, dowoi . . .*" By evening the entire barracks had been disassembled and loaded onto the trucks. All that remained were the wooden supports set in the ground and the latrine hole.

Oma and I tried to be unobtrusive and helpful to our unwilling German hosts. I offered to work around the farm, and Oma worked in the kitchen, cooking our spartan meals without interfering with the farm woman's routines. The butter the Russians had given us when Mutti was first shot was long gone, and we ate mostly boiled potatoes and bread. We survived.

I met the farmer and his old father, the only other people who lived on the farm. The old man was nice, and he liked to talk. He told me they used to have many more horses, but had given them to the Wehrmacht. He thought the one old horse that was left should be able to enjoy his final days in a meadow grazing rather than pulling a plow. But this old horse was all they had, so he had to work until he died. "We also had many farmhands," he confided in me, "but they were drafted into the Wehrmacht, too. I don't know where they are or if any of them are still alive." I felt the old man probably never had the opportunity to talk. With me around, he could say whatever came to mind; he didn't expect answers. I rarely saw the farmer. He rose early in the morning to work in the barns or in the fields. I seldom saw any activity in the village. The villagers stayed inside their homes, or worked in their gardens and the fields. Upon sighting a stranger, they quickly went inside.

With Mutti in the hospital, I constantly worried about our future. Before our long journey had begun, I had thought only of play; the future had been taken care of by my mother. I thought about my grandparents—Oma Grapentin was with us, but I didn't know what had happened to Oma and Opa Samuel nor to Opa Grapentin. I wandered through the village and its surroundings, always on the lookout for signs of danger and for food. I missed school. I no longer felt like a child, even though I was only ten years old. I didn't know what would come next, now that Mutti was ill, but I knew my future revolved around my mother. She just had to live. If she didn't, what then? I couldn't allow myself to think that way. There was no future for me without my mother in it, period.

By Friday, July 13, we had spent two full weeks on the farm. There was no word from Mutti, nor had Llydia returned. I went begging for food as I had done ever since Mutti was shot. Ingrid could not beg, she was too young, and Oma was too old. Our family depended on me to find food. I didn't beg in our village. Unfortunately, there were not enough villages nearby, and I found myself going back to the same farmers over and over again. They soon knew me by sight, and, if they saw me coming, many simply would not answer their doors. I walked through the fields barefoot, as I had always done in summer for as long as I could remember. The warm, soft sand felt good between my toes. I crossed the meadow. The skeleton of a Fieseler Storch liaison plane sat in its middle. Farmers had removed the plane's cloth skin. Nothing remained except a tubular frame with the two seats looking strangely exposed. The instrument panel was still intact, and the engine and the propeller were in place. Every time I passed the plane, I dreamed of flying. I often sat in the pilot's seat and in my mind soared high above the land. But soon I would remember why I was there.

I headed straight for the one farmer who usually gave me something, or at least had a kind word if she had nothing to give me. I crossed the quiet, deserted village street. When I reached the garden gate, I carefully opened and closed it without making a sound, as if I would bring down someone's wrath on me by slamming the gate too loudly against its post. The garden was colorful with the varied greens of onions, carrot tops, parsley, several kinds of lettuce, beans, and other vegetables. Hardy pansies bordered the red brick walk, and climbing roses showed their blooms around the front door. I knocked timidly on the old oak door. I'd come too often, I knew. After waiting several minutes I knocked more forcefully. Then I heard the familiar shuffling of feet, and the door opened wide. The old woman leaned on her walking stick, looking at me with piercing green eyes.

"*Guten Tag,*" I greeted her. "I wonder if you could spare anything to eat for my little sister and my sick mother?"

"Your mother is still sick?" she replied in a brittle but surprisingly strong voice.

"Yes, she is still recuperating from her war wound. Such wounds heal slowly," I said. "Thank you for asking about her." The old woman walked past me into her garden without saying any more.

"Here, take this knife." She pulled a paring knife from her sweater pocket. "Cut this lettuce." She pointed at a specific section of leaf lettuce that was about to go to seed. I took the knife and cut the lettuce, putting it into a net bag I had brought along for the purpose. When I finished and tried to hand her the knife, she hobbled over to the carrots and pointed at several with her stick. "These you may pull." I pulled the designated carrots and added them to my leaf lettuce. She walked slowly back toward the house. I ran after her hastily and handed her the knife.

"Thank you for your generosity, dear lady," I said, and prepared to leave.

"Not so fast, young man," she called after me in her unusually strong voice.

"Yes, can I do something for you? Help you with a chore? I'd be happy to do it."

"No," she commanded, "wait here."

Dragging her right foot slightly behind her and assisted by her walking stick, she slowly made her way into the house and disappeared into what was probably the kitchen. Several long minutes later, she returned with the cane in her left hand and three brown eggs in the palm of her right. "Cook these for your mother," she said in a softened voice. "I hope she gets well soon. Come back again." And she firmly closed the door behind her. I could

Messenger of Death

hear the iron key turn in the old-fashioned lock. I was taken by surprise at her generosity. She usually had something for me from her vegetable garden, but she had never given me more than one egg at a time, and now she had given me three without my asking for any. I carefully placed the eggs amongst the lettuce leaves to protect and conceal them. I decided to try two more farmers in the village to see if I could get a few potatoes. No one answered the door at the first house I came to and I saw no one in the yard, even though several barn doors stood ajar indicating recent activity. I knew they had seen me coming. I also knew that even if I got them to open the door they probably wouldn't give me anything. I kept trying.

I walked to the last farm in the village. My timid knock on the door was answered with a terse response. The woman who opened the door was big-boned and strong; she looked well fed. A blue scarf held her hair in place, and a white rubber apron covered her front. She looked like she was going out to milk the cows. "Why are you here again?" she shouted, not allowing me to say anything. "You were here just last week begging. People like you should be thrown in jail. In Hitler's time this wouldn't have happened. Now all sorts of *Gesindel* is allowed to roam the roads. Don't let me see you here again. If you do come back, I'll put the dog on you. Now, away with you." She slammed the door in my face.

I had met rude people before, but no one had ever threatened me with a dog or called me riffraff. I was ashamed of having to beg, but I had no choice. We had to eat. Tomorrow I would beg again, but today I quit. As I passed the Fieseler Storch, I didn't dream of soaring above the clouds. Instead, carrying my few leaves of lettuce, my carrots, and three precious eggs, I felt empty and helpless, humiliated. I tried to focus on the old woman who had shown so much kindness. Oma was pleased when she saw what I brought. It was enough to carry us to the next day. Our farm woman had taken a liking to Ingrid and fed her morsels of food for breakfast, lunch, and dinner. Never a real meal—an apple here or a slice of buttered bread there. The woman took care of my sister, and I appreciated her generosity. It was that much less food I needed to beg or steal from someone's garden.

Late that afternoon, as I was sitting in the yard listening to the old man talk and watching fat field pigeons peck around the dung heap, a young man on a bicycle rode up to our open foyer door. The foyer, with its brick floor, was always pleasantly cool this time of year. The kitchen and our room were opposite each other across the foyer. I watched the young man go inside and stop for a moment to cool off, wiping sweat off his forehead. Then he knocked on the kitchen door and disappeared from view. Moments later I saw him emerge and quickly ride off without looking at us. I felt his visit to be unusual. Something about it made me uncomfortable. The old man was still talking when I walked into the foyer. There, I found my grandmother in tears.

"What is it, Oma?" I asked. A premonition took possession of me. My stomach tightened. Maybe she had received news about Opa. She looked at me and sat down on a chair in the foyer, handing me the note the messenger had delivered. Written in pencil on a scrap of paper, it said, "*Flüchtling* woman from barracks in Hanshagen died this morning of typhus fever." I didn't want to understand what I read. "Oma," I said, "do they mean Mutti died?"

"Yes," Oma replied in a voice that revealed her deep despair, "my Hedwig is dead."

"But this doesn't say that my mother is dead," I objected. "Maybe it is someone else. Where did this note come from?" I didn't want to deal with the content of the note or its implications. It could not be true! I desperately wanted to hold on to a glimmer of hope. My mother couldn't just die and leave us by ourselves. Not my Mutti. She wouldn't do that. God wouldn't let her do that.

Between sobs, Oma said, "The young man who dropped off this note was from Sievershagen, the village where we were interned. Since we don't have a post office or a telephone, the hospital called Sievershagen. The Sievershagen postmaster took the message and had the young man deliver it to us. Someone must have told him how to find us. Who else could it be except my dear Hedwig? My dear Hedwig is dead." Oma continued her lament. I took Oma in my arms and let her cry. I was the only "man" in our family, I thought, and I had to act like one, no matter that I was only a boy and wanted to run into the fields to be alone with my own grief. Oma's sobs were deep and painful. I held her until she stopped crying. Finally she sat down on the chair, bent over, her hands in her lap, her face streaked with tears, a few strands of her usually tidy hair hanging down the side of her face. Although I was stunned by the unexpected message, tears would not come for me. My mother couldn't be dead, I insisted to myself. I silently spoke to God again. "You wouldn't let this happen, God. I just know you wouldn't do this. You wouldn't allow it. It isn't her time. We need her. You

Messenger of Death

have always helped me when I needed you. Why would you desert me now? And besides, I am much too young to lead my family. I don't know what to do!"

I clung to the stubborn belief that it was a mistake. The note did not have her name on it. Therefore, it couldn't be true. Clinging to this thin thread of hope, I turned to Oma and took her hands. "Oma," I said loudly, "let's go to Sievershagen and telephone the hospital." Oma nodded her head. It was something to do. In the meantime, the farmer's wife had joined us. I let her read the note, and for once she showed signs of humanity. Quickly she got out fresh rye bread and butter and made all three of us sandwiches liberally covered with butter and sugar. Ingrid took hers and went off into the kitchen to stay with the woman, who by now had become her friend. Oma and I took our buttered slices of bread and started our walk to Sievershagen to call the hospital.

On the way out of the village, we passed no one. Everything was quiet on that sun-drenched July afternoon. We walked down the tree-lined cobblestone road holding our sandwiches, neither one of us eating, just walking quietly side by side. Tears jumped out of my eyes as we passed the wrecked Wehrmacht truck with the pontoon bridges. I couldn't help myself. But I didn't want to upset Oma, so I made sure that not a sound came out of my mouth by keeping it wide open. I couldn't do anything about the tears. They ran down my face in a steady stream. Then I became angry at myself. My mother was not dead! The note didn't say Mutti had died. It didn't have her name on it. I wiped the tears off my face with the back of my hand and ate my sandwich. Deep inside, I knew I was fighting against reality, pushing confirmation of the truth a few more minutes into the future. My mother was dead—Oma knew it and I knew it. At the post office Oma timidly opened the door.

"We are closed," said the man behind the counter.

"Please," said Oma. "Please help us. We had this note delivered by a young man. It says that my daughter has died in the hospital in Grevesmühlen. Can you tell us more about it? Was it you who took the telephone call?"

"No," the old man replied, straightening his blue coat, "what's on the note is what I was told by the hospital, word for word. I can't tell you any more. I can get them on the telephone if you would like to speak to them?"

Oma hesitated. "Yes," I answered for her, "we would like to speak to

Messenger of Death

Left to right: Wilhelmine; Hedy, age seven; Wilhelm; and Marie, Hedy's older sister: the Grapentin family after church in 1921. Those were happy days for the veteran of the Great War and Verdun. Fate was to be especially cruel to Wilhelm and Marie. Hedy would barely survive an ordeal she could have never imagined in her nightmares.

Willi and Hedy in Schlawe, Pomerania, not far from the beaches of the Baltic Sea, in 1934. The occasion was the introduction of Willi's twenty-year-old bride-to-be to his parents.

Left to right: Hedy and Anna and Wilhelm Samuel, my grandparents, on the steps of there home where I spent many happy vacations as a young boy.

Hedy (left) and Willi (right) and their newborn son Wolfgang in the spring of 1935. Hedy continued to live with her parents in a village near Strasburg. Willi is shown in his new Luftwaffe uniform after transferring from the cavalry.

Me, my sister Ingrid, and Hedy in 1941 in front of our apartment house in Sagan.

Willi and Hedy in Sagan, Lower Silesia, in 1938 on the occasion of his promotion to Leutnant in the Luftwaffe. At this time they were genuinely happy.

Ingrid and me in Sagan in 1943. My mother made me hold Ingrid's hand. She had our picture taken every year and took great pride in dressing us well.

Railway carriages like the ones we frequently traveled on in the 1940s.

In April 1945, we fled with a column of German military police over cobblestone roads like these.

Me in front of our rotting
former Wehrmacht bar-
racks in 1949, wearing my
prized possessions–an
English army jacket and
American army pants.

Ingrid and me (right) and
Hedy and Ingrid (below)
inside our barracks apartment
in 1949. My mother is wearing a dress she sewed from
window drapes.

Ingrid, Hedy, and me in front of a C-47 transport aircraft at an open house at RAF Fassberg in 1949.

This C-54 transport crashed upon take-off at RAF Fassberg in January 1949.

Trucks at RAF Fassberg loaded with ten tons of coal for Berlin-bound C-54 aircraft.

Two friends, Hedy, and Leo in 1949 at Mom's Place in Fassberg, a bar which catered to American servicemen.

Leo and Hedy's hospital wedding in Fürstenfeldbruck in 1950.

Hedy in Munich in early 1950, standing in front of a Fiakar, a horse-drawn tourist carriage. Note the ruins behind her that were so typical of the Germany of the late 1940s.

Hedy and me on the deck of the USS *Goethals* during our stormy, eleven-day Atlantic crossing in January 1951 from Bremerhaven, Germany, to New York City.

My grandparents, Wilhelm and Anna Samuel, and me in front of their new house in Elmpt, Germany, in 1958. At the time I was an airman stationed in London, England.

My son Charles and me in 1964 on the flight line at Forbes Air Force Base, Topeka, Kansas. In the background is an RB-47H electronic reconnaissance aircraft in which I flew against the Soviet Union.

My commanding officer, Major General Blood, at Headquarters United States Air Forces Europe, Wiesbaden, Germany, awards me a third Distinguished Flying Cross earned while flying with the 355th Tactical Fighter Wing out of Tahkli, Thailand, in 1970. (Courtesy of U.S. Air Force)

someone at the hospital." The postmaster, who was also the storekeeper, took the receiver off the hook and turned the crank on the left side of the phone several times. A voice answered from an exchange, and the postmaster asked to be connected to the hospital in Grevesmühlen. I found time to wonder how so soon after a war the phones were working. People like the postmaster and our farmer and his wife were going to work and doing what they had always done. The postmaster motioned for Oma to come around the counter and take the phone. She hesitated.

"Go ahead and take the phone, Oma," I whispered. She put the strange instrument to her ear. It was the first time in her life she had used a telephone, and she spoke hesitantly into the black, horn-shaped speaker.

"Hallo, is this the hospital?" She continued to talk. Her voice was so low I couldn't hear what she was saying. She had her back to me, and I couldn't watch her face either. There was a long silence. Oma pressed the receiver to her ear, her mouth almost on top of the speaker. Finally I heard her say something again, and then she said loudly, "*Vielen, vielen Dank,*" and hung up. When she turned around she was smiling. My mother was alive!

I wanted to shout and tell people that my mother was alive. She was not dead! I heard birds chirping outside, and I wanted to run out of the store and run and run and run and laugh at the sun and tell the world my mother was alive, my mother was alive! I love you, Mutti, I really love you, Mutti, I rejoiced! I need you so much. I am so glad you are alive. I just want to be with you and have you hold my hand. I am so alone without you. My dear Mutti is alive. Thank you, dear God. Thank you for saving my mother. I lifted my face toward the ceiling of the store. Oma's hand taking mine brought me back to reality. I was in the Sievershagen post office, and Oma was saying, "Say *auf Wiedersehen* to the Herr Postmaster."

"*Auf Wiedersehen,*" I shouted joyously and gave the old man a bow and tumbled outside. It was even more beautiful outside than I had thought. I could smell the fragrance of the linden trees and hear the cooing of the pigeons, the chatter of the sparrows. It was a wonderful day. My happiness encompassed my entire being. I had never experienced such euphoria in my life.

"Oma, what did they say?"

"Well, it took awhile before they knew what I was talking about and who I was," she said. "Then they said Frau Samuel was doing very well. She took her first solid food by herself today, and she has even taken a bath. We should come out and visit her as soon as we could. She is recovering rapidly."

"What about the note, Oma?"

"Oh, the note was correct, too. The woman who died was the older of the two sisters from Berlin who lived in the room next to us in the barracks. She, too, had contracted typhus fever, just like our Hedwig, right after she moved out of the barracks. When she died, they didn't know her name. She had told them she was a *Flüchtling*, had a boy of ten, and lived in Hanshagen on a farm. That's how the mistake was made. The people here at the post office thought of us when the call came. They didn't know about the other family. They had heard about us for some reason. It was just coincidence, just coincidence," Oma muttered. We walked to Hanshagen in silence. I was so joyous and full of pent-up energy that as we passed the wrecked Wehrmacht truck I couldn't contain myself and jumped into the cab to play driver. I sat there holding the steering wheel and imagined driving down a tree-lined road in a place where they knew no war.

When we entered the farmyard, the farmer's wife was waiting for us at the door. Gleefully I told her that my mother was alive. For an instant I thought she was disappointed in the news. Maybe she felt she had wasted her sympathies, as well as her bread and butter. Her expression quickly changed to almost a smile, and she told us that she shared our joy.

The next morning I set out for Grevesmühlen to visit my mother. It was too far for Oma to walk with her bad legs, and she felt she should stay with Ingrid anyway. There was nothing that could have stopped me from going. My walk was long and lonely. I saw no one on the road. About halfway to Grevesmühlen I passed a Russian army camp, the first time I had seen Russians in large numbers. In a meadow a hundred trucks or more were parked in neat rows, painted a dark green. American trucks. Dodge trucks. Russian soldiers lived in tents in the adjacent forest. It was probably the camp where our dismantled barracks had been taken. I arrived in Grevesmühlen three hours after I had left the farm that morning. After asking several people for directions, I finally found the hospital. A nurse dressed in her professional white habit sat behind a desk in the hospital foyer. I approached timidly, not sure of what I should say. To my surprise she addressed me first, with a smile on her face and a kind voice.

"What are you looking for, young man?"

"I am here to visit my mother. Her name is Samuel and she was shot through the neck."

"Oh, yes," the nurse said, "I know where you can find Frau Samuel. Why don't you have a seat"—she pointed to a bench up against the wall—"and wait a moment and I will have someone escort you to your mother's room."

The hospital smelled of ether. Ten minutes later another nurse approached and said, "Please, come with me and I will take you to your mother. I am sure she will be happy and surprised to see you." She, too, smiled as she spoke. We climbed a flight of stairs and walked down several corridors. Then she stopped and pointed at a door ahead of us. "That is your mother's room. You may enter. She is awake."

My heart pounded. I thought of knocking. Then I just pressed down slowly on the handle and opened the door a crack. There were two beds in the room; the far bed by the window was occupied. I could not see the face of the woman in the bed. I quietly entered and said softly, "Mutti?"

The woman turned her head toward me slowly. It was my mother. A smile crossed her face as she recognized me. "Wolfgang, come over here and give me a kiss." I ran to her bedside and kissed her on the cheek. She still wore a bandage around her neck, but the color of her face was normal and her eyes no longer showed black-and-blue rings.

"My dearest Mutti," I cried. And I put my head in her lap and sobbed. She let me cry. Then she wiped my face with a washcloth lying on her nightstand. I told her about Ingrid and Oma and how Llydia had helped us. I assured her that we had enough to eat. I told her the story of the message the boy on the bicycle delivered. She listened without interrupting. She kept smiling at me and looked so much better than I remembered her. It seemed as if she had never been shot and never had typhus. The fever was gone; the bullet wound had not become infected but had healed miraculously on its own. The nurses gave me soup made from dried vegetables, and I was permitted to stay overnight. The next morning I left the hospital with Mutti waving to me from her wheelchair, which was placed next to a window looking out on the street.

"I'll be home soon," she said. "Llydia will drive me home." On my long walk back to Hanshagen, I wondered about the typhus. Maybe the water from the pump in the barracks was contaminated and that was how Mutti and the woman from Berlin were infected at the same time. I remembered that the water pump was near the toilets. A week later Llydia brought my mother home, and Mutti made immediate plans for our return to Strasburg. We would be on the move again. Our reluctant hosts, the farmer and his wife, seemed delighted we were leaving, although I thought the old man was sorry to see me go.

Chapter 12

THE LIST

utti was determined and wasted no time in getting us ready to
leave for Strasburg. It was the last week in July. After our long
and difficult journey from Sagan, we had come within thirty kilometers of Lübeck—we were thirty kilometers from freedom. Circumstances
trapped us in the Russian zone of occupation. Even if somehow we had
reached Lübeck, I knew Mutti would have returned to Strasburg to reunite
her mother and father. Beyond that, I don't believe she had a plan. While
I thought I understood the difference between living on the other side of
the new border, under American or English occupation, and living in the
east under the Russians, I wasn't sure my mother did. If she did, it appeared
to be of no immediate concern to her. She seemed to think that she could
solve problems as they occurred, rather than anticipating them, as I was
learning to do, or better yet, avoiding them altogether if that was possible.
But maybe I was wrong about her. All I knew was that I feared the Russians
and everything that was called Communist.

Mutti made final disposition of our horses to the Sievershagen farmer. A
condition of the deal was that if she found her father in Strasburg, and if he
agreed to return with her to Sievershagen, then she could have the horses
back. Llydia picked us up in her Russian staff car. She drove us to the train
station, where we bought four one-way tickets to Strasburg, back to the
town we had fled in terror before the Russian army only weeks earlier.

"*Auf Wiedersehen*, Llydia," we cried. "You've been such a true friend. You helped us through difficult times," Mutti said to Llydia with tears in her eyes. Oma cried. I thought she was crying because she was happy and going home. I cried when I hugged Llydia because I thought I was losing a friend who had been there for me when I was in great need. Llydia, too, cried, but quickly remembered her makeup.

"All the tears are to stop," she ordered, and we laughed with relief.

"*Auf Wiedersehen*, Llydia, and thank you for your help," I said to her as she gave me a final kiss on the forehead. I knew I would never see Llydia again. The train to Strasburg was just like the one we had taken from Berlin to Strasburg in March, uncomfortable and slow. March and Berlin seemed years ago. At least the trains were running again. The following day we arrived in Strasburg, exhausted from sitting and sleeping on the uncomfortable wooden benches of the third-class coach. We walked from the train station up Bahnhofstrasse to the *Marktplatz*. The antitank ditch that had run through the old cemetery into the street had been filled in.

From the post office onward to the *Marktplatz*, most of the houses had burned. The three-story facades with their empty window and door openings stood like skeletons reaching for the sky. The Strasburg streets looked much like those bombed in Berlin, except that the house ruins were not as tall. Most of the stairwells in the burned houses were empty shafts; the wooden stairs had gone up in flames and collapsed. Many of the upper floors had collapsed also. The charred remains formed heaps of rubble on the ground floors. Each burned building looked like every other one—empty shells smelling of ash, plaster, and mold. Occasionally a rat peeked brazenly out from under debris. Unlike in Berlin, though, there probably were no dead people in the ruins to feed the rats. On the west side of the *Marktplatz* the department store had burned, as had the *Rathaus* on the *Marktplatz* where the mayor and the Nazi Party once had their offices. On the east side of the square the buildings still stood. The gallows had been removed. Oma's house was burned to the ground, as were the other houses on her street and on several streets to the east and west.

"Let's go to Marie's house," Oma suggested as we stood in front of her burned-out home, "and see if it is still standing." With our three battered suitcases we trudged through the war-ravaged streets of Strasburg to Mutti's older sister's house. On Marie's street the houses stood untouched by war. Marie's apartment fronted a cobblestoned backyard. Her house had been built as a servants' quarters and was behind the main house. We entered the yard by way of a passage through the main building. Marie's house sat at the far right of the yard. We knocked on the kitchen door, and Heinz, the youngest of Marie's three children, promptly opened it. Oma was home again and she was overjoyed. Vera, the oldest, soon arrived. Käthe was ironing with an iron filled with glowing charcoals. In the early evening Opa Grapentin came home from work. Oma's joy was complete. Soon Marie's husband, Paul, also arrived and joined the growing gathering of the Grapentin family. The family was nearly complete except for Ernst, Mutti's younger brother, and Marie. Everyone hoped Ernst was a prisoner of war of the English or the Americans. Marie had died in June of typhus.

Paul had been a manual laborer before he was drafted into the Wehrmacht. His apartment had only two rooms and a kitchen. In the summer of 1945 nine of us lived there with him. The outhouse was behind the kitchen. The water pump stood in the center of the yard. In the kitchen was a four-burner, cast-iron, wood-burning stove, with iron rings over each burner to accommodate different-sized pots. At night we carefully scraped the hot coals into a heap, covering them with ashes to preserve the glowing embers until morning. The first one up, usually Oma, added kindling to the remaining embers and built up the fire to make ersatz coffee and cook breakfast. The stove was the only source of heat for the kitchen. The family room was heated by a tile oven. The other room, a bedroom, had no windows and no heat. Ingrid and I slept in the kitchen under the table. We were used to sleeping that way.

Vera soon told us what had happened after we fled Strasburg on that dreary night in April. She didn't know how the fires had started. "There probably was some fighting in the center of town. It was too far away for me to hear much." As it became obvious that the Russians were about to enter Strasburg, a woman, a party member and BDM leader, assembled the young BDM girls and told them that the Russian animals would rape them over and over again, and when they were of no more use they would kill them. She suggested that they cut their wrists and slowly bleed to death. It was painless, the woman said, and preferable to the fate that awaited them. Many of the young girls followed her advice. Those who were too timid to cut their own wrists received help. Someone cut Vera's wrist for her, but the cut wasn't deep enough. The bleeding soon stopped. While other girls around her bled to death, Vera decided dying wasn't for her. "I wanted to take my chances with life," Vera said. She quickly left the mass-suicide scene and hurried home.

Opa Grapentin hid Marie, Vera, Heinz, and Käthe in an orchard behind Marie's house. When the Russian soldiers came, they went through the house and into the orchard, yelling, *"Frau. Wo ist Frau?"*

"They seemed to know where to look," Opa said to Oma and Mutti. "They found our hiding place." Nothing happened to Heinz and Käthe. Marie and Vera were repeatedly raped by groups of soldiers. The violence went on for days, as different soldiers came day and night to repeat their cruel acts on the women. A Russian officer finally reserved Vera for himself. Every afternoon for two weeks he sent a carriage for her and made her stay with him overnight. In the early morning hours Vera would be driven home, only to be picked up again that afternoon. One afternoon Marie and Vera finally found a secure hiding place. The Russian soldiers searched for them for hours. They finally left and didn't return again. The rapes stopped. In June Marie fell severely ill with typhus. "We tried to make her comfortable. There was no hospital to take her to, and she died quickly. Even before her death, maggots were crawling in her decaying body," Opa said with tears in his eyes. "I was thankful when Marie died. I built a simple casket from pine boards, dug her grave and buried her myself in the cemetery."

Hearing my grandfather talk, I felt deep sorrow for the old man. I knew so little about him. I remembered the owl calling every night in June when we were in the barracks in Hanshagen. Oma decided that the owl had quit calling the night Marie died, June 26. What Oma believed must have contained some truth. Surely there were things on earth which no one understood or could explain.

I remembered an incident in Sagan in 1943 when Mutti heard a knock late at night on our apartment door. I heard it, too. Only one friend of hers had ever knocked like that. We both heard the knock twice. We sat quite still for a moment, neither one of us saying anything. The only person who knocked like that, a soldier Mutti knew, was supposed to be somewhere in Russia. He simply couldn't be in Sagan. I finally got up to see if someone was really outside the door. There was no one. "He's dead," Mutti said. "He's dead." Several weeks later Mutti received a black-bordered death announcement in the mail from the soldier's mother. Had it been his knock? I don't know. Mutti, I knew, believed it was possible for two people in different places to communicate in times of great stress. She believed in messages of death.

Soon after Paul's capture by the Russians in April 1945, he had been released. He was proud that the Communists were in power because he had always been a Communist himself, or so he said, and finally the people ruled. Paul must have been telling the truth about himself being a devout Communist, because he was already a member of the local police force. His new police uniform looked exactly like the old Wehrmacht uniform, which is what it was. Mutti didn't like Paul. She never had. Mutti began looking for a place for us.

"We have to get out of Paul's place," Mutti said to me, rolling her eyes. Looking through the main house, we found that its sole occupant was an old lady, a widow. The rear entrance to the house was usually unlocked during the day, and Mutti and I took a look around the rooms on the first floor. The old lady always stayed on the upper floor. Her husband must have been a game warden, because the foyer as well as the downstairs rooms we looked into were decorated with many sets of professionally mounted deer and elk antlers. We peered into what seemed to be a formal dining room. Its two windows looked out onto the street. Mutti pulled the heavy drapes and let the daylight flood in through the sheer curtains. The bright light made the room appear warm and inviting. It had a beautifully decorated white tile oven and was furnished with a dining table, chairs, easy chairs, and a cabinet full of crystal and silver. The walls were hung with numerous sets of roe deer antlers.

Mutti spoke to the old lady about our moving into that room temporarily. Although the old woman was reluctant to take us in, Mutti convinced her that it was in her own best interest. "It is better to have us living here with you rather than have a town official requisition the house because it is empty. With more people living in the house, the chances of the town confiscating it should be lessened. We will take care of your things," Mutti assured her, "and we will move out as soon as we find something more suitable." Reluctantly the old lady agreed. We moved in that day, leaving Oma with Opa at Paul's. The old lady gave us two single beds from an upstairs bedroom, one for Mutti, the other for Ingrid and me. July turned into August.

In exploring the neighborhood, I quickly found that the boys there were much like the ones I had encountered earlier that year in Oma Grapentin's neighborhood. They didn't like city boys or officers' sons, and I was both. They showed their resentment by attacking me, always as a gang. I learned to cope by avoiding them or running away if I saw them coming. The gangs managed to bloody me up plenty. Often enough they went away with their own bloody noses. I didn't like the situation. Every moment I spent outside I had to be prepared to fight. My cousin Heinz set me up in an ambush once by luring me to a remote area under false pretenses. Heinz curried favor with the gangs by telling them my father had been an officer in the Luftwaffe. I was, therefore, automatically branded as decadent and a legitimate target for their violence.

I had never before been particularly interested in my father's military rank, but to these boys it mattered, and it gave them a reason for beating me. They proudly proclaimed that their parents were true Communists, and had always fought against Hitler and his henchmen. Having been only simple soldiers who had done their duty in the war, no more, they were "the people" and were now taking their just revenge. I didn't know where the new language came from, and I didn't understand it. I understood, though, that I was not "people" as they defined the term. Instead, I was an exploiter of "the people," the son of one of Hitler's henchmen, and a blood-sucking leech, among many other terms they used to describe me in public harangues. It was very real and frightening.

My grandfather had found employment with the town of Strasburg soon after the war ended. He took care of the town horses. He was good at that, having tended horses in his younger days before coming to Strasburg to work in the newly built sugar refinery. The sugar refinery had burned, too. Opa told me that French forced laborers took revenge when the war ended and set the refinery on fire. On weekends Opa and I went to the *Schlammberg* where he had his tiny plot of land. I helped him tend the carrots, potatoes, cabbage, and other vegetables which we would need to stay alive through the winter. Other than on the black market, there was little food available.

I often went to the *Schlammberg*. There I was alone, unmolested by the gangs of revenge-seeking ruffians. I could relax and watch birds flying and huge rats swimming in a foul-smelling pool next to the railroad tracks. At one time there had been two sets of tracks so that trains could go in opposite directions at the same time. One set had been dismantled and shipped to Russia. The tracks, glistening in the sunshine, fascinated me. Looking west, I imagined that they led to faraway cities, even to other lands, places that were kinder than Strasburg. I was stuck in Strasburg, poorest of poor towns in Germany. There was no way out that I could see. I felt as trapped as the rats in that stinking pool. We were prisoners. Although we were allowed to run free in this town, our stinking pool, we lived in constant fear of being arrested or of disappearing, never to be heard from again. We had to get out of Strasburg one day.

The warm summer days of 1945 passed into a gentle autumn. I helped Opa harvest carrots, cabbage, and potatoes on the *Schlammberg*. Most of our bounty we stored right there on our land by covering it with straw and dirt to protect it from the winter's cold. It would be our major food source for the winter; there was none other we could count on.

With great anticipation, I started school again in late August, but the experience turned out to be a disappointment. I was put in a class with the same rowdies who had harassed me throughout the summer. Most of them couldn't read or write well and knew little about numbers. The level of instruction was geared to them and their abilities, so I learned practically nothing new. I spent most of my time in class trying to figure out how to escape from the bullies who wanted to beat me as soon as school let out. They didn't have to search for me anymore. All they had to do was wait for me at the door. There were no textbooks; the old books, no matter what their subjects, had been withdrawn because they might be tainted with National Socialist ideology. Much of the time in class was taken up by our teacher talking about the greatness of Communism. If Communism was so great, I thought, why was there no food? Why were we afraid to talk? Why were we in fear of being arrested? I was smart enough not to ask those questions in class. Instead, I sat at my desk quietly. I knew that sounding off would bring trouble to Mutti, Opa, and me.

As the year entered its last few weeks, the days grew shorter and colder. It was the constant dampness that made me really uncomfortable. We were lucky in that our new room had a tile oven. Firewood was abundant. I hauled it in from a nearby forest using a handcart. In the evenings when Opa came home from work, I grabbed the other end of the saw and we sawed the logs into pieces. Opa showed me how to split the wood so it would fit our ovens. After school, with Opa still at work, I often split logs in the yard. Neither Paul nor Heinz ever helped.

Although we were able to provide heat for ourselves, there was no light. Electricity had yet to be restored in our neighborhood. That really didn't matter at Paul's place, since it had never had electricity in the first place. Our room did have electric outlets and lamps. We used kerosene lamps, but the problem was finding kerosene. One grey, damp November day I saw people gathered around a diesel pump. Two old men, who appeared to be town employees, were emptying the tank using a hand-operated pump. They were spilling an excessive amount of the fuel into the gutter. I quickly decided it was not by accident that they were spilling so much diesel fuel. They were good men helping people by being sloppy. I heard people say that if salt was added to the diesel fuel it wouldn't smoke, and then it could be used in our lamps. People scooped up the spilled fuel with tin cups and poured it into milk cans. I ran home, grabbed our two-liter milk can and a tin cup and quickly returned to the place of the fuel spill, hoping there was some still left for me to retrieve. There was. The old men took their time transferring the fuel from the underground tank to a drum, spilling much of it. I filled our milk can and hurried home with my treasure. I told Oma about the salt. She seemed to know what to do. That evening, while Mutti, Ingrid, and I sat by the light of the lamp using my fuel, I felt proud at having contributed to my family's welfare.

While the Russians themselves were not much in evidence, the German police were. The *Volkspolizei* wore old Wehrmacht uniforms, and carried German army rifles and pistols. As a policeman, Paul became more obnoxious toward us each day. He would come into our room without knocking and just stand by the wall near the door insulting Mutti. He wore his police uniform pants and his long-sleeved undershirt with the suspenders on top of it. He usually took his tunic off before coming over. In his clumsy way, I thought, he was trying to get Mutti to go to bed with him. More than once he made suggestions of that nature to her in front of Ingrid and me. Mutti reminded him that it was unseemly, that he was her brother-in-law, and that he should not make such suggestions in front of the children.

One evening Paul's vindictive questions and comments carried a more sinister message. "Hedy," he said, "do you know that your father will be picked up soon like so many others who committed crimes against the people during the Hitler regime?"

Mutti was shocked. I saw it in her rigid posture and her face, suddenly turned ashen. "What did you say just now?" Mutti asked Paul.

"I said Wilhelm will be arrested soon. It is common knowledge. You should have heard about it. Haven't you?" It wasn't common knowledge to us. We had never heard about this from anyone.

"Why would anyone want to arrest my father?"

"Oh," Paul said expansively, "you remember when Wilhelm was in the Volkssturm, and he was assigned to guard Russian prisoners of war?"

"Yes?"

"Well," continued Paul, "you probably also know that one day as he was escorting the prisoners past the *Schlammberg* they broke away from him to help themselves to some raw potatoes. Wilhelm came after them with a stick and beat them."

"No, I didn't know about that."

"Well, being in the police gives me access to important information, and, of course, I can't share everything with you. Many know who is on the list of enemies of the people. If I can be of assistance to you, just let me know. All you have to do is be nice to me, Hedwig."

For once Paul left without being asked, grinning from ear to ear as he closed the door behind him. Mutti did remember the incident Opa was involved in back in April. So did I. Mutti also knew that Opa regretted it. He had a temper, like Mutti herself, and it got the best of him at times. The incident had been forgotten in the turmoil of the closing days of the war. Suddenly it was back with a terrible vengeance. That night Mutti waited until Opa came over to say *Gute Nacht*, as he did every night. She asked him if he knew about the list the Communists put together of people who were to be arrested over the next several weeks.

"I have heard of the list," Opa said, "and I have heard that my name is on it." He paused in apparent puzzlement. "Why would anyone want to arrest me, Hedwig? I haven't done anything. I know about my mistake when I beat the Russian prisoners earlier this year. I am sorry about it. But no one is going to throw me into a concentration camp for that."

"Yes, they will," Mutti shouted, totally losing her composure. "Don't you see, Father? They are giving you ample warning to pack up and leave and save your skin. God only knows what will happen to you once they arrest you."

"You worry too much, Hedwig," Opa said calmly. "They need me to tend to the town's horses; no one here knows anything about horses. If it weren't for me, many of the horses would have died by now. They need me, Hedwig. Believe me, they need me."

The List

"Father," Mutti pleaded, her hands grasping his broad shoulders, "they don't need you! They will get along without you. You must leave now. We can go to Mecklenburg, where I left two horses in the care of a farmer. He would love to have you. You can take care of his horses, and for the first time in your life you would have your very own horses, too. You will be safe there. Don't you know that I came back to Strasburg for you, dear Father? I deliberately made arrangements to allow us to return to Mecklenburg. I was worried about this very thing happening. Now it is happening and you won't listen to me."

Mutti's tears ran over her high cheekbones, down her hollow cheeks, and into her mouth, some dripping onto the floor. Only she and I seemed to comprehend that the quiet since the end of the war was not going to last, and that the time was coming when the Communists, our new masters, would act to define their world and cleanse it of those who they thought did not belong. I did not belong in their world, I knew that already, nor did Opa Grapentin. These were people who took revenge seriously, and now that they were in power they were about to act. Although he listened patiently while his only living daughter pleaded with him in an effort to save his life, Opa's eyes revealed to me that he couldn't or didn't want to understand what she was saying.

After a moment's silence, he spoke. "Hedwig, I can't leave here. This town and the village you were born in are the only places I've ever lived and worked in. Yes, I served in the kaiser's army during the Great War, and I survived the gas at Verdun. That's all I know about the outside world, and I don't want to know any more about it. I am too old. This is my home. I will stay here. It won't be as bad as you fear. Everything will be all right. I know the people on the police force. They are good people. They know me. They wouldn't do anything to harm me."

Mutti stared at him in comprehending exhaustion. She knew she could not say anything to change his mind. He simply would not and could not see the changed world he lived in. "*Gute Nacht,*" Mutti said to Opa. She kissed him on the cheek. Opa left to go to bed. That night I heard Mutti sob into her pillow, crying late into the night. I finally fell asleep. I had never heard her cry like that. Opa went to work day after day, caring for his horses. We forgot about the list. Now and then I heard some woman in a food line saying that so-and-so had not been seen for some time and had probably been taken away, that so-and-so had been on the list. The list was real. People on the list were arrested and taken away, always at night, and were never heard from again.

One cold evening in late November, about nine o'clock, I heard a loud knocking at our front door. The knock was repeated several times, insistent and without letup. I looked over at Mutti. She nodded her head. I opened the door. Two *Volkspolizei* stood there, rifles with fixed bayonets slung over their shoulders. I knew what it meant when the police knocked on your door at night. "Mutti, the police are here," I shouted at her across the hall. I was very afraid. Mutti came to the door, and one of the policemen politely asked if they could speak to Herr Wilhelm Grapentin.

"Yes," she replied, "I believe he is next door."

"Would you please get him?"

"Yes," Mutti answered stoically, leaving Ingrid and me standing at the door with the police. Mutti returned with Opa. He wore his wooden clogs; his pants were held up by suspenders over a long-sleeved undershirt. As the policemen saw him approaching in the corridor, they stepped forward and met him at the door to our room. Everyone entered. Mutti closed the door.

"Herr Grapentin," one of the policemen said, "you are under arrest for crimes you committed against the people." Opa seemed visibly confused. He brushed his hand across his eyes.

"This must be a mistake," he replied after a brief pause. "I haven't committed any crimes against any people."

"That is not for us to determine. We are just doing our duty. It is up to the people's court to decide your guilt or innocence." The other policeman, the quiet one, proceeded to search our room for incriminating evidence, and, judging from the way he went about his search, it seemed to me that someone had given him directions. He found an army backpack given to me by the German soldiers we had accompanied on our flight from the Russians across northern Germany earlier in the year. I had put that prized possession on top of the high tile oven where I had thought no one would find it. The ornamental tiles at the top prevented the rucksack from being seen from anywhere in the room. The policeman went right over to the oven, grabbed a chair, and pulled my rucksack down from its hiding place.

"Are you hiding other military goods or weapons, Herr Grapentin?" asked the policeman conducting the search.

"No," I answered for Opa, "that's just a rucksack which I need to carry things in. Someone gave it to me as a present. My grandfather has nothing to do with it."

"This was German military property," said the policeman, ignoring me, "and, therefore, it belongs to the people." Turning to Opa they motioned for him to move. "It is time to go, Herr Grapentin." Both policemen walked toward the door, one ahead of my grandfather, the other behind. He still wore only his pants, an undershirt and a vest, and his clogs.

"Can I quickly go and say *auf Wiedersehen* to my wife and pack a few things to take along?" Opa asked.

"No," said the spokesman for the two policemen. "Let's go." They grabbed Opa by the arms and ushered him outside into the street. I ran into the hall to the coatrack on which Opa hung his jacket when he returned from work. He and the two policemen were already down the front steps and on the street when I caught up with them.

"You need this, Opa, it is cold tonight." I handed him his jacket. "Will you come back soon?" The policemen slowed their pace and allowed Opa to turn around to face me.

"I will be back soon," he replied. Then he and the two policemen with their rifles and mounted bayonets walked off into the cold mist of the night. Opa, taller than either of the two, his jacket casually held in his right hand, walked upright, like a man who had nothing to fear. I screamed, "Opa! My dear Opa! Come back soon!" He waved with his left hand without turning around. I feared I would never see my grandfather again. I felt devastating sorrow at seeing him being led away by the police. Mutti went over to Paul's place to tell Oma that Opa had been taken away. I didn't go along. I didn't want to be there when she told Oma. Paul had not come home that night.

After Opa's arrest we worked harder than ever to put food on our table. Mutti started to tell fortunes by reading palms and playing cards. There were many in Strasburg who believed in the supernatural. Mutti had learned these skills in a perfunctory fashion from friends she had met in Sagan. It used to be a way for her to entertain guests at her parties. Llydia had taught Mutti some of the finer points of fortune-telling. Mutti used these skills now to make a living for us. When she began fortune-telling, she first mentioned it to a friend of hers who was a hairdresser. The hairdresser mentioned her in casual conversation to her clients, and soon Mutti was getting all the business she could handle. She developed a sizeable following of women, old and young. Many returned regularly every week. They paid with food or articles one could trade for food, such as jewelry, since money was nearly worthless.

Paul grew ever more officious after Opa's arrest. Mutti continued to rebuff his clumsy advances. One day he informed her that her fortune-telling was a degenerate activity which undermined the authority of the state and could not be tolerated any longer. "It must end immediately or I have to report you, which will result in your arrest and confinement."

"Paul, don't do this to me. We are your family. My sister was your wife." Mutti tried to reason with him. Begged him.

"You are not family anymore," he said. "You never accepted me and always looked down on me. Now, when I am important, you want favors from me. I will do no favors for you, Hedwig. Also, I am going to move into this room. Find yourself another place to live. Since you make no contribution to the welfare of our state, you have no right to a nice room like this in our new society. Anyway, my apartment is too small for the children, your mother, and me. I need to get another woman, too. She couldn't live over there. Be out of here by next week." In one short, venomous outburst Paul robbed Mutti of her means of support as well as a place for us to live.

The shooting war had ended seven months earlier. In the Russian zone of occupation, a new war raged—a war of survival, as bitter as the one that had just ended. There was little food. No new clothing replaced what had been worn threadbare. The dreaded knock on the door at night was back again. People disappeared without trace, just as they had in years past. Another cold winter loomed ahead of us. Strasburg was like one of my frequent nightmares. The only difference was that when I awoke the nightmare was over; Strasburg was still there.

Chapter 13

A WINTER NIGHTMARE

W e moved out of our comfortable room the week following my grandfather's arrest by the Communists. There was no use arguing with Paul. Some of Mutti's women friends knew of a room with kitchen privileges near the train station, across from two sugar warehouses which belonged to the burned-out refinery. The move was easy and uncomplicated. We had so few possessions it was only a simple matter of packing our three suitcases again and carrying them to our new home. As we trudged through Strasburg, I thought about the many times we had made the three-suitcase trip—from Sagan to Berlin, from Berlin to Strasburg, from Strasburg to near Lübeck, to Strasburg again, and to yet another place in Strasburg. I saw no reason why this should be the last trip. Our new home was a simply furnished room with a table and four chairs, a bed on one side of the room, and a couch without a back on the other. A *Schrank* sat to the right of the door. There were two double windows with deep sills facing the street.

In the winter of 1945, food became ever scarcer. I felt a sense of desperation pervading our lives. It seemed that people would do anything for a bite of food, a cigarette, or a drink of schnapps or vodka. Some would go to the police to turn in a neighbor for real or manufactured wrongs in the expectation that something good for themselves would come out of such desperate action. My family, like many others, had no stocks of food. We lived from hand to mouth, from one day to the next. When we thought of food, we thought of potatoes, rutabagas, and sour bread. Meat and butter were luxuries only rarely available, and then mostly on the black market. Oma spent most of her days with us. At night she went back to Paul's in case Opa should return. She wanted to be there when he came back. On a grey day in late December 1945, the word was out that one of the town horses had died. We knew the next day there would be meat available from the horse carcass. I knew the horse the townspeople were talking about, a skinny old nag that had died of old age. In school my friends told me the carcass had been hauled to the one butcher in town and that it was being processed that night.

I was up early the next morning. When I got to the butcher shop, the line was already long; it was made up mostly of women wearing ill-fitting grey or black coats and shawls wrapped around their heads to protect them against the bitter cold. Most of the women had sallow faces and missing teeth. There were no other children in line. I arrived at seven; the store would not open until one o'clock in the afternoon. The line grew longer as the morning progressed. The damp cold seemed to penetrate to my bones, and my feet felt like lumps of ice. A low-hanging cloud deck made the day seem even gloomier. The two women behind me talked incessantly. By eleven o'clock their talk turned to me.

"He has lice," one woman said to the other. "Can you see them?"

"Yes," said the other woman loudly, "one is crawling across his back."

She let out a loud shudder of disgust. I knew I didn't have lice. We washed our hair daily because of the threat of lice from other children. Every afternoon Oma looked at Ingrid and me to make certain we were clean and had not picked up lice from other children. One of the two women started to complain even more loudly.

"Why do we have to stand behind a louse-infested boy? We'll probably catch lice ourselves, just because we want to put meat on the table for our hungry families."

The accusatory, loud chatter from the two women continued without letup. After a while, all of the grey-looking, shawl-clad, scrawny women in the long line stared at me, while the two women behind me kept up their accusations. Finally, I couldn't take it any longer. I did what they wanted me to do. I left the line. I arrived home in tears. Mutti rushed over to comfort me. I told her the story of the two women and how after five hours in line I couldn't take any more of the things they were saying about me. Mutti looked me over and then took a dead louse off the back of my overcoat.

"One of the women probably put that louse on your back, Wolfgang, to get you out of that line. When you left, they were one space closer to getting meat for their families. They can be pretty cruel to children. Let's go back and see if there is still some meat left. I should have known not to leave you there for such a long time by yourself." We walked to the butcher shop together. It was a long walk across town. The line was gone, and so was the horse meat. Mutti talked the butcher out of a bone which she used to make soup. Our incessant search for food continued.

On another day we heard that salted herring had arrived at a store on the east end of town. Mutti sent me over as soon as we heard about it; again I was too late. When I got near the store I couldn't see a line, and I knew the herring was gone. I went inside the store anyway to look for myself at the empty barrel, half full of brown brine with fish scales floating in it. A surly salesgirl saw me looking into the barrel, and, with a sardonic grin on her face, she said, "Yes, the herring is gone. You need to get here quicker the next time."

I ignored her. How could I get places more quickly? The only way to find out about such things was through contacts, and I didn't have any. I went home knowing that all we would have to eat that evening were potatoes from our cache on the *Schlammberg*, with salt. Mutti viewed the matter differently. When I told her about the empty fish barrel, she announced, "Tonight we will eat make-believe fish and real potatoes." She grabbed our all-purpose two-liter milk can, which in the past several weeks had held everything imaginable except milk, and off we went to the store. Mutti politely asked the girl behind the counter for permission to take some of the brine. The salesgirl said to go ahead and take all we wanted. "We'll just throw it out anyway," she said, with that same condescending grin on her face. That night we poured the herring brine over our potatoes after first straining out the fish scales. Dinner tasted extraordinarily good in contrast to a meal of only potatoes and salt.

It became still colder. Snow fell. We were hungry most of the time. We became thinner, bonier-looking. Christmas came and went just like any other day. The Communists did not encourage church activities, and so our Christmas passed at home without a tree and without celebration. The old church near the *Marktplatz*, the church in which my mother and father had been married and I had been baptized, was locked. I remembered that only a year ago Mutti, Ingrid, and I had spent Christmas in our comfortable home in Sagan with the biggest tree ever. It almost reached the ceiling, and was decorated with tinsel, colorful handblown glass birds and angels, white paraffin candles, and sweets for Ingrid and me to eat on New Year's Day, the traditional day for tree plundering. That was a year ago. I pushed the thought out of my mind. I wouldn't have known where to find a tree anyway, even if Mutti had asked me to get one.

One of my teachers, in contrast to most others, had not turned into a devout, overnight Communist. He was a tall, thin, quiet man who taught *Naturkunde*, natural history, and I loved his class. Although we had no textbooks for use in our classes, he showed me where I could find the old ones in the basement of the school. The books had stamped on their front and back covers "Property of the Strasburg School District." In the middle of the stamp an eagle with spread wings rested its claws on a swastika. I took an armful of the books, carefully hiding them under my coat as I exited. I practically memorized those books, which were about flowers, grasses, mosses, trees, and mushrooms. I learned how living things developed and grew and how the flowers bloomed and why. I read about the role of insects in fertilization and about many other interesting subjects. The books allowed me to escape my dreary existence and enter a life of learning on my own. I was grateful to the teacher for allowing me to take the books, which had been destined to help heat the building.

I also knew that he could get into serious trouble if I mentioned his kindness to anyone. The same teacher asked my class to memorize several old Christmas poems. During our last class of the year, on *Heiligabend* (Christmas Eve), we presented our poems in front of the class. We all brought gifts, which we exchanged, and a true spirit of Christmas embraced our class as the day waned and big snowflakes lazily drifted by the windows. For many of us children, it was the only Christmas we knew that year. It was for me. It was a Christmas of the heart and of the spirit. For a brief shining moment, we forgot the terrible times we lived in. Now and then the classroom echoed to our laughter. Before we broke for the afternoon, we sang the old carols *"Leise rieselt der Schnee"* and *"Oh, Tannenbaum."* I walked home that afternoon feeling warmth in my heart and hope for the future. As I passed through the cemetery, my thoughts wandered back to

Sagan and the days of Christmas past. Those were wonderful times when our family was together—safe, warm, and not hungry. It was enough just to have good memories, I thought. And I should not forget to be thankful, I reminded myself, that all three of us were still together, and that we had survived this dreadful year.

The winter of 1945 seemed every bit as harsh as the previous one had been. Low-lying clouds covered our region for weeks; it seemed like the sun was only a memory and that the snow would never melt. My clothes were thin and worn; Ingrid's were in no better condition. Both of us were growing out of our clothes, as well as wearing to shreds what little we still had. We were cold and hungry all the time. Mutti tried to find food for us in every way possible—buying, begging, stealing. It was never enough. I could see the desperation building in her face day by day, she not knowing where the next bite of food was coming from for her children. I didn't want to be a burden, but I didn't know how to help. I thought of Hansel and Gretel in Grimm's fairy tale, and I suddenly understood the gruesome truth behind it.

Mutti met some Russian officers who were assigned to the *Kommandatura*, now located in the former post office building. Some of the officers had their wives with them by now, and Mutti was successful in interesting one of the Russian women in her fur coat, hand muff, and fur hat. In return, Mutti received salt pork, Russian army bread, and brown sugar. By this time, Paul was refusing to feed Oma, so Mutti had one more mouth to feed, one more burden weighing her down. The last of the potatoes and carrots Opa Grapentin and I had harvested together the previous autumn and stored on the *Schlammberg* received frost during an especially cold night. As a result the potatoes tasted sickeningly sweet when we tried to eat them, and the carrots turned to mush when they thawed. We were totally dependent on whatever food Mutti could procure, however she was able to do it.

From our windows, we could see the sugar refinery warehouses. The buildings were guarded by Russian soldiers who lived there in an administrative building. The Russians posted a guard at the gate to the warehouse compound. On a cold and utterly desperate afternoon, Mutti put on her only pair of warm boots and her flimsy summer overcoat and wrapped a shawl around her head for warmth. Then she walked up and down in front of the warehouse gate. That night a tall Russian in a bright green uniform jacket, brown riding pants, and new black knee-high boots came home with Mutti. He spoke excellent German and smiled and said he was a Ukrainian, not a Russian. I thought he was a *Kommissar*. He wore a flat hat with a short, black bill. On the front of his hat he wore a badge with a red star, a hammer and sickle superimposed over it. Ingrid and I went to bed on the narrow, backless couch against the wall opposite from Mutti's bed. Mutti blew out the candle. The Russian undressed in the dark. I heard his boots drop on the floor. He went to bed with my mother. I heard them moving in bed and whispering. My desperation reached new heights as I realized what I did not really want to know—that my mother was sleeping with the Russian so we would have food to eat.

"Mutti," I said out loud, unable to stop myself, "you shouldn't be doing what you are doing. Only Dad should sleep with you." For a while I heard no movement. There was no reply to my comment. The movement resumed. I pulled the blanket over my head. When I awoke the next morning, the Russian had gone. I noticed that one of the windows was ajar and that there was a two-liter milk can on our windowsill. I moved the can inside and took off its lid. Steam smelling of food billowed out into the chill of our room. It was a thick noodle soup with pieces of chicken floating in it. All four of us had enough to eat that day, for the first time in a long time. The *Kommissar* came every night, usually after Ingrid and I had gone to bed. In the morning I would find the usual can of noodle soup on the windowsill. One morning when we tried to eat the soup, we found that it had been contaminated with salt. That night the Russian *Kommissar* told Mutti that the soldiers had put salt in the soup out of spite.

"I can no longer bring soup for you and your family," he said, loudly enough for everyone to hear. "Also, I am being transferred back to the Soviet Union this weekend." I was happy to hear his news and to see him go even if it meant losing the food he had provided every morning. The torture of knowing he was in bed with my mother and of having to listen to them every night had become unbearable for me. I overheard women talking about my mother and about other women who slept with Russian officers. They called the women whores. I didn't know how to deal with that term when it was applied to my mother. I knew my mother was not a whore; she only wanted to feed her children. Ingrid and I had to eat, or we would die. My school friends were hungry, too. I could see it in their gaunt faces. I wondered if I looked that way to them.

One day I overheard three of my classmates whispering in the hall. They stopped talking when I approached. I figured it wasn't any of my business so

A Winter Nightmare

I didn't ask about their secret. The next day my three friends were not in school; no one knew where they were. All three had vanished, and neither parents nor friends knew what had become of them. We assumed it had to be the German police. Three days after their initial disappearance, two of the missing boys showed up again, looking even more haggard than they had before. They refused to talk about where they had been and what had happened to them. Two weeks later the third boy came home. Tall and thin to start with, he now looked like a walking skeleton covered with skin and hair.

I learned that the three had broken into one of the sugar warehouses across from our house to steal some of the unrefined brown sugar. They had done so several times without getting caught by the Russian guards. Unfortunately, the three bragged about their previous successes, and an informer told the Volkspolizei, who then informed the Russians. When my classmates made their next attempt, the Russians had been forewarned. The boys nearly got away, except that during the escape one of them injured an ankle. He couldn't run fast enough and the other two wouldn't abandon him. They never spoke of the treatment they received while they were held captive. Their eyes continued to express terror.

In February 1946, I turned eleven. It was no cause to celebrate. I was just one year older. On my last birthday I had been in Berlin. Then we were bombed by the Americans by day and by the English at night. We weren't being bombed anymore, but we faced dangers much more unpredictable than the bombing had ever been. On a grey and cold February afternoon, after school, a number of us decided to go to a lake on the west side of Strasburg. We believed the lake would be frozen solid. Although we had no skates, we thought it would be fun just to run out on the lake and skid across the ice. There were eight of us, and I was the last. Not being a swimmer, and after nearly drowning two years earlier in the Bober River, I had developed respect, if not fear, for water, even in its frozen state. I lagged behind my friends on purpose. One of my friends was the boy held by the Russians for three weeks after they caught him in the sugar warehouse. He was the first to skid onto the ice; two other boys followed, skidding toward the middle of the lake, laughing and shouting with delight. I was the last one sliding onto the ice, and as I came to a halt I looked down and nearly died of fright. I could see the bottom of the deep lake. Fortunately it wasn't really thin ice,

A Winter Nightmare

as I had feared; it was just clear. The fright was enough to cause me to get off the ice immediately and back on solid ground.

I became aware of screaming in the distance, and I could see some of my classmates running back toward me, trying desperately to get off the ice. My tall friend had broken through near the center of the lake. When he surfaced, his two companions tried to pull him out. Then they, too, started to break through the ice and had to run for their lives. Two town employees eventually showed up in their blue linen work suits, the same two who had pumped the diesel fuel into the road. Slowly and carefully they felt their way across the ice, making sure it could hold their weight, pushing a flat-bottomed boat ahead of them. They had come to retrieve the body, not to save a life. They brought grappling hooks, and after an hour they pulled the body of my classmate from the icy water. By the time the two men got him to firm ground and loaded him onto the back of a horse-drawn flatbed wagon, he appeared to be frozen stiff. Lying in the open wagon, my friend's corpse was driven through town for all to see. As the two workers and their gruesome load disappeared from sight, heading down the cobblestoned road toward the cemetery death house, I saw the left forearm of my tall friend sticking up in the air, waving around aimlessly, as if he were making a last grasp for life that had eluded him in a boyish whim of playfulness. Walking home I felt tired and old. Much older than eleven.

During the bleak winter days, our lives focused on getting food for the next day and on staying warm. Sleep was the only relief from the repetitive greyness of our daytime pursuits. I slept on the couch in our one-room apartment; Ingrid slept at the other end, her feet toward me. I again began having frequent nightmares. They were always the same. Either I fell into a black abyss, knowing that when I hit bottom I would die, or my mother left on a train and I could not move to reach her, nor would any sound come out of my mouth when I tried to call to her. When Mutti heard me screaming, she would rush across the room to comfort me. I would gain consciousness with her holding me and stroking my hair, as I pressed my head against her bosom. I dreaded going to sleep. Ingrid always seemed to sleep through my nightmares. If she heard me, she never said anything.

After Opa's arrest in November, Mutti tried to find out where the police had taken him. At first her efforts were tentative; then they became more and more the focus of her daily existence, other than obtaining food. She quickly learned that most people in our Communist society could be bribed.

Sometimes Mutti used flattering words to gain information; at other times it took money or articles of value coveted by the informant. And sometimes she had to use herself. She nearly always took me along when she went hunting for likely prospects who might have knowledge of my grandfather's fate. I was her protection from the men who coveted her body. Although most of her contacts proved fruitless, she persisted in her search, believing that in time, if she kept trying, she would find out what had happened to her father.

After many fruitless attempts, we went to visit a distant relative of Mutti's, an uncle once or twice removed. I had never met him, nor had anyone spoken of him in my presence. She tried to make her first visit look casual, as if she were just stopping by to say hello to a relative she had not seen in a long time. He was a thin man, emaciated and constantly coughing, a heavy smoker who looked as if he had tuberculosis. After they exchanged greetings, Mutti talked about Ingrid and me and how hard it was to find clothing for growing children. We soon left. On our way home, after walking in silence for ten minutes, I couldn't restrain myself any longer and nearly shouted, "He is not my uncle, Mutti," trying to put into words the utter revulsion I felt for this repulsive man. "I don't like him, and I don't want you to go back to him. He is evil." I grasped her hand and looked up at her, hoping she would agree.

She didn't break her stride or give any outward sign in response to my emotional outburst. Looking straight ahead, she said, "I don't like him any better than you do, Wolfgang. We have to be practical if we want to help your grandfather. Why do you think I have not gone to see him sooner? Because he is an awful man and I am afraid of him. But if there is anyone in town who can help us, he can. It is only a question of *if* he wants to help and *if* we have anything he might want in exchange for his information." Two days later we went back again. He was not home. We waited an hour, standing in the cold, drafty hallway of his house, until a neighbor told us that she had not seen him all day. We finally gave up waiting and left. We returned the following day about four o'clock in the afternoon. This time he answered the knock on his door and bade us to come in. His sparsely furnished room was damp and stank of stale air and cigarette smoke. A rumpled bed was pushed up against one wall under a dirty window. A table and two chairs sat in the middle of the room. The floorboards were worn, and there were cracks between some of them. A chest of drawers and a

A Winter Nightmare

Schrank pushed up against a wall completed his furnishings. A water bucket with a ladle hung inside stood in a corner next to a stove. Plaster was peeling off dirty, whitewashed walls, and a single, flyspecked lightbulb dangled from the ceiling. Mounds of cigarette butts filled saucers and tin cans. Cigarette ashes were everywhere.

He lay in his bed smoking, one leg pulled up toward his scrawny body, the other stretched out. He made no effort to rise when we entered the room. "Come over, Hedwig," he called to Mutti, using her old-fashioned first name. She stood near his bed, just out of his reach. I turned around in the doorway to leave, but Mutti said, "Stay, Wolfgang, there is no reason for you to go." I remained standing in the doorway—watching, listening.

"Do you know where they took my father?" Mutti asked bluntly. She took a wad of money out of her coat pocket and held it out to him while she waited for his answer. He put his cigarette in his mouth, took a long drag, and inhaled deeply. Then he took the money from her, examining it briefly as the cigarette smoke slowly oozed out of his mouth and nostrils, and casually pushed the money into his left pants pocket. What would he buy with the worthless money? I wondered. His cigarettes were Russian. The front half of the cigarette was tobacco, the back half a hollow tube. He certainly must have access to Russians to smoke cigarettes like that, or maybe to other Germans with access to Russians. Nobody gave anything to anyone without receiving something in return. He had given something for the cigarettes, and I doubted if it was worthless German money. What did the repulsive man have to offer to others?

Mutti's negotiation with him did not seem to be going well. I heard her begging for information, any information about Opa. "You are family," she reminded him. "Please, help me find out about my father. If you know someone who can help, please, give me his name so I can contact him. I won't mention your name. Won't you try to help a relative?" I knew this was a desperate move; her appeal to family hadn't worked in the past when she had tried it on Paul. The dirty man was stalling, that much I could tell. Maybe he didn't know anything.

Then he said slowly, with the words sort of squeezing out of his thin mouth, briefly exposing his discolored teeth, "I promise you information soon, Hedwig—if you would just lie down next to me." He looked her in the eyes.

"I will think about it," Mutti said. He rose from his reclining position, stubbing out his cigarette in an already-full ashtray on the floor next to him. He rested his chin in his right hand.

"This information you are asking for, Hedwig, is sensitive." He sat on the side of his bed looking at the floor. "I have to take great risks to pass it on to you. One never knows," he reminded Mutti. "People talk. Pretty soon I'm gone, too."

"I'll be back next week, any day you say," Mutti replied.

"I will be able to tell you something by next week," he promptly responded, looking at her with leering eyes. A slight smile formed around his thin lips. "Come back next Tuesday, Hedwig. In the afternoon, about two. I'll have something for you then. Remember," he said loudly, "information is hard to come by and it costs. It always costs, Hedy."

On our way home, I again expressed my disgust to Mutti about the ugly man. She listened patiently. Finally she said, "He always has been an informer, Wolfgang. You have to understand that about this man. That's how he makes his living. He informs the police about the goings-on in Strasburg. He did the same thing under Hitler. Nothing has changed. I came to him because I don't know what else to do. He may be the only person who actually knows what happened to Opa, other than the police. I have to find my father, Wolfgang, no matter what the cost. You can understand that, can't you?"

I knew Mutti had tried many other people over the past weeks and gotten nowhere. There were farmers in town who were important because they had food to trade and who were also Communists from the old days. Mutti met with them, and I went along to some of those meetings. The farmers knew nothing and had no way to get such information. All they thought of was taking her to bed. They did not hesitate to ask her bluntly, in my presence, to sleep with them. And they didn't mean some day in the future—they meant then, right there in that room. I was a child. I could be sent outside to wait.

Another contact was a newly formed theater group. Mutti attended several meetings. She had mixed feelings about anyone in that group having access to the kind of information she was seeking. One evening she returned in tears. She told Oma it was the final rehearsal for the group's first public performance. Each actor or group of performers, who she had thought were novice actors like herself, had chosen a song or a ballad, a musical rendition, a speech, a dance, a short one- or two-person play, or an impersonation of something or someone. Mutti had thought of tap dancing, but she couldn't locate shoes, or taps, or a proper costume. She remembered the red poetry book the German soldier had given her the day before we surrendered to the Americans. She memorized the Schiller poem *"Der Handschuh."* She practiced her lines several times in front of me. At the rehearsal she saw that the songs and dances and speeches and plays were about farmers and workers and capitalist oppressors. She almost decided not to do her poem. Then she did, out of defiance, I believe. They never let her finish. Halfway through they began to whistle at her and shouted, "Get off the stage. Throw her out. Get out, you capitalist whore." She ran away crying, leaving behind her things, including the red poetry book. She never returned to retrieve the book or any of her other belongings.

On Tuesday afternoon Mutti and I went to see her uncle. This time he said he had information, but that she really would be better off not hearing it. "I insist you tell me whatever it is you know," Mutti pressured him.

"Come over here, Hedwig." When she leaned over him, he whispered into her ear. She looked at him in astonishment.

Then she came over to me and said, "Go home, Wolfgang, please. I will come home soon," and she closed the door behind me. I heard the iron key turn in the rusty old lock. I walked home dejectedly. I knew what the man wanted from my mother. I also knew she had no choice but to pay his price. I hope he dies soon of TB, I said to myself, as I walked alone through the desolate streets of Strasburg. The air was damp and cold, the clouds low and oppressive. The huge portraits of Lenin and Karl Marx by the post office building sneered down at me from their red banners. I felt a deep hatred well up inside of me for the Communists, for German Communists who took away the freedom and dignity of their own people. Mutti came home late that afternoon. She looked tired and beaten. She didn't want to talk.

"Leave me alone, Wolfgang. I don't have anything to tell you," she responded curtly when I asked her what she had learned about Opa.

"You have to tell me, Mutti. I need to know what happened to my grandfather," I persisted. "I love him just as much as you do. Please."

She turned toward me. Her features had softened, and she said gently, "You are too young, Wolfgang. Some things are better left unsaid. Just think of your grandfather as a brave man who loved you." She pressed her hands against my cheeks. Her brown eyes were filled with tears, and she looked lost and helpless.

A Winter Nightmare

"Mutti," I begged, "I have to know."

She walked around the table several times, her head down, her hands uncharacteristically clasped together in front of her. Then she grasped my hand, and we sat down on the floor in a corner of our room. Maybe she had to talk to someone, and I was the someone. Ingrid was in the kitchen with Oma.

She put her arms around me and said, "You must be brave, Wolfgang." I knew her news wouldn't be good. As she spoke, tears ran down her cheeks. Her voice remained steady. She always had control when she needed it, a quality I had recognized in her before and admired. "You must promise," she said, "never to say anything to Oma or to Ingrid."

"I promise," I said, without knowing what I was agreeing to. She looked at me for a minute or two before she spoke again. "They took Opa away," she said almost in a whisper, "and that night they put him in a cell with other men. The men received no food or drink or blankets to keep warm. The next morning he was put on a truck and driven with the others to another town east of Strasburg, not far from here. Pasewalk or Prenzlau. There he was told why he had been arrested, for beating starving Russian prisoners of war." Her voice was breaking. Her shoulders shook as a deep sob broke from her chest. "Then they beat Opa for days, with a stick. Just like he supposedly had done to the Russian prisoners. The beatings were so painful he tried to climb the walls of his cell with his bare hands to get away from them. They beat him until he died. My uncle was there when my father died. His last words were for you, my son. 'What will happen to Wolfgang? What will happen to Wolfgang?' he cried over and over again, until he became unconscious and then died. He loved you and cared for you, my son. I know it's true from the way it was told to me. Oma can never know about this, you understand that, don't you?" I nodded my head in agreement.

I was totally bewildered. I had never heard or read of such brutality. If only he had listened to Mutti, he would now be with his beloved horses, plowing a field on a farm, doing the things he loved to do most. Why hadn't he listened to her? Why couldn't he have taken her advice and gone west with us when he knew what Mutti said was true? Maybe he just couldn't believe that his own people would do anything to him. They knew him as a hard-working man who never got into trouble. And then he made one mistake and had to die for it. I told myself I couldn't think about it anymore, or I knew I would never sleep again without dreaming about his death. I knew I had to be strong, like Mutti. I had to help her and be a support to her, not a burden. I wiped the tears from my face with the back of my hand and rose slowly. I stood there confused, staring into the darkness of the room. Mutti had gone. I needed to be near her. I had to touch her, to feel her presence. I really wanted to be on her lap with her arms around me. I found her in the kitchen.

Although Oma Grapentin stayed with us every day, she still returned to Paul's in the evening. She wanted to be there when Opa returned. She was sure he would just walk in the door one evening and kiss her on the cheek as he always had in days gone by. I didn't know why she thought he would come in the evening and not during the day. Mutti, Paul, and I knew that Opa would never greet Oma again.

We continued to live from hand to mouth, from meal to meal. On many days the food we ate, whatever it was, was all we had, and there was no more for the next day. Some days there was nothing to eat. It fell on Mutti to provide food for the four of us, and I helped where I could. My help was much too little. Mutti tried many ways to obtain food. Now it was the black market. Through some of her women friends, she made contacts with the Russians garrisoned in our area. She became the intermediary between Russian officers and farmers, who each had something the other wanted. The farmers had vodka and the Russians had sugar, cigarettes, leather, and cloth, things they had confiscated from German stores and homes. The vodka was made from potatoes or anything else that fermented, such as grains and fruit, and could be turned into alcohol. The Russians didn't care how the vodka tasted; what mattered was that it had a high alcohol content, because they wanted to get drunk.

Mutti's part of the black market transaction was a cut of the food, cigarettes, sugar, cloth, or whatever else was being traded for vodka. The best situation for her was when the Russians gave her fresh loaves of bread from their army bakery, because we could eat the bread right away without additional processing or trading. The worst situation occurred when Mutti received a sack of grain. Then she had to find someone to transport the grain to the miller, who kept half of the flour for the service he rendered. Then she or Oma would take the remaining flour to one of the two bakeries in town to have them bake bread. Of course, they took their cut, too. A sack of black market grain didn't realize much bread for us. It depended on how

A Winter Nightmare

greedy and dishonest the in-between processors were. Mutti was able to go on feeding us by trading on the black market. One disadvantage of this method was its unpredictability; it required that the farmers had vodka and that the Russians were accessible for trade. Neither was the case all the time.

I had just returned from school one day when I heard Mutti rush into the house. Instead of coming into our room as she usually did, she turned into the kitchen where Oma was washing dishes. Mutti put her arms around Oma's neck and her head on Oma's shoulder and bawled like a little girl. Oma saw me looking from the doorway and quickly shut the kitchen door. The door was too flimsy to keep sound from traveling into the hall. When Mutti stopped crying, I overheard her tell Oma that she had gone to the nearby Russian compound. A soldier wanted to trade something for vodka. Her contact took her to a barracks and the two of them went upstairs to the soldier's room. "I was uneasy about the situation from the start," Mutti said to Oma. "About going into a barracks, and especially into someone's room. I always try to stay within hearing of others and in public places. Several soldiers were in the room, and it seemed all right for me to go in. The soldier who wanted to make the deal started bargaining, and in the process of making the deal the others quietly drifted away. Once I realized I was alone with him I knew I was in trouble and tried to leave." Then she started to cry again. "He closed the door, threw me on his bed, and raped me. When he finished with me, he opened the door and the other soldiers reappeared and tried to make deals. I acted as if nothing had happened, but I only wanted to get out of there. I am never going to that compound again, Mother. Never."

I was ashamed that I had listened to her story. I still was not sure I fully understood what rape was. I only knew it was something men did to women against their will. The way Mutti spoke of it, I knew it must be awful and painful. After this incident, Mutti temporarily quit trading on the black market. When she resumed, she was much more careful about where she met with people. But we had to eat no matter what happened. There was food on the regular market, of course. The rations were small and availability was unpredictable. Obtaining food was as much a matter of having contacts as it was having a ration card. A year after the end of the war, food was scarcer than ever. The only things plentiful were the red banners strung across roads and buildings proclaiming the everlasting solidarity between

A Winter Nightmare

the German and the Russian peoples. These banners showed hammer and sickle emblems and the faces of Lenin, Marx, and Engels.

In April, Ingrid's seventh birthday passed quietly, just as my eleventh had in February. Since our situation had not improved and because it was early spring, I decided to try my hand at fishing, hoping that I could contribute toward the needs of our family. Rambling around the countryside with some friends, I had noticed ponds on one side of town, the result of peat digs many years ago. I saw a neighbor come home with several giant carp which he had caught in one of the holes. No one had fished that particular hole for years, and the carp had grown to immense size. He cleaned the carp in the backyard. No one expected him to share any of his fish. As he cleaned the fish, I asked him if he could loan me a hook. He laughed.

"You need more than one hook if you want to catch fish. You'll lose at least one a day, maybe more if you are unlucky." I don't know where he got his hooks, but he generously handed me several, each a different size, and explained to me how to use them. I needed a pole and fishing line. For the pole I cut a young tree sapling. Strong string had to serve as my line. I had just enough real fishing line for use as a lead for my hook. I obtained a float from the same man and used scrap lead from old batteries lying around in the burned-out refinery to fashion weights. A sunny day soon came, and I headed out to the ponds. Cattails and reeds grew near the ponds, and there I found insect larvae which I used to bait my hook. My improvised fishing gear with the heavy string and the clumsy knot near the hook didn't bother the fish. They bit over and over again. At first I had trouble setting the hook, but once I got the knack of it, I pulled in a good number. They weighed from a quarter pound to a pound. I could hardly wait to get home to show them to Oma. She was pleased with my catch and immediately set to cleaning the fish. That night we ate fresh fish for dinner. It was a real delicacy. Best of all, there was enough for all of us.

I continued my fishing with more or less success. On some days the fish would bite and on others I caught nothing, even though I was doing everything the same way. One day I encountered the really big fish, *the one that got away*. As I sat at the edge of the pond watching my float for signs of activity, all at once it just disappeared below the surface of the water and stayed down. I jumped up and yanked the line out of the water—hard. I was too forceful in my excitement, and yanked the hook right out of the fish's mouth. The fish came flying toward me and flopped into the shallows at my feet. I threw myself on top of the twisting fish and tried to grab it. Every time I had it in my hands the slimy fish slipped away. It finally flopped itself back into deep water, and all I had to show for my effort was a fish story and totally messy clothes.

I decided to try a larger lake nearly six kilometers from Strasburg. I left early one morning because I had heard that was when fish bit best. "Bite, fish," I said out loud, sitting on the bank of the lake. "I'm here. Bite." I watched the early morning mists rise from the water. I took a deep breath, wishing the moment wouldn't pass. I caught a number of smaller fish that day. I went home with over thirty assorted fish weighing half a pound or less. Their size wasn't a problem for Oma. "If they are too small to fry, then I cook them," Oma said, and she proceeded to make a fish soup. I hadn't thought she had it in her to fix something other than potatoes and white gravy. Oma added onions and some peppercorns for flavoring. It was a delicious soup, I thought.

In addition to my fishing, I returned to the *Schlammberg* to see what I could plant for the coming season. I took a spade, turned the soil and raked it properly the way Opa had taught me, and then put in lettuce and carrots from seeds we were able to buy in a store. Later I planted potatoes. I took a potato and cut it into sections, making sure that an eye was in each section. Then I put the sections into small holes and covered them with dirt. Once green shoots started to sprout, I heaped dirt around the plants. I knew that by August or September we would have a crop of new potatoes. The lettuce and carrots didn't turn out so well. Rabbits developed a taste for the succulent young plants, so they didn't get a chance to develop. I tried to catch the rabbits with homemade snares, but they were smarter than I.

On the *Schlammberg* I felt the presence of my grandfather Grapentin. Here I could think of him without feeling pain. When I worked the soil, I sometimes thought I could hear him speak to me, giving his approval at what I was doing. I would stop working and look around, but there was nothing—only the wind, the clouds, and the crows.

A Winter Nightmare

Chapter 14

SUMMER 1946

Tere still were not many men around. Most had been killed or were prisoners of war. The men in Strasburg were, for the most part, either old, very young, crippled by war wounds, or active Communists. In the burned-out sections of Strasburg, groups of women could be seen with hammers in their hands and babushkas around their heads pulling bricks out of ruins and cleaning and stacking them in neat piles. They were working to help feed their children, and it was hard work. On my way home from school, I noticed that one of the house ruins was being rebuilt with such reclaimed bricks. I watched the house being put back together day after day as I went to and from school. It turned out to be a bakery, the first building to go up in Strasburg after the war. They finished the building on the inside; the outside, however, did not receive the customary coat of plaster and continued to look unfinished and ugly. Once the bakery opened for business, bread was never displayed on its shelves. It was always brought out from a back room after the store formalities had been settled. That way it was easy for them to say, "Sorry, we are out of bread. Try again tomorrow." They were always out of bread when I went there.

On a cloudy, damp, and still-cold Saturday in early May, our lives changed again. About nine o'clock in the morning, several battered Russian trucks drove into our street and stopped in front of two makeshift air raid shelters. One shelter was located directly across the street from our house.

From my Berlin experience, I knew that shelters such as these could never have stopped a direct bomb hit; rather they were intended to provide shelter from falling debris and deadly steel shards produced by exploding bombs. The shelters consisted of two steel boilers from the sugar refinery which had been buried in the ground and had entrances on either end shored up by railroad ties. The tops of the shelters were also covered with wooden railroad ties and a layer of dirt.

Although the Russian soldiers didn't speak German, they quickly got their message across to us. We were to evacuate our houses at once. At once meant right now. "*Dowoi, dowoi, dowoi, raus, raus . . . ,*" they shouted, gesturing with their hands to emphasize their intent. We assembled in the street, watching the soldiers unload boxes of explosives and carry them into the shelters. Then they attached detonators to the explosives and ran detonation cord out to one of their trucks. They attached the cord to a box with a plunger and then stood around for a while, smoking and talking. All of us watched the goings-on in disbelief. It finally dawned on everyone that this wasn't an exercise, that they actually intended to blow up the shelters. I moved away from the shelters along with the crowd. Several women protested loudly to the soldiers, to no avail. The soldiers tried to chase the women away. When they refused to move, the soldiers ignored them. Without further warning, one of them walked over to the box to which the detonation cords were attached, a hand-rolled *papyrossi* dangling from the corner of his mouth, and pushed the plunger.

It was a horrendous blast. Debris flew high into the air and shattered nearby houses. The soldiers had placed the explosives in the center of each shelter. They had not sealed the entrances. As a result, much of the blast effect came straight out of the entrances, blasting debris into our houses like shot from a gun. Many windows and doors were completely blown out. The midsections of the shelters, directly below the explosives, also blew, throwing old railroad ties up into the air and out into the street. Surprisingly, no one was injured. The Russian soldiers jumped into their trucks and left, never to return. The stench of explosives lingered in the air for the rest of the day. People removed debris and railroad ties from their front yards and from the street and began to repair the damage to their houses.

Mutti was away during the explosions. She had gone to visit a girlfriend who was the town's sole telephone operator. She liked visiting her at work and listening in on what she described as often hilariously funny telephone conversations. Anyone in Strasburg who had a telephone was either a Communist official or somehow connected to those in power, such as the police. The Russians had their own telephone exchange. Sometimes Mutti's girlfriend learned whom the police were going to arrest next and when, but she couldn't do anything about the information she had without endangering herself. Another time she learned that one man's wife was sleeping with the police thinking she was saving her husband, who, she had been told, was on the list, but he wasn't. The police had just made that one up and hinted to the woman that if she was nice to them they would postpone or even overlook his arrest. They thought it was funny and laughed loudly when they spoke of it on the phone. Mutti's girlfriend had a crippled left hand. She was one of the young BDM girls who had tried suicide at war's end by having someone cut her wrist, but the person had cut only her tendons.

When Mutti returned home, about noon, she was aghast to see what had happened in her absence. It was time for us to move on again. Our room in its present condition was no longer habitable. It was not only the glass in the windows that was broken but also the frames. Debris from the blast was scattered over our room. Mutti was faced with a situation in which she had to find a place for us to live even more quickly than when Paul had evicted us. "There is one hotel in Strasburg," Mutti said, thinking out loud rather than speaking to me. She meant the Bahnhof Hotel. "That's the only place in town where we might find a room quickly, Wolfgang. If it is full, then I don't know where we could go. We may have to stay here overnight. At least we have a roof over our heads, and we won't get rained on." Mutti laughed, looking at me. I laughed back at her. There was nothing funny about our situation, but we had been in worse predicaments before and come out all right. Our room stank of cordite.

"Some time ago," Mutti continued, "I was in the hotel and I looked around inside. There were several unoccupied guest rooms, nicely furnished. There weren't any *Flüchtlinge* living in the rooms, to my surprise. You stay here and watch Ingrid, I'll go and see what I can find for us." Mutti did not go directly to the hotel, as it turned out. She thought of a better plan on the way. Since it was Saturday, she was able to find a Russian officer with whom she had traded more than once. Mutti had acquired a fair fluency in Russian, and the officer agreed to accompany her in her quest for a place to live. She just wanted the officer along to give her words authority. Such a plan had worked once before when her friend Llydia impersonated a Russian woman in Mecklenburg. Why shouldn't it work this time? This time she had a real Russian with her.

"The Russian major never said a word to the dour hotel proprietor while I negotiated with him," Mutti explained to Oma after her return. "I told him I was the officer's girlfriend and the major wanted us put up in the hotel until we found something better. The Russian just followed me around as we went through the hotel looking at empty rooms. I persuaded the proprietor to let us have one room facing out to the street and a smaller room right across the hall facing the backyard. Really nice rooms"—Mutti grinned from ear to ear—"better than what we now have." We were packed and ready to go. We said *auf Wiedersehen* to our distressed landlady, who was still in shock, as much from the arbitrary nature of the events of that morning as from the actual damage sustained by her house.

Across the street from the hotel was the *Sportplatz*, with a soccer field and a burned-out ruin of what once had been the town's sport center and *Jugendheim*, youth center. The hotel's worn wooden stairs led from the foyer to the guest rooms on the second floor. The larger of the two rooms was really nice, I thought. Its two windows overlooking the *Sportplatz* were hung with floor-length green velvet drapes and sheer lace curtains. The room was generously furnished with a four-poster bed, a settee, a coffee table, and an overstuffed chair with a high back and large ears. The pine floor was covered with a fine-looking Persian rug. The walls were papered and hung with pretty hunting prints. Across the hall, the smaller room had only one little window, which looked out on the backyard. That room was much simpler in its appointments; it contained a single bed, a table with four chairs, and a simple dresser with a water pitcher and porcelain basin on top—no carpet, wallpaper, or pictures. A single lightbulb hung from the ceiling of the room. A built-in wall closet at the end of the hallway between our two rooms was also at our disposal. It had served as a linen closet when the hotel really was a hotel. We would cook with the other hotel "guests" in the downstairs restaurant kitchen, and would use hotel kitchen utensils and dishes. Mutti had solved our housing problem as quickly as it had arisen.

On my way to or from the *Schlammberg* to tend our vegetables, I frequently took time to explore the burned-out sugar refinery. The refinery had several huge molasses storage tanks with inspection doors two feet off the ground. The doors stood open, and I could see the molasses nearly reaching up to them. It was contaminated by human waste. The inside of the refinery buildings was a jumble of heavy machinery and pipes running everywhere—steam pipes wrapped in thick asbestos blankets, water pipes, waste pipes, molasses pipes. The upper floors had collapsed onto the first floor's heavy machinery when the beams were weakened by fire. I sawed off sections of charcoaled beams and took them home to provide fuel for cooking. The beams made excellent firewood and gave off a steady, nearly smokeless heat.

A railroad spur ran from the train station into various places in the vast refinery area. One spur ran past the molasses tanks out to the *Schlammberg*, where they used to deliver the beets and wash them. Over the years the residual dirt from the beets had accumulated to form the *Schlammberg*. For weeks I had eyed some of the railroad cars standing on that spur, particularly one smaller flatbed car. I thought I could move it. On a sunny day I set to work, and, with persistence and a Herculean effort, I got the rusted brakes to release, and the flatbed car began moving downhill, gaining speed as it went. I jumped on the car and rode it all the way into the middle of the refinery compound, standing tall and laughing loudly, my arms spread out and the wind tousling my hair. It was a thrilling ride. For a brief moment while I was standing on that railroad car, I felt as if I had been freed from all my troubles and I was flying into another life. Then the car came to a halt, ever so slowly, and as its momentum died so did my dream.

Mutti resumed her black market trading. One day she came home with a section of wild boar shot by Russian officers on a hunt in a nearby forest. The boar meat was a welcome change from our monotonous diet of potatoes, sour bread, and ersatz coffee. Oma always brewed ersatz coffee, and I had grown to dislike it, but there was nothing else safe to drink. I dreamed of drinking lemonade. Our water was not safe to drink unless it was first boiled. I drank boiled water only when I was really thirsty, remembering the deaths and disease caused by contaminated water when we were interned in Sievershagen by the Americans. Ersatz coffee, made from roasted barley and in apparent plentiful supply, was bitter, but it was safe to drink. When we had sugar, Oma added lots to my cup to kill the taste. We had sugar only infrequently. I kept dreaming of lemonade.

The Russian officer who had helped Mutti get our rooms in the Bahnhof Hotel now asked for a favor in return. He wanted to have a party for three of his friends. What he needed was privacy, he told Mutti. She was invited to join them if she cared to. My mother declined, but thought having the party wasn't a bad idea. The hotel proprietor had begun to ask uncomfortable questions about why her Russian friend never came to visit. The Russian officers came one afternoon loaded down with bread, butter, onions, and several bottles of vodka. We didn't see much of them. They laughed more and more loudly as the afternoon progressed into evening. By the time I went to sleep, one was playing a harmonica, and the others were dancing and singing. I was familiar with the routine. I just hoped they wouldn't do anything to my mother. I went to bed under the table with Ingrid at my side. The following morning, having totally forgotten about the party next door, I opened the door. The four Russian officers were lying about the room in grotesque poses, totally drunk, sleeping off the vodka. They awoke sometime that afternoon and left quietly.

We hadn't eaten butter or lard, any fats for that matter, for a long time, except for some tasteless margarine Mutti obtained on our ration cards. Mutti decided to visit the farmer in Sievershagen, the man who had taken our horses and proposed marriage to her. She thought maybe there she would be able to get some bacon or lard. The farm had lots of animals when we left a year earlier. Mutti didn't know what she would find once she got there but thought it was worth a try. We had nothing to lose. She took the train to Grevesmühlen, returning ten days later. She was loaded down with a rucksack full of smoked sausages, smoked ham, salami, and a large chunk of suet. We rendered the suet and used it as spread on our sour bread; with added salt, it tasted fine. Mutti said she couldn't go back. The farm had been taken over by the Communists and been collectivized, another new term for me which I didn't really understand. The farmer who once owned the place still managed it, but now he was just one of the workers and had no more rights than anyone else. Our horses were still there, but it was too late to get them back, even if we wanted to. They belonged to the collective now, and the collective belonged to the people. There was that strange word again.

"Who are 'the people'?" I asked Mutti.

"Nobody," she said with a sarcastic smile crossing her face. "The state is the people. The Communist Party is the state, you already know that, Wolfgang."

In July we were surprised by a most unexpected but welcome visitor, Herr Schmitt, the man we had stayed with in Berlin for several weeks early in 1945. He appeared one afternoon and greeted us with a happy smile, as if he had found long-lost relatives or friends. He was considerably thinner than I remembered him, but he had not lost his sense of humor. We had potatoes for dinner that evening with salt herring. Herr Schmitt loved the potatoes, and even got me to look away through a trick of his while he licked his plate. I thought a grown man licking his plate was funny. Mutti found an empty room in our hotel where he could spend the night. He suggested I come and stay a week with him in Berlin.

"Of course, Wolfgang will have to bring a rucksack of potatoes along for food; food in Berlin is really scarce," he said. I was delighted to have the opportunity to get away from Strasburg and to accompany my dear friend to Berlin. We had enough early potatoes from the *Schlammberg* to fill a rucksack. Herr Schmitt and I left the next day. Berlin was a shock to me. When I had been there in March 1945 there was destruction from the bombing, but much of the city was still intact. Now, nearly all I saw was rubble—row after row of burned-out houses. Herr Schmitt no longer lived in his fine apartment. It, too, had been destroyed. He and Frau Schmitt now lived in a makeshift basement apartment. Frau Schmitt was happy to see me. Most of all she was happy to see my rucksack bulging with potatoes. That was why Herr Schmitt had come to Strasburg. He was no longer quite as jovial as before, and Frau Schmitt didn't smile much at all. He liked having me around, though, and, just as we had done before, he walked with me through the Berlin that once was. He didn't say much on our walks anymore. I thought about it for a long time, and, on one of those walks through war-shattered Berlin, I finally asked the question that had been on my mind. "Have you heard from your son, Lieutenant Schmitt?"

Herr Schmitt put his hand around my shoulder as we walked. Finally, he said softly, in a tremulous voice, "I don't know what happened to Hans, my dear boy." After a long pause, he added, "I think he died fighting for his country." I took Herr Schmitt's hand in mine and held it as we continued our walk. I hoped it would make him feel better. By the time I left Berlin, we both were laughing again. It was the way we affected each other. With me around, Herr Schmitt seemed to be able to recover some of himself, some of what he had been before the war changed us all. When I said *auf Wiedersehen* to the Schmitts after five days and told them I really had to get home again to help my mother, they had tears in their eyes. The destruction in Berlin was so total that I was glad to get back to Strasburg. I had never thought I would ever say that.

My uncle Ernst, Mutti's younger brother, returned to Strasburg in July

Summer 1946

from an English prisoner-of-war camp. The English had released him in June. Ernst took a train to the border between the English zone of occupation and the Russian zone, and then he walked all the way to Strasburg, nearly two hundred kilometers. Oma was ecstatic. The arrival of Ernst, her youngest child, raised Oma's spirits. I was sure she thought maybe now that Ernst had returned, Opa, too, would be coming home soon. Uncle Ernst promptly found his former girlfriend in a nearby village, where she worked on a collective farm. He married her and joined the farming commune. I went to visit with him once in August. I got up really early that morning and walked through town, heading west on the Woldegker Chaussee, the same road we had traveled in April 1945 to escape the approaching Russian armies. I arrived at Ernst's village in a couple of hours, just in time to jump on a wagon with him and go out to the fields. Only one horse pulled the wagon. I knew a farmer always took two horses to do plowing, if he had two. I said nothing to Ernst. When we got to his field, he unloaded the one-bladed plow from the wagon and reharnessed the horse to the plow. As he went off plowing a field that had lain fallow since the end of the war, I went walking. It was a beautiful day, and for a time I just soaked up the warming rays of the sun.

I could see the Woldegker Chaussee ahead of me, old trees lining its ancient cobblestones. Someone had planted them before the century began, I thought. How different things must have been then. No airplanes, no tanks, no bombed cities. Right here nothing had changed much since those days. Looking at Ernst plowing the field, walking behind his horse, making sure that his furrows were straight, I saw a scene out of my fairy tale books, a scene hundreds of years old. I knew Ernst worked just as hard as they had two hundred years ago. Then they were serfs, owned by their masters. In 1946, the land Ernst was plowing still didn't belong to him. All he had was a roof over his head, and that didn't belong to him, either. It seemed to me that maybe nothing had changed in two hundred years. I knew there must be a better way. I also knew that better way would never arrive under the Communists, or as the result of people working on a collective farm.

Looking west, I noticed three burned-out Wehrmacht trucks up the hill and near the edge of the forest. I ran over to inspect them. Fighting had taken place there after we had passed that night in April 1945; I noticed bullet holes in the open doors of the trucks. One had been a communications truck—the radio equipment was a burned jumble of dangling wires.

Near the forest was an 88 mm antitank gun, its barrel pointing threateningly east. Around the gun lay shells, randomly thrown about. I walked across the untended field to the gun. The gun had many white and some yellow rings painted around its barrel, with dates inscribed on the rings. Each ring must have been for a tank destroyed; maybe the yellow rings signified ten tanks, or even airplanes.

Playfully I reconstructed a tank battle in my mind and imagined myself loading rounds into the gun, my crew aiming, firing, and destroying tanks. As I imagined the battle scene, I picked up one of the rounds with multicolored bands painted around its tip, and tried to load it into the gun's breach. It was too high off the ground. I couldn't quite reach. I heard someone yelling from the road. Engrossed in my play, I paid no attention. I was too involved in my imaginary battle and continued to try to get the shell into the breach of the gun. I was suddenly shocked out of my dream world when a man came rushing up, out of breath. He looked like a recently released prisoner of war, like Ernst had looked when he returned in his worn army uniform with no belt around the jacket, without insignia of rank or unit emblems. The man dropped the pack he was carrying and held out his hands toward me, saying, "Please, hand me that shell very carefully. Do not drop it on the ground or it may explode and kill us both."

I stood there, feeling foolish, no longer in the middle of my imaginary tank battle. I didn't know what to do, so I held on to the artillery shell, which only a moment ago had been just a plaything to me. Now it appeared evil and life threatening. The former soldier came toward me slowly, lifted the shell from my arms, and gently placed it on the ground. He didn't seem angry, only relieved. He retrieved his pack, telling me, "Don't play here anymore. This old ammunition is dangerous. It has lain here in rain, snow, ice, and sun for a year and could explode at the slightest touch. The round you were holding is a phosphorous round. It is especially dangerous. The smallest amount of that stuff on your body will burn right through you. Don't touch any of this ammunition again, please."

The man walked off toward the road to continue on his journey with two others who looked just like him, dressed in the same old worn uniforms. When I looked at the gun again, it no longer brought visions of heroic battle, but seemed like what it was, an abandoned relic of war, still deadly. I was glad when I got home that evening to the security of my simple bed under the table.

Summer 1946

In the late summer days of August, the sun was especially warm and comforting, and life assumed an almost pleasant quality. People seemed nicer toward one another, and led what appeared to be an almost normal existence. It wasn't. We still didn't have enough food, and our worn clothes would not be adequate for the coming winter. I tried hard not to think of those things. When standing in a food line one day, I heard three old women talking excitedly. They had heard from "people who knew" that Strasburg would soon go to the Americans. The occupation zones had been realigned, and, as a result, the Russians would be pulling out and the Americans would take over. For an instant I felt a flash of incredible happiness.

"The Americans will be here not later than January or February of next year," one old woman said, "and then everything will change for the better. In the American zone the stores are full of food, and no one goes hungry. People are given winter clothes to wear." And then she whispered, still loudly enough for me to hear, "There is no secret police, and people are not arrested and taken away." She paused for a moment. Then she looked around to make sure no one else had been listening and said with finality, "Everything is different there than it is here." After my initial euphoria I decided the old women had to be wrong. I didn't know where she got her information, but I was sure it was wishful thinking. I wished for the Americans, too, but I knew it couldn't happen. Days later, Oma told me the same rumor, which she claimed was true. "If everybody is talking about it," she said, "it must be so."

"No, Oma," I said to her, "that will never happen." She was disappointed by my response, and saddened because I wouldn't share her dream.

"Maybe this time you are wrong, Wolfgang," she said, her disappointment showing in her face. "Let's hope you are wrong, and I and the other people are right." I knew I was right. Summer was nearly over.

I befriended a boy in the house next door to our hotel. His family lived comfortably in comparison to us, and they always seemed to have food. The boy bred rabbits and kept pigeons. When several of his rabbits had little ones, I asked him for one or two, and he agreed to let me have as many as I wanted. I built several rabbit hutches in back of our hotel and stacked them on stilts, because I had heard that otherwise a fox might get to the rabbits. It was easy to build the hutches. All I needed was old boards, nails, and chicken wire. Boards and nails were plentiful in the burned-out refinery, and the chicken wire came from my new friend next door. He gave me four young rabbits and a guinea pig to rotate among the hutches. "He will keep them healthy," he said. Succulent greens for the rabbits grew abundantly near the refinery. I liked to watch them eat the food I brought them. In winter, I thought, I would feed them carrots and rutabagas, as my friend did. I hadn't yet figured out who was going to kill the rabbits once we decided to eat them. The eating part was equally abstract to me, since I didn't think that I would like to eat my own rabbits. But we had rabbits, and I was caring for them, which was fun. I was also thinking of the future for my family, as my grandfather would have wanted me to do.

In late August school started again. I was in the sixth grade. In reality I hadn't had any useful schooling since January 1945. Maybe things would change. In October I realized I wasn't learning anything new. Many of my teachers were there only because they were devout Communists, not because they had studied to be teachers. I grew rebellious. My attitude toward school became hostile and affected my ability to learn even in the classes where the teachers were qualified and did their best to teach us something. One new subject that was mandatory was the Russian language. I refused to learn Russian, the language of our occupiers, of the Communists. All I accomplished by this was to relegate myself to the ranks of the incompetent students, and there were many of those. As long as I didn't cause trouble and sat quietly at my desk, the teacher didn't seem to care much whether I chose to learn Russian or not. I was anything but passive, and I tried to influence other students to join me in my boycott of Russian.

During our long forty-five-minute lunch breaks, some of us always went into the schoolyard and played soccer using an old tennis ball. At times a rock had to do. The class after the long break was Russian. I was certain the Russian teacher and the principal had discussed my attitude. For some reason they chose to do nothing, waiting for me to do something openly disruptive. They didn't have to wait long. One day, when the five-minute warning bell rang for us to return to class, I proposed to my classmates that we skip our Russian class and play soccer instead. "Who needs Russian?" I argued. "None of us will ever speak Russian. And besides, it is boring and we are having fun playing soccer." Five others joined me, and we stayed in the yard playing soccer instead of going to class. The final warning bell rang one minute before the start of classes. The others hesitated briefly. I hollered, "Let's play," and their inertia was broken. The five boys stayed. We continued to play yard soccer.

Summer 1946

I knew something my playmates didn't, that this was not a spontaneous cutting of a Russian class. It was my own, premeditated plan to disrupt the class, and only the timing for its execution had I left open. About twenty minutes after the start of classes, a school employee came and told us to stop playing and report to the office of the *Herr Rektor*. I began to feel guilty, not because we had not gone to Russian class, but because I had gotten the others into trouble. It was my fight, not theirs, yet I had made them part of it. I hadn't thought out the consequences of my action. I didn't know what the *Herr Rektor* would do to us. Whatever it was, the others were going to suffer because of me.

I felt bad as we walked into the office. The *Herr Rektor* was a man I had never met before. He wore a white laboratory coat of the kind I had seen on doctors and nurses. He looked about fifty, older than most of our teachers. He was short, stockily built, and bald, with the look of an angry bulldog. The *Herr Rektor* glowered as we entered the room. Then he planted himself directly in front of us, feet apart, hands on his hips, and screamed at the top of his lungs. While he was berating us, he looked me straight in the eyes. I stared back at him defiantly. He screamed about the greatness of Communism, about how he had suffered under Hitler and had escaped the Nazis, and about how he had found asylum amongst his Russian brothers; now he was back to set things right. Part of setting things right was that we Germans would learn the language of our brothers. Then he said in a lowered voice (for a second I thought maybe he was tiring), "No one is going to defy me and go without punishment." I was wrong. He wasn't tiring. He was just getting started.

"Line up. One behind the other," he screamed with the vigor of the tyrant that he was. I stepped forward to stand at the front of the line, feeling responsible for what was happening. I should be the first to receive whatever punishment he was going to mete out. He grabbed me by the shoulders and unceremoniously marched me to the rear of the lineup. "Stay there," he ordered. Then, with his left hand, he grabbed the first student in the lineup by the front of his shirt, and with his right he slapped the boy's face. Back and forth—slap, slap, slap. When slapping did not elicit the desired response, the *Herr Rektor* punched my friend in the face and in the stomach until he bled from nose and mouth. When the Herr Rektor finished with the first student, he roughly shoved him toward the door. "Return to your class," he shouted, panting from exertion.

Summer 1946

The *Herr Rektor* proceeded to beat the other four boys in the same manner, only stopping when they were bleeding and crying, or when he had to
catch his breath. I was the last and prepared myself to receive an especially
severe beating. I promised myself not to cry, no matter what he did. But
instead of grabbing me by my shirt and hitting me, he rubbed his hands
together as he stood in front of me and stared into my eyes. His hands were
bloody and showed signs of cuts where he had hit my friends in the teeth.
Suddenly, he leaned against his desk and put one hand over his heart, as if
he were in pain. After what seemed an eternity, he turned toward me and
screamed, *"Raus!"* I left his office without further prompting.

Instead of returning to my Russian class, I hid in a waste barrel just outside the classroom. I couldn't bear to go into the room without a mark on
me. It would look as if I had sold out my classmates. When the bell rang, I
stayed in the barrel until the classroom was empty and then entered the
room to retrieve my books and my pouch. From that time on, we played no
more soccer during break, all of us were punctual to our classes, and we
studied our Russian lessons diligently. The brutal experience was demonstration enough for me that a new regime was in power and that it would react
quickly and cruelly, regardless of the level at which it was challenged. The
lesson was not lost on anyone who was involved or who knew about the
incident—which was everybody, students and teachers alike. I continued to
feel guilty about my role in the episode, and I finally decided that the *Herr
Rektor* had outsmarted me. I believed it was his plan all along not to beat
me as he did the others, because he knew I was the leader of this rebellion
to his authority. He wanted me to watch as he brutalized my friends. He
wanted to make me look bad. He succeeded. I wasn't so sure he didn't have
other, more sinister, things in mind for me in the future.

Autumn days turned the leaves to gold; soon the sunshine faded, and rain
and overcast skies were the rule again rather than the exception. The leaves
remaining on the trees shriveled and turned black before they finally fell to
the ground. The mood of the townspeople turned bleak and somber again,
as we stared another threatening winter in the face. After the brutal beating
episode in school, I never quite recovered my spirit. It depressed me to think
I had absolutely no rights whatsoever as a human being. Anyone in authority could do to me whatever they wanted. If they wanted to take my grandfather and kill him, they could do that. If they wanted to imprison and abuse
some hungry kids whose only offense was to steal raw sugar to moderate their

hunger, then they could do it. If they wanted to beat some schoolchildren who skipped class to play soccer, they could do that, too. If they wanted to rape my mother and blow up my house, or nearly so, they could do it. They could do anything. I could do nothing but stoically accept my fate. And if I didn't? I knew the consequences.

I was not a stoic, and I didn't think I could take this slave-like existence without a fight too much longer. I felt certain there was no life for me in Strasburg. We had to leave soon. I began to hate them, whoever they were, those who inflicted all this pain on their own people. I hated the Germans who did this to us, not the Russians. I hated the prison I lived in. And I was afraid of what they would eventually do to me when they found out that I could not submit to them. I knew someday I was going to suffer a fate similar to my grandfather Grapentin's, because I could not be like them.

I had no warm clothes to wear for the coming winter, and it was getting colder by the day. Everything I owned was either full of holes or had been outgrown. Oma mended my socks so many times I could hardly see a sock any more, just one patch sewn next to or over another. My Hitler Youth pants, my only pair of long pants, were worn out. My short pants were getting too tight. I had no stockings to cover my legs. I spoke to Mutti about my lack of clothes, and she said she knew, but she could find nothing for me that fit other than the pair of shoes with the plastic tops and the wooden soles.

"I have a section of camouflage tent," I said to her, "which I have hidden since May of 1945. Why can't you have someone tailor me a pair of pants and a jacket from it? I don't care what it looks like." I showed her the tent section I had hidden for so long, and which the German police had not found when they had searched our room in November 1945. Two weeks later Mutti and I went to a friend of hers who was a seamstress. The seamstress measured me and then announced she had enough material for a jacket and a pair of long pants.

"I want pants which blouse at the bottom so I can tie them off at the ankles and stay warm," I told the seamstress. "And I want a jacket that looks like what the American soldiers wore. Short. Just down to my waist, with buttons down the front."

"I can do that, too," the seamstress said with a smile. I left in great anticipation of what her creation would look like. Two weeks later Mutti came home with my new camouflage suit. Once I saw what the seamstress had sewn for me, I was pleased and excited. At first people stared at me when they saw me on the street, but eventually everybody got used to seeing me in my strange-looking suit. The pants chafed the insides of my thighs for a while until I got toughened up. For a belt I still used the same old leather tent straps I had been using since the American soldier had confiscated my German army belt as a souvenir. My new clothes were waterproof, and they kept out the wind well. They were not warm.

We still had no word as to where my father was or what had happened to Oma and Opa Samuel. Mutti had written repeatedly and sent her letters to old addresses, hoping maybe one letter would find its intended addressee. Her letters vanished into a void. Then, one dreary day in November 1946 a letter arrived from my father. He had addressed his letter to Oma's old address in Strasburg, to the house which burned. The letter had taken several weeks to reach us, and, surprisingly enough, it had not been opened. Mutti read the letter, and only after much prompting did she share its contents with me. He wrote, "No matter what happens, sometime in November or December I will come to Strasburg to look for you and take you back to the English zone. I am living near Fassberg in the Lüneburg Heath." For once I was speechless. Just when I was seeing nothing but continued gloom in our future, my father had popped up unexpectedly and promised to take us to the West. I had been totally unsuccessful in my efforts to persuade Mutti to consider escaping to the West; she didn't even listen to me anymore when I brought up the subject. Mutti was as surprised by the arrival of the unexpected letter as I was. I didn't think she was looking forward to meeting my father. I wasn't sure if he could even persuade her to escape to the West. I worried about my father, too. I had heard from friends that former officers who returned from American and English prisoner-of-war camps were picked up by the German police. The rumor was that they were sent to prison camps in Russia. I promised myself I wouldn't say anything to my friends if my father came. I didn't want anything to happen to him.

As I watched Mutti reread Dad's letter for the third or fourth time, I realized that I actually didn't know my father well. I had been born in 1935 and it was now 1946, almost 1947. I was nearly twelve years old. I could only vaguely remember back to 1939 when I was four and my father still lived with Mutti and me in Sagan. I remembered most vividly the birth of my sister, Ingrid, in April of that year. My clearest memory of my father was of a day later in that summer when he brought his secretary home for dinner.

Summer 1946

That's the day I discovered him on top of her on the couch in my room. I did not understand what happened that day. I knew he had committed a terrible wrong, and Mutti said she would never forgive him for what he had done. Soon after that awful day, a war started between Germany and many other countries and my father was mostly gone. Through the war years I saw him only briefly, when he returned on military leave from France or Holland, where he was stationed at German airfields as an armaments officer for Dornier bombers. When he was home on military leave, there was always friction between him and Mutti. The talk between them nearly always involved other women. The secretary who had come to dinner at our home in 1939 frequently came up in conversation, and one day I overheard that the woman had a baby girl.

One day in the summer of 1944, when Mutti and I had been walking into Sagan to go shopping, she had said to me out of the blue, "I am going to divorce your father as soon as the war is over." I didn't really know what divorce meant, but I assumed that Mutti and Dad would no longer be together. Then who would I live with? Who would be my family? She really scared me. When I visited my grandparents Samuel in Schlawe for my annual summer and fall visits, I learned more about my father's upbringing. He was their only living child, and Oma had doted on him, Opa Samuel said. My father went to the *Gymnasium* in Schlawe, and after he graduated he wanted to emigrate to the United States. He was born in Gnesen, which in 1919 had become part of Poland. Therefore, my father was classified as Polish by United States immigration officials. "The Polish immigration quotas were small," said Opa Samuel, "but your father found a distant uncle in Detroit who had emigrated years before the war. He was willing to sponsor Willi to the United States and even had a job lined up for him in an automobile factory."

The same week my father received a visa granting him entry to the United States, he also received an acceptance into the one-hundred-thousand-man German army. Oma Samuel easily persuaded my father to stay. Oma convinced him he would have a prestigious and secure career in the German army. So, my father joined the cavalry, the same unit my grandfather had once served in. In 1933 he volunteered for the new Luftwaffe. He met Mutti in the spring of 1933 while he was still in the cavalry, and they married in 1935, shortly after I was born. It seemed that they were happy in those early years from what I could remember. In early 1940, after his affair with his secretary, he volunteered for paratroop duty to get away from the mess he had made at home. He was assigned to a parachute regiment for the invasion of England, which luckily never came. Then he was assigned to the 7th Parachute Division, and, only days before they jumped into Crete, he was reassigned because the Luftwaffe was short on armaments officers, which was his primary occupation. I knew little about my father, and much of what I knew was colored by the unhappy affair with his secretary and the constant quarrels between him and my mother.

Whatever had happened was in the past. I fervently hoped that he would come in November or December to take us to the West as he promised in his letter. A low level of excitement began to build in me in anticipation of his arrival. For once I did not share Mutti's misgivings. I hoped that whatever had happened between them would resolve itself and that Mutti wouldn't dig in her heels and decide not to go. I didn't want to have to choose between him and her. I wouldn't know what I was choosing, my father or the West. Please, Father, I prayed every night lying in my bed under the table, please come and get us. Don't forget about us.

November came to a wet and blustery end, and my father had not appeared. I didn't think anyone except me remembered that he had promised to come and get us. Through every dreary day, as I trudged off to a school whose only aim seemed to be to make a good Communist out of me, I thought of my father's promise. Throughout the school days I remained quiet, for fear that any questions would give me away—that I was not and never would be a Communist. If they found me out, then they would want to take revenge on me. They could just pick me up and send me somewhere, I thought, and Mutti would never know what had happened to me. I had to just go to school and act like everyone else.

I waited for my father to arrive and take us to the West. To come and save us. To save me.

Summer 1946

Chapter 15

ESCAPE TO THE WEST

I returned home from school on an early December day to find my father sitting in the easy chair with the big "ears." I was totally surprised to see him. Speechless might be a better way to describe my astonishment. Although I had tried to believe that he would come to get us because he had said so in his letter and I had prayed for his arrival every night before I went to sleep, deep down I felt it would never happen, that it would be one of my many dreams which would never come to pass. I approached him slowly and said, "Dad, you came." I didn't know what else to say. It had been such a long time since I had seen him last, over two years, and so much had happened. I didn't quite know how to act toward him. We were strangers.

His response was an easy, carefree smile. He took me in his arms, hugged me, and held me close. He said, "Dear Wolfgang." He didn't need to say more. I understood. I couldn't recall, though, if he had ever hugged me before. I didn't think so. I stepped back from his chair and remained standing there, gaping at him, mesmerized by his presence. I marveled at how he looked, so relaxed, with an openness in his manner such as I didn't see around town often. He spoke like a man who was not afraid, like a man who was not from Strasburg, where everyone was afraid. He looked like a free man, I decided, that's the look he had about him. I knew I wasn't free. I was afraid of so many things, not the least of which was that one day I was going to disappear like my grandfather Grapentin and die in some dark cell, with nobody ever knowing what had happened to me. I wondered what I looked like to my father, or what Ingrid or Mutti looked like to him. Could he see our fears in our eyes? Could he see my nightmares?

His face was thin and his body lean. When I had last seen him in Sagan in 1944, I thought he had a worried, restless look in his eyes, which never left him the whole time he was there. He didn't look worried now. He was calm and his eyes were steady. I had interrupted a conversation between him and Mutti when I came into the room. He had been speaking about his time as a prisoner of war. I sat down on the floor next to Ingrid, facing him, hoping he would continue with his story. He didn't.

"What's for dinner?" he asked. Boring. Dinner was never exciting. We ate what we ate, whatever it was. We didn't have the luxury of choices for dinner. He didn't know that. How could he?

"Königsberger Klopse," Mutti replied.

"Königsberger Klopse is one of my favorite dishes, as you may remember, dear Hedy." I remembered my father was always polite when it came to complimenting Mutti on her cooking. That hadn't changed. Then he asked her the question I had asked myself many times before. Why he asked it at this time, so soon after his arrival, I don't know.

"Why didn't you come to Fassberg when I asked you to, Hedy?" I could see Mutti stiffen. "I wrote you three letters and you only answered one, and then you didn't even respond to my urgent request for you and the children to join me immediately. I knew that everything was coming to an end and that Fassberg was safe. I wrote you at some risk to myself, you must have known that." He paused, looking at her intently. "Outgoing letters were being censored, and if I had been caught saying the wrong thing it would have been my head. I felt I had to risk it for my family." I was certain that my father had not made a wise decision to raise this topic with my mother. "One reason Fassberg was safe was because it would be occupied by the English or the Americans. We knew that. Not by the Russians, that's what was important. You know better than I how the Russians treat women." He said "Russians" through his teeth, as if it were a distasteful word. "I had a house assigned for you and the children—a furnished house, which we could be living in right now, Hedy. I will never understand why you took such a risk with your own life and the lives of our children." I cringed at his criticism.

Escape to the West

Mutti answered none of his questions. She had been ironing when I first came into the room, and she continued ironing the same blouse over and over. After a long pause she stopped and simply said, "I made a mistake, Willi. Now I have to get dinner ready." I had never expected her to just admit she made a mistake and then walk away. Thank you, Mother, my eyes said to her as I watched her leave the room.

"Oma, Opa, and I are living in a barracks in Trauen near Fassberg, in the Lüneburg Heath," my father continued, speaking to me. He looked out the window at the burned-out shell of the *Jugendheim*. "Fassberg was where I wanted your mother to bring you children when the war was ending in March 1945. But she never listens to me." Suddenly anger and disappointment clouded his blue eyes and distorted his face. I thought I understood why my mother had not taken his advice to join him in Fassberg. I didn't think he would listen to me if I tried to tell him. So I said nothing. He just didn't seem to understand that she had not forgiven him for what he had done to her. And he surely didn't know how close Mutti was to her parents. She didn't have the heart to leave them once we got to Strasburg. When the war caught up with us that April night in 1945, my mother knew she had made a mistake by staying. Then she did the best she knew how to save us. When he turned his face back toward me, the frown was gone and his eyes were clear again. He clasped his hands behind his head and said, "Trauen, you may not know, was part of a German research laboratory for *Vergeltungswaffen*, as the great Führer of all time, our great Austrian leader Adolf Hitler, referred to them." A sneer passed over my father's face like a cloud darkening an otherwise blue sky on a sunny day. The look passed quickly. "At Trauen they did research on the V-2 rocket. The facility is right next to the Fassberg *Flugplatz*, on the opposite side from the town. Few people knew of its existence; certainly the British and the Americans did. For their own reasons they chose not to bomb Trauen." He paused and looked apologetic. "Here I go on about war when you probably want to know about your grandparents. Right, Wolfgang and Ingrid?" We both smiled at him.

"Well, Oma and Opa Samuel stayed in Schlawe through the Russian occupation. Your grandfather decided they were too old to run. And you know your grandfather. He isn't afraid of anything. Opa speaks some Russian and even more Polish, so he was able to communicate with the Russian troops who occupied their house. Since Schlawe became part of Poland, they were deported in late 1945 to a camp in the English zone. When I was released from detention in March of '46, I visited camps which held *Flüchtlinge* from Pomerania, looking for them. I found them in a camp in Schleswig. We then traveled by train to Fassberg and I found us two rooms in a barracks, which all three of us now share."

I was overjoyed to hear that my dear grandparents were alive and well. I loved my Oma and Opa Samuel, and I longed to be with them again. My father kept on talking. I didn't hear anything he said anymore. My thoughts were of my grandparents. Mutti came into the room with the cooked hamburgers. Oma Grapentin had set the table, and we sat down to eat. The table was crowded with five people. The meal was tasty. When we finished eating, Dad complimented Mutti profusely on how good the *Klopse* tasted.

"Well," Mutti said, with just the slightest of smiles playing around her mouth, "it was only horse meat, Willi, that is the best we can get around here."

"As I said," he replied, "it was really tastily prepared hamburger; you can make it again for me, anytime."

"That's all there was," Mutti responded. "Meat is hard to find in Strasburg. Any kind of meat." I thought it was wonderful to have just a simple family conversation around the dinner table. Oma got up to clear the table, and Mutti and my father went into her room to talk.

"Willi," I heard her say, "this is not the West, and you may not be aware of what things are like here. You could be in danger of being arrested." My father listened attentively. "The neighbors probably saw you come in."

"No, I don't think so," he interrupted. "I was careful, and I met no one in the hall."

"They saw you," Mutti interjected in a firm voice. "At the end of this hallway there is a room right next to the stairs. It is occupied by a man, a former prisoner of war of the Russians. He is always friendly to me, too friendly. He is also always at his peephole in the door, no matter when I leave or when I come home. He doesn't know I know that he is a police informer. I have a girlfriend who is the town telephone operator, and she warned me about this man when I moved in here. I know that anything that happens around this hotel he reports to the police. He is a little afraid of me, I believe, because I had Russian officers up here several times, and he doesn't know what to make of it. Let's hope you are right that he didn't see you."

"I am here to take you and the children back with me, Hedy," my father said bluntly. Mutti didn't respond. She got up and fluffed the pillows on the couch. I left the room, not wanting to hear anything that might destroy my dreams of going to the West.

The next day was dreary, typical for Strasburg in December. In me the sun was shining. My father had come; he hadn't forgotten about us. My father would take us to the West, to the English zone, away from the Russians and the German Communists and all those who enjoyed hurting people. I couldn't think of anything else all day long. In anticipation of our departure, I thought I had better make arrangements to get my grade book. I knew I had to be careful in the way I went about it. There was one teacher whom I trusted—the man who had had the Christmas party for my class last December, and who had given me some of the old textbooks to read. He taught my last class of the day. At the end of that class, I stayed in the back of the room, acting busy. When the last student had left, I stepped up to him. "*Herr Lehrer*," I said timidly, "would you please have time to talk to me?"

"Of course," he replied, looking down at me. He was a tall, thin man. "I always have time for you, my boy." He said that with true affection in his voice, which surprised me. Then he went over to the door and closed it quietly. "Now what troubles you, my child?"

I got cold feet. I wasn't sure I was doing the right thing. I had not discussed this with my father first, and I thought I probably should have. My impulse seemed foolish now, and dangerous. I began to stutter. My teacher took me by the shoulders and walked me over to the window. He sat in one of the chairs and motioned for me to do the same. I looked at the floor and blurted out, "We may be leaving soon, and I need my grade book to take along to my next school. Could you get it for me?"

He looked at me for what seemed a long time. His eyes were friendly, yet expressed concern. "Your family is going to the West," he said simply.

"Yes," I answered truthfully, figuring that since he knew, there was no sense in denying it. "My father has come to get us," I added.

My teacher took my hands into his and bent forward to face me. "You won't need your grade book, Wolfgang, where you are going," he whispered. "Just go. Don't say anything to anyone. Do you understand what I am telling you? Don't say anything to your friends, to other students, but especially not to any teachers. Say nothing to anyone."

Escape to the West

"Yes, *Herr Lehrer*," I answered, realizing that I had probably made a grave error which could cost all of us our freedom, and maybe my father his life. I was stricken by the magnitude of my mistake in telling anyone of our plan. I could feel myself blush, and I looked down at the floor in shame and embarrassment for being so naive.

He rose and said, "Go now, my dear boy. Remember not to say anything to anyone," and he squeezed my hands in parting.

"*Auf Wiedersehen*," I said to him.

"*Auf Wiedersehen*, Wolfgang, and may God be by your side on your difficult journey," he whispered. Suddenly tears sprang to my eyes, and I impulsively put my arms around him. He patted me on the back and said, "Everything will be all right for you."

I left quickly. I didn't know if I would be back to school the next day; it depended on Mutti's and Dad's plans. That evening I continued to be troubled by my indiscretion. I said nothing to either of my parents about what I had done. I trusted my teacher. I felt certain he wouldn't say anything to anyone. We ate dinner early, around five o'clock in the afternoon. At the table Mutti told us that when she was preparing dinner our neighbor, the informer, had showed up unexpectedly, using the pretense of also needing to cook earlier than usual this day.

"He started a conversation with me about my visitor. I told him that you were my husband, Willi, and that you had just been released from a prisoner-of-war camp. I asked him if he would be so kind as to keep it a secret. He assured me that not a word would pass his lips and our secret would remain safe with him. What else could I do?" she said. "He knew you were here. He saw you, and now he wants to find out more about you. I figured that letting him in on a little secret which he already knew might keep him from running to the police right away."

I watched my father's face. He seemed to take Mutti's comments casually, without showing alarm. Maybe he doesn't really understand the brutality of this place, I thought, as I observed his calmness. I got worried about his lack of concern. I hoped he was not as foolish as Opa Grapentin had been. After dinner I withdrew to my room and crawled into bed under the table to be by myself. Mutti and my father remained in her room, Ingrid sitting in his lap. Mutti closed the door. It was unusual for her to close her door, except at night when she went to sleep. Maybe they were trying to figure out what to do next and didn't want anyone to hear. Our neighbor worried me. If he went to the police, which I knew he would, then they would come and arrest my father as they had Opa Grapentin. Please, Dad, I prayed, please, get worried and do something. I heard hurried footsteps in the hall, and suddenly my cousin Vera stood in the open door.

"Where is Tante Hedwig?" she demanded, panting and out of breath.

"In the other room," I replied, puzzled and worried by the urgency in her voice. I crawled out from under the table. It was obvious that Vera had been running. Perspiration streamed from under her wind-blown hair, down her forehead and into her eyes. Sweat rings had spread on her dress under her arms. She wiped the sweat off her brow before knocking on the door, and quickly entered when Mutti answered.

"Tante Hedwig," I heard Vera say, still trying to catch her breath, "Willi has to leave right away. My father came home just now to tell me that a man from this hotel reported that your husband, a former German Luftwaffe officer, was with you, that he had just arrived illegally from the West after release from an American prisoner-of-war camp. My father sent me over to warn you that you have two hours before the police will be here to pick up Willi. You must leave immediately. My father also wanted me to tell you that there is a train leaving about eight this evening for Neubrandenburg. It's in the general direction you want to go."

My father didn't give any outward sign that he was afraid. He had listened to Vera and remained calm. Mutti seemed to take the news in stride, too. It wasn't totally unexpected to her; she had just miscalculated. The informer hadn't waited but had run to the police right away with his information. Mutti and Dad rose from the sofa together.

"Thank you for the information, Vera. Thank your father, too," Mutti added. "I know Paul didn't have to do this. It is risky business for him to send us a warning. Please, thank him for Willi and me." Vera hurried off.

"Ja, Willi, let's get ready to leave. The decision has been made for us," Mutti said to my father. She moved decisively, as I'd seen her do many times before. We packed our three worn suitcases. Running away from someone will never end for us, I thought. We were always packing our suitcases and running. But, oh God, I was so happy we were leaving Strasburg again. Oma could hardly believe her eyes when she saw us packing.

"Are you coming with us, Mother, or are you staying?" Mutti asked bluntly. She already knew the answer.

"I have to stay behind this time and wait for Wilhelm," Oma said, with sadness in her voice. We had been together a long time—since March of last year. "I will go to your brother, Ernst, and stay with him," she said. "You must go with Willi, Hedwig. You must go with your husband."

Mutti took Oma by the arm and led her into the next room, where they talked. I saw Oma nodding her head and heard her say, "Don't worry, Hedwig, I'll take care of her." Then Mutti came over to me and said, "Wolfgang, Ingrid won't be going with us. She'll stay with Oma. They'll move in with Ernst and Lotte. I will come back and get her as soon as I can. She is not strong enough to accompany us on such an uncertain trip this time of year. We don't know what we'll run into. It is best this way. Now hurry, Wolfgang, and change. We must leave quickly." Then she took Ingrid and Oma aside and spoke to both of them. Mutti picked up Ingrid and held her, kissing her several times. Then Ingrid threw her arms around Mutti, and they both cried. Mutti said in a tear-choked voice, "I'll be back soon, my dear little girl. I'll be back soon to get you. Oma will take good care of you."

In forty-five minutes we were packed. The informer had not yet come back from the police station. I walked down the hall noisily, just to make sure. I saw no eye in the peephole on his door, and I went back to report my finding. The three of us carefully walked down the hallway, down the creaky wooden stairs to the foyer, and out into the darkness of a damp and cold December night. Maybe, just maybe, I thought, nobody had seen us leave. In the dark, three people dressed in drab clothing were difficult to see on an unlit street, and we melted away into the night, heading toward the *Bahnhof*. We walked close together. I missed Ingrid. We had never been apart before like this. At the train station, my father bought round-trip tickets for Neubrandenburg so as not to arouse suspicion. Had he bought tickets for the western border of the Russian zone, the agent would probably have called the police to report us. The agent had a telephone, I knew that. Most train stations had telephones. My father knew it, too.

The train was late, and it was cold on the platform. I paced back and forth, worried and staring at the station clock as if by doing so I could make the train arrive more quickly. There was an advantage to our hurried departure. Mutti and Dad had had no time to argue about when or if we were going to leave. The police informer had made that part of our flight easy. The train arrived nearly forty minutes late. A small engine pulled several old cars. The cars had the same type of compartments as the train we rode from Berlin to Strasburg in the spring of 1945, with access only from the outside to each compartment. No one could walk down an aisle as in the more modern cars and look into each compartment. It would be more difficult for the police to find us if they came looking. But, of course, they could stop the train if they wanted to and then search it by going from compartment to compartment.

The train sat in the station for what seemed an eternity. The engine huffed and puffed, belching clouds of white steam, until finally I heard a whistle; the cars momentarily rattled back and forth as the locomotive made a jerky start. The train slowly moved out of the station. I felt an indescribable sense of relief as we left Strasburg behind. Nearly two and a half hours had passed since Vera had brought us the news. It was ten minutes to nine. I wondered how close the police were to us, and I wondered if my father was anxious. He sat across from me looking unconcerned. An hour later we got off the train in Neubrandenburg. There was no place to go other than the public waiting room. There were no more trains scheduled that night.

The public waiting room was open all night, allowing travelers to sleep on wooden benches in the unheated room. It had gotten perceptibly colder outside. Winter was finally upon us. My father went looking for a train schedule. He found a station attendant who told him there was a train leaving at seven in the morning for Wittenberge. Again, none of us had thought to bring food when we made our escape. Twice before we had fled under similar circumstances—first from Sagan in January 1945 and then again from Strasburg in late April. In each case we hadn't taken food because we were in such a hurry. We hadn't learned a thing, it seemed. The three of us sat in the cold room huddled as close together as we could get.

With morning came December snow. Visibility outside was poor, and I didn't see the train, swathed in a combination of fog, steam, and snow, pull into the station until it was almost upon us. The wet cold seemed to penetrate to my bones. I shivered in my thin camouflage suit. We boarded the train, a *D-Zug*, and found an empty compartment. The passenger cars were more modern than those on the train from Strasburg. The long cars had an entrance on either end, and a corridor ran down one side of the car. The passenger compartments were located opposite the corridor and could be accessed through sliding doors. The cars were second class, and instead of wooden benches we had the luxury of upholstered seats—two bench-style seats, face to face in each compartment. Best of all, the train was warm. I put my hands over the heat duct on the compartment floor below the win-

Escape to the West

dow. The obvious disadvantage of these cars was that the conductor could walk through checking tickets while the train was in transit. So could the police. My father was questioned several times by the conductor and by a police patrol about his destination. The questioning appeared casual, and my father smiled at the men and spoke to them in a cordial manner. He told them we were going to visit Mutti's old and ill parents. My father explained to us that before he had come he had spoken to several people who had crossed the border more than once. They had told him how to act in certain situations and where the best border crossing points were located.

"Once we get to Wittenberge," my father said, "we will change trains and go on to Salzwedel. From there we will walk across the border near Lüchow. There is no other way. The final few kilometers we have to walk." My father didn't say how many kilometers that was. "Although it is cold, the weather is in our favor." I could see the wind outside driving the snow across open fields and into drifts. We changed trains in Wittenberge without incident and arrived at our destination in Salzwedel just as it got dark. The public waiting room at the Salzwedel station was filled with people. It smelled of sweat, cigarette smoke, and urine. We were hungry, not having eaten for twenty-four hours. Mutti and Dad went to see if they could find some food. They found only cold water, and Dad traded several English cigarettes for half a loaf of bread. I ate the sour-tasting bread hungrily. My father spoke to several men who looked as if they were there to cross the border. He agreed to lead three of them and their families across the *Zonengrenze*. He seemed to think there was safety in numbers. We slept uneasily through the night, shifting positions constantly on the hard benches. We had to sleep sitting up because there were so many people in the station.

At eight o'clock, as it was getting light outside, my father decided it was the right time to leave for the border. I felt tired, dirty, and hungry again. Mutti wiped my face with a wet handkerchief. The combination of the wet cloth and the firm pressure of her hand made my face feel fresh and clean. The storm had intensified overnight. At least ten inches of snow lay on the ground, and in places it had blown into high drifts. We tightened our bootlaces. My wooden-soled shoes with the plastic tops didn't keep out the cold, and my feet were chilled even before we ventured outside. The wooden soles slipped on the snow. I had long ago worn away the thin rubber sole that had been nailed to the wood. My old camel-hair coat barely fit around my shoulders, but it provided extra warmth. Mutti and I were poorly dressed to withstand the cold. My father wore a warm, quilted jacket, woolen pants, and sturdy leather boots, and he had long underwear. My camouflage suit kept out the wind, but it didn't provide warmth.

"It's about three kilometers to the other side," my father said. I didn't really appreciate how far that would be walking in a blizzard. We each took a suitcase. I carried the smallest. The other three families joined us, making a total of fourteen. One family didn't have any children, another had three. One by one we exited the welcome warmth of the smelly waiting room and stepped into the chill of a merciless winter storm. It was a frightening shock as the icy wind grabbed me and wrenched the warmth from my body. We followed my father in single file. He set a slow, steady pace everyone in the group could follow. We had not gone far when I saw several men coming toward us in the distance. They walked bent over, shielding their faces from the cold wind, and appeared to carry rifles on their backs. My father stopped and set down his suitcase. I stopped next to him. The men were German border guards dressed in what were formerly Wehrmacht uniforms and carrying what were formerly German army rifles. They were supposed to be looking for people like us. I could tell they really didn't want to find us. But here we were, fourteen of us; they couldn't pretend we didn't exist. I looked closely at the scarves wrapped around their mouths to keep the cold wind from freezing their faces and at their hats pulled low over their ears and at their overcoats crusted with snow. The guards carried leather ammunition pouches for their rifles on their broad belts, and every man had his hands pushed deep into his coat pockets.

"Where are you going?" one of the guards asked my father. I was sure he knew where we were trying to go. My father responded for the group, which had by now caught up with us and stood around him, apprehension clearly showing in their faces.

"We are trying to rejoin our families on the other side and are looking for a crossing. We would appreciate it if you could point us in the right direction." I was astounded at his honesty, even asking the guards for directions. But then, what could we possibly be doing in the cold and driving snow except wanting to cross the border and flee to the West? The guard listened, wiping snow and frost off his brows.

"All of you look like you are frozen," the guard said. "Why don't you come with us and have something warm to drink and then we can talk about what to do next." We fell in behind the three guards and followed them to their station. Ten minutes later we were in the warm border police station. I could think of nothing but thawing out my frozen body. I was so cold I could hardly talk. It was difficult to purse my lips and get a coherent word out. I was glad the border guards had come along. I don't believe I would have made it to the other side. An iron stove stood behind a wooden rail dividing the room. I wanted to run over to the stove and let it roast me first on one side and then the other, but I couldn't, because the stove stood behind the railing in the office area, not in the public area where we waited.

We stood around, walking in circles, stomping our feet to get warm. The three policemen moved behind the wooden railing to stack their rifles and removed their caps and coats. They disappeared behind a door. No one else seemed to pay attention to us. One of them returned with a pot of ersatz coffee and four dented aluminum cups. He placed the metal coffee pot on the potbellied stove and, without looking at us, said, "It'll be hot in just a moment. Please, come in and help yourselves. These are all the cups I can spare, so you have to share them." Pointing to a door on the other side of the room, he said, "There is running water in there to rinse the cups." He left and returned to the back room. My father and the other three men went over to the potbellied stove and filled the four cups with the steaming black liquid. The cups were passed around until every man, woman, and child had a sip of warming ersatz coffee. We emptied the pot quickly. Two women from our group took the cups and the empty pot and washed them before we returned them with many thanks. A border guard officer emerged from an office across from where we stood and walked slowly toward us. He stopped at the railing and looked us over. Then he beckoned to my father with a gesture of his head. My father took my hand, and the two of us walked across the room, through the gate in the railing, over to where the officer stood. The officer didn't have his blouse on. He wore the pants of a German army officer and the usual suspenders over his long-sleeved under-shirt. As we approached, he turned toward his office. We followed. He sat down behind a desk, leaned back in his chair with his hands clasped behind his head, and looked us over.

"What is your name?" he asked in a neutral tone of voice.

"Samuel," my father said. "Willi Samuel."

"Where are you going, Herr Samuel, in such a terrible winter storm?" I could see his jacket hanging on a rack by the door. It looked like a German officer's jacket with the rank of major on the shoulder pieces. Strange. There was no German army anymore, yet all of the men looked like they were in the Wehrmacht.

Dad responded to the major's question slowly and deliberately. "I am trying to take my family back to a town called Fassberg, just across the border. I have only recently been released from a prisoner-of-war camp and was lucky enough to find them. Now I want to reunite them with other members of our family and start a new life."

"What was your rank in the war and what service where you in?"

"I was a captain in the Luftwaffe and served as armaments officer in several bomb wings in the West. Toward the end of the war I commanded an antiaircraft battery. I was captured by Americans and sent to a prisoner-of-war camp in Alsace-Lorraine. I was released this past March."

"*Ja*," said the major, "I was an army officer, and now I have this distasteful job of arresting my own people. I tell you this, I can't take you to the border myself, but what I will do for you and your people is give you the schedule of the Russian patrols. Don't get caught. If they catch you, I can't help you. No one will ever hear of you again. You understand what I am saying?"

"I understand fully."

"The Russians don't always stick to their schedules, so maybe it is best if you take one or two of those men out there"—the major pointed with his thumb over his shoulder toward the room filled with the rest of our group— "and reconnoiter the *Grenze*. Wait until you see a Russian patrol, then come back here, get your family and the rest of them, and head straight for the *Grenze*. There will not be another patrol for two hours after that one passes. Use cover and stay out of sight as best you can. Use the skills you learned in the military. Don't let them see you. They will shoot first and ask questions later."

"Thank you, Major," Dad replied. "I will be forever grateful and in your debt."

"Go now, man," said the major. Dad reached across the desk and shook hands with him. Then he rendered a military salute. The major returned the salute, and we went back outside to rejoin our group. My father huddled briefly with the other men, telling them what he planned to do. Since each of them had army experience, he took all three on the search for the Russian patrol. They returned an hour later, frozen through and through. They had lain in the deep snow to hide themselves from the passing patrol. For twenty minutes the men warmed themselves by the potbellied stove, passing around another cup of ersatz coffee to take the chill out of their bellies. Then everyone grabbed bags and suitcases, and we again braved the raging blizzard.

The wind blew hard from our right and slightly from behind, so it wasn't as bad as it could have been if it had blown directly in our faces. We walked as fast as we could. Three kilometers was a long walk in a blizzard. In the beginning I stayed warm from excitement and from the pace set by Mutti and Dad. The other families behind us followed in three clumps, their bodies bent under their loads. The snow, driven by the wind, built up on our clothing, clinging tenaciously to the fabric. This is like Siberia, I thought. We were going to freeze to death on these barren, icy fields along a border of what had once been one Germany. My father left the main road and followed a drift-covered *Feldweg*.

"It's more direct going this way, I believe," my father said, as he made a path for us through a snow drift. "It is also time for us to leave the road. The Russian patrol uses the road right here along the border." I looked at the bushes on one side of the rutted farm road. If necessary they would provide a place for us to hide, but we probably would freeze to death if we had to lie down in the snow for any length of time. I saw no border markings. My father seemed to know where he was going.

"We will know for sure we are across the border when we get to the next village," he said, as if in response to my unspoken question. We plodded silently onward through the deepening snow, lifting our frozen, unfeeling feet as if we were machines. Step—step—step—step—on and on and on. Don't stop. Keep moving. My wooden soles gave me little grip in the snow, making my progress even more exhausting. Don't think about anything. Just keep on moving one step at a time. I dragged my suitcase behind me on top of the accumulated snow. Step—step—step—step—on and on.

The others followed in our path through the snow, but had fallen far behind us. I couldn't hear them, and I felt too cold and weary to turn around and look again. I felt nothing anymore—neither cold nor warmth. My camouflage pants were covered with frost and snow; they were hard and brittle and hurt my thighs as I walked. At least I still felt something, so I thought I must be all right. If I hadn't had my old camel-hair coat over my camouflage jacket, I might have frozen to death. Weariness overcame me. I felt I couldn't go on any more. I just wanted to lie down in the snow and go to sleep. I stopped. Then I went on again. Step—step—step—step.

Escape to the West

As I looked up, I saw my father, followed by Mutti, far ahead of me. They were encrusted with snow and frost, bent over, looking unreal, not like people. In the distance I saw the faint outlines of farmhouses. They seemed to huddle in the snow like a flock of birds trying to stay warm. Their low-hanging roofs, covered with a deep layer of snow, appeared to touch the ground. I tried to pick up my pace as the anticipated warmth and safety of the village beckoned. I couldn't. I was too exhausted and could barely walk anymore. My suitcase seemed to be welded to my hand with snow and ice, and I no longer had feeling in my arm. I stumbled on toward the village through sheer will power, stoically denying the ever-increasing weakness which made my knees wobble. Suddenly a rush of warmth flooded through my body. I have frostbite, I thought. I am freezing to death, that's why I feel this way. I had read about frostbite in a book about Alaska. The book told of men who felt warm and comfortable just before they froze to death. It didn't matter. I couldn't do anything other than what I was doing, moving my feet forward one painful step at a time. I tried to call out to my mother and father, but my mouth was frozen and refused to move.

We entered the village of Lübbow in the English zone of occupation. I saw its train station in the distance. My father was heading for it. Again I tried to pick up my pace, again I couldn't. My legs barely followed my commands. My father opened the door to the station and then looked back. He saw that I was far behind. He ran back toward me and pried the suitcase from my hand, grabbed me under my arms, and carried me the rest of the way into the warm waiting room. I collapsed in front of a cast-iron stove which had a lively fire burning within it. The severe pain of my thawing body made me cry out. I rolled around the floor in agony, unable to restrain the tears. I got on my knees and rocked back and forth in pain. Then I stood up, slapping my hands against my sides and stomping my feet on the floor to deaden the pain. None of it helped. As the pain abated over time, I slowly regained my composure. Then I noticed that my hands were covered with blood. I stared at them in disbelief, having no idea where the blood had come from. Becoming aware of wetness between my legs, I looked down and saw black patches on my camouflage pants near the insides of my thighs. It was blood. My thighs had been rubbed raw by my stiff, frozen pants. The wounds burned fiercely.

"Mutti, I am bleeding," I whispered to her, "and it hurts so bad." She stared at me with uncomprehending eyes, exhaustion marking her face. Then came sudden awareness and she reached for my hands.

"Oh, my dear child," she whispered, bending down to examine me. The kind old stationmaster brought a wet rag. Mutti cleaned the blood off my hands, thighs, and pants as well as she could. The bleeding stopped. The pants hurt me every time they touched the raw wounds. We had no bandages, no rags. I just had to bear the pain as best I could. My father bought three tickets on the next train.

"The train only goes one place—out," said the stationmaster, chuckling. He was a friendly old man, dressed in the usual blue uniform worn by German railroaders on both sides of the border. "This is the end of the line. Once it went on to Salzwedel, but no more." He had watched me with sympathetic concern. The other three families arrived and crowded around the stove, the children going through gyrations similar to those I had performed only minutes earlier. We filled the waiting room to capacity. One of the women had a roll of gauze, and Mutti wrapped it around my wounds. At least I could walk without pain.

Late that afternoon we boarded the train for Lüchow and Dannenberg. At Dannenberg we changed trains to travel the rest of the way to Munster-Lager. The compartment was warm. My father was talking to Mutti. I was too exhausted to comprehend anything he was saying. All I heard was the comforting sound of his voice. We were safe now, and with that comforting knowledge I went to sleep.

When I awoke, the train was moving slowly. Mutti had her head on my father's shoulder, her eyes closed. He, too, was sleeping. The thought entered my mind that our long journey to the west had begun nearly two years earlier, in January 1945. I pressed my forehead against the steamed-up window and watched the snow-covered landscape glide past. Two long years had changed us all. It seemed much longer than that to me. I felt much older than I was. I sat back in my seat, lifted my legs, and looked at the blue-and-yellow plastic of my wood-soled shoes, at my strange-looking camouflage suit with the dark bloodstains between my legs—and suddenly understood that none of that mattered. What mattered was that I had a family, that we were together. I looked at my father, asleep, who had come to rescue us; I looked at my mother, alive only by the grace of God, who had saved us in spite of everything. I loved them in different ways, but I loved them both. None of it was their fault. The tears that sprang to my eyes were tears of joy and gratitude, not tears of sorrow.

Escape to the West

Chapter 16

THE TRAUEN BARRACKS

E arly the next morning, we reached Munster-Lager. For most of the night, the train had sat in the station at Ülzen. It was warm in our compartment, we were alone, and sleep made us forget that we were hungry. By morning, though, I was feeling weak from lack of food. As we got off the train in Munster-Lager, my father mentioned that he knew someone in town and we could at least wash up there, maybe get some breakfast.

A short walk from the train station stood a high-gabled house with grey plaster walls and a red brick roof, one of many just like it on that street. My father went up the steps to the front door and rang the bell. After a minute or so, someone came to the door and fumbled with the lock. Then the door opened a crack, and I could see a woman's face peering out. Recognizing my father, she opened the door wide, spread her arms in a welcoming gesture and shouted "Willi," not seeing that Mutti and I were standing by the garden gate. When she saw us, the smile vanished from her face and her arms dropped to her side. She quickly regained her composure and said, *"Kommen Sie doch rein, bitte,"* directing the invitation to my mother. I gratefully followed into the warm kitchen, where the woman continued changing the diapers on a baby girl. While my father introduced the woman to Mutti, I sat down on a kitchen bench. I felt weak in my knees.

"The boy has not eaten for more than a day," my father said. The woman got out bread and marmalade and set the table. She apologized, "I'm sorry,

236

this is all I have to offer." I ate and felt better almost immediately. The bread wasn't enough for any of us, but it staved off the worst hunger. I sensed that Mutti wanted to leave. The welcome by our hostess probably extended only to my father, not to the family he had brought along. He and Mutti thanked the woman for her hospitality. I shook her hand, and then the front door closed behind us. We hadn't stayed more than half an hour. My father led us to another train station; a narrow gauge ran between Munster-Lager and Celle. The village of Trauen, our final destination, was one of its stops en route. The train was ready to leave when we arrived. It was a short train, only three cars. We rode in silence the last eight kilometers.

Later, Mutti and I crowded around my father on the windswept platform at Trauen. He pointed south, up a road paved with square granite stones. Melting snow made it glisten like a silvery ribbon. "There are the barracks," he said. "We are home." About half a kilometer along the road, up against a pine forest, stood three former Wehrmacht barracks. They looked forbidding in their squat greyness. If our new home didn't look welcoming, at least I was grateful that our odyssey had come to an end. A sense of elation briefly showed in my father's face as he stood there, pointing at the barracks. He had returned safely from the Russian zone and brought his family home. He deserved that fleeting moment of triumph.

To the right of the forest sheltering the barracks were open fields covered with wind-blown snow. I could make out the shapes of military aircraft in the distance, across from the fields and along the edge of the forest. As we crossed the railroad tracks, I asked Dad about those strange airplanes. "They are old German bombers," he said, looking at me. "This is the outside perimeter of what once was the Fassberg *Flugplatz*. There are hundreds of old Luftwaffe planes parked in the forest and along old runways. No one needs them anymore now that the war is over." From a distance, the planes looked alive to me, ready to start their engines and taxi out onto a runway and take off for some distant war. There was no war anymore, and I was glad.

We walked quietly for the remainder of the way, approaching the barracks on a narrow dirt path parallelling the road. Mutti and I fell in behind my father. He turned between the first two barracks and stopped at the first entrance of the one to our right. He entered a foyer and opened the door to the left. There stood my grandmother Samuel, her eyes lighting up as she saw us. Her gnarled, rheumatic hands held an aluminum pot she was just taking off the cast-iron stove. She put down the pot carefully, wiped her

The Trauen Barracks

hands on her apron, as she had always done in Schlawe, and, smiling broadly, called out loudly, *"Alter,"* referring to my grandfather Samuel, "come quickly, the children are here."

Oma's joy at seeing us did not cloud her powers of observation. She immediately set about fixing sandwiches and hot chocolate for me. I had not tasted anything as delicious since we left Sagan two years earlier. The hot chocolate tasted rich, smooth, and foreign. I cradled the tin cup in my hands and sipped the precious liquid slowly, so as not to miss any of its flavor. Oma wiped my face with a hot, wet towel. Then she did the same to my hands. Opa Samuel handed me a piece of yellowish-looking bread spread with real butter and jam. It had a sweet taste to it, almost like cake, not sour like the bread we got in the Russian Zone.

"What is it?" I asked Opa. "Cake?"

He explained with a laugh, "That yellow color is corn, Wolfgang. American corn. What we call *Mais.* Some well-meaning person in America sent ships loaded with American corn rather than rye or wheat. Now it has to be eaten. The bread is a little dry, but it's wholesome. And we have to thank the Americans for it." Opa looked at me with his kind blue eyes and laughed again. An embracing, happy laugh. Oma took me next door, and I lay down on a real bed with blankets. I believe that I was asleep before she left the room.

I awoke the next morning to see sunshine reflecting off the snowy field beyond our barracks. Everyone was already in the kitchen sitting around the table. The chairs were an odd assortment of castoffs. The table was homemade. A stand by the door bore a wash basin, and a tiny mirror on the wall was used by the men for shaving. A shelf below the mirror held shaving brushes, a bar of real soap, razors, and well-worn toothbrushes. Oma poured hot water into the basin, and I washed my hands and face and combed my hair. The others had already finished breakfast—that *Mais* bread again and real butter. Oma quickly brought me a cup of steaming cocoa. I felt good after breakfast—I was warm, clean, and rested. The hunger of the day before was already a fading memory.

I accompanied Opa on his errands, eager to learn from him about everything that had happened to them over the past two years. "I'll tell you in time, my boy," he said, as he got a basket out from under the table. "I'll tell you in good time. We survived, and we are together now; that's all that matters." He looked at me, his eyes steady and firm. I nodded my head. The subject was closed. I knew he wouldn't talk about the past ever again. "We must bring some firewood or Oma is going to get after us," he said, as he slipped on a thick, fleece-lined grey winter jacket which reached to just above his knees. He saw my questioning eyes and said, "An American church group gave me this jacket in the internment camp in Schleswig. I had nothing to keep me warm. They are good people, the Americans." He placed the basket, which he had woven himself from supple willow branches, over his right arm, and we stepped out into the cold. I grabbed his gnarled, rough hand. It felt reassuring to hold on to my grandfather's hand again. The sun, low on the December horizon, shone through broken clouds scudding across the sky. The blizzard had passed.

We walked past a water pump into the pine forest, following a narrow, well-worn path leading to a two-story brick barn. Opa unlocked the door to what had once been a horse stall. Inside was a neatly stacked pile of firewood and a chopping block with an axe stuck in it. I immediately picked up the axe to try it out. "You'll have plenty of opportunity to chop wood around here," Opa said, his eyes laughing. I put the axe down. In the dim interior of the windowless room, I saw several nesting boxes and a rack on which hens perched, some of them cackling in a low, resentful manner, signifying their level of annoyance at being interrupted in their rest. "Don't go over to them," said Opa. "You'll disturb the laying hens in the boxes. They don't lay much in winter. Some get confused, though, and now and then we have a few eggs."

My grandfather's face was covered with the usual beard stubble. In his teeth he clenched a cold pipe. Little had changed since I had last seen him. "All right, my boy, why don't you take the basket of firewood to your grandmother," Opa said, interrupting my observations, "and I will tend to the chickens. You can come back and help me split wood if you still feel up to it."

"Yes, Opa, right away," I replied, feeling happy that I could be of help. I grabbed the basket, which was surprisingly heavy and bulky. I staggered off under the load toward my new home.

Over the following weeks, I had ample opportunity to become familiar with barracks routines and our surroundings. There were three barracks in our compound, each filled with *Flüchtlinge*. Our apartment, which now housed five, consisted of two rooms, one on the front side of the barracks and another on the back, separated by a thin wall of pine boards. I learned

The Trauen Barracks

quickly that there were few secrets in the barracks, because anything said above a whisper was overheard by someone and quickly became common knowledge. Neighbors heard when people coughed next door, turned in their beds, or made love.

The three barracks were arranged in a U-shape. The area bounded by the barracks had once been a well-kept lawn adorned by a flagpole, according to my father. The flagpole had vanished long ago into someone's stove. The grassy area had been divided into garden plots where people grew vegetables. The barracks on the east side sat parallel to the road leading to the former Trauen V-2 *Versuchsanstalt*, a rocket research center. Our barracks was situated on the north side adjacent to a potato field. The third barracks, to the south, sat next to a pine forest. All three barracks faced inward. Nearly every door and most windows were located on the inward-facing sides. Everyone looked at everyone else all the time. There was no privacy.

At the open end of the U, to the west, stood a smaller barracks, the community latrine. At one end were two private toilets. The remaining toilets were located in one room with five holes on each side facing each other. I discovered that at this time of year, with the cold wind blowing and temperatures below freezing, I should not linger in the latrine. On my first visit, I discovered my mistake in not bringing paper. Fortunately, an old newspaper lay on the floor.

On the day of our arrival, the barracks setting had seemed tranquil and serene. The snow had covered the ugly scars made by the inhabitants of an overcrowded compound filled with refugees, most coming from the former eastern regions of Germany but some from lands once occupied by the German army. These scars would soon become visible once the snow melted. There were public washrooms in the barracks, but no running water. And, of course, there were no kitchens, since at one time the barracks had housed soldiers who were fed at a mess hall on the air base. Each family had obtained a wood-fired stove. A flat piece of aluminum was nailed to the pine floor in front of the stoves to make sure that hot embers did not ignite the floor. A stovepipe ran from the back of a stove up through the ceiling and the roof. The roofs of the barracks were covered with tar paper. Everything was flammable. The stovepipes, which became extremely hot when in use, caused many burns on those who inadvertently touched them, the fate at one time or another of every child living in the barracks. Such burns were ugly wounds, healing slowly.

The Trauen Barracks

Electric heaters owned by some residents, and carefully hidden, represented the real fire hazard. "They're only a problem in winter," my father told me the first time the lights went out, "when some people turn on their heaters for a little extra warmth, putting all of us at risk." The aluminum wiring was designed to provide electric current for lamps, not to carry the enormous electric loads required by a resistance heater. When someone used an electric heater, the fuse for that barracks in the central fuse box would inevitably blow. Occasionally, heater use would cause a short circuit and start a fire under someone's roof area. Then men would frantically run around pulling apart wires and splicing them and trying to find out who was at fault. The real culprits were never found, and convenient scapegoats, usually single women, took the blame, even when there was no proof that they even owned heaters. The punishment consisted of a vicious campaign of slander and epithets directed publicly against those who were accused of being guilty.

Upon his arrival, my grandfather had taken the initiative to have a well drilled and a hand-operated water pump installed near our apartment. I don't know where people got their water before the pump was installed. The one pump provided the water used in the barracks for all purposes—cooking, washing, and watering of plants in our gardens in spring and summer. Each family had several water buckets which stood on benches in the kitchen areas. Waste water was accumulated in a slop bucket. When full, the bucket was emptied in the garden to water and fertilize the vegetables. No one worried about contaminating the ground water with soap, since it was a nearly unattainable luxury. What we bought in lieu of soap was really refined clay and provided absolutely no bubbles, no matter how hard anyone scrubbed.

Opa tried to persuade people not to empty their slop buckets near the water pump, because he feared that the waste would contaminate our drinking water. He was only partially successful in his efforts, and eventually convinced the potato farmer in Trauen for whom he worked to drill an even deeper well to decrease the chance of an epidemic. Opa was a veteran of the First War, and he told me once that he had lost more soldiers to foul drinking water than to enemy bullets.

Every morning at about seven, an English Royal Air Force (RAF) truck drove up near the pump and sat there idling for about five or ten minutes, spitting out foul-smelling exhaust fumes. The truck had an ugly flat nose, with the engine located in the driver's compartment. The truck picked up men and women who worked at the air base and brought them back at five-thirty every afternoon. It was an open-bed truck with a tarpaulin draped over the back to keep out the rain. Usually the women sat on folding benches and the men stood, holding on to the metal frame while the truck bounced over the cobblestoned roads. Sometimes we children sneaked onto the truck and rode into Fassberg. The men would shield us from the driver. Although the driver was German, his instructions clearly were not to let anyone other than air base employees ride the truck. In the evening, when the workers returned, most of them brought home some food. One especially prized item was English bread. The bread was white (made from bleached Canadian wheat flour, I was told) and soft, with a brown crust. It tasted delicious, I thought, almost like cake.

Some fortunate people brought English coffee home from work—real coffee, not the German ersatz. The smell of real coffee was precious to me. For such a long time we had no good smells in our lives. Sometimes, without warning, the memory of the smell of gunpowder, of burning rubber, uniforms, and people would creep into my nostrils. Just the thought of those smells made my stomach churn. Smells colored my world, and much of my world had been black and grey, ugly and putrid. The smell of English coffee made my world seem warm and joyful; it conjured up a world at peace, not war. The best smell, though, was Palmolive soap. A clean smell. It drove out of my mind the smells of burning people and gunpowder.

Those German workers who were fortunate enough to work at the air base enjoyed showing off the goods they brought home. In our world, where everyone was a *Flüchtling* and possessions were at best a used bicycle or the old clothes on our backs, anything new and different bestowed status upon its owner. English white bread with real jam on it was a status symbol. Children frequently paraded their thick slices of English bread covered with English jam outside for all to see, eating their precious possession slowly and deliberately.

Most of the women were employed as maids in the households of English officers or sergeants in Fassberg. Others worked in the airmen's canteen or at the officers' mess or as cleaning women in various offices and maintenance shops. The men worked in the motor pool and as carpenters, electricians, and in other skilled trades the English had a need for. My father did not work in Fassberg; he worked in Munster-Lager, usually referred to as

Munster. He had taken a job there as an electrician in an English searchlight battery after he was released from the British prisoner-of-war holding camp in Munster. No truck ran to Munster, and, of course, there was no public transportation. So my father walked the eight kilometers to work and back every day. He didn't seem to mind. He, too, brought home English bread and coffee now and then, along with English cigarettes, which he traded on the local black market for food.

My grandfather had found work at the potato seed farm in Trauen. He tended their horses and worked in the potato fields when it was planting and harvesting time. Less than two years earlier he had been a respected director in the *Finanzamt*, the internal revenue service office, in Schlawe. Opa just laughed when I mentioned that to him. "That is life, my dear boy," he said when I expressed my surprise at the work he was now doing. "The past is past. I can't do anything about it anymore. But the future we can shape. You must know how to help yourself no matter what the situation, my child. Learn from the past and shape your future. Don't make the mistake of trying to redo what happened yesterday. It's history."

Working on the farm gave Opa valuable benefits for our family and the barracks community as a whole. He was able to get the well drilled and the pump installed to benefit all people in our compound. The potato farm provided potatoes and a daily ration of milk. I soon found myself going into Trauen in the late afternoon to collect our milk ration. The pay my father and Opa received for their labors was not important, because there were few goods to buy with the nearly worthless German *Reichsmark*. Jobs provided access to food and other goods, which were either used or traded on the black market for the things we desperately needed. Shelter, fuel for our stoves for heat and cooking, water, food, and clothing were our priorities during the winter of 1946. I quickly learned that most of our family's activities would revolve around these five things.

All five of us slept in the back room on metal army cots and straw mattresses. I slept on the floor most of the time because I found the floor more comfortable, or maybe I had just become used to it. Because of our crowded conditions, on work days my father elected to stay at the English base in Munster. As the December days passed, my mother became more and more restless. Just before Christmas she persuaded my sixty-six-year-old grandfather to return with her to the Russian zone to get Ingrid and my cousin Vera, if Mutti could talk Vera into coming. Vera was the pretty fifteen-year-old girl who had warned us that the *Volkspolizei* were coming to arrest my father. I believe Mutti felt she owed it to her dead sister, Marie, to give Vera a chance at a better life. Maybe my mother also saw herself in Vera and was drawn to her.

My grandfather's willingness to join Mutti in this hazardous venture didn't surprise me. I knew that fear for his personal safety was no longer a consideration for him. I had never known him to be anything but resolute and courageous. Although Opa never spoke of the Great War, my father told me that he had won a battlefield commission for bravery in Rumania, and a fistful of medals which he showed to no one. He probably saw this rescue as a duty, if not a welcome opportunity to again do something meaningful. The two of them, Opa Samuel and Mutti, were a good match, I thought.

The day before Christmas Eve, December 23, my mother and my grandfather left Trauen, each carrying a rucksack filled with enough food to sustain them until they arrived in Strasburg and a change of underwear. Nothing more. I wasn't certain if I was going to see either one again. I knew Mutti had to get Ingrid, and it weighed on her mind. I noticed how perky she looked as they left for the Trauen train station. I suspected that my mother had gotten used to taking risks; maybe she even got a thrill out of doing so. Their plan was simply to catch the train to Munster and then retrace the route we had followed only three weeks earlier.

Christmas 1946 was just another day. Oma prayed, as she always did on *Heiligabend*, with her hands folded and head bowed. We thanked God for keeping us alive through the dangers of war, for bringing us back together as a family, for keeping us healthy, and for giving us shelter and food. We prayed for my mother and Opa and their safe return. At age eleven I had acquired a simple faith. While my family had never felt strongly about attending church, there was the pervasive presence of a strong and fundamental belief in the Almighty, a belief found in farmers most anywhere. The Bible was never far from my grandmother's side, and the word "God" never passed her lips lightly for fear she was committing blasphemy.

According to my grandmother Samuel, God was always near us in good times and in bad, and he heard and saw everything we said and did. Or at least his emissaries were always near us and watching, his *Engel*. God himself was obviously busy with many, many important things and, according to my grandmother, he had legions of angels tending to those things of lesser consequence which he could not personally oversee. "Everybody has an *Engel*," Oma said to me in a manner that left little doubt of her conviction. "You too, Wolfgang, have an *Engel* who watches over you. *Ja*, you have an *Engel* for sure, my dear boy, and your *Engel* will take care of you." Then she turned toward me, shaking a finger in my face, and said, "Yours is a girl *Engel* for sure." She laughed when she said that. I loved my grandmother and her quirky ways. Since our dramatic escape from the Russian tanks in early May 1945, when our wagon had broken down by the side of the road in a hail of rocket and artillery fire, I had believed deeply in God. It was not something I shared with anyone. Oma was right. I must have an angel—how else could I explain the many coincidences that had saved my family from certain death on so many occasions?

January 1947 was bitterly cold. The frigid winds swept the snow before them, piling it into high drifts around our barracks. In Opa's absence I tried to do the chores he would have done—hauling and splitting wood, feeding the chickens, and looking for eggs. There were no eggs. The hens didn't lay in winter. When there were no chores to do, I sat by the stove to stay warm and talked to Oma as she cooked, cleaned, or sewed. As the month came to a close, my father began to talk about how it was high time for me to start school again. I had not had any meaningful schooling for nearly two years. I knew my education was seriously flawed. I myself worried that I would never be able to catch up with others my age whose educations had been less disrupted. If I attended a village school such as the one in Trauen, I believed, my attempt to get an education would be doomed forever. My father quieted my fears. He thought I could go to school in Fassberg. The Fassberg school, he explained, was much larger and had facilities and resources far superior to those of the Trauen village school. He knew the principal of the Fassberg school and thought that he could get him to make an exception so that I could be admitted. On the first Monday in February when the weather was nice and the ground frozen and dry, my father and I set off for Fassberg to attempt to enroll me in school.

It took nearly an hour to walk the four kilometers of undulating *Feld-* and *Waldwege* before we reached the school in Fassberg. It was a new red brick building. The principal's office was on the second floor. We waited in the hall outside the faculty lounge, next to the principal's office, until the class break. Soon after the bell rang, Herr Soffner, the principal and my father's friend, came down the hall toward us with long, sure strides. He

The Trauen Barracks

immediately recognized my father, and, increasing his pace, stretched out his hand in a genuine gesture of welcome. Herr Soffner's greying hair was combed straight back. His appearance was one of extraordinary neatness. He invited us to join him in his office, and he closed the door behind us. Dad and he spoke without sitting down.

"My next class starts in ten minutes," Herr Soffner apologized, "and I can't be late for it." He reached into his jacket's breast pocket and removed a silver cigarette case. He opened it and offered it to Dad. My father took a cigarette, and, while Herr Soffner took one for himself and replaced the case in his jacket, Dad got out an English Ronson lighter and offered a light to his friend. Then he lit his own. The two men briefly enjoyed the smoke of their cigarettes; then Herr Soffner, who had sat down on the corner of his desk, said, "What can I do for you, Willi?"

"This is my son, Wolfgang." My father gestured toward me. "He needs to get back into school." While my father spoke, Herr Soffner looked at me with his stern grey eyes; I believed I detected a welcoming glimmer in their deepest recesses. "He has been in the east zone for nearly two years, and his education is seriously flawed. For him to catch up he needs to attend a school such as yours. The Trauen village school is just not able to deal with his many deficiencies."

"I understand," replied Herr Soffner, smoothing back his hair with his right hand and rising from the corner of his desk. "How old are you, Wolfgang?"

"Twelve. I just turned twelve on the second of February," I replied, taken aback by his direct question.

"Well, then you should be in the sixth grade, right?"

"Yes, Herr Soffner."

"Willi, I must go." He stubbed out his cigarette. "Leave Wolfgang with me. I will take care of everything. Give my best regards to your wife and do visit when we have more time to talk. *Auf Wiedersehen.*" He shook my father's hand vigorously and took me by the shoulders, ushering me into the hall. Five minutes later I was sitting in a classroom. I was back in school—a real school. I hadn't thought it could happen so quickly. My joy was tempered by the curious faces looking at me from behind their desks.

The short February days passed quickly as a result of my being back in school, with its discipline, schedule, and routines. One Saturday afternoon I was looking idly out our back window, watching the train arrive from

The Trauen Barracks

Munster. After the ancient steam engine with its three equally old cars departed the station, I noticed a tiny clump of people walking toward the barracks. That was nothing unusual. The people coming up the dirt path approached slowly, and as they got closer I saw that there were four of them. I sensed something familiar, something about the way the man walked. He walked like my grandfather Samuel, slightly dragging his left foot. It was Mutti, Opa, Ingrid, and Vera! I bolted outside and raced down the path to meet them.

After dinner Mutti and Opa finally gave in to my badgering and told me about their trip. "When we left Trauen, Opa and I took the train to Munster. There we transferred to a train that took us near the border. From Lübow we walked." Mutti paused. "The weather was much better this time. There was no snowstorm. We thought we had nearly made it across when we were surprised by a Russian patrol."

Opa picked up her story. "First, Hedy and I were thrown into a cell after each of us answered a few perfunctory questions. Soon, that same day, the Russians released us from the cell to clean latrines. They assigned us a regular room in a barracks with two army cots with the usual straw mattresses and two blankets. No pillows. Not enough blankets to stay warm in the unheated room. We slept with our clothes on, not that we would have taken them off anyway. We cleaned latrines for several days. When I asked a guard for firewood, they gave us wood for our stove. The food was simple, yet adequate. It was the same food the Russian soldiers ate. Black bread, a chunk of butter and some jam in the morning, and bread and cabbage soup in the evening."

When Opa paused, Mutti laughed her infectious, carefree laugh, and said, "Every day I practiced my Russian on the commander of the small Russian border unit. After several days he became quite friendly with both of us. We continued to clean their latrines, split wood for them, polish the officers' boots, and do any number of things they wanted done. Finally, I talked him into releasing us. I convinced him that Opa and I were coming home after escaping from the British zone." I broke into a loud laugh when she said that.

"Do people really escape from here to go to the Russian zone?"

"I don't think so," Mutti replied between laughs. "But the story worked, and, after being detained for four weeks, we were let go by the Russian major. Once we got to Strasburg we found Oma Grapentin and Ingrid with Uncle

The Trauen Barracks

Ernst and Lotte. Oma told me then that in December we had escaped the *Volkspolizei* just in the nick of time. They arrived at the hotel around eight that evening. They searched the rooms, but of course found nothing. Oma told them she didn't know where we had gone, that she thought we would be back shortly. They waited for a while. When we didn't show they got impatient and left to look for us at the train station."

"I remember," I interjected, "the train to Neubrandenburg was late that evening, arriving about forty minutes after eight. The police must have missed us by only minutes. Maybe they even saw the train pull out of the station?"

"We were lucky," Mutti added. "Oma getting them to wait for us for a few extra minutes may have made our escape possible. I still don't know why they didn't call the police in Neubrandenburg to arrest us. Maybe they did and they had already gone home for the night. Who knows? I hate to think what would have happened to Willi if they had caught up with us." Everyone was silent. Mutti and Opa rose from the table to go to bed. I continued to pester them for more details about their trip.

Oma finally intervened on my behalf, saying, "You owe the boy an explanation, *Alter*. Wolfgang was worried about you."

"There isn't that much left to tell," Mutti interjected as she and Opa sat down again. "Ernst and Lotte had no room for us. So we walked back to Strasburg to see if Vera could put us up."

"I was really surprised when Aunt Hedwig and Opa Samuel showed up," Vera said, her cheeks flushing red with excitement. "My father had moved into Aunt Hedwig's former place with his housekeeper, so we had some room to spare for her and Opa. It took me just minutes to pack my suitcase when Aunt Hedwig suggested I accompany her and Opa to the English zone, right, Aunt Hedwig?"

"Vera, please call me Hedy, would you?" Mutti replied, shaking her head at Vera's use of her given name. "You know I can't stand being called Hedwig."

"Yes, Aunt Hedwig," Vera replied. We laughed loudly.

"We stayed three nights with Vera. Vera's father, Paul, never came by while we were there. We deliberately stayed out of his way so as not to put him in a compromising position. I think it was the sixth of February when we left Strasburg, right, Opa?"

"Yes, that's about right, Hedy. Yes, I am sure it was the sixth. We didn't

The Trauen Barracks

think it wise to return the same way we came. What if we were caught by the same Russians who had caught us before? When they released us, they made us sign a paper saying we would not attempt to escape from the Russian zone, and, if we were captured in such an attempt, we would be put before a military court and sent to prison. We headed toward Magdeburg, further south," Opa explained.

"Ernst was nice enough to give us bread and lard for sandwiches," Mutti added, "and Vera brought more food. We were much better prepared this time, Wolfgang."

"It took the four of us two days before we arrived in Magdeburg." Opa picked up their story again. "We sat in the train station trying to think of what to do next, when I noticed a coal train coming into the station, slowing and stopping on a distant track. The train was headed west. I knew there weren't any large cities west of Magdeburg, except in the English zone. A plan began to evolve. I started a conversation with one of the station attendants and learned that coal trains occasionally came through on their way to the English zone. He told me the trains were closely guarded when they crossed the border. Now I had our plan!

"That afternoon it started to snow lightly. As it became dark around four o'clock, the coal train still sat in the station. A local passenger train arrived shortly after four. We took our things and walked to the far end, where the platform was darkest, and, after the passenger train pulled out, we quickly crossed the tracks. Then we crawled between the coal cars to the far side of the tracks, hoping no one had seen us. No one had. We climbed on top of an open coal car and huddled together for warmth in a corner. We were sheltered from the wind and from prying eyes. It was cold and getting colder as the hours passed. We started to shiver in spite of our best efforts to stay warm. Our little Ingrid hugged Hedy so closely she was almost invisible." Opa smiled at Ingrid and pulled her up on his lap. "And she never, never complained." Opa pulled Ingrid close to him, took his ever-present pipe out of his mouth, and said, "Now give your old grandfather a hug."

"After midnight, the train moved. Less than an hour later, it slowed again and stopped at a lit siding. We were at the border. It was snowing hard. We heard guards talking in the distance. Then two of them walked past our car and stopped—one climbed on the car behind us and the other climbed on our car. The guard was right above us. We didn't breathe or move a muscle. After what seemed an eternity, I heard him climb down.

The Trauen Barracks

The two guards walked down the train, repeating the process over and over. It took a long time. We were so cold that time began to lose its meaning. Finally the train moved again. The next time the train stopped, we were in Braunschweig. We quickly got off."

With Vera's arrival, we now were five adults and two children living in two small rooms. My father helped out by continuing to sleep at his place of work. With Opa's help Vera immediately found work at the potato farm. Ingrid was going on eight years old, and she had had almost no formal schooling since she turned six. Dad took her to the two-room schoolhouse in Trauen and enrolled her. Ingrid learned quickly. The modest pace at the village school allowed her to catch up with other children her age. She received much individual attention from the schoolmaster, who coped with a flock of students of different ages, abilities, and backgrounds. Ingrid thrived in the Trauen village school.

Mutti and Dad spoke to each other when they were together. They did not sleep together. I overheard them talking about divorce. They discussed how they would go about getting a divorce with the least impact on the family. My father agreed to be the guilty party, since under German law one of the two had to be guilty of a transgression that would warrant a divorce. He promised to admit in court that he had slept with other women and not to contest Mutti's request for a divorce and custody of Ingrid and me. Several days later, though, they had a fight, and he said he wouldn't give her a divorce. Things quickly went back to the way I remembered, loud arguments and accusations. Although I wished that things were different, a divorce wouldn't really change anything for either Ingrid or me. Oma and Opa Samuel were our grandparents, and nothing my mother or father could do was going to change that. I knew for sure that one day they would get their divorce.

Every day I walked the four kilometers from the barracks to my new school in Fassberg. I liked being back in a real school. They taught real academic subjects, not political theory. My teachers were real teachers who had gone to school to be teachers, and they expected their students to study and learn. We did. I studied geography, German, mathematics, biology, and music. Once a week we had gymnastics in our well-equipped gym. I couldn't take English even though I wanted to, because my classmates were already too far ahead of me, I was told. My sixth-grade class was nearly equally divided between girls and boys, and by fall a number of the boys would go to a *Mittelschule*, a middle school, in another town, which meant that some of them would eventually be allowed to go to the *Gymnasium* or even the university. I didn't know how the decision was made about who would go to school where. I sensed it had long-term implications for our futures. I was happy to be in a good school, and I didn't worry about why I didn't have the opportunity to go to an even better school. I realized that I was poorly educated in comparison to my classmates. I just wanted to do well where I was.

My first few weeks were a period of adjustment and making new friends. I quickly got into fights with classmates because I wanted to play soccer with them in the school yard during recess. They let me know that if I came into the yard they would beat me up. I didn't know if they meant it. I was both troubled and scared by their overt hostility. It seemed as if I were back in the kind of environment I had known in rural Strasburg. A girl who overheard the threats took pity on me and invited me to play with the girls on their side of the school yard. I accompanied the girls, who played girl games and asked me to join them. I got so embarrassed that I instantly overcame any fear of my classmates and went over to the boys' side of the yard to face whatever awaited me there. It wasn't long in coming. A tall boy who was recognized as the informal class leader and who was also the "big gun" on the Fassberg Youth Soccer Team, sent over one of his bullies to teach me a lesson. That boy looked surprised when I punched him squarely in the nose and made it bleed. He bloodied mine. Our fight was a draw. Recess was over at that point, and we went inside. If the teacher noticed that two of us had bloody noses, he said nothing.

On the following day, I went outside during recess and stood my ground when selections were made for school yard soccer. Teams were picked in sequence by the team leaders, and, as I expected, I was left standing like a lone carrot in an empty field. "Hey," I said firmly, "I am playing, so you better decide whose team I am on, or I am going to select my own team." They ignored me and started play. I jumped in and started playing, too. In only seconds, punches were flying again until one of the team leaders called a time-out. "Hey, you," he said looking at me, "if you are any good we'll find out soon enough. Play on the other team, all right? Now, let's go and play before recess is over."

I scored several goals. My opposition complained bitterly because I was wearing shoes with wooden soles; they claimed I hit them in the legs and that was why they couldn't stop me. They called me a *Bolzer*, a chopper. Yet I knew I hadn't hit them in the legs. I was especially careful, because I was aware that, while all of them wore leather boots, I wore clumsy plastic shoes with wooden soles. I had to be more aggressive to prove that I was as good as they. And they were trying to prove the opposite. My shoes were intimidating to look at, and that may have been of help to me. After that game, however, I had no more problems getting selected for a recess soccer team.

School made me acutely aware that I was different in other respects from my classmates. I was a *Flüchtling*. I never thought much about being a refugee other than that it meant my family had to flee from where we once lived because of the war. Being a refugee meant that we had lost our possessions and that we lived in crowded, substandard housing. My status did not appear unusual to me. What my classmates saw, however, was that I was one of only two *Flüchtlinge* in our class. Since I lived in barracks I was, if not looked down upon, at least different. In Germany being different has always meant being an outsider. Most of my classmates tried not to show their prejudices, and they probably didn't consciously think about them. They were only reflecting their parents' feelings and attitudes. I could sense that they were uncomfortable with me around after school. Only one boy thought of inviting me to his home, and no one invited me to play or to come to anything such as a birthday party. Going to school with me was one thing; being friends was another. I did become friends with the other refugee boy, Arnim, who also lived in a barracks.

I liked Fassberg. It was whole and clean, with no reminders of war. The town was built in 1933 right after Hitler came to power. A concrete road ran to the main gate of the air base, and the town was laid out around this road. There were three housing areas: the red, the white, and the grey. The red area had the best houses. Built of red brick, they were for officers and senior managers. Most had balconies, patios, or verandas, or all three. In 1947, British families lived in many of these houses. The red housing area also had a butcher shop, a bakery, a drugstore, and a grocery store. My school and a church were across from the shops. A barber, a watchmaker, a tailor, a ladies' hairdresser, and a florist all operated out of their homes. In the white and grey housing areas, the exteriors of houses were either white or grey plaster, and the houses had few balconies or verandas. Fassberg had no hotels. The streets were covered with asphalt rather than with the traditional cobblestones found in older towns, and the houses had gardens surrounded by unpainted picket fences. Much of Fassberg had been built in the middle of a pine forest, the only kind of tree other than oak and birch that seemed to thrive in the poor, sandy soil. Many of these trees had been left standing when the houses were built, and the town had a pleasantly woodsy character.

Every day as I left the squalor and poverty of the barracks behind and came closer to Fassberg, a load lifted off my shoulders. With its clean, orderly tranquility, in contrast to my world of stress and deprivation, Fassberg became a refuge, a place of solace, healing, and peace. When I stepped out of the forest onto the paved sidewalks and walked through the English housing area, I began to feel clean and free. Fassberg offered the promise of future improvement, the promise that I would not have to live forever in the crowded, squalid, and depressing conditions of the Trauen barracks. Every Monday, Wednesday, and Friday, a wonderful event occurred at school. On those mornings a group of volunteer women served each student a cup of steaming hot chocolate and a handful of Spanish peanuts. The peanuts were exquisitely delicious; I felt as though I had never eaten anything as divine. I didn't know what they were—whether they grew on a tree, a bush, or some other plant. I sipped the hot chocolate while it was still hot enough to burn my tongue. I was often cold when I arrived in school, because I had to walk so far in my thin clothes and plastic shoes. The hot chocolate warmed me for the rest of the day. I didn't miss a Monday, Wednesday, or Friday; I didn't miss any day of school. Each school day was precious to me.

I came down with the flu in the winter of 1946. I dragged myself to school every day so as not to miss the peanuts and hot chocolate. Often I went to school without eating breakfast. Our classes started at eight o'clock in the morning and ended at one in the afternoon. By the time I walked home it was two or later before I had anything to eat. I didn't mind. I had gotten used to doing without food. But I couldn't do without hope. Fassberg and my school gave me hope for a better future.

Chapter 17

REFUGEE LIFE

Barracks life imposed its own crushing burdens on our family. While we no longer feared for our physical safety, day-to-day life had become just as dispiriting and oppressive in the English zone of occupation as it had been in the Russian zone. With five adults and two children crammed into an exceedingly small area and with little or no privacy, our situation became one of daily degradation. The thin apartment walls meant that lives were shared with family and neighbors on a twenty-four-hour basis.

Spring arrived. With the cover of snow gone and the ice melted, the ground in our compound turned into soft, squishy mud, and the true squalor of our barracks life became visible. A permanent lake of dirty water and mud surrounded our water pump. Every family living in the barracks had to get water at least once a day, usually more often. There was no choice but to stand in the mud while pumping water. It helped to have rubber boots, but few of us did. It rained often in the Lüneburg Heath, nearly always a slow, persistent rain lasting for days. Twice each workday the RAF truck drove into the compound to pick up or return those men and women who worked at the air base. With its huge tires, the truck turned our compound into a nearly impassable quagmire, where one could easily sink into mud up to the ankles. The truck ensured that the area remained in that deplorable state by crushing any dry path that someone might have tried to build between a barracks and the pump. In time, no one did anything anymore. Our waste water had to be disposed of, too, and it ended up in the centrally located garden plots. Much of that water then drained to the lower-lying areas—around the water pump and in front of our doors. Mud, mud, and more mud. And when it finally got warm, the mud turned fetid. The stench reminded me of the smells of the nearly medieval section of Strasburg where my grandparents Grapentin once lived.

The three barracks held a hodgepodge of old and young, mostly from the eastern part of Germany and also from some of the lands once occupied by the German army during the war. Regardless of their place of origin, most people turned petty, narrow-minded, ugly, and conniving because of the terrible conditions. Many of the inhabitants soon looked just like the barracks in which they lived—grey and worn. One exception was a Dutch couple and their daughter, a nice-looking young woman in her early twenties. The Dutch family lived on the north end of the barracks adjacent to the road leading to the former V-2 research center. They must have arrived in 1945 before the war ended, because they had a larger than usual apartment and their own furniture. Both husband and wife were heavy people. Their pretty daughter was slim and blonde, always nicely dressed. Rumor had it that the Dutch couple were Nazi Party people who had escaped Holland before the English and the Americans liberated the area from German occupation. I only knew them as nice people who kept to themselves.

I took notice of another couple, young and nice looking, which set them apart from most of the others. They, too, kept to themselves. She was a tall bleached blonde, or at least that's what my mother called her, with a little envy in her voice. He was a former Ju-87 Stuka pilot. He was strong and husky, not as tall as his wife, with naturally blond hair combed straight back. A strand of hair always seemed to be falling into his face, and he would throw it back with a nearly automatic flick of his head. He wore his old flying boots and Luftwaffe uniform, except for the insignia. I assumed that his uniform was probably the only clothing he owned. I spoke to him once while both of us were getting water at the pump. "Do you miss flying?" I asked brashly.

"Yes, I miss flying," he answered, with a quick smile lighting up his face. "I would fly any airplane, for anyone, anytime, anywhere, just give me an airplane," he said, with vigor in his voice and a brightness in his blue eyes that hadn't been there moments before. He continued pumping water.

Refugee Life

When he turned his face toward me in response to my subsequent questions, I saw an intensity in the flyer's eyes that made me wish to know more about him.

"Did you like flying the Ju-87, the Stuka?" I asked.

"Ja, I did like flying that airplane." He stopped pumping. "It was slow," he continued more thoughtfully, looking into the distance, not at me, "but I knew how to fly it well. There is nothing to worry about when you know your airplane. Do you understand what I mean?" He gave me a quick look, his eyes clouding over, reflecting none of the earlier brightness. He was sorry he had spoken to me, a child who couldn't possibly understand. He was right. I didn't quite understand what he meant to say. I wanted to talk to him more about flying. He yanked the full bucket off the pump, and, without looking at me again, rushed off.

There was a Polish family, the Paschmionkas. They had two hulking boys in their late teens, big, muscular men, and another my age, slighter in stature. The older boys worked for the English and were always trading on the black market to bring in extra food for their family. Their parents were big people, too. The old man was nearly immobile. In contrast, his wife, although large in stature, was quite agile and did the work around their apartment. Whenever the weather permitted, the old man sat in front of his apartment in a rickety rocking chair. He never did any work as far as I could tell. I never even saw him walk anywhere, except to and from his chair. When my grandfather Samuel passed by on his way to the barn, Herr Paschmionka would invariably call out, "Herr Samuel, you are working much too hard again; you should slow down a bit and enjoy life as I am doing." Opa would politely acknowledge him with a tap of two fingers to the bill of his ski cap and continue on his way. Opa, I knew, had the opposite point of view about enjoying life and living a long time. According to his philosophy, people had to keep moving, especially when they were older.

Of course, the barracks also had a Communist. For some reason he singled me out to tell me how wonderful it was to live in the Russian zone, in the people's paradise. For reasons he did not divulge, he never packed up and moved to live in the paradise of which he spoke so glowingly. He had met his wife in the barracks, and she was pregnant. She ran around in a dirty dress with a soiled apron over her swollen belly, bringing me face-to-face with the concept of birth. I had, of course, seen babies before, but never thought about how they were made and where they came from. I thought about it now because of the woman parading around the compound with her big belly, as if it were an award or a badge she had earned in a contest.

Some *Flüchtlinge* made vivid impressions on me. They colored my life not by who they had been or where they had come from, but by what they did to each other. One such couple lived in the middle of our barracks in a larger than usual apartment with all of their own furniture. They, too, had arrived in Trauen and settled into the barracks before the war ended in May 1945. They said they came from Köln. "We were bombed out," the daughter who was my age told me, as was commonly said when a house was lost in a bombing raid. Yet they still had their furniture. How could they have been bombed out and still have their furniture? To me it seemed even stranger that the man, who was tall and handsome, had not served in the Wehrmacht. The only explanation I came up with was that he, too, was a *Flüchtling*. Unlike those of us who had fled the former German lands east of the Oder River, he probably was a *Flüchtling* from his political past. I figured he had once been a ranking party member or in some police organization, which kept him out of uniform. His wife was short and attractive in her own way, with a sure, arrogant walk, a flowing mane of hair, and an oversized head. Rumor had it that she would perform abortions—for something in return, of course, other than worthless *Reichsmark*.

The couple from Köln had two children, a boy Ingrid's age, and the girl, my age. The boy was short like his mother, forever parading in front of his barracks with a piece of white English bread thickly covered with butter and English orange marmalade. His father worked at the air base, like most everybody else, and his job seemed to give him access to an unlimited supply of bread and marmalade. The girl was my height and had a large head like her mother. The few times I played outside with barracks children, an unmarried fat woman, whom everyone called *Dicke* Bertha, would invariably be leaning out of her window and comment on what a beautiful couple the girl and I would make. She embarrassed me to death when she said so out loud for everyone to hear. The girl had a flat face like a pancake, couldn't she see that? I didn't want to be a couple with her. I knew *Dicke* Bertha meant well, but she annoyed me with her comments. Besides, I hadn't quite figured out how girls fit into my life. I was beginning to feel some disquieting things happening in my body, which somehow made girls appear more attractive. I told myself that I had no time for such nonsense and tried to suppress the existence of my occasional hormonal surges. The changes in my body were terrifying and disturbing to me. I had no idea how to deal with what was happening to me nor anyone to talk to. I also noticed that my voice was changing. The girls in school laughed out loud when I broke into a high-pitched squeal.

Two women who frequently had English soldiers for visitors lived in separate apartments in the barracks at the edge of the forest. One was a schoolteacher, in her twenties and unmarried. She was from Ostpreussen, of average height with lovely brown hair, quite good-looking and well proportioned. Aside from the Stuka pilot's wife, the schoolteacher was without doubt the best-looking woman in our compound. In the evenings I often saw English army jeeps parked in front of her apartment. The soldiers usually stayed overnight and didn't leave until early in the morning. The other woman was divorced. She was a redhead with two young children, a girl and a boy. She and the schoolteacher went out together, and, when the schoolteacher had English visitors, the redhead was invariably at her place, too. On those days her children had to fend for themselves.

On my way home from school one gloriously sunny day in May, I walked past the barracks where the two women lived. The redhead was leaning out of her window enjoying the sunshine. I was shocked at the sight of her. I had not seen her for a while, and her appearance had changed dramatically. Her once-beautiful bright red hair had faded and thinned out to the point where I could see her scalp. She wore a pink, short-sleeved sweater, and on her arms and face I saw ugly sores. She smiled as I passed by her window. When I saw her again in June, the sores had disappeared, although her hair was still as thin as before. Later that month she went to a nearby former Wehrmacht hospital. She soon died of syphilis, and her former husband came and took the children away.

The redhead's death opened up a tiny apartment—two rooms the size of one of Oma and Opa's. Mutti spoke to the redhead's husband and acquired the furniture. Then Mutti, Vera, Ingrid, and I moved in. At about the same time in June when the redhead was in the hospital dying of syphilis, I saw the pretty schoolteacher several times a day walking back and forth between her room and the apartment of the "bombed out" woman from Köln. This went on intermittently for two weeks, and then, suddenly, I didn't see the schoolteacher anymore. I noticed the absence of English jeeps at her apartment, too. She died shortly thereafter from an infection in her belly. The barracks rumor had it that the Köln woman had performed an abortion on the schoolteacher using extra-long knitting needles and that the teacher had contracted an infection and died. Whatever the truth of the rumor, the schoolteacher was dead.

Some ugly tongues took pleasure in the fate of the two women, consider-ing their deaths well-deserved punishment for sleeping with English soldiers. I knew nothing about sin and punishment and who deserved what fate. I felt that the two women did not deserve to die but should be sharing life with the rest of us. After the death of the schoolteacher, the "bombed out" woman from Köln was seldom seen outside her apartment. When she did venture out, she seemed even more arrogant in her demeanor. I took the two deaths in stride as I had others in the past. Life went on. The two women were soon forgotten. More important topics fed the insatiable gossip mill. However, I could not completely forget the two and their sad fates. To me they were casualties of the war that had supposedly ended in May 1945. They just died in different ways.

Summer arrived, and in summer even the bleakest situation seemed to look more positive and less threatening. I knew that delusional feeling from living in Strasburg. Food and clothing remained scarce. It seemed as if after the war nothing new had been grown or manufactured in Germany. I heard rumors about war reparations to the Allies in return for damage done by the German army. While I was still in Strasburg and working on my little plot of land on the *Schlammberg*, I had often seen freight trains heading east on the single track, loaded with the machinery of whole factories. They went to Russia, people said. Most of the dismantled factories came from the American zone. An old forest across the street from our barracks had also been cut for shipment to England. But not everything manufactured or grown was shipped to Russia and England, or was it? Why wasn't there more food and clothing available? Farmers farmed their land; they cared only about their fields and animals, about rain and sunshine, not about war and politics. I remembered seeing farmers in the fields on the last days of April in 1945 as we fled from the Russians. Nothing kept farmers from their fields, not even war. What happened to the food they grew in 1945 and 1946? Did it go for war reparations? I couldn't believe that. Yet there was little food to be found anywhere.

We were lucky to be living in the countryside compared to people in the cities. At harvest time I could go into the fields where the potatoes had already been harvested and find plenty that had grown deeper than the potato machine had been set for. Some varieties of potatoes were harvested as early as July, others in August and September. I had scavenged potatoes in the summer of 1944 in Sagan. I really hadn't had to do that at the time, since our rations were ample. Now scavenging was a necessity. Living in the barracks, I became good not only at scavenging potatoes but also at finding mushrooms. The heath country received lots of rain, and I learned quickly that the white champignon mushroom liked wet areas. All summer long I brought home these tasty mushrooms, which Mutti fried with onions and served as a main dish. I found other varieties and learned quickly to keep the locations to myself. I usually went into the forest looking for mushrooms after a rain. Then they seemed to pop out of the ground at incredible speed. There were poisonous mushrooms, too. Most I could easily identify by their showy colors or their thin and fragile bodies. If there was any doubt, I let them be or took them to Frau Paschmionka. She knew all about mushrooms.

I went into the adjacent pine forest one Saturday afternoon. It had rained in the morning until about ten. Then the sun came out. It turned into a hot, steamy summer day. I had on my airplane tire sandals, shorts, and a worn short-sleeved shirt. I headed into a section of forest I had not been in before and came across what looked like bomb craters, which made me curious. In one crater I noticed a colony of extra-large mushrooms. Some of them measured over one foot across the top. Their tops were grey with the edges curled upward, and they had thick stems. They looked as if they had sprung up only that morning. I looked into other nearby craters and found several more filled with these giant, fleshy fungi. Since I had no idea whether or not these mushrooms were poisonous, I took one and ran home with it. My first stop was the Polish woman. She wasn't in. I had to make a decision. I grabbed two shopping nets and went back to the place of my curious find. I filled both nets until they couldn't hold another mushroom and returned home about five o'clock that afternoon. Mutti was home. Frau Paschmionka still was nowhere to be seen. I showed Mutti my find, and she quickly agreed they would make a great dinner.

"I don't know if they are really edible or not," I cautioned her. Our mutual greed and lack of dietary variety convinced us to be experimental and brave.

"My mother told me once that if you are unsure of a mushroom you should put it into boiling water for a few minutes with an onion," Mutti said, "and if it is poisonous the onion will turn blue or black."

"*Ja*, let's do it," I said, throwing caution to the wind. We boiled our test mushroom with an onion, and, when it didn't change color, we proceeded to fry about half of the mushrooms in bacon fat with onions. Ingrid and Vera arrived. Vera set the table. The mushrooms were done and smelled delicious. We sat down at our all-purpose table and looked at each other. No one touched anything. I knew what the question was. Who would try them first? I picked up my fork and began to eat. They tasted wonderful to me. Still, no one followed my lead. "Are you waiting for me to have stomach cramps?" I asked, looking around the table. "They are the best mushrooms I've ever tasted. If you don't start, I will eat yours, too." Everybody laughed and started eating. After dinner I went outside. It was still light, a beautiful summer evening. I began to have second thoughts about my bravery. I could still stick my finger down my throat and throw up, I thought. I walked past the Polish woman's apartment, and, looking through her window, saw that she was in the kitchen. I ran back to our apartment, grabbed one of the largest mushrooms and took it to her.

Frau Paschmionka opened the door and immediately exclaimed, "Ah!" She then said, "That is a beautiful *Habichtpilz*. Where did you find this? I have never seen one this large before."

"They are not poisonous?"

"No, no, my boy," she nearly shouted with glee. "They are some of the best eating mushrooms you can find. I just didn't know they grew around here." I was so elated with what she told me that I offered to take her to the place where I had found them. She accepted immediately and got her youngest boy to come along. I grabbed my two nets again and we set off. Between the three of us, we picked every last one of the mushrooms. I returned frequently during the summer, hoping to find new growth. The so-called *Habichtpilze* never grew back again.

When I wasn't thinking about food, I thought about wood for our stove. We had a one-burner stove in the first of our two rooms. We cooked on it, and it also heated our apartment. Like all such stoves, in winter it turned the immediate area hot while the rest of the apartment stayed cold. In summer it made every room hot and uncomfortable. As with Oma's stove, which had several burners, our stove vented through a pipe which ran through the ceiling and the roof. I watched carefully to see that the ceiling didn't catch on fire when the stove was in use.

One constant problem for me was to find kindling, which I needed every day to relight the fire. On a warm August day I went exploring on the grounds of the former V-2 research institute. Everything was empty—barracks, a motor pool with many work areas, vehicle maintenance shops, and related buildings. Every structure on the installation was empty. There were no abandoned trucks, no burned piles of weapons, nothing lying about. The thought struck me that the English had probably taken everything and everybody to England. If the Germans had evacuated the place just before the war ended, they would have destroyed much of it. There was no rubble. Every building was neat and clean and empty. One building looked like it might have been a hospital. Its doors were locked. I didn't break them open. Next to the hospital was a garage. One of its doors appeared to be unlocked. Although it was dark inside, I could see that the garage was stacked high with wooden hospital beds. I decided I would take several home for our use. I carried them first to Opa's barn. Later, at night, Opa and I assembled two in their apartment. Both Opa and Oma liked their new beds. Every day I carried side boards to the barn, where I cut them up. I had solved my kindling problem. I carried the sides for fifty beds to the barn, chopped them up, and fed them into our stove for the rest of the year.

Our primary source of firewood was the forest. A forester kept an eye on the woods near the barracks, because he knew people cut down trees, and he attempted to prevent that. While we tried not to be too obvious, the forest near the barracks gradually became thinner and thinner. People cut down trees in the darkness of night. I cut some, too, but it wasn't enough to get us through the winter. Opa Samuel went about it the right way and received permission from the forester to cut trees designated by him for that purpose. The designated trees, however, were in a forest ten kilometers from our barracks, on the Munster-Lager artillery range. This presented two problems. First, we had to get a wagon and horses to transport the logs from the forest to our barn; second, we had to find out when the English were not practicing with their artillery so we wouldn't get hit. The forester obtained the range firing schedule for us. Sunday was the only day the range was not in use. Opa was able to get the horses and a wagon on loan from the potato farm where he worked. One August Sunday, Opa and my father took our saw and set off to cut down the trees the forester had marked for us on the Munster artillery range.

Felling the trees was the easy part. Cutting them into lengths which allowed us to manhandle the logs onto a wagon was harder. It took two trips for Opa and my father to finish the job. On a subsequent Sunday at five o'clock in the morning, Opa and I went to the potato farm and got two horses and a wagon. By six o'clock my grandfather had harnessed our team, and we were on our way. The horses moved at a slow and deliberate pace. They were powerful animals and bred to pull heavy loads. It felt good riding in the wagon, sitting next to my grandfather. He smelled of tobacco from the pipe that rarely left his mouth. It was a familiar smell to me, the smell of a man who had lived a lot of life. I always felt a great sense of security when I was with my grandfather Samuel.

He held the reins loosely, like a man who knew about horses. We said little on the bumpy ride. There was no need. It was enough for me to sit next to him. We arrived at our destination deep inside the Munster artillery range two hours later. The trees my father and Opa had cut on the previous two Sundays lay fairly far apart. Opa parked the wagon on the *Waldweg* so the horses could pull straight ahead once the wagon was loaded. Opa unlimbered the horses, but kept them tethered to the wagon tongue. This way they could move about and feed off the grass on the edge of the *Waldweg* but still be secured. The trees that had been cut had died either from damage inflicted by insects or from artillery fire. The forester wasn't about to release healthy trees for cutting in his beloved forest, even on an artillery range.

By noon I was grateful when we took a half-hour break. Opa had brought a bottle of water, and Oma had prepared several sandwiches. The bread was generously spread with butter and filled with thick slices of hard salami. Oma knew logging was hard work. I wondered where she had got the salami. My father had probably traded English cigarettes to a farmer for it. Dad could get nearly anything for English cigarettes; they were the closest thing we had to money. The sandwiches tasted good, and the water was refreshing. Opa and I sat side by side on a fallen tree eating our lunch. Sunlight gently filtered through the trees, throwing splotches of light and shade onto the *Waldweg* and the feeding horses. Big forest flies constantly pestered the horses, who tried to chase them away by flicking their long tails and shaking their heads. We finished loading by three o'clock in the afternoon and started for home. Although the wagon was fully loaded with timber, the horses leaned right into the load. Once we were out of the forest and on the main road again, they moved just as easily as when we had traveled with an empty wagon earlier that morning. While the horses had looked lazy and bored then, on the return trip they looked alert and seemed to enjoy pulling the heavy load.

Once we left the tricky sandy soil of the *Waldweg* behind, Opa relaxed and lit his pipe. The horses seemed to know where to go on their own without any real intervention on his part. He gave me the reins. "Keep them loose," he said. "Apply just enough pressure for them to know you are there. They'll know that you have the reins now and they'll do little quirky things to test you. Just remain steady and they'll settle in again and accept you." The horses did as Opa said they would. "This place is an old friend." Opa leaned back against the backrest of the wagon bench, relaxing, enjoying his pipe.

"Why is that, Opa?"

"Well, many years ago, before your father was born, I was detailed here to Munster-Lager as a young sergeant in the kaiser's army." He paused, taking several puffs from his pipe. "I was twenty-six years old then. The kaiser had acquired a number of colonies in Africa, and in 1904 there was a rebellion in one of them. The Herero tribe in German Southwest Africa tried to throw us out. They almost succeeded. It took us several years before we put down the rebellion. I trained recruits right here in Munster-Lager for that nasty war. I am glad I never had to go myself. Many of our soldiers came back with diseases which no one knew how to treat." Opa fell silent. His pipe went out. The sounds of creaking leather, wagon wheels crunching against cobblestones, and the clip-clop of laboring horse hooves were comforting and reassuring.

"You can never stand still, my son," Opa continued. "The world keeps changing and you must change with it. Those who don't are left behind. Don't you ever be left behind, my dear boy. Keep your eyes on the future." Opa looked me in the eyes. "Have faith in yourself. Your time will come. You will know when it does." He put his hand on my head and stroked my hair back slowly, lovingly. When we arrived at the barn, Dad helped unload the wagon. It was hard work and made us sweaty and hungry. Opa drove the empty wagon back to the village. Before he could come home, he had to clean and feed the horses. It was eight o'clock in the evening before Opa finally walked through the door. I knew he had gotten up at four-thirty that morning and he wouldn't go to bed until ten. I slept like a log that night. Later in the autumn we cut each log into lengths that fit our ovens, and then we split the sections into smaller pieces, which we stacked in a pyramid outside the barn so they would dry properly. When we finished cutting, splitting, and stacking, all three of us had callouses on our hands as a result of handling saws and axes day in and day out for several weeks.

On my daily walk to and from school, I learned to love the pine forest and the heath with its juniper bushes. In places, the junipers grew densely enough to make their own forest. Some of them had weird shapes, and at night could appear to look like men. I would stop in my tracks to ascertain that a juniper bush really wasn't a stranger coming toward me. In every case it was just a bush tricking my mind into thinking it was a human form, putting a scare into me. The heath was especially beautiful in August and September, blooming in purple splendor as far as the eye could see. I would stand at the edge of the forest for minutes at a time and gaze at the sea of flaming purple. I was almost always alone. Few people had cause to follow the paths I walked, and no other children from the barracks went to school in Fassberg. Sometimes when I stood still and listened carefully, I would think I could hear the tranquil sound of absolute stillness. For that instant, only the forest, the heath, and I existed. Then the moment would be gone. The trill of a meadowlark rising straight up from its nest and hovering in one spot about ten to fifteen meters up in the air would remind me that I shared nature's beauty with other living things. Then suddenly the lark would stop singing and plummet straight down to its nest.

My path from the barracks to school in Fassberg took me first along potato fields and then through the pine forest, which extended right into the town of Fassberg itself. What was now a potato field had been an open area used as a runway by Luftwaffe planes during the war. In the middle of the field stood a battery of five 20 mm antiaircraft guns, like the guns my father had once commanded. The guns were clustered in a tight circle, their barrels pointing threateningly at a sky which no longer bore enemy aircraft. They were rusting relics from a time which was receding rapidly into history. I tried not to think of those days; they were too terrifying to recall. But with all the remnants of war around, I couldn't help but ask myself on occasion what had happened and why. I had no answers to those questions.

A scant half kilometer away from our barracks, the Luftwaffe graveyard began. Most of the planes sat on the perimeter of the forest facing runways which were little more than level ground. On my way home from school, I explored the abandoned planes. Of the hundreds of aircraft parked in the forest, most were Junkers Ju-88 twin-engined medium bombers and Heinkel

He-177 heavy four-engined bombers. I enjoyed climbing into the cockpit of one particular Ju-88, sitting in the pilot's seat, holding the control column, and imagining myself flying. The thought of flying was inspiring. The aircraft smelled of plastics, rubber, aluminum, paint, fuel, and sweat. Surely there was the smell of sweat mixed in with all the other odors, or did I imagine that? People sweated when they worked hard, when they were afraid, and when they were happy and excited. When I sat in one of the planes in the forest, the smell of man and machine made them more to me than just old airplanes, more than just pieces of abandoned metal. The planes represented the challenge of flying, and also courage and valor, the things I admired in my dad, in my grandfather, and especially in my mother.

My father had told me once that the last large combat mission flown from Fassberg was in June of 1944 against a Russian air base at Poltava. "Sometimes the Americans did not return to their own air bases in England or Italy. They flew on to Russian bases. An He-177 from Fassberg followed one of the American B-17 groups to Poltava, and that night the Luftwaffe attacked, destroying many of the American B-17s on the ground. After that mission we were nearly out of fuel for our airplanes, and we didn't fly any more for the remainder of the war." I thought back to the second Sorau raid I had witnessed in late May of 1944. Those Americans hadn't turned back; they had kept flying east with a different-looking aircraft in trail. I remembered clearly that odd aircraft far behind the B-17s. Maybe it was a Heinkel-177.

Aside from the Ju-88s, there were well over a hundred He-177s parked among the trees. Some had been vandalized as people had come and removed instruments or tires. Aircraft tires were cut up for sandals like the ones I wore. Me-109s were also scattered throughout the area. Some of them sat in the middle of a runway with English roundels painted on their wings and fuselages. The English had flown them when they occupied the base in 1945. One section of the aircraft graveyard held miscellaneous planes, some of which were damaged during a raid by American fighters. Among them was one lone Ju-87 Stuka. Up close I was surprised to see how small the Stuka was. A German company had begun to cut up the planes, loading sections of wings and fuselages onto a railroad car parked on the single siding in the Trauen rail yard. When the car was loaded, it was picked up by the morning or afternoon train, and another empty car was left behind. The wrecking crew moved methodically from the miscellaneous aircraft area into the Ju-88 area. It appeared they would do the He-177s last. I knew that when they finished their task, my flying dreams in the old airplanes would be over, too.

That summer Mutti got a job on the air base. She worked at the Navy, Army, and Air Force Exchange (NAAFE), where soldiers and their families shopped. She was served lunch there and was able to bring home some food for us. She took the English truck in the morning, just like everyone else who worked on the base, and came home in the evening on the same truck. At the base she met an English airman named Ken. Ken worked in the motor pool and occasionally drove up to our barracks in a new Volkswagen built for the English in the Volkswagen factory in Wolfsburg. The factory was not far from Fassberg, right up against the Russian zone border. The Volkswagen was a simple car with almost no instruments, something I looked for since I was familiar with aircraft instrumentation, and the seats were not comfortable either. But it was a military car. Maybe they were different from others.

Ken had been a coal miner in England before he joined the RAF. He spoke fluent German. I didn't know where he had learned German, and he never gave me a straight answer to my questions. Ken was nice enough, and, like all the other men who got close to my mother, he wanted to marry her. Although Mutti saw Ken now and then, I could tell she wasn't really serious about him. I urged Mutti to marry Ken so we could go to England and escape. I figured England had to be better than the Germany we were living in. I knew my request was selfish, but I was getting desperate. Mutti didn't share my enthusiasm for going to England. "No," she said with laughter in her eyes as I urged her to marry Ken, "Ken is a nice man, Wolfgang, but I am not going to be a coal miner's wife." She broke out laughing at my youthful naivete, not knowing that desperation and depression were behind my strange request. Ken was transferred back to England in October of 1947. He wrote Mutti several times. She didn't open his letters. I felt sorry for Ken. I opened his last letter, in which he told her how much he loved her and wanted her to come to England. He had papers ready for her signature, he wrote; it wouldn't take long for them to be married. He also wrote that since his release from the RAF he had not been able to find work, but he was confident that in time he would find something. I felt sorry for Ken and wrote him a letter telling him that I didn't think my mother was ever going to marry him. I didn't tell Mutti. Ken never wrote again.

One evening early in October, just before Ken went home to England, he rode up to our barracks on a three-speed military bicycle. When he left that evening, he gave me the bicycle, cautioning me not to ride it through the English housing area or past the main gate. The bicycle was easily identifiable, painted in RAF blue with an RAF roundel on the front main brace. It wasn't my first bicycle, but it was my first new one. (In 1946 in Strasburg I had assembled a bicycle from scrap. My bike rode quite well and I received many compliments on it. Mutti had traded it for food, just as she had traded her fur coat and the watch the German soldier had given us in May 1945.) I stored my precious new bicycle in our private toilet, which had come our way when we took over the apartment from the woman who died of syphilis. The toilet had a simple lock. One morning in October when I went to get my bike, it was gone. For a moment I thought maybe Opa, Dad, or even Mutti might have taken it. But I knew it had been stolen. I also thought I knew by whom. A man and a woman lived about half a kilometer from our barracks in the forest near a group of Heinkel bombers. The man always looked unkempt and dirty. He had removed a number of bomb bay doors from the He-177 aircraft which served as walls for a simple one-room house. He had built the roof from various other aircraft parts and insulated his airplane-house by stuffing dried heather between the bomb bay doors that served as outer walls and the chicken wire, tarpaulins, and other odds and ends that served as inside walls. I had been in his airplane-house several times. He had an iron stove which he fed continuously with wood from the surrounding forest. He told people that he and the woman living with him were married, and they even wore wedding bands, but I didn't believe him. Once I had seen her kissing another man. I assumed they lived together because it was convenient. It made no difference to me.

He had been in the Luftwaffe and worked as an electronics technician. He removed parts from the abandoned aircraft and built radios which he then traded for food. His radios worked well, and he couldn't build enough of them. I had watched him build them. I went to see him because he taught me things, but he also frightened me. I could never totally relax around him. Several times I accompanied him on scavenging expeditions through aircraft looking for radio parts. He taught me about vacuum tubes, capacitors, inductors, and resistors—what their functions were and how I could tell their electrical values from markings on the components. He showed me how to match components to each other and how to construct a chassis for the radio from aircraft aluminum, how to fit the tube sockets inside the chassis and wire them up from underneath. He was a talented teacher, and I was fascinated by what he taught me. Still, I remained afraid of him.

He always needed housings for his radios; it was the one thing he couldn't salvage from aircraft. "I promise you fifty marks for each housing you bring me," he said to me more than once. On the way home from school one day, I peeked through a window of a vacated English house in the red housing area. I saw an empty radio sitting on the living room floor. The basement door was unlocked. I took the housing to the radio man. He didn't pay me then. He promised to pay "some other day." Several days after the theft of my bike, I went to his place to get the promised fifty *Reichsmark*. He had asked me to come by that particular morning, promising to pay for sure. As I entered his airplane house, I saw that he was still in bed. Unshaven, wearing underwear full of holes, his hair hanging in his face, he looked awful and smelled of alcohol and cigarettes. I hesitated at the door and started to leave. Feelings of disgust and revulsion rose within me. He beckoned with his hand for me to come close. I slowly walked toward him, taking care to stay out of his reach.

"Come closer, Wolfgang," he said, with a touch of annoyance in his voice. "I am sorry I am not up yet, but that isn't important."

"I just came for my money. The money you promised you would pay for sure this time, if I came early this morning."

"Yes, the money"—he slurred the words—"you'll get your money, don't worry about that. Now, why don't you just come over here." He reached with one hand toward me. The woman was nowhere to be seen. "If you do, I'll give you even more money."

"Why do you want me next to you?"

"I would like to touch you, that's why. It won't hurt and you will like it."

"Touch me where?" I said in childish innocence.

"Your penis, of course. I like to play with boys. Don't be afraid. Everybody does it. Boys in Trauen let me do it. You know the boys I mean. They really enjoy it." I stood there in the middle of his foul-smelling room, stricken with terror. The man was worse than I had imagined. He was the kind of man my parents had warned me about when I was still a young child. He leaned over toward me, reaching for me with his left hand. I bolted into the fresh air of the forest and didn't quit running until I was well away from his house. I told Mutti he wouldn't give me my money. I never mentioned a word about what he had tried to do to me. I was too ashamed. That after-noon Mutti walked over to his shed with me and demanded the money he owed me. He paid immediately.

I was convinced that the corrupt man had stolen my bicycle. In my small world I knew everyone and everything. I also thought I knew just about what individuals were capable of. No one living in the barracks would have stolen my bike, I knew that for sure, just as I would not have taken theirs. I remembered that the radio man had seen me one day as I returned from Fassberg. I passed within one hundred meters of his place. I didn't stop, hoping he wouldn't see me. Of course he had. On another day he had even brought up the subject of bicycles and how people stole them and how one had to lock them up. Foolishly I told him that I locked my bike in our latrine every night. I had told him everything he needed to know. Once I decided he had to be the thief, I walked straight over to his house. My anger was stronger than any fear I felt over what he had tried to do to me the day before. He was inside, standing by his work table testing one of his radios.

"Someone stole my bike," I blurted out at him, "and I think you know where it is."

"I don't know where your bicycle is," he answered, laughing loudly. "You know English bikes are in demand and someone in your barracks probably took it. I wouldn't think of doing anything like that to a friend." He looked at me with a knowing grin, showing his uneven, yellowed teeth. I under-stood that he wanted me to know that he had taken my bike. He got plea-sure out of my loss. He was no friend of mine or of anyone else's. The only friend he had was himself, and he didn't take care of that friend. I had never told him that it was an English bike. He would have known that only if he had seen it up close, and that would have been possible only if he had stolen it. I looked at the radio man with hate in my eyes. He looked back at me, standing by the work bench in his shapeless, grey pants and dirty shirt, a long strand of blond hair hanging in his face, and the stump of a dead cigarette sticking out of one corner of his mouth. He shook his head, grin-ning. I would have to get used to walking to school again.

Chapter 18

WINTER OF DESPAIR

Our principal, Herr Soffner, who was also our homeroom teacher, now, informed us that the State of Niedersachsen had decided that my class would receive an extra year of schooling, a ninth year, because in 1945 so many children had missed a considerable amount of instruction. My teachers were competent and motivated in their respective fields, and I learned quickly. In many subjects I was better read than my classmates, because I had always been a voracious reader. However, the fact that most of the others had received better formal schooling than I clearly showed in mathematics, a subject with which I struggled.

Ingrid, at age eight, either stayed at our apartment or slept at Oma and Opa Samuel's. More and more she stayed with our grandparents. I didn't know her reasons for doing so, and I didn't ask. My mother didn't seem to care where Ingrid slept as long as she knew where she was. Ingrid's clothes were worn and patched, just like mine. We wore other people's cast-offs if we could get them. There was no second dress for Ingrid or second pair of pants for me, only the clothing on our backs. Ingrid's long stockings had been darned so many times they had lost their shape. Her dress was too short. Her only jacket was too tight in the shoulders. Her shoes were badly scuffed, her big toes showing through. In her hair she wore a bow, giving her a cheerful look, which belied her deepening sadness.

In the spring our grandfather had brought a black lamb home from the

271

potato farm where he worked. Ingrid promptly adopted it as her own. She carried the lamb everywhere she went, feeding it milk and trying to be a good mother to it. Two weeks later the lamb died. Ingrid was deeply saddened by the loss. It was the first living thing she had ever loved as her own, and it had died on her. I was taken aback by how much she grieved. As I watched her, it became obvious to me how much love she needed and how little she received.

We did have the pleasure of our dog, Teddy. My father adopted Teddy as a puppy in Munster and brought him to the barracks. A white spitz, he was a friendly, feisty dog, who took care of himself. He seemed to be the only truly happy being in the barracks. He was spoiled by my father, who always brought him scraps of food from the English mess in Munster. Teddy was generous with his affection and totally integrated into the family structure, with his bed of rags behind the stove in Oma Samuel's kitchen. We loved Teddy and his carefree, unpredictable ways. If only we could be like him, I thought.

Although Ingrid and I had been together since her birth, I could not say that I really knew my sister. She was quiet, almost withdrawn. We were also four years apart, perhaps too much for a brother and sister to be close. With Ingrid going to school in Trauen and me attending school in Fassberg, we grew even further apart. In early November, Ingrid became deathly ill. Mutti took her to the former Wehrmacht hospital where our neighbor had died of syphilis. Ingrid had rheumatic fever. She remained in the hospital for weeks, recovering slowly. Mutti and I went to visit her once. It was a long walk, and Ingrid, although weak, greeted us with her usual smile. We could tell our visit was draining her strength, and we soon left. I figured Ingrid was better off staying in the hospital than living in the grey bleakness of our barracks.

Mutti also fell ill and walked to the same hospital for treatment. Her eyes and face appeared yellow. She had hepatitis. I was alone, except for Vera, who was at work most of the day and gone in the evenings with her new boyfriend. I got lonely and went to Oma Samuel to share my pain with her. She knew immediately what needed to be done. She pulled Dad's old uniform jacket from the closet, brushed it off, and put it on me.

"That'll keep you warm," she said, without further explanation. "Tomorrow morning you go and visit our Hedy and Ingrid." I left early the next morning after Oma filled me up with ham sandwiches and ersatz coffee. I

Winter of Despair

thought it would take me three hours to walk the eight kilometers. Oma had made a sandwich for me to take along. About an hour into my walk, I decided to eat my sandwich. Since I had been thinking about it all the time, it seemed that I might as well get it over with. I sat under a birch tree by the side of the road, eating slowly. It was quiet. There was no traffic. I watched the wind make waves in the tall brown grass in the roadside ditch. It was turning into a nice day for late November. The birch trees lining the road looked graceful with their white-and-black dappled trunks and thin, long, nearly leafless branches waving in the breeze like the hair of a woman. The birches stretched along both sides of the straight and narrow road for as far as I could see. Somewhere in the distance they seemed to merge until all I could see was trees, no road at all.

At eleven o'clock I sighted the hospital. I politely explained the purpose of my visit to the nurse on duty. "Please, have a seat," she said, smiling. The openness of her smile took me aback. I wasn't used to people being kind to me for no reason. "I'll be right back," she said. "Why don't you have a seat." Five long minutes later the same nurse reappeared, pushing my mother before her in a wheelchair. Mutti was happy to see me. She put her arms around me and hugged and kissed me. I was embarrassed by her unconstrained affection in front of the nurse. The nurse smiled again and went about her business. I pushed Mutti to her room, which she shared with another woman. I had lunch with them. The nurses brought an extra bowl of soup for me. That afternoon we saw Ingrid. She still looked frail, but that didn't keep her from trying to cheer us up. Her nurse soon cut our visit short, saying curtly, "She needs her rest." The nurse took Ingrid to her room.

As I was about to leave that evening, Mutti said, "Wolfgang, it is so late already and you have such a long walk ahead of you in the dark, why don't you stay overnight. I have talked to the nurses and they have a bed next door you could sleep in. The room doesn't have any lights, but you don't really need that. The nurses will make up the bed for you and wake you at first light. Will you stay?"

"Of course, I will, Mutti." I was relieved at not having to walk home alone in the dark. The room was dark, as Mutti had described it. I took off my shirt and pants, slipped under the sheet, and went right to sleep. The next thing I remember is being shaken awake by a nurse the following morning.

Winter of Despair

"It's time for breakfast," the nurse announced with a laugh. I liked it that the nurses were all so friendly. Our barracks were not a place to foster smiles. I had forgotten that people could smile for no reason. "Why don't you go down the hall and wash up," the nurse suggested. "Here is a towel for you and a facecloth. When you finish, please join your mother in her room for breakfast. Don't come back to this room. I'll put your jacket in your mother's room." Mutti was happy to see me again, and my bowl of hot porridge was already waiting for me on her table. I ate hungrily.

Mutti confided, "I should be home in another week. Ingrid might take longer." Briefly my mother's face lost its smile, and in that short moment her eyes unintentionally revealed the depth of her exhaustion. I wished she could stay longer in the hospital, or at least stay away from the barracks. I was worried about her. Ten days later Mutti did come home. She looked much better physically than when she had left. It felt good to have her back again. Without her, there was no home. It was just two drab barracks rooms. While she was in the hospital, Mutti had lost her job at the English NAAFE. The English were leaving Fassberg. I had watched their slow departure since early summer, and finally they moved out the few remaining airmen. In the English housing area, fewer and fewer houses were occupied. I used to see Spitfires taking off in the early morning hours or late in the afternoon. Now, no aircraft flew into or out of Fassberg anymore. Losing her NAAFE job meant that Mutti also lost her access to extra food. Again we were forced to live off our rations, the yield from our garden, which at this time of year was sparse, and whatever any one of us could scrounge. We had potatoes. Sometimes I would see a certain look in Mutti's eyes when she didn't know I was watching, an exhausted look, a look born of too heavy a burden carried for too long. I knew she was worried about our future. I wanted to put my arms around her and tell her how much I loved her and that she had done well, that none of it was her fault. I never did put my arms around her. I began to worry that my mother might despair and do something awful.

Every evening around five or five-thirty, I went to the village to get our ration of milk, which we had because Opa worked at the potato farm. The milk was important to us, especially for Ingrid when she got home. There was only one way to go to the village—down the road, past the railroad station, and across the bridge spanning the little river Örtze. Past the railroad station on the left side of the road sat a ramshackle store run by a

lecherous, thin, short-statured man with an ever-growing family. He and his
rotund wife had several children, and he tried to interest every woman who
came into his store in having sex, or so I had heard. People were hungry,
and mothers would do whatever was necessary to put food on the table for
their children. It wasn't all that difficult for the man to succeed.

I was still learning what terrible damage the war had done to people's
lives and how its aftermath continued to affect people like us, the *Flüchtlinge*
nobody wanted. We were the people who had nothing and lived from hand
to mouth. We were the human debris of that evil war. We had no reserves
of food, clothing, or anything else that sustained life. We were desperate
people, easy to exploit. The storekeeper's eldest son was my age; his brother
was a year younger. Other children ran about the place with runny noses
and clothes as dirty as their faces. I had played with the two boys once or
twice. I soon found out that they were liars, and were constantly scheming
about what to steal or vandalize next. They reminded me of two marauding
dogs. I knew I had to watch myself as I passed their place on my way to get
our milk.

Then I began to notice the two brothers hiding behind juniper bushes
near their store and watching me as I passed. One day as I returned from
the farm with a full pail of milk, they both sallied forth from their hiding
places wielding boards with nails sticking out. I put down my can of milk
carefully. My aim was to attack them head-on rather than wait for them to
get to me. I suspected that courage was not one of their attributes. Even so,
they wielded dangerous weapons, which I knew they would use. The two
boys began to slow down in their approach as I ran toward them. They
hadn't expected that. I got to the younger boy first and punched him in the
mouth as we met. Both dropped their fearsome-looking weapons in their
hurry to get away. I retrieved my can of milk and continued my walk home.
I didn't think they would try anything like that again. Just in case I was
wrong, though, every time I went near their place I was prepared to fight. I
carried a stick in the sleeve of my jacket or a rock in my fist. I hated going
into the village. Every milk run turned into a tension-filled trip.

My grandfather acquired a piglet and kept it in the barn along with the
chickens. Our monotonous winter diet of bread and potatoes was occasionally augmented by a few eggs from the chickens, which were not prolific egg
layers, and by the occasional chunk of ocean fish or salt herring provided by
an unpredictable food distribution system. Usually we received dry bread,

still baked with corn added to the rye, and a not-so-tasty jelly which defied identification as to its possible ingredients. Basic staples such as meat, sugar, fats, and flour remained rationed and were hard to get. Our only grocery store was the Trauen store owned by the lecherous little man. Fassberg had a larger store, but it was too far away to be a practical alternative. Some people occasionally took the train to Munster.

On a bleak December day just before Christmas, Mutti came home from shopping at the Trauen store. The expression on her face was bitter. She carried a basket filled to overflowing with bags of sugar, flour, and hard candies. Two pounds of butter, a pound of margarine, lard, baking powder, jars of jelly and jam, and other items filled the basket. Mutti's face and the full basket told me everything. My shock must have been plainly written on my face. I knew what she had to do to get that food for us for Christmas. I ran outside into the cold mist and wandered across the fields aimlessly. I wished she hadn't done that to herself. I could survive on bread, potatoes, and salt, I thought. That's all I needed. I returned home after dark, cold and dispirited, and went to bed without eating. I made matters worse by not eating any of the food she had acquired at such a high cost to herself. I still had no idea of what sex really entailed. I knew from listening to people talk that it was something that should be private and personal between a man and a woman. People said that if a woman had sex for food or money she was a whore. I knew my mother wasn't that at all. She had done it for Ingrid and me—mostly for Ingrid, who was back from the hospital and needed better food than potatoes and bread if she was to get well again and stay well. But understanding why did not make it easier for me.

Several days later, as I passed the store, the two boys stepped out from behind a juniper bush, calling to me. They appeared eager to talk. They didn't mean to do me any harm, they said. I stopped, set down my milk can and put my rock firmly into my right fist just in case they changed their minds. I stood in the middle of the road. They came as far as the last juniper bush near the edge of the road. "Would you like to come in and play with us?" the eldest asked.

"I don't think so," I answered.

"We have something that you would really like to see," the younger brother blurted out.

"What could that possibly be?" I answered disdainfully. "I can't imagine you having anything that I would like to see."

"Yes, you would," he insisted. "You know, up in the attic of our house, above the room next to the store, there we have a hiding place."

"What is that to me?" I said, getting ready to pick up my can of milk to leave.

"We made a small hole in the ceiling, and when our father has sex with a woman, we watch." I knew what was coming next; they had set me up.

"That's disgusting," I replied, picking up my can of milk, hurrying to leave quickly.

"The other day we watched our father have sex with your mother," he shouted, and they both laughed loudly. I was enraged not only at what they said, but also because I had let them trap me into the conversation. I ran toward them to vent my rage. They turned and ran, laughing loudly as they escaped into the store. I was devastated. In that same instant, though, I knew that I loved my mother even more for her sacrifices.

I tried to withdraw into my Fassberg life, where families appeared to be living as families should, in real houses and apartments with bathrooms and kitchens. Fassberg was clean; it had sewers and running water for kitchens and bathrooms. Our barracks had a stinking outhouse and only one water pump for a population grown to over one hundred; we had no sewer or bathrooms, only slop buckets emptied into our gardens before our doorsteps. Fassberg had paved streets. We had mud, fed by rain and slop, nurturing teeming populations of flies and mosquitos from early spring into late autumn. I started to feel dirty, inside and out, every time I entered our compound. In contrast, a feeling of cleansing relief would come over me when I got close to Fassberg. These were feelings and thoughts I could not share with my mother, who, I sensed, was entering a phase of personal desperation in her unceasing struggle to feed and clothe her two children. I was certain she appreciated my help—the mushrooms, the firewood, potatoes in season, and vegetables from the garden. But my help wasn't nearly enough, had never been enough. For the first time since we had left Sagan in 1945, I began to feel that my mother was losing her fight with the world in which we had to live. My father stayed away more and more. In Munster he had a room with a nice bed, indoor toilets and showers, and a workers' canteen where he received hot food as part of his pay. He was doing all right for himself, while Mutti faced a terrible time. Ingrid and I were his children, too—couldn't he help more at a time like this? We remained her burden. I

Winter of Despair

felt torn by my recognition of the situation. Fear entered my life again—fear for my mother's life.

Nearly everyone in our compound had lost their jobs at the air base, just as Mutti had. The only remaining employers were the potato farm in Trauen and the English army base in Munster. They had few jobs available this time of year. In Fassberg the beautiful houses in the red housing area stood empty. I thought how nice it would be if we could live in a house like that. But those houses were for winners, not for losers like us. The fields were barren again. Cold winds blew off the storm-whipped North Sea and rattled the windows of our aging barracks. The pine forests seemed to close in upon themselves in anticipation of winter's icy grip. The few leaves left on trees, brown and shriveled, hung on until some ferocious gust of wind came along and tore them off, driving them to the ground where they lay rotting in puddles of dirty water. The people in the barracks seemed to be shriveling, too, just like the leaves on the trees. Hopelessness had raised its dispiriting head again. If it didn't rain, then a fine, cold mist persisted in the air, chilling our bodies and our spirits. The first snows came gently at first, then more persistently. Finally winter arrived with a vengeance. The mud around the barracks froze into steel-hard ridges and valleys, making it difficult to walk to the pump. The danger of fire was ever present as I pushed wood into our stove by the basketful. I kept an eye on the ceiling, hoping to catch a fire before it became uncontrollable.

A piece of tin surrounded the stovepipe where it entered the ceiling. That piece of tin isolated the hot pipe from the tinder-dry ceiling boards and kept the pipe from setting the ceiling on fire. When I kept the stove going all day, the piece of tin became as hot as the pipe, turning the ceiling brown, even black in places. I usually slept in the room with the stove and never went to sleep until the stove had cooled; then our apartment turned bitter cold. When the wind howled outside and drove the snow before it, I could feel the frigid air come through cracks in the walls, through the floorboards, from under the door, and around the window frames. The wind drove the snow into the room and onto my bed. We slept with our clothes on, with every blanket and coat spread over us. By morning our water buckets were frequently covered with a thin layer of ice.

Loss of work meant the loss of meals once provided at work. It meant the loss of opportunity to augment meager diets from the scraps of food discarded by the English mess or given by English families to their grateful maids and housekeepers. Loss of work meant having nothing to trade on the black market for the essential items of food and clothing needed to sustain a family. Loss of work was totally dispiriting. The leaden skies, grey barracks walls, and persistent cold made winter a period when we measured life in hours and minutes, not in days, weeks and months. Just getting from one desperate minute to the next took as much energy as any of us could muster.

We students planned an *Elternabend* for our parents in late January, with each of us to make a presentation of one kind or another. I had nothing to wear for the occasion that I would not be ashamed of when standing before the parents of my classmates. I spoke to my father about my problem. On weekends he came home to check on his parents. I told him my problem to get it off my chest, not expecting him to be able to do anything about it. My father listened patiently, as he always did. Then, after a moment's reflection, he said, "I think I can help."

I was surprised by his unexpected response. "How can you possibly help me? I don't want to wear your old Luftwaffe jacket," I told him, thinking that was his solution.

"Just be quiet for a moment, Wolfgang," he replied in mock sternness, and he hurried into the back room. I heard him rummaging around in the *Schrank*. He came back into the kitchen grinning, holding in his hands a package wrapped in brown wax paper, held together by string. "Aha!" he exclaimed. "I've been waiting for the right moment, and this is it."

"What are you talking about, Dad?"

He unwrapped the parcel. It was a bolt of cloth—not a large one, but of some size. "Where did you get this material, Father?" I asked in astonishment, feeling its fine texture between my fingers.

"Believe it or not, Wolfgang, I've carried this bolt of cloth with me since I left my last duty station in France in 1944. I saved it for this moment." The material, brown with a reddish thread running through it, was of excellent quality. He watched my rising excitement with pleasure.

"How did you get this through the Americans?"

"The Americans confiscated the cloth when I was admitted to the *Gefangenenlager* in Alsace-Lorraine. They returned it upon my release. The American sergeant who returned my personal belongings said, 'This has no military value, Captain Samuel, and we have no use for it. You better take it, because you'll need it.' He was a nice man, the American sergeant. Tomorrow afternoon, provided it doesn't rain or snow, we will go to Fassberg to a tailor I know and we'll have a suit made for you."

The next day my father and I walked to Fassberg as he had promised. He knocked on the door of the tailor's home. After several minutes we heard footsteps, and the door opened a crack. The sallow face of an older man peered out from behind it. Dad doffed his hat. *"Guten Abend,"* he said cheerfully. My father was always polite to everyone. The man stepped out from behind the door once he recognized his caller. "I am sorry for the lateness of our call. This is my son, Wolfgang."

"Come in, come in," the tailor said, opening wide the door to the house and gesturing for us to enter. Once we were in the foyer, he closed and locked the door and quickly moved past us to open the door to his work-room, a bedroom converted to a workshop. "Please, take off your hat and coat," he prompted my father, "and let me hang them up for you." He was a polite man, too. His workroom had several unfinished jackets and pants hanging and lying about in various stages of completion. When the formali-ties were completed, Dad handed the material to the tailor, who looked at it with trained eyes. "Good material," he said, looking up at Dad. "French," he added, matter-of-factly.

"Yes," my father responded.

"I assume you want me to make a suit for your son, correct?" The tailor sized me up with experienced eyes.

"Yes, of course," Dad responded, momentarily flustered. "Do you think it will be enough?"

"Well, let's take some measurements and see what we can come up with," the tailor replied. He removed the tape from around his neck and took my measurements: arms stretched out, with my elbow bent, arms hanging by my side, shoulders, waist, hips, inner and outer seams for my trousers. Next he measured the material. He was quiet for a while and then said, "Yes, I can do it. There is just enough for a suit, just enough." My father and the tailor agreed on a date for delivery, the day of my presentation. They both whispered about arrangements to pay for the work—not money, money bought nothing. After we had left the tailor, Dad chuckled as we walked home side by side.

"Why are you laughing?"

"You remember the tailor saying, 'There is just enough material for a suit'? You remember him saying that?"

Winter of Despair

"Yes, I do. So?"

"Well, Wolfgang, I know there is more than enough material for a suit. What he meant to say was that there was enough material for a pair of short pants or a jacket for his son. That's how it works. What matters is that you will have a nice suit in which to make your *Vortrag*. He is an accomplished tailor." The *Elternabend* was the last Friday in January. My suit was ready that afternoon after school. It fit too perfectly. There was no room for me to grow, but I didn't care. I had a beautiful new suit to wear for an important occasion. Dad gave me one of his shirts, a tie, socks, and a pair of his shoes, and for the first time since leaving Sagan I was nicely dressed. My father came and listened to my presentation. I was happy he did. Everyone seemed to like my *Vortrag*, I thought; the parents appeared to be looking at me with more than the usual attention.

When I mentioned that to my father later in the evening, he laughed and said, "Of course, Wolfgang, they liked your presentation. They also liked your new suit. It looks nice on you and fits you perfectly, and it's made of such excellent material. Nearly every parent who has a son came up to me to ask where I had gotten the suit for you. They wanted to buy a suit like yours for their own sons. I told them the truth, and they went away disappointed." Then he said, "I enjoyed listening to your *Vortrag* and having you look so nice for the occasion. You have learned much, my son. Keep on learning." My father's words were a great gift, I thought, maybe even greater than the new suit.

Although the *Elternabend* was a temporarily uplifting occasion, it changed nothing about our life. I turned thirteen that February, nearly three years after the war ended. There was no thought of a birthday celebration. Few celebrations took place in the barracks at a time of nearly total unemployment. Slowly, people were coming to see themselves as being at the end of their wits; they were beginning to doubt their ability to sustain their families. No amount of ingenuity could hold the old uniforms and ancient pieces of clothing together much longer. Everything was worn out and worn through. Clothes were permanently stained with rings of sweat and the dirt of years, dirt that was impervious to hard water and the bars of clay used in place of soap.

The sun had not shone for weeks, and for a time it never stopped raining. Our compound swam in a sea of mud. The constant rain revealed the true state of our aging barracks. The roofs were leaking, and we had nothing with

Winter of Despair

which to fix the problem. Drip, drip, drip was a sound I dreaded; it was repeated over and over from too many leaks. I ran out of containers for catching all the water and had to give priority according to where the leaks occurred. Some I had to ignore, letting the water run through the rotting floorboards. I tried to keep our beds dry. The smell of dirt and decay wrapped itself around us, smothering the little spirit we had left. I felt myself being pushed down into the cold, wet, grey quagmire at our doorsteps. Spiritually I began to feel as if I were slowly drowning, sinking into the sea of ooze around me. In this bleak environment I became obsessed with finding something to hold on to, something to give me hope for a better future. One night lying in my bed of straw, I suddenly remembered the German soldier who had stopped for us in Strasburg in April 1945 amidst the chaos of a fleeing army. He had rescued us from the Russian army. The memory made me feel better. I fell asleep thinking about the soldier and his selfless act.

On subsequent nights I tried to recall other people who had given us a helping hand since we had lost our home and become refugees. There was Llydia, who had gotten rid of the phoney Communist teacher, kept the barracks from being torn down for another day, and helped us find a place to live. Llydia had found a hospital for my mother when she was wounded with a Russian bullet through her neck, and saved her life. It instantly made me feel better about myself thinking of these people. I remembered the schoolteacher in Strasburg who had given me the condemned textbooks so that I could learn, and who had not told anyone about my father being there, nor about our plans to escape to the West. What about Lieutenant Schmitt? I thought. Where would we be if he had not come back to put us on a train out of Sagan? Would we have died in the fiery hell of Dresden? Even Paul, who had seemed so awful at the time, had reached out to us when he tried to warn us of Opa Grapentin's arrest, and a second time when he sent Vera to tell us that the police were on their way to arrest my father. Maybe Paul was not as evil as I had thought he was. As the nights progressed, I began to see things differently. I discerned some light on my dark horizon. When I recalled the numerous selfless, frequently courageous acts of people who had held out a helping hand to us, I began to feel better about my present life. I quit feeling sorry for myself. In the long nights of the winter of 1947, it was the memories of what others had done for us that gave me comfort and strength.

In late February, it turned bitterly cold. A blizzard blew up off the North

Sea, reminding me of ones I had read about in my books about America. I looked out our window, thinking that this was what it must have been like on the Great Plains when the winter storms struck in the late 1800s. Ingrid didn't go to school that day and remained curled up in her bed covered with every blanket Oma could find. Oma cautioned me not to go to school. I didn't listen to her. How could she know that I had to go, that nothing could keep me from going to my school. Nothing.

Fortified with a cup of hot cocoa, I stepped resolutely into the raging storm and began my four-kilometer walk to Fassberg. The wind blew the snow horizontally across the frozen fields, coming from the north in powerful blasts that grabbed me and forced me to run if I wanted to stay upright. At times I felt as if the wind were sucking every bit of warmth out of my body. High snow drifts made my going slow and difficult until I reached the shelter of the forest. I wore a warm English army parka with a hood. My father had left the parka behind for me to wear on cold and windy days. Still, the wind was merciless and found its way into my clothing to chill my body. I carried my schoolbooks in a worn English army ditty bag slung over my shoulder.

The wind died down a bit when I entered the forest. Wherever there was an old Luftwaffe runway cut through the trees, the wind regained its strength, building up high drifts. A few of the old Luftwaffe aircraft still stood in their parking places at the edge of the forest, looking like fearsome weapons of war covered in their mantles of snow. I battled on, looking forward to reaching my school and the warmth of my classroom. My feet froze in my plastic shoes with their badly worn wooden soles, and my thin socks provided no warmth. I staggered through the forest thinking of the hot stove that awaited me, blanking out the painful cold working itself up my legs.

Since my group's schooling had been extended a year, the building was short one classroom. The principal had a basement room converted. The school custodian installed a coke oven which he personally fired up every morning before class. I crossed the railroad tracks running into the air base. I hadn't seen a train on the tracks in many months, and the rails were rusting. They were mostly covered with a thick layer of snow, only barely discernible in places where the wind had laid them bare. I followed the air base perimeter fence past the closed Officers' Club and finally emerged from the forest at the main gate. I turned right, down the concrete road. Normally I cut through the red housing area, but, with the English families gone, the streets were covered with huge snowdrifts. I chose instead the main road, which was longer but easier for me to walk. When I arrived, I saw no one; my classroom was empty. The door was locked when I tried the handle, and I could see that there was no fire in the stove. I wanted to cry. I was exhausted and very cold. Maybe they are just late, I thought, trying to console myself. I decided to wait. Maybe the others would come soon. Nobody came, and my heart sank as I stood outside my empty school with my feet so cold I could no longer feel them.

I started the long trip back. Since I was walking directly into the wind, going home was much worse. Then the wooden sole on one of my shoes split down the middle. I tied my belt around my foot so that I could continue to walk. By the time I got to Oma's, I had no feeling in my feet; they seemed like clumps of ice which didn't belong to me. I couldn't speak because my facial muscles wouldn't respond. Oma undressed me. She poured hot water from the ever-present kettle on her stove into two bowls. She made me sit and put my head, which she covered with a towel, over one of the bowls. "Breathe the steam deeply into your lungs, my dear boy," she said. She put my feet into the second bowl. I cried with pain and tried to keep my feet out of the water. Oma insisted I keep them in the hot water and suffer the pain.

"Would you want to lose your toes, my child?" she asked, not expecting an answer. "No, you don't, and I won't let you. So, keep your feet in the water. The pain will be gone soon." Later, Opa rubbed my feet forcefully in his warm hands to get my blood circulating, and then Oma put me to bed in the back room. She covered me with blankets and coats until their weight became nearly too heavy for me to bear. By evening I had a high fever. Sweat poured out of every pore in my body, drenching me in my cocoon of blankets. Oma wouldn't let me out from under them. She continued to make various poultices, which she put on my forehead and chest. In the middle of the night I awoke, painfully cold, my teeth chattering loudly and uncontrollably. Chills racked my body. Oma piled more blankets and coats on me, but it didn't help. Finally, in total exhaustion, I began to feel hot again; the fever had returned. As I lay sweating profusely, Oma seemed pleased.

"Keep on sweating, my dear grandson," she consoled me. "The fever will soon break." It happened as Oma had predicted, and I fell into a deep sleep. I slept all day and all the following night, with Oma at my bedside the entire time, Opa later told me. I awoke with a ravenous hunger and thirst the following morning, two days after I had staggered into Oma's kitchen, frozen by the blizzard and its howling winds. The storm had passed, and the sun was shining. I was still weak and stayed in bed for another day. During the day I hopped out of bed and went into the *Schrank* to look for something to read. I found a book which belonged to my father. It was by Wyk van Mason, an American writer, and was long, which pleased me. It was a story about the American War of Independence against the English and about fast clipper ships, blockade running, and life in coastal America in the late 1700s. I read until the winter light faded.

The day I returned to school, massive snowdrifts remained as the legacy of the blizzard. My grandfather had repaired the broken sole in my shoe. The bright winter sun shone on the wintry landscape. It was incredibly beautiful. Here and there I could see tracks in the snow made by rabbits and foxes, and the occasional cry of a bird pierced the absolute stillness of my world. When I arrived at school, I said nothing about having come to Fassberg during the storm. I apologized to my teacher for missing class because of sickness. "Fine," he said, "the school was closed for several days. You didn't miss anything."

In mid-March, Opa decided that our pig had achieved its desired weight of over two hundred pounds, and early one morning the pig was killed and processed into hams, sausages, pork chops, bacon, and lots of lard. Processing the pig was a happy event. Opa had located one of Oma's sisters living in barracks similar to ours near the town of Verden, a day's slow train ride away. She was a spry old lady who knew the rituals of processing a pig, especially how to properly prepare and season the various kinds of sausages, from liverwurst to blood sausage. For her early-morning-to-midnight labor, Aunt Minna received an equitable portion of everything the pig provided. Our family's meat and fat problem was suddenly solved for the remainder of the year. When we ran out of meat from that pig, our new piglet should have grown to the desired size to take its place in our food chain. It was a pleasure to eat bread again, now that we had something to put on it. Opa was the happiest person around, because his planning and hard work had finally paid off. The hams, bacon, and sausages Opa took to the potato farm and hung in the smoke room until they were properly cured. The lard was rendered into earthen jars, and some of the meat was similarly stored and covered with salt. Nothing was wasted from that great pig. Everything was eaten, from snout to tail.

The hot chocolate and peanut breakfasts at school were discontinued. I had enjoyed every cup of cocoa and every handful of peanuts I had received. March passed with its eternal greyness. Life returned in April. Maybe things would get better in 1948? After the grey and cold of this terrible winter, people abandoned the prison of their rooms and spent every minute they could outside in the rare and invigorating sunshine. Windows were opened and old bedding aired. There was no paint, but people scrubbed walls and floors with water and rags and felt better afterwards, even though the grey pine boards looked no different from how they had before. There were smiles on people's faces now and then, and the women emerged from their barracks warrens with their babies and young children and stood in groups gossiping, many with hands held over swollen bellies. People-watching and gossiping became the activities of the idle once again. There were many men among them, since the RAF base at Fassberg was still closed, and everyone who had worked there was still out of a job. When I wasn't in school, I cultivated our garden plot and planted seeds for a future harvest. Directly under our two windows was a narrow dirt embankment which I carefully dug up and planted with hardy pansies, those indestructible little flowers known to survive even the worst of frosts. For me they represented hope and perseverance.

Mutti had met a German man in early March while on a trip to Celle trying to find shoes for me. The man came back with her. He was nicely dressed, polite and friendly, and he took no offense at the sight of our meager existence. He said he was on a business trip in the area and that his home was in a small town near Dortmundt. He asked Mutti to accompany him on his return trip to meet his mother. Mutti accepted. I was happy to see her leave the barracks, if only for a few days. She returned the following week and brought back pictures of the man's house and of him and his mother. One picture showed him in an army officer's uniform. He wore a Knights Cross around his neck and the Iron Cross First Class and the silver *Verwundetenabzeichen* on his left breast pocket. "He asked me to marry him, Wolfgang," Mutti said when she returned from the trip. I wasn't surprised. I didn't know what it was about my mother, but her men friends always proposed marriage.

"Did you say yes?" I asked, knowing her answer.

"No, I told him I would think about it." I wondered what it was she was looking for in a man or if she even wanted to ever get married again. That man had everything she would want, I thought—a home, a business, a way out of our squalor to a normal and regular life. Maybe that was what I wanted, not what she needed.

"His wife was killed in a bombing raid in 1944, and he doesn't have children," Mutti said. "He also said he would be glad to have you and Ingrid as stepchildren." In the following weeks her new friend wrote several letters. One day I asked Mutti why she didn't answer him. "No," she said, "he is just a friend; I don't want to marry him." She laughed when she said that. A nice, girlish laugh.

"Why don't you at least answer his letters?" I persisted.

"I don't know. I think this way is best. I like him, and I don't want to hurt him. I know he isn't right for me."

"Look, Mutti," I persisted, "he has a house, and he said he would take care of Ingrid and me. How can you say no?" She looked at me with strange eyes, as if I had broken a trust between us. She said nothing. She didn't have to. I was embarrassed at what I had just blurted out. I put my arms around her and hugged her, and she hugged me back. In time the letters from her friend stopped coming.

Mutti and my father reconciled their bitter differences sufficiently and again agreed to go through with their divorce. Both of them took the train to Celle, the county seat, and they petitioned the court for a divorce. The court granted the divorce based on my father's admitted transgressions with other women. Afterwards, they seemed to get along much better. With the arrival of April, the dark, sinister, and dispiriting winter of 1947 came to an end. All of us living in those aging barracks knew that we had survived a difficult period. The warming rays of the sun not only dried out our wet and rotting barracks but also warmed our bodies and raised our spirits. There were signs, too, that better times lay ahead. On Fassberg air base there was renewed activity. The English started hiring again.

Chapter 19

RETURN OF THE AMERICANS

I n addition to sunshine and warmth, spring brought rumors of the Russians closing off roads and waterways to Berlin and delaying trains with coal and food at the border checkpoints, not letting them pass until many days later. In April the Russians even stopped an American military train on its way to Berlin and attempted to enter and search it. The Americans refused to submit to the Russians. After that incident, they began flying their supplies out of Frankfurt and Wiesbaden to their Berlin garrison. Suddenly, there was activity at RAF Station Fassberg. This time it was not Spitfire fighter planes I saw but twin-engined Dakota transports bound for Berlin.

Shortly after the arrival of the Dakotas, the former Trauen V-2 rocket research center was turned into a German labor camp. In May hundreds of German men arrived in English army trucks. They wore British uniforms dyed dark brown and strange-looking berets, just like the English soldiers. With childish curiosity, I watched the men as they pitched their four-man tents on the grounds of the Trauen center.

"What do they call you?" I asked one of the workers who was busy with three other shirtless men erecting their tent. He straightened up, wiped his forehead with the back of his hand, and, putting his hands on his hips, said, "They call us GSO men, young man. That stands for German Service

Organization." Then he laughed. "But that's just a fancy name for plain laborers. Now, why don't you run along and let us finish our work."

The Paschmionka boy whose older brothers again worked at the air base told me that the GSO men were former German soldiers who couldn't find work. "They unload trucks and trains, and load English aircraft with supplies for Berlin," he said to me. "They work for their clothing, housing, one hot meal a day, and a little money." Then, laughing, he added as an afterthought, "But the food is good." With the reopening of the air base, there was again enough work for everyone. Trucks resumed picking up barracks people in the morning and returning them in the evening, as they had done before this last horrible winter. No longer were my walks to and from school quiet and tranquil moments for reflection. Instead, I heard the intermittent thunder of straining aircraft engines overhead, the sound of trains, their heavy cast-iron wheels again putting a shine on the rusty rails, and the distant roar of heavy trucks.

In April and May the haunting call of the cuckoo sounded through the forest and across the heath. Larks rocketed into the sky from their carefully hidden nests. Daisies popped up at the side of the road, and the heath began to assume a green hue as it rejuvenated itself. Flocks of grayish-black heath sheep with long, shaggy coats grazed on succulent shoots of grass, on young heather, and on upstart pine trees. All which was so familiar to me was joined by the new sights and sounds from the air base.

In addition to the arrival of spring and the return of the English to Fassberg, there occurred an event of even greater significance to us *Flüchtlinge*. The *Währungsreform* was an event of such magnitude that it profoundly changed the lives of every one of us. With this currency reform, I decided that the war was over for me. The shooting might have stopped in May 1945, but I had never really felt that the war had ended for us Germans. During the three years after the war, our suffering had continued unabated. In many respects, it was worse *after* the shooting and bombing stopped. The dying continued; now, though, the victims were mostly women, children, and the old, and the causes of death were different. For me, war was not just the shooting of guns and the dropping of bombs. It was all the other things created by war which continued to make life difficult for many and impossible for some—fear, hunger, disease, exploitation and abuse, and rape of women of all ages by force and through circumstance. Until the conditions we had been enduring changed, there was no peace for me. I hadn't known how it would happen, but, with the implementation of the *Währungsreform* on June 20, 1948, two days before the arrival of summer, I knew that this war had finally ended for my country, for my family, and for me.

My mother and I walked the four miles to Fassberg that day and stood in a long line to receive our share of the new deutsche mark, or D-mark, as it was quickly christened. Each of us, Mutti, Ingrid, and I, received forty deutsche mark. The remarkable power of the new money was immediately apparent. At the instant of its distribution, goods appeared on long-empty store shelves, things which few of us had seen for years, much less owned and enjoyed. Clothing, shoes, and food were available and for sale without the need of a ration card. The world I had believed I was going to find when we first crossed the border fleeing from the Russian zone of occupation in December 1946 had finally arrived. Like mushrooms after a warm summer shower, peddlers on bicycles appeared, flooding our barracks compound with cheap goods. Many people spent their good, new money on bad, old things at grossly inflated prices. But no one knew what something should cost. It had been a long time since people had purchased goods only with money, without ration cards or without giving something else in return. A state of persistent poverty and despair was replaced by a nearly euphoric view of life. The bad times were behind us, or so most people believed. We could begin making plans again for the future. The timing for the introduction of the new money couldn't have been better. With the confrontation between the Russians and the Western Allies over Berlin, there was plenty of work now at the Fassberg air base, work paid for with money of real value. An unaccustomed degree of prosperity and optimism enveloped our tattered community.

It wasn't only the purchasing power of the new money that so fundamentally changed our world of subsistence and deprivation, but, even more, it was what the money represented—a new beginning, a fresh start. Maybe it would provide the means for a transformation from what we had become to what we secretly wanted to be. Maybe the new money would end the despised black market, which represented the darkest aspect of our daily lives. It was, above all, a market that traded in sex. It deprived young women of their dreams and forced mothers to view themselves as chattel, as goods, valued by another as being worth a few cigarettes, a pair of nylons, two candy bars, a bar of soap, or a can of coffee. One pack of cigarettes was the value of a woman, the value of my mother, my friend's sister, my neighbor's daughter, the ex-Stuka pilot's wife. With the pack of cigarettes or the can of coffee she received for letting a man possess her, the mother, sister, daughter, or wife would try to obtain on the black market the food she needed for her children or aged parents, who were waiting for her in a home no more than a ruin or in an abandoned Wehrmacht barracks. For me the black market at its worst was the memory of a milk can filled with soup, the soup that kept my sister and me from starving to death in the brutal winter of 1945.

Although everybody at one time or another had to fall back on the black market to obtain something to keep a family functioning, it was not a frivolous choice. It was usually an act driven by the necessity to stay alive, to maintain the body if not the soul. The family that did not count a young woman among its members was at a disadvantage in the day-to-day struggle for survival. The black market, the conditions of scarcity it thrived on, and our years of living in the rotting Wehrmacht barracks had stripped our lives to their bare essentials. Sex was so pervasive in our environment that it had become currency for us, the destitute. Personal humiliation had become our daily norm, and most of us didn't even recognize it for what it was anymore. The dirt of our lives was not only under our fingernails and on our unwashed bodies but had penetrated our souls. Barracks life, poverty, untold needs, and the usurious market that satisfied them ate away at our self-respect. With the *Währungsreform*, I had hope that the black market would at least change its nature.

The warmth of the spring sun, the new money, a new job, and the general excitement surrounding the reopening of the air base changed my mother, too. No longer did I see the haunted look of past violence and fear of the future in her eyes. Her face again looked younger as she smiled and laughed. I looked at her closely over dinner one evening. I could barely discern the roundish scar on her neck made by a Russian bullet three years earlier. I knew there was a corresponding scar on the other side. It was almost unnoticeable, but I knew it was there. I admired this brave woman, my mother, my hero, my friend.

Mutti again took the train to Munster to look for shoes for me and Vera. I had only a pair of sandals remaining, homemade from German aircraft tires. They were no substitute for real shoes, especially when it got cold

Return of the Americans

again. Vera needed shoes, too. At least she had one pair made of real leather which she wore when she went dancing or to a movie in Munster. Vera went barefoot to work in the fields. Mutti returned from Munster late that afternoon with one pair of shoes which fit both Vera and me, since we wore the same size. She had been able to find only one pair in our size or larger. Mutti gave the shoes, made of raw undyed leather, to me, reasoning that Vera had one pair while I had none. We sat down to dinner—Mutti, Ingrid, Vera, and I. Vera ate sullenly.

"I should have the new shoes," Vera said suddenly, looking straight at Mutti. I could see smoldering hostility, maybe even hate, in her eyes. Her demeanor was challenging and demanding. A long silence followed. Vera kept staring at Mutti.

"Wolfgang should have the shoes," Mutti replied with finality. "All he has is a pair of sandals, and they are not even real sandals, only pieces of airplane tire. Don't you understand that, Vera?" Mutti looked at Vera as a mother would look at an errant child. Vera stared into her soup for several minutes, her spoon held in suspension. Then she rose from the table and threw her soup spoon noisily into the plate.

"I am working," she said loudly. "I need shoes even more than he does. I have to go barefoot into the fields. I am tired of you, Hedy." She dropped the customary and polite prefix "aunt." "You favor Wolfgang over me because he is your son. I am fed up to here with you." Vera raised her right hand to her neck.

"You need to wash your neck," Mutti responded simply, ignoring Vera's outburst. "It's still dirty from your work in the fields today." Vera ignored Mutti, grabbed the few things she owned, shoved them into a bag, and stalked out of the room, saying, "I am never coming back." Vera was eighteen years old. I was taken aback by her hostile departure. Hadn't her aunt risked her life to rescue her from the Russian zone?

"Finish your meal," Mutti said to Ingrid and me. She looked troubled. Vera went directly to the barracks across from us and moved in with another woman who had a room there. Since Vera had found a boyfriend among the GSO men, she would now be free to bring him home, something Mutti had not allowed her to do.

The GSO workers flooded the village of Trauen. There was little for them to do. Soon a stranger from Hamburg built a tavern across the street from the barracks. He named it Rote Laterne, a name more suited to the raucous sailor quarter of Hamburg-St.Pauli than to the staid landscape of the Lüneburg Heath. The red lantern was a well-known symbol for prostitution, promising girls and sex; at least, that's what I heard people say. In its back rooms the Rote Laterne operated unobtrusively as a brothel for the hundreds of GSO men living nearby, while in its front rooms it conducted the normal business of a bar. The building itself, constructed of grey, concrete blocks, remained unfinished on the outside, an ugly eyesore even compared to our rundown barracks.

Some GSO men formed a chess club. They met at the Rote Laterne once a week. I went over and watched the men play. I picked the game up quickly and asked the club's president if I would be permitted to join and play in their tournaments. He was excited to have a young boy join the club. He started me off playing in practice games, and, when he thought I was ready, he allowed me to enter their tournaments. I was good at the game and soon was the club champion.

In early summer 1948, some very personal and confusing things began happening to me. I could not ignore the fact that hair had started to grow on my face. Much more embarrassing was my voice, which no longer just made the occasional squeak it had the year before but began to change in earnest. My friend Arnim's voice was changing, too. The girls laughed loudly when our voices broke while we were speaking or singing in class. Mutti said it was natural and not to worry about it, that I was turning into a man. I wasn't ready to be a man yet, with all the responsibilities I thought a man had to assume; I wanted to stay a boy. And the hair on my face and my cracking voice weren't all that was bothering me. I couldn't talk to Mutti about what really perplexed me, nor my father, nor my grandfather Samuel. At night I often awoke experiencing a different feeling in my groin. I had no one to talk to about that. I had no books to read on the subject, and I was too shy to ask anyone. Girls began to hold a strong attraction for me, and I lost the ease with which I had been interacting with them. I began to comprehend many of the things I had seen and heard after the war. I thought I was even coming to understand the implications of the word "rape."

In our biology class we studied the human body. The drawings and sketches used by our teacher were neither male nor female. At first I thought maybe the teacher would eventually get around to discussing the parts of our bodies about which we speculated and would help us understand what was going on inside ourselves. He never did. The course ended without any mention of sex. We were disappointed that our study of the human body omitted the one thing that was so powerfully occupying our minds and raging through our young bodies. We never spoke of sex amongst ourselves, and so we continued to grow up more or less in ignorance of something that was ever present in the world around us and changing our perceptions of one another.

The apartment of the barracks Communist was right behind ours. He and his wife had to pass our door through a small foyer to get home. I had never been in their apartment. I knew her bed was up against the wall next to my room. The couple had one girl, and I noticed the woman again had a swollen belly. I wasn't surprised. All winter long I had had to listen to him groan on the other side of the thin wall. She never made a sound. There was no way to pretend we didn't hear him. Often it was late in the afternoon, and Vera would say to me, "Listen, there they go again," pointing to the wall. I tried to hide my face in embarrassment whenever Vera said that. Mutti ignored the noises and acted as if she heard nothing. Every afternoon or evening, day after day, if I was around, I listened to him having sex. I felt ashamed overhearing something I believed should be private. Of course, there was nothing private in the barracks.

Our new pig was growing fast. Every evening after the meal at the GSO camp, I grabbed a slop bucket and walked to their mess tent. I had received permission from the cooks to pick up the leftover food the GSO men pitched into a barrel by the tent after dinner. They ate well. In the slop was white English bread, remnants of rice, potatoes, meat, and whatever else they may have had for dinner and couldn't finish. I had made a ladle from an English biscuit tin and a broom handle, and I used it to scoop the slop out of the barrel. Opa inspected the slop, mixed it with chopped grain, and then poured the mixture into the trough. The pig loved the stuff. I often watched him eat until he had finished and had licked his trough clean.

At RAF Fassberg, the level of activity had been increasing rapidly since April, when the Russians first attempted to restrict road and rail travel between Berlin and the western zones of occupation. The few English Dakotas I had seen taking off in April had increased in number, and soon I began seeing American C-47s, too. The C-47 was the same airplane as the Dakota. By early May, takeoffs and landings had become frequent occurrences, and aircraft noise could be heard at all hours of the day and frequently at night as well.

All at once American soldiers appeared on the streets of Fassberg; their presence provided me with a deep sense of security. I knew the Americans had chosen to be here with us Germans, placing themselves on our side, trying to save our Berlin. Their coming meant to me that we were not some-day going to be part of the expanding Russian empire. The day-to-day pres-ence of the American soldiers gave me, I thought, what new money could not buy and what war had lost for my country—friends. Good friends, I hoped, who would be there each tomorrow to help if we needed them. It was a never-ending thrill to watch the American planes take off and land and to see them overhead as I went to and from school. I knew there was a better life ahead for us Germans with friends like the Americans.

There were so many wonderful things for a young boy to discover about these American soldiers. They were different from soldiers I had known before, mostly men whose faces were hard and whose fingers were never far from the triggers of their guns. These Americans carried no guns. Their numbers grew by the day; they flooded the town of Fassberg with their pres-ence. Soon a *Gasthaus* catering exclusively to them opened its doors. Called Mom's Place, it was filled with young Americans from early afternoon until late at night. The place was only a few houses away from my school, and on my way home I could see the soldiers sitting there, laughing, enjoying the German beer they liked so much, and smoking endless packs of cigarettes. If they weren't smoking or drinking, they were chewing gum, just like the American soldiers of 1945.

They wore what looked like tailor-made uniforms of fine-quality mate-rial, fitting for a Sunday suit, with shoes and socks of matching color. They wore their hats at a jaunty angle, which matched their friendly dispositions, their carefree looks, and their relaxed and easygoing manners. Their uni-forms were impeccable, except for the hats, which looked as if they had been crushed, the sides drooping down. I learned that the crushed look came from the headphones they wore over their hats while flying. They also seemed to have lots of the new German money, and they spent it freely. An influx of merchants who wanted to sell their wares to the prosperous Ameri-cans quickly provided the opportunity. The merchants erected their porta-ble tables near the main gate of the air base and sold everything from fine

Solingen knives with artfully carved stag handles to Bavarian beer steins, from Black Forest cuckoo clocks to fine jewelry from Idar-Oberstein.

Among the tradesmen were money changers who operated mostly out of the pockets of their overcoats. When I watched them exchanging D-marks for dollars, I found out that an American dollar bought nearly twenty-four of the new German marks. I had no idea how money was valued and by what measure an American dollar warranted twenty-four marks. I had received only forty D-marks when the new currency was issued—not even two dollars in American money. Women not from Fassberg appeared in town. They stood along the garden fences near the main gate trying to find American boyfriends. Many of them did, and suddenly there was a high demand for rooms in Fassberg. The supply of available rooms was limited. For the right price, though, families were willing to double up and rent a room to an American and his girlfriend, who didn't mind paying the high prices they asked for. Some of my classmates had to give up their rooms when their parents rented them to Americans. They smiled when they told me. Their families were suddenly prospering with the influx of so much money, money which bought real goods.

Mutti initially took a job at the English NAAFE. She soon switched to the American post exchange, or PX, as the Americans called their store. She was hired as a salesperson because she spoke English, unlike me, who couldn't speak a word of it yet. The PX was a store, as Mutti described it, carrying everything from expensive Swiss watches to the much-prized nylon stockings and American cigarettes. Such items were not yet available on the German market. Nylon stockings began to show up on the legs of Fassberg girls, a sure sign of who was going out with an American. The Americans sold their Lucky Strike, Camel, Pall Mall, Old Gold, Chesterfield, and Philip Morris cigarettes right outside the main gate in plain sight of the military police. The cigarettes came in wax-paper-wrapped cartons of ten packs, called a *Stange*. I knew that when an American airman exited the main gate with a brown paper bag under his arm, most likely he was carrying a *Stange* of cigarettes, which he would sell before he had walked a hundred meters.

I continued to observe the American airmen every chance I got. They drank wine and beer, and the few stores in town carried a wide variety of German wines to meet the demand of their free-spending American customers. Most of the Americans remained friendly even when they drank too much, in contrast to the Russian soldiers I remembered. The Americans drank for different reasons, mostly for enjoyment, while the Russians always drank to get drunk. There were English airmen stationed at Fassberg, too; after all, it was an English air base. But the English kept to themselves. Most of them didn't bring their families this time, and the nice houses in the red housing area continued to stand empty.

Late one afternoon, our barracks Communist joined me on our front steps as I watched English Dakotas pass overhead. "Soon the capitalists will be gone," he said, smiling broadly. He made me uncomfortable. "Then the proletariat"—a word I didn't understand—"will unite in East and West and we will live in peace as brothers and sisters, united in harmony, working toward a common goal. Ours will be a world of peace and plenty," he said emphatically, his voice rising. I was appalled. Memories of life under the Communists flashed before my eyes—the spies, the beatings, the knock on the door at night, the prisons. Facing him, I shouted, "I have lived under your wonderful secret police. I know what you Communists are like. Why don't you take your family into the paradise in the East if you like it so much. No one is stopping you. I would rather die than live like that again." He jumped up as if stung by a hornet, looked at me with undisguised hatred, spit on the ground before me, and walked into his apartment.

In late June, people were saying that the Russians had stopped traffic into Berlin and that the city of over two million was totally isolated except for three air corridors leading to Berlin from Hamburg in the north, a central corridor near Fassberg, and another corridor from Frankfurt in the south. It was only a matter of time, people speculated, until Berlin was out of food and coal and would become part of the Russian zone of occupation. By the middle of July, even more English Dakotas and American C-47s were flying out of Fassberg. I didn't know for sure what it was they were flying to Berlin. I thought it probably was food for the Berliners and for their own garrisons. Then, in the beautiful month of August, almost overnight a large American airplane showed up at the Fassberg air base. The new transport was different from the Dakotas and the C-47s. It had four noisy engines, and the aircraft did not sit on its tail like the others did when on the ground. Instead, it had a nose wheel and sat straight and level on its landing gear. Within a week, the English Dakotas had left Fassberg, and the base was filled with American C-54 Skymaster transports.

From the day the C-54s arrived, they flew into Berlin, and not only dur-

Return of the Americans

ing the day and in good weather, but day and night, seven days a week, rain or sunshine. When the wind blew down the runways from the northwest, as it usually did, the C-54s turned over our barracks every three minutes. At night I watched the exhaust flames from the four engines as the full airplanes strained to gain altitude before entering the northern corridor only thirty kilometers east of our barracks compound. When walking to school, I often met full coal trains arriving, or empty trains leaving, heading for the Ruhrgebiet to be filled again, to return and repeat the cycle. The GSO workers shoveled the bulk coal into American duffel bags left over from the war, and then loaded the bags onto ten-ton trucks, I was told. "One truckload fills one airplane," my friend, a GSO worker, told me over chess in the Rote Laterne. "We load the airplanes by handing twenty thousand pounds of coal from hand to hand. The two-engined Dakotas and C-47s carry only two and a half tons, that's why they don't use them anymore." My GSO friend was all wound up and kept talking excitedly about the *grosse Luftbrücke*, neglecting our chess match. Lowering his voice, he said, "The RAF and the Amis fly into Berlin along the northern and the southern corridors, and the empty planes return down the central corridor. I bet you didn't know that." He paused. Then, with his hands, he drew an imaginary grid in the air depicting Berlin and the corridors and said, "The Russians will shoot down any English or American planes that stray out of those narrow corridors. They are only twenty miles wide, and it's easy to stray out of them."

"That's pretty wide," I postured, trying to sound like I knew something about what was going on.

"No, no," he said. "That's not wide at all, my boy." I felt myself blushing in embarrassment. Then he gently explained, "When you fly at 170 miles per hour, it takes less than seven minutes from one edge of a corridor to the other. At night and in bad weather it is easy for a pilot who flies down the middle to drift left or right. There are winds up there, you know, and they don't just blow from one direction and at a steady velocity." He pushed the chess set aside, leaned forward on his elbows, looked straight at me, then whispered, "It makes me feel good to work with the Amis," and his eyes shone brightly when he spoke. "Let me tell you something else, my young friend. You know the Fassberg planes fly their coal into Gatow, don't you?" I nodded my head, although I didn't know that. "It takes them an hour to fly to Berlin. They fly a straight-in approach to Gatow, and, if they miss for whatever reason, they have to turn around and return to Fassberg. There is no second try. It's like an assembly line in an American automobile factory. A plane takes off right after one has landed, and that cycle repeats itself hour after hour, day and night."

"You are exaggerating," I said. "I can't believe that. They don't have that many airplanes." Another GSO man who had joined our table said, "Werner is right. They fly and they fly and they fly, like it is a war they are fighting. The Russians will not get Berlin going against the Americans." He pounded the table emphatically with his fist, making our chess pieces jump. "I'll take any bet on that."

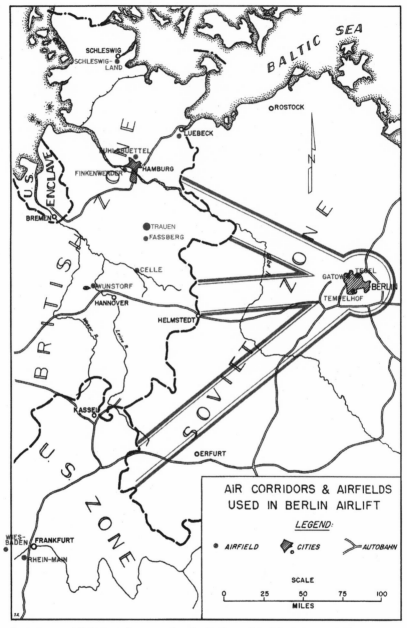

American and British air bases used in the Berlin airlift. *The American Military Occupation of Germany 1945–1953*, Headquarters, United States Army, Europe, 1953, 141.

Chapter 20

SERGEANT LEO FERGUSON

My mother liked working for the Americans. Occasionally she came home accompanied by American officers. Pilots. They wore silver wings on their jackets and silver bars on their shoulders. The Americans brought chocolate and cigarettes. They never stayed long. I could see in their eyes that they hadn't expected to find the poverty, squalor, and depressing greyness of the barracks next door to the clean and seemingly prospering town of Fassberg. It was a shock for them to see that people lived as we did. The sight of kids still mostly dressed in the oldest of clothing, the deteriorating barracks, the mud, the flies, and the always-present smell of the latrine made them want to return quickly to their clean, antiseptic quarters. If that didn't do it, once they saw the interior of our apartment—the stove with its pipe going through the ceiling, the water buckets, the worn furniture—they didn't want to stay around much longer. For whatever reason they had accompanied my mother home, they didn't seem to remember it once they got there.

August was always the most beautiful month in the Lüneburg Heath. One sunny day followed another, and the heath bloomed in purple splendor. All the German aircraft had been removed, including the airplane house, and I could enjoy the beauty of the land without the presence of the decaying tools of war. I had learned to love the land, in spite of the hard times our family had endured living there. I abhorred the barracks, but I loved the

301

heath and Fassberg, which, in their own way, had shared my desperation. They had become friends who were there with their healing and sustaining powers when I needed them. When the heath was a blanket of purple stretching before my eyes to the horizon, I felt rewarded and rich for being able to share in the beauty of the land. Bees buzzed through the heath by the thousands, collecting honey for the long winter ahead. Shepherds emerged with their flocks of heath sheep, and the juniper bushes stood as silent guardians. I knew that one day I would leave the heath. I also knew that it always would remain a part of me. The American C-54 transports flew overhead, struggling to gain altitude in the warmth of the day. They, too, had become friends, and, like the heath, they belonged here.

One day Mutti came home from work accompanied by an American sergeant. The sergeant wore the usual brown uniform with the Ike jacket and the large stripes on his sleeves. He was tall and lanky. I was immediately attracted to him, a feeling I never had about any of my mother's friends. I watched him carefully. Standing in front of our barracks across from me, he slowly and deliberately took a pack of Camels from the left breast pocket of his meticulously pressed Ike jacket. He hit the pack several times against the side of his left hand, then pulled a red cellophane string which neatly took off the top of the cellophane wrapper. He peeled away a section of paper about the width of four cigarettes, and finally appeared ready to remove the first cigarette from the pack. He did this by again hitting the pack against the side of his left hand. A cigarette popped from the tight package. He pulled it out and put it between his lips, smiling at me when he noticed I was watching. I smiled back. Before lighting the cigarette, he replaced the pack in his breast pocket. He was so deliberate about the entire process that he had totally captured my attention. Then the sergeant pulled an English Ronson lighter from his pants pocket and unhurriedly lit his cigarette. Leaning his head back as if to say that there was nothing better in life than a good cigarette, this cigarette, he took a long first puff, and blew the smoke out of his mouth up into the air.

"My name is Leo Ferguson," he said, in twangy, slow, American English. "Call me Leo." He stretched out his hand to shake mine. I noticed that his fingers were long and slender, his nails clean and manicured. I didn't understand everything he said, and he could tell. "Leo," he said again. "I am Leo."

"Ich bin Wolfgang," I replied. He smiled, his teeth regular and white, and his brilliant blue eyes laughed at me.

Sergeant Leo Ferguson

"W-o-l-f-g-a-n-g," he repeated slowly, as if savoring the sound of the strange name. "That's a fine name. I like it." We both laughed. I could tell he liked me as much as I liked him. I knew he wasn't seeing any of the things the others had seen in me, in my family, in our barracks—my worn-out clothes, my sandals made from German airplane tires, the mud, the flies, the smell of the latrine, the snot-nosed kids. And I hoped he wouldn't leave like the others had. Mutti joined us on the worn wooden steps in front of the barracks where Leo and I had sat down, side by side, close together. I knew everyone was looking and that they would be saying things about us. I didn't care. I liked the American, and I liked being near him.

Two girls of three or four with dirty faces and dirty dresses scampered up, sticking their fingers into their mouths as they came near. They wore no panties, and their thin dresses barely covered their fat bellies. They obviously had been playing in the dirt in front of their barracks. There was nowhere else for them to play. The girls stood in front of us, smiling, sucking on their dirty fingers, looking at the sergeant, at Leo. Leo reached into his jacket and pulled out a yellow pack of Juicy Fruit chewing gum, the same kind of gum the American soldier had given me in 1945. He held out a stick to each of the girls, who removed their fingers from their mouths, giggled, and hesitantly took the offered gift.

"*Danke schön*," they said in unison and ran off skipping and laughing to their apartment across the way to show off the gum they had gotten from the nice American soldier. Leo, Mutti, and I went inside. Mutti served a simple dinner of potatoes and hamburgers fixed in a brown sauce, *Königsberger Klopse*. After dinner they talked, and then the sergeant rose to leave. He came over to me, shook my hand and said, "*Auf Wiedersehen*."

"*Auf Wiedersehen*," I replied, jumping to my feet. I knew he would be back.

After Leo had gone, Mutti told me that the sergeant had been coming to her PX counter for a number of days. "He stands around and acts like he is looking at something. I knew he was trying to work up the courage to speak to me. Finally, after looking at a watch for a long time, he asked if he could see me after work. He blushed like you do when you tell a little lie, Wolfgang. I told him I lived four kilometers from the gate. If he wished he could walk me home." She paused, then said, "Do you like him?"

"Yes," I said quickly, "he seems like an honest and nice man. Yes, I like the American. His eyes are gentle and warm and have no hate in them."

Sergeant Leo Ferguson

"I thought you would like him," Mutti responded with a satisfied smile on her face. "I like him, too."

Leo walked Mutti home whenever he could. Then, one day, he bought two bicycles. It wouldn't take so long for them to come home after work now, and it would be easier for Leo to get back to the base by eleven o'clock, before curfew. It soon became clear to me that the relationship between Mutti and Leo was different from those she had had before. She and Leo seemed to care for each other. They spent most of their time together on weekends. With their new bicycles, they were able to get around easily. Often they went to Müden, a picturesque village on the road to Fassberg, where the Americans had requisitioned a restaurant and hotel and turned it into a sergeants' club. There they could eat, drink, and dance, and even watch American movies. One weekend the Americans trucked in children from nearby villages and fed them dinner, with Coca-Cola and cake for dessert. They had a funny clown, and the children shrieked and laughed. They were nice people, the Americans, people who cared for children. At the age of thirteen, I was too old to attend and could only watch the party through a window.

Leo gave Mutti some pieces of uniforms for me to wear, items which he no longer needed or decided he could spare. I acquired one pair of precious American uniform pants, a brown army sweater, and green undershirts and underpants, of which I had none. I had not owned underwear for a long time and had forgotten the good feeling of wearing it. Now that I owned underwear, I had to wash it, too, which I did every five days, or when I thought it was dirty. I frequently rode out toward the air base on Mutti's bicycle, when she chose to ride the truck, and met Leo halfway between our barracks and the base, at the edge of the forest where the ugly Heinkel-177 bombers used to sit. I waited for him if he wasn't already there smoking a Camel. He always shook my hand, then sat down again to light another cigarette in his usual ornate and deliberate manner. He would sit there for a while enjoying his cigarette. He seemed a man totally at peace with himself. Although I enjoyed watching him smoke, I never wanted to myself, and he never tried to get me to smoke.

I didn't speak any English, but I wanted to talk to Leo and tell him things. So I spoke to him in German. Occasionally he would nod his head in response to what I said and smile, or he would say, "Okay." He spoke to me in English. I listened attentively to what he said, and sometimes I picked

Sergeant Leo Ferguson

up a meaning because some words seemed to be similar to German words. Then I would nod to him and smile and laugh. Neither one of us fully understood what the other said. We didn't need to. We both felt we communicated with each other, and, with every day that passed, I thought, we became closer friends. I was drawn to Leo as a son to a father. I felt his caring warmth. In Leo's presence I began to feel whole, sheltered and protected, a feeling that I had lost in those awful days of 1945 when my childish world came crashing down. I had fewer nightmares now that Leo was around, and the faces of the dead I saw in my dreams had softened, their eyes no longer reaching for me.

One Saturday Leo asked me if I would like to accompany him to the base. We left from the barracks riding our bicycles, taking the *Feldweg* across the potato fields into the forest, past the site where the 20 mm guns had once stood. Instead of crossing the railroad tracks, we followed the *Waldweg* alongside the tracks right into the base. There were no guard posts or sentries. We rode across the base to one of the former German aircraft hangars, which were steel structures with flat roofs. On top of the hangar roofs, as on some of the buildings at the Trauen Research Center, was a layer of dirt with grass, heather, and young trees growing in it. Parked inside the cavernous hangar were twin-engined C-47s, the smaller transport plane no longer used for airlift duty. Leo's room was at the top of the hangar, directly under the roof. We climbed an iron staircase that led to a balcony near the roofline which ran along three sides of the hangar. Leo's room contained four neatly made-up cots, their blankets tightly stretched. He took a coin from his pocket and bounced it off the blanket on his bed. "Regulations," he said, smiling at me. At the foot of each bed was a green footlocker. Two metal cabinets stood up against the wall. Each occupant shared one half of a cabinet. I saw no locks anywhere.

Leo took off his jacket and undid his tie. He removed his shirt and indicated for me to do the same. Then he took two towels, two bars of soap, and a bottle of shampoo from his cabinet and motioned for me to follow. I did, with some trepidation. We walked down to the showers. Leo handed me a towel and a bar of soap and then pointed to one of the shower stalls. He undressed and stepped into one. I watched him turn on the water. Steam soon rose from the floor. As Leo began shampooing his hair, he saw me still standing there. I didn't know what to do. At thirteen, I had never taken a shower. I hadn't even had a real bath, in a real bathtub, since 1945. Leo

Sergeant Leo Ferguson

again pointed at a shower stall. I reluctantly started to take off the remainder of my clothes. I couldn't get myself to take off the new shorts Leo had given me, so I entered the shower with my shorts on.

Once I got the water temperature adjusted I really enjoyed showering. It felt wonderful to have hot water bounce off my body. What a luxury! I took the bar of reddish soap and lathered myself all over, then rinsed with more of the glorious hot water. The soap had the word "Lifebuoy" imprinted on it, and it smelled strangely of iodine. I thought about taking off my shorts. I just couldn't. Leo was already out of the shower, dried and dressed when I finally got out. He said nothing about my shorts. When I started to dry myself, I decided I had to take the step and take off my wet underpants. I did, then dried and pulled my pants on. I didn't know what to do with my wet underpants. I was sure Leo was laughing inside at my modesty and at the predicament I had gotten myself into. On the outside he remained un-noticing and helpful. Once we were back in his room, he handed me a pair of dry shorts, without comment, and I put them on.

"Come on," he said, after I was finally dressed again, "let's go and have a Coke." For once I understood clearly what he said. After taking the shower, I liked Leo even more. For the first time in several years, I felt really clean—not only on my body, but also inside where the grime of hopelessness and despair was slowly washing away. I was grateful for the soap he had given me and for the hot water. And I was especially grateful that he had not laughed at me for wearing my underpants into the shower. We rode our bikes to the post exchange and parked them in an old, rusty bicycle stand. The PX build-ing was near the flight line where they parked the airplanes. On the back side of the building was pine forest. A rusted chain-link fence ran through the forest, erected by the Luftwaffe years ago to keep unauthorized persons off the airfield. The Americans seemed to be unconcerned about fences and keeping people in or out. They had expanded the open area in front of the PX entrance by having a bulldozer clear and level the area of trees, bushes, and wartime debris. The bulldozer had pushed the debris, including an old German FW-190 fighter, up against the rusting fence. One of its wings had crumpled and was bent upward, sticking straight up against the fence, show-ing its light-blue underside and black cross. No one but I paid attention to the old Focke-Wulf fighter. Times had changed. I liked the new times.

We entered the PX and came to a sign proclaiming Snack Bar. I knew what the word "bar" meant, and I thought "snack" must mean sandwich. A

Sergeant Leo Ferguson

bar where you buy sandwiches. That was an interesting twist on words, I thought. Who had ever heard of a bar for food? Only the Americans would think of such a name.

"Would you like a Coke, Wolfgang?"

"Yes, please," I replied in English, hoping that the unfamiliar words would come out sounding right. They must have, because Leo got both of us a Coca-Cola. The drink came in heavy, shaped glass bottles. Leo also brought two glasses with straws and ice. Ice?

"*Setzen wir uns bitte,*" Leo said. I was surprised. I didn't know he knew that much German. He must have picked up a few words, or more likely Mutti was teaching him. We sat down, and I watched the comings and goings of the American airmen. Most wore their work uniforms, baggy coveralls with oversized pockets, and caps on their heads with the bills turned up. It was so funny to see soldiers running around looking like that. They didn't look military. There wasn't any saluting going on either, and no heel clicking at all, as the German and English soldiers liked to do. The airmen in their baggy work uniforms came and went on clumsy-looking American bicycles with fat tires. The Coke, as Leo called it, was an exquisite drink. I tasted coffee in it, or maybe caffeine. I let the Coke run over my tongue slowly so I could absorb its full flavor and not forget the pleasant experience too quickly. I was sure I had never had a cold drink that tasted this good. It was much better even than lemonade. I looked up at Leo, and he was smoking one of his Camels again, looking relaxed and at ease.

After our Coke, Leo and I went to another area of the PX. I was overwhelmed by the new smells enveloping me, smells I had never experienced before. A strange mixture of pleasant odors emanated from boxes of candy bars and chewing gum, from brewing coffee, and from other things to eat such as donuts laid out under a glass counter at the snack bar. Donuts, I could see, were *Berliners* fried in fat with a hole in the middle rather than jelly. My eyes must have been wide and wondering. Leo just let me be. No hurry. He seemed to have a wonderful sense of knowing when another person needed time to absorb the new impressions rushing in upon him. He lit another cigarette instead and went over to the snack bar, where he got himself a cup of coffee and a Hershey chocolate bar for me.

Airmen were everywhere, laughing, pushing, jostling, talking, smoking, and, of course, chewing gum. Some read comic books while they drank their coffee and smoked their cigarettes. Many looked very young. I had never

Sergeant Leo Ferguson

seen a whole book of comics before. Why would grown men read comic books? I wondered. I thought comics were for children. I didn't know how to ask Leo that question. He must have followed my eyes and seen the questions arising within me, because he took me over to the magazine racks where the comic books were.

"You stay here, Wolfgang," he said, "I have to go and buy cigarettes. I'll be right back." He left me standing in front of the comic books. I looked at the colorful covers—monsters, a crazy-looking duck, a man flying through the air with a cape around his body. One comic was called *Superman* and another *Captain Marvel*. The young airmen read their comics the way I read my Karl May books, totally engrossed, with expressions passing over their faces as they turned the pages. Leo returned. "Did you have enough for today?"

"What did you say?" I asked Leo in German, not understanding what he meant.

Leo repeated his question in German. *"Hast Du genug für Heute?"* That was simple enough. I tried to remember the English words as we walked to our bicycles. I silently repeated to myself over and over: "Did you have enough for today?"

Leo took time to be with me when he and Mutti weren't going anywhere. Once I talked him into riding our bikes to Munster. When we started out that day, the sun was shining. We rode silently alongside each other, stopping occasionally for Leo to smoke a cigarette by the side of the road. I felt that Leo liked the countryside as much as I did. On the way home, the weather changed rapidly. The sky clouded over, and within ten minutes it was raining heavily. Neither Leo nor I had brought a raincoat. I didn't own one, of course. We took shelter under a tree. An English army truck approached, heading for Munster. The driver saw us huddling under the birch tree and stopped. He got out of his dry cab, running through the rain toward us. I couldn't understand what he said to Leo because of his strange accent. Then the driver took his jacket off and gave it to Leo, pointing at me. I was wearing only a shirt; the rain was cold and I was shivering. Leo handed me the English soldier's jacket and gestured for me to put it on. The jacket felt warm and comfortable.

"Okay?" the smiling English soldier said, looking at me. I nodded my head.

"Sorry, mate, I can't take you to Fassberg. Maybe the jacket will keep the

Sergeant Leo Ferguson

boy warm." He waved at Leo and me and then ran through the rain to his truck. His shirt got soaked in the heavy downpour. We waved back at him as he drove off in a cloud of blue gasoline fumes. I was touched that an English soldier would stop his truck to lend me his jacket so that I, a German boy, could stay dry and warm. The rain soon stopped, and we cycled home. Leo took the jacket to the base the next day and left it with the guards at the main gate.

Opa and Oma Samuel spoke of building a new house. Knowing my grandfather, I understood that it was no idle wish. He would build another house, even though he was already in his mid-sixties. It was just a matter of where and when, not if. School began again, and now I did not arrive at school hungry. Also, for the first time in three years, I had real clothing to wear; I was no longer uncomfortable and ashamed to be seen by my classmates or their parents. At school I was given a new name—Ami, which was short for American, because of the clothes I wore. I wore my American uniform pants every day, my American army shirt and sweater, and my English army jacket if it was cold. I really wanted to own an American Ike jacket, but I didn't dare ask Leo for one; I could only dream. Being called Ami was good-natured fun and I took it as such.

A bookstore had been added to the shops across the street from our school. On my class breaks when I was not playing school yard soccer, I went to the new store to look at the books. I was especially excited over a detective magazine about a private eye and his adventures in New York City. Every other week a new edition of the magazine appeared, and at fifty Pfennig a copy even I could afford it. The lead character was Kenney. Kenney's turf was New York. Kenney lit a cigarette first thing in the morning, drank lots of black coffee, ate only nearly raw beefsteaks, and always tracked down his man somewhere in the canyons of Manhattan. I would buy the new edition of the magazine the minute it came out and read it overnight.

Since I could use either Mutti's or Leo's bicycle, I could get back and forth to school much more quickly. We kept the bikes in our apartment at night, so that no one would be tempted to steal them. The man who had once tried to molest me and whom I had accused of stealing my English bike the year before had moved into the village of Trauen when the wreckers tore down his airplane house. There he continued to build and sell radios, having stripped sufficient parts from the German aircraft to keep him busy for years to come.

Sergeant Leo Ferguson

October, November, and December passed. In December it didn't get light until after eight in the morning, and it was dark again by four in the afternoon. The rains came, too, as they always had, with sleet or hail between showers. The American transport planes flew every day and night, without interruption, regardless of weather. They now flew to the new airfield of Tegel in the French sector of Berlin. At our weekly chess club meeting, my GSO partner told me, "There are now three airfields in Berlin—Tempelhof, Gatow, and Tegel. Do you know about Tegel?"

"Know what about Tegel?" I replied. "I don't know anything about Berlin airfields."

"*Ja*," he said expansively, "Tegel was built in only three months by the Berliners themselves. The runways were built from the rubble of bombed-out buildings. Isn't that amazing?" I agreed with him. "And then," he said, "we have just opened a new American air base in Celle. They fly their coal to Gatow."

"Who flies food to Berlin if Fassberg and Celle only fly coal?"

"*Ja*, the Americans have other bases in Germany, and they fly food out of Frankfurt and Wiesbaden. I flew once out of Wiesbaden early in the war when I was in the Luftwaffe," Werner said, continuing his tutorial. "It's a beautiful city."

At night, lying on my straw mattress, I thought about what Werner had said. I thought about the Americans who were able to assemble a huge fleet of planes to supply Berlin from the air, just as they had once assembled fleets of B-17 bombers to bomb Berlin. I heard their transports turn over my barracks as I lay there thinking about them. Even when I knew rain clouds were nearly touching the tips of the tallest trees in the surrounding forest, I could hear the drone of the planes above my head. I thought about the pilots, those brave men sitting in their cramped cockpits holding on to their control columns, staring into what must seem to them impenetrable cloud. I wondered if they were ever afraid to fly, and how they found their way to Berlin, and why they didn't crash in weather like this.

On a clear December night, a C-54 turned over our barracks and fell like a rock out of the sky. I didn't see it happen or hear it crash because I was inside at the time. I heard the commotion outside. Some men had watched the C-54 turn and had seen it fall to its death. They heard the explosion when the plane crashed. "Not far from us," one of the men said to me, "probably on the Trauen Center." Later I learned from Leo that the coal

Sergeant Leo Ferguson

had shifted inside the aircraft as it made its turn. The plane crashed outside the fence line of the Trauen Research Center. The crew of three was killed. I went to the crash site after the Americans had removed most of the debris. The site was black from oil and fuel that had seeped into the soft, marshy ground. One engine lay half buried, and another was underground, buried too deeply ever to be seen again. The airplane had dug itself deep into the marsh. I felt sorrow for the American pilots who had died for us Germans. Only three years ago they were fighting against my country, and now they were dying for us. The Americans were strange people, and I didn't really understand them, even though I had read about them and met them first in war and now in peace. I wondered, as only a child can wonder, what made these people do the things they did.

Opa Samuel had raised another pig, and he butchered it just before Christmas. Now we had plenty of ham, sausage, bacon, lard, and meat. The difference between this winter of 1948 and the one of 1947 was that everybody had work, new money, and hope for a better future. Christmas 1948 was a simple celebration, our first in three years with a Christmas tree. I spent Christmas with Oma and Opa Samuel, as I had the year before. Mutti and Leo went away for the holidays, the first time since 1945 that Mutti had had a vacation. Ingrid was with my father, who had met a German woman, a war widow whose husband had been killed in Russia in 1942. The widow had two children, a boy and a girl. Dad and Ingrid went to spend Christmas with them.

The cold weeks passed in repetitive monotony. School remained the highlight of my days. I disliked the weekends, when I had to stay in the barracks; then I helped Opa chop wood and feed the new pig, or did chores for Oma. Mutti continued to work in the PX, and Leo came to visit less frequently because of the weather. I missed him. The American transports kept on flying day and night. They had become so much a part of my life that at times I didn't even hear them anymore. In February of 1949 I turned fourteen. Since we had flour, sugar, and butter, Oma baked a cake with a candle burning on it. I blew out the candle as she asked me to do. I was supposed to make a silent wish, which I couldn't tell anyone or the wish wouldn't come true. I didn't wish for anything. I felt happy. I couldn't think of anything I needed just then.

Leo bought chocolates, coffee, and cigarettes at the PX, as most soldiers did, and he and Mutti sold them on the black market. The black market

Sergeant Leo Ferguson

was different from how it had been before the *Währungsreform*. Now, goods were sold for money; they were no longer traded for other goods or for sex.

As it got warmer and the days turned sunny, Leo frequently brought friends along with him. On sunny weekend days, they sat in front of our barracks talking. They would send me to the Rote Laterne, where I would buy beer for them. Leo and his friends were generous with their beer and cigarettes, sharing with the German men who lived in the barracks and came over to talk to the Americans. On Saturday afternoons, it was not uncommon to see a group of Americans surrounded by their German friends in front of our barracks, drinking beer and talking about the airlift and America. Leo and his friends gave me chewing gum and candy bars as my reward for getting beer for them from the Rote Laterne. I saved the candy bars and the gum. I felt I didn't want to get used to the taste. When I had accumulated a fair amount, I started to sell them to children in the barracks. The word got out quickly, and, before I knew it, kids were coming from as far away as Trauen village to buy my chewing gum and candy bars. When I had a few marks saved up, I decided to talk to Mutti about an idea I had entertained for some time.

At the dinner table I tried to ask for her advice. My timing was bad. Mutti had decided to tell jokes, something she always did badly. She laughed at her own jokes so hard that I rarely got the punch line. I tried several times to interrupt but didn't get anywhere. "Here is one more story you have to hear, Wolfgang. Leo, you, too. Then I stop," she gasped between laughs. Her laugh was full and genuine, free of pressure and worry. It had been a long time since she had laughed with such abandon. "So," she said, "Wolfgang came to visit me unexpectedly in the hospital. You remember, Wolfgang? November of '47?" She translated for Leo. "I was so happy to see you. I was depressed by my illness, for being confined to a hospital bed when I knew you didn't have enough to eat. Then, suddenly, there was Wolfgang like a ray of sunshine out of nowhere brightening my day. My dear son." She became serious, not laughing anymore.

"This is something I have wanted to tell you for a long time," she continued, looking at me. "That afternoon when I asked you to stay overnight, I thought there wouldn't be a problem finding a bed for you to sleep in, because we usually had one or two empty rooms in the hospital. When I spoke to my nurse, she informed me that the hospital was full. Every room was occupied. Every bed was filled. We thought and thought about what to do,

Sergeant Leo Ferguson

until the nurse had an idea. The room next to mine, the one you slept in, was the room where they put the dead for a night or two until they were picked up for burial. They had two corpses in there. The nurse put one corpse on a roll-away and put it into the operating room. There was no place to put the other corpse, so she just left it in your room, covering it with a sheet so you wouldn't see it. The nurses made sure there was no light in the room by removing the light bulb and pulling the window shade. They made up the bed from which they had taken the first corpse, and that's where you slept. I am so sorry. I couldn't tell you at the time, and I've wanted to tell you ever since. Are you angry with me?" She looked at me with apprehensive eyes. How could I have been angry? It was my turn to laugh. I laughed so hard I nearly fell off my chair. Mutti and Leo joined in my laughter.

I remembered that I had been wanting to ask her and Leo a question. There was a moment of silence, and I saw my opportunity. "Mutti, I have a question for you and Leo now."

"Yes, what is it?" she said, smiling.

"Can Leo buy me some boxes of candy and chewing gum with the money I've saved from selling my gift candy? Would you ask Leo, please?"

"Sure, I will do that for the boy," Leo responded, and lit a cigarette. He always lit a cigarette when something pleased him. He didn't ask me why I wanted the candy and the chewing gum. It was like Leo to assume I had a good reason for my request. I was saving my money for a pair of boots, boots like the American airmen wore. Instead of wearing their issued shoes, the Americans had boots made to order by German boot makers. The boots came to just above the ankles and were easy to get into. I had daydreamed for months of owning boots like that. On my walks to and from school, I would imagine what the boots would look like on my feet and how well they would go with my American uniform pants, sweater, and shirt and my English army jacket.

The boots cost 147 D-marks. Leo's friends kept giving me candy and chewing gum for running their errands, and I kept selling it. Sometimes I asked Leo to buy me an additional box of candy or gum. Eventually I saved the 147 marks, and, by May of 1949, I owned a pair of boots like the ones I had envied on the feet of the American airmen. They were my first real leather shoes since 1945, and I had bought them with my own money. With money left over, I bought a watch. Leo and I went to Fassberg to select a waterproof watch. I told the watchmaker how much money I had to spend.

Sergeant Leo Ferguson

He took a few D-marks off the price of the watch I liked, Leo added a few marks of his own, and I was the proud owner of a seventeen-jewel, water-proof watch. Seventeen was the minimum number of jewels acceptable for a good watch, according to my school friends. I couldn't settle for anything less, because they would scrutinize my watch in school, and it had better say seventeen jewels on its face. For the moment, my worldly wishes had been fulfilled. Except for the unattainable American Ike jacket, I had everything I could think of. As more and more merchandise showed up in the stores of Fassberg, Mutti was able to buy several dresses and pairs of women's shoes with high heels for herself. She, too, had had no new clothes for many years. The nicest-looking dress she had owned before she met Leo she had made herself from curtains which hung in our barracks apartment when we took it over from the woman who died of syphilis.

The black market was thriving with the introduction of the new German money. The new black market, however, provided goods otherwise unavail-able, and it served a useful, rather than a sinister, purpose. I listened to Leo and my father talk one afternoon in front of our barracks. Leo mentioned that at the air base they had arrested a sergeant who wasn't selling just cigarettes and candy bars. The sergeant, who worked in the motor pool, had taken several tanker trucks loaded with aviation fuel and driven the trucks to Hannover, where he sold both the fuel and the trucks on the black market.

My father marveled at the ingenuity and brazenness of Americans. "No wonder you won the war," he said to Leo. Both laughed loudly, each taking a sip from their beer. "The black market and the new German money are made for each other," my father continued. "You want our new money, and we Germans need everything you are willing to sell. So, everybody is happy. Ja, Leo?"

"Ja, Willi. Everybody is happy." They laughed at each other, two friends sharing a beer. Leo and Willi liked each other and got along well.

The American planes continued to fly their never-ending relays to and from Berlin. Another transport from Fassberg had crashed in January. There were rumors that the Russians were reopening the roads and rails to Berlin. Then the Russians halted the trains again. The Americans kept on flying. "We are bringing more into Berlin than the Berliners are consuming," Leo told me, "and we are building up stockpiles for any future blockade by the Russians." It wasn't enough for the Americans to beat the Russians and to

Sergeant Leo Ferguson

supply a whole city of two million with their essential needs. Now that the Berlin airlift had become routine, they made a game of it. At an open house on Fassberg air base, I saw a huge banner draped across the front of one of the hangars. BEAT CELLE it read in large black letters.

"What does it mean?" I asked Leo.

"Fassberg is competing with Celle to see who can fly the most coal to Berlin in the month of May and every month thereafter," he said with pride in his voice. I found it so American for them to make a game out of a necessity. The Americans liked games, I had observed, and they liked winning, too. I didn't know who finally won the competition, Fassberg or Celle. By June 26, 1949, the first anniversary of the Berlin airlift, the Russians had reopened the rail lines and highways to Berlin. The Americans were gleeful that they had beaten the Russians without firing a shot. At Mom's Place the victory celebrations went on all day and night. There was talk that the blockade was broken. I was sorry to hear that in a way, for I feared that our American friends, and Leo most of all, would leave us once the airlift ended. My father announced his intention to marry the war widow whom he had met the year before. I didn't mind. Mutti and Dad were divorced, and I knew they had to build new lives for themselves. In June my father married, and Ingrid decided to live with them. Mutti was saddened by Ingrid's leaving. She didn't say anything, but I read the pain in her face when she was confronted with the situation. She could have made Ingrid stay, but that wasn't like her. She let Ingrid do what she thought would make her happy.

After the Russians reopened the rails and roads to Berlin, fewer American flights left Fassberg. The intervals between planes became increasingly longer. The drone of straining C-54 aircraft engines overhead became infrequent during the day, and ceased at night. At dinner one night, Leo mentioned that everyone at the base expected orders for transfers. I knew that once the *Luftbrücke*—the Americans called it Operation Vittles—was over, there would be no reason for Fassberg to remain open. On July 29, American and English troops had a parade at the air base in honor of those who had died in the airlift. On July 30, Leo came home and told us that an announcement had been made that the *Luftbrücke* would officially end on October 31, 1949. The next day the last C-54 flew from Celle to Berlin. Celle was closing. On the evening of August 27, Leo said that the last C-54 loaded with coal for Berlin had flown from Fassberg and that everyone had celebrated the occasion. He was slightly tipsy when he arrived that evening.

Sergeant Leo Ferguson

"We'll be going soon," he said to Mutti. There was no need for her to interpret. On August 31, Mutti came home early with a wan smile on her face.

"I've been laid off. That means I don't have a job anymore, Wolfgang," she lamented. "I don't make any more money. Everything is closing." She added in disbelief, "It's all happening so fast." The GSO men also began to leave. Soon they would be gone and there would be no more chess club in the Rote Laterne. When I arrived home from school a week later, Mutti was waiting for me at our front door. She greeted me as I rode up on Leo's bicycle.

"Hallo, Wolfgang. How are you? Come in, quickly, I need to talk to you." I was puzzled. She had never greeted me like that before when I returned from school. Something important must be happening. She didn't look worried, so it couldn't be bad. I parked my bicycle against the barracks wall, locked it up, and went inside. "Come sit by me," she told me gently as I entered the room. I sat close to her. She put her right arm around my shoulders and stroked my hair out of my face with her left hand, as she liked to do at times.

"You are getting so tall, Wolfgang. Where has the time gone? I was so worried about putting food on the table, I may have missed something as you grew into a young man. You are fourteen now? Yes, of course, you are fourteen years old already, my dear boy." I wondered where she was heading with this strange conversation, which made me uncomfortable. "You have suffered so much in your young life already," she continued. "I am sorry." She took her arm off my shoulders and moved to face me better. "Wolfgang," she continued, "next week Leo is being transferred to an American air base in Bavaria. He is going to Fürstenfeldbruck, near Munich." There was a lengthy silence. "Leo has asked me to go with him. Do you mind if I go?"

"No, Mutti, of course I don't mind if you go with Leo to Bavaria." My response was instinctive. I had expected something like this.

"Will you be able to stay by yourself?" she inquired, looking worried.

"Yes, Mutti," I replied, wanting to dispel any fears or reservations. "I am a big boy now, as you just told me a minute ago. I can live in this place until I graduate from school next year. Then I probably have to go into some sort of apprenticeship, if I can find anyone to take me. If you are not back by that time we may have to give up these two rooms. There is no reason for

Sergeant Leo Ferguson

you to worry about that now. Next year is far away. Go to Bavaria with Leo, Mutti." I got up from the couch so she could not see the emotions in my face. Mutti got up, too, put her arms around me, and kissed me on both cheeks.

"You are such a good boy," she said, "and I am so proud of you. I'll write and I'll come home to visit. It'll just be for a little while."

The following week, in the middle of September and just before the first storms of autumn, Leo showed up with a surplus army jeep with the letters USA and ARMY painted in white letters on its sides. On the hood of the jeep was a white American star. Leo drove, and his friend sat next to him. Mutti and another woman sat in back. Their things were packed and stuffed all over the jeep. The little car looked hilarious with its four occupants and every bit of space filled with gasoline cans, bags, and boxes. The four of them set off, waving to Oma, Opa, and me, laughing loudly. They were having a good time. I wished I could go with them. I envied them. As the jeep disappeared on the road to Trauen, I thought that for Mutti the barracks were a thing of the past, finally out of her life forever.

On September 27, 1949, Fassberg went back into caretaker status, and the Americans were gone. The bars that had opened for them were closed. The American airmen and their money were a thing of the past. The girls disappeared, too. The merchants who sold wares to the Americans from their portable stands along the main road no longer came to Fassberg. At the main gate, German guards in brown GSO uniforms controlled access again as they had before the Americans arrived. An English soldier sat in the guardhouse where the American MPs had once sat. It was as if the Americans had never been there. I suddenly missed the Americans and their airplanes. I missed being around those noisy, confident, and carefree people, the people who liked to play games—to win.

Sergeant Leo Ferguson

Chapter 21

BAKER'S APPRENTICE

I was alone in our two-room apartment. Mutti had gone with Leo. Ingrid had gone with my father. I felt abandoned, vulnerable, and afraid. I knew I couldn't let such feelings persist. I thought of my grandparents Samuel, of Fassberg, and of my school. I quickly focused on these, the constants in my life, and drew from them the strength I needed to be on my own for the first time. At the age of fourteen, I had a year of school remaining. Then I would have to learn a trade and make a life for myself. I knew I didn't want to be just a common laborer, but finding a place to learn a trade was something to worry about. My classmates with older brothers told me that it had taken their brothers a long time to find anything, and then it wasn't necessarily the trade they wanted to learn. My biggest problem was that I had no idea what my talents were, or what I wanted to be. I did know that I wanted to read more, learn more about everything, and not just work with my hands. But that sounded like more school, and I knew that wasn't going to happen. Something would surely come along. Next year was still far off.

My class, the extended eighth grade in our ninth year, was now the most senior class in school. We were a close-knit group. I had made two good friends, Arnim Krüger, the other refugee, who lived in the old German army barracks near the main gate, and Wolfgang Luthmer, whose home was in the grey housing area. I no longer felt as different from the other boys and girls as I had during my first two years in Fassberg. With the new money, plenty of jobs, and ample goods in stores, resentment against *Flüchtlinge* had waned. After school, the three of us often rode around on our bicycles, turning circles on the street in front of the stores or at the main gate to the base.

Our teachers organized a sports competition for our class in early September. The boys assembled near the soccer field to compete in the 50- and 100-meter run, broad jump, high jump, and 250-meter relay. The girls didn't compete; instead, they made up the certificates for the winners, and they watched. We were to compete by year groups—1934 and 1935. During the first hour of the event, we were given time to practice. I discovered that I could beat everyone in my 1935 year group. I asked the principal if I could compete against the 1934 group. He agreed. While I knew I would be competing against one fellow in particular who was much taller than I, and who because of his longer legs could jump farther and run faster, still, I wanted it to be a true competition for me. If I stayed with my own year group, it wouldn't be. The tall fellow beat me in high jump, as I had expected. I came in third. He beat me again in broad jump and in the two races; I came in second in both. I also came in second in the overall standings for the 1934 year group. For me it was a real competition of my own making, and I liked that. I had striven mightily to beat my taller and longer-legged adversary, and I didn't mind losing to him. He had made me try much harder than I would have if I had stayed with my own group. It was the competition that was important, not the final outcome.

At night I sometimes missed having my mother around. As it got colder, I didn't light the stove. I piled more blankets on my bed to stay warm. I ate my meals at Oma and Opa's. Oma fussed over me just as she always had when, as a little boy, I had visited her in Schlawe. Since I was with her nearly constantly now when I was not in school, she took full advantage of her opportunity to spoil me. She always managed to come up with a special egg dish or a cup of hot cocoa. I loved hugging my grandmother and giving her a kiss or two on the cheek, because she always acted like she didn't need that sort of thing. I knew better. She protested loudly when I kissed her and put my arms around her.

"Wolfgang, stop that," she would admonish me, laughing loudly. "You are such a foolish boy. You are getting my apron all ruffled, can't you see that?" And she would shuffle off laughing, straightening her apron. I loved to get Oma worked up.

In December 1949, Mutti came on a short visit from Fürstenfeldbruck. She had written of her plans, and I met her at the train station. I was happy to see her again. She looked healthy and rested. That night she fixed dinner for us two, and it was almost like old times, but not really. I knew she would leave soon, and I would be on my own again. Over dinner she told me that she and Leo wanted to get married. I was surprised that she had finally said yes to someone.

"Leo is starting the application process. It is complex and tedious," she explained. "There are so many forms to fill out and interviews. I've come on this visit to get some of the paperwork started, since Fassberg is our permanent place of residence."

We went to the Fassberg city hall the next day, and the first thing the clerk did was issue Mutti and me a *Flüchtling Ausweis*. I was puzzled. Over four years after the war, we were still categorized as refugees, second-class citizens in my eyes, and they even gave us an identification card to certify our status. Mutti filled out papers for her marriage application certifying that she had no criminal record, had not been a Nazi, had no outstanding debts, and was a German citizen. The next morning she left again. During the dreary winter months, I kept busy with school, helping with the never-ending chores, and now and then seeing a movie in Munster. In the evenings I sat at the kitchen table next to Opa, watching him smoke his pipe and repair baskets with willow reeds, baskets that he had woven himself when he first came to the barracks in 1946. I looked at his gnarled hands. A Rumanian bullet had passed through one of his hands in another, long-forgotten war. The light reflected off his silvery hair as he concentrated on his task. I tried to imagine the things he had experienced in his life, all the decisions he had had to make for himself and for others. He and Oma once had built a house and furnished it, and they had lost it all to war. They never complained. Never. The two old people were instead planning to build a new house again. They didn't seem to need anybody else, only each other. They were truly self-reliant. Sitting at the table watching them, I thought that I wanted to be like them—independent and self-reliant.

Since my family had first come to the barracks in late 1946, little had changed. Of course, the two neighbor women had died in 1947, and Vera had come. The blonde Dutch girl had married her supervisor at the potato farm and left to start her own family. The two hulking Paschmionka boys had succumbed to the good money they were told they could make as coal miners in the Ruhrgebiet after the Fassberg air base closed for the second time and they had lost their jobs again. Their parents and the younger boy stayed. Vera had a baby girl in 1949 and the father, a GSO man, had moved in with her. Many more babies had been born to other women. The barracks Communist's wife was pregnant with her third child. There was no sign that the man was going to join his comrades in the East. The abortion lady and her family moved out in March of 1950. They rented a railroad car for their furniture. The next day the regularly scheduled passenger train came by and picked up the car. They climbed aboard and with their belongings were on their way back to Cologne. A family in the barracks who needed more space moved into their empty apartment. When the air base closed on the first of October, most people had lost their jobs for the second or third time. They went to work on farms in nearby communities to earn a meager living. It was time to leave the barracks. It seemed that there was no permanent work in this poor region of Germany.

On April 2, 1950, Palm Sunday, my classmates and I, except for two who were not Evangelical Lutherans, were confirmed in St. Michael's Lutheran Church. Once a week for the past year and a half, we had remained in school for two additional hours of religious instruction. Our pastor was a former U-boat chaplain. We studied the New Testament and learned the Ten Commandments. Mutti came from Fürstenfeldbruck for the occasion, and my father came from Munster. I bought myself a pin-striped, dark blue suit with money Mutti and Dad gave me, as well as new black shoes and a white shirt. Dad gave me a nice-looking silk tie as a gift. The new clothes felt good once I had everything properly tied and buttoned up. It was a typical April day in north Germany—cool, overcast skies, but no rain. All three of us walked from the barracks to Fassberg. My mother and father walked together, deep in conversation the entire way. I walked behind them. I was proud and pleased that they both had come to be with me on a special occasion in my life. I felt this was probably the last time I would see my mother and father walking together like this.

The church service was a plain Lutheran service. We were given permission to take Communion, to take bread and wine in honor of the Lord. The pastor delivered a lengthy sermon about the importance of confirmation to the church and to our own lives. He called out our names precisely and loudly, twenty-one boys and sixteen girls:

"Horst Boschatzki." Called first, according to the alphabet, a short, feisty boy. I liked Horst.

"Klaus Gerlach." A slightly built, blond boy whose pilot father had died early in the war.

"Eberhard Gundlach." Tall and blond, teeth as white and regular as those in a toothpaste advertisement. His father was a gardener.

"Arnim Krüger." My best friend, the other refugee.

"Alfred Mrotzek." The tall, successful soccer goalie of the Fassberg Youth Soccer League.

"Gerd Pauline." Going to England, following his mother, who had married an English airman.

"Wolfgang Samuel." At the sound of my own name I was surprised, then pleased. I walked forward in my new suit. The pastor's face was stern as he handed me my certificate.

"Karl Töpritz." Planning to be a streetcar driver.

Then came the girls:

"Ursula Bleckert." Pretty and tall.

"Helga Kretschmer." Arrogant and bright.

"Irene Schweitzer." Always smiling and friendly.

"Sigrid Wolf." The last in the alphabet.

We were fourteen or fifteen years of age, and the pastor presented each one of us with a certificate attesting to our confirmation in the Lutheran church. I looked around at the thirty-six others, and I knew that our closeness was coming to an end. Where would we be next year? Where would we be in five years? What were our futures? I felt uneasy. School was coming to an end, my family was split up, and soon I would have to earn my own living. I was going to be totally on my own. The constants in my life—school and family—were melting away.

I became increasingly restless, worried about my future. I should get started arranging my life, I thought. I needed to learn a trade. It was April; school would be out later that month, and I didn't have a *Lehrstelle* yet. I spoke to my grandfather, and he agreed to accompany me to Celle, the county seat, to help me register at the *Arbeitsamt* for an apprenticeship. Two days later, we rode our bicycles to Celle. Opa always had been a man of his word, and he did everything he could to help me find a place to learn a useful trade. I had thought that maybe learning to be an electrician, a metal worker, or even a plumber would be useful. But there was nothing of that sort available, not in Fassberg and not even in Celle, a much larger town. Only two positions were offered me by the *Arbeitsamt*—one as a furniture carpenter's apprentice in a shop in Hermansburg, a smallish town not far from Fassberg, and the other as a baker's apprentice in Hannover. I wanted to get away to a city. Opa said we would look at both positions. The *Arbeitsamt* made appointments for us to meet with each of the two masters, who were qualified and authorized to train apprentices in their respective trades. Since Hermansburg was the closest, Opa and I went there first. I didn't think much of the idea of going there, no matter how nice the position might be. I wanted to get far away from the barracks, from the memories of my past, and live in a completely new place.

Hannover sounded exciting. It was a real city with museums and parks, and most of all a library. After my interview, the master in Hermansburg offered the position to me. I was to let him know within a week. "No," I said to Opa as we left the shop. "I am not going to be a carpenter. It's not in my hands."

"All right, let's try the big city," Opa replied, with a smile in his voice as we mounted our bicycles to return to the barracks. "I will write the shop master that you will not be available for the position. Let us hope that you like what we find in Hannover."

On the appointed day Opa and I traveled to Hannover to meet with Herr Franz Krampe of the Rheinische Bäckerei at Detmold Strasse 1. We took the train to Hannover and walked the rest of the way to the bakery. It was a Saturday afternoon, and the business was closed. Herr Krampe turned out to be a balding man, maybe six feet tall, with a layer of fat around his middle and a slightly protruding belly. He immediately asked us to step into his apartment located above the bakery. Frau Krampe joined us to welcome Opa and me into their home. She was a brunette, a little taller than Mutti, and on the stout side like her husband, as if she also ate a little too well. Over her dress, she wore a white frock similar to one worn by a medical doctor, and her right arm was amputated below the elbow. I stared at the stump and its ugly red scar. She wore nothing over the arm to hide the scar. Herr Krampe saw me looking at her missing limb and explained that it was the result of a bombing raid in late 1944.

They asked us into their dining room, where the table was set with delicious cakes and pastries. Frau Krampe entered from the kitchen with a steaming pot of coffee, real coffee. I loved the aroma, but I didn't like to drink it. Opa Samuel returned the customary greetings, and then we sat around the table for coffee and cake. Opa ate heartily and savored the coffee, having several cups. Another young woman entered the room belatedly and joined us. She, too, was pudgy, like Frau Krampe, but taller with a bigger frame, and she carried her weight better. She introduced herself as Emma, Frau Krampe's sister. Emma seated herself at the table with us. From the ease with which she slid into the chair, I assumed it must have been her customary place.

"My sister," Frau Krampe said, "manages our other store in downtown Hannover, and she makes the home deliveries." Emma, who looked remarkably like Frau Krampe, smiled at me. The table conversation was mostly about me, where my family had come from and how I liked school, what my grades were. I concentrated on eating while Opa and Herr Krampe talked. Then Herr Krampe turned toward me and said, "Let me tell you about the bakery. In addition to several sales personnel, I employ four other bakers, people you will work with. One is a second-year apprentice, another is a journeyman, the third is a master baker, and the fourth is also a master in cakes and other fine bakery goods. They are all good people. The bakery is below us, and I will show you around in a moment. On Saturdays we close at noon. That's why you don't see anyone working this afternoon. We start on Monday at four in the morning. For you, as the first-year apprentice, it will be even earlier than that, because someone has to get the ovens ready before the others arrive. Our days are long and don't usually end until four in the afternoon." Herr Krampe rose from the table and gestured for me to follow.

I followed him into a cobblestoned backyard. In the yard stood a three-wheeled delivery truck, an ugly little vehicle with one wheel in front and two in the rear. On the delivery truck's door was written RHEINISCHE BÄCK-EREI, INH. FRANZ KRAMPE. I noticed that above the fourth floor the building was a ruin, probably bombed out sometime in 1944 or early 1945. The war seemed so long ago. The building across the yard was a total ruin. I followed Herr Krampe down a narrow concrete staircase into the basement.

"Here," he said, "we have a small sales area where my wife sells bakery goods to people from the neighborhood. We only do it as a convenience for the people who live around here. Our store is located on a busy shopping street in downtown Hannover. You'll see the store in time and you will make deliveries there." I noticed that he was speaking as if I were already an employee. He was nice enough, so I didn't mind. Then we went over to the other side of the basement, to the actual bakery. There were two tables on one side of the room, and across from them were two ovens built into the wall. Pointing to the ovens, he said, "We keep these going constantly during the early morning and well into the day. As we quickly unload one oven and reload it, the bread is baking in the other oven. When that load is done, the process starts over again.

"Early in the morning, we mix and knead the dough. We place the dough on these tables, and with dough cutters"—he picked one up and held it up for me to see—"we cut off a pound of dough and roll it carefully, quickly, into a round ball, which we place on long boards beside these tables. The balls of dough will rise as they sit. Then they are shaped into loaves just before we put them into the ovens; we put three cuts across the face of each loaf, brush the loaf with water to give it a shiny surface, and into the oven they go. As you can imagine, once we start in the morning, the pace is hectic. Then, when the baking is done, the pace slows down. The cake baker works by himself in a back room, and he uses the ovens when we are done baking bread and rolls." I noticed that the entire room, floor and walls up to the ceiling, was tiled. It was also clean. Herr Krampe stood and watched me for a moment as I looked around. Then he said, "Have you seen enough?"

"Yes," I replied. What was there to see? I would hate to spend my life in such a cramped and probably hot room. I started to sweat just thinking of what it would be like. I followed Herr Krampe back upstairs. Opa and the two women were laughing as we came into the room. Herr Krampe and I again sat down at the table.

"Any more coffee or cake?" asked Frau Krampe. I declined. One cup of that coffee and the caffeine in it had made me feel jumpy. Turning to Opa, Herr Krampe said, "We will, of course, provide a furnished room for the boy as well as three meals a day. He will receive the customary pay for an apprentice, which isn't much, but it goes up every year until he passes his journeyman exam after the third year. Let me show you his room, Herr Samuel." He rose again to lead the way. Herr Krampe was businesslike. Opa and I both got up and followed him down the hall to view my room.

Baker's Apprentice

"Looks fine," Opa said, and I agreed. It was close to the Krampes' living quarters. I wouldn't have any privacy. It'll work out, I told myself.

"When can you start?" Herr Krampe asked, turning toward me.

"Right after I finish school."

"How about April 30?" Herr Krampe suggested. We agreed on that date.

"We need to sign an apprentice contract," Herr Krampe mentioned in passing, "but we can do that after you get here. Oh, by the way, you also have to go to trade school twice a month during your apprenticeship."

"What do you think, Opa?" I asked him on our way to the train station.

"I don't know, Wolfgang," he replied. "Krampe wants you pretty badly, and there really isn't anything else available right now. I suggest you take it. Three years isn't that long. You'll survive."

We walked the rest of the way to the train station in silence. I noticed the ruins. Little had been rebuilt. There were heaps of cleaned bricks. I remembered the women I had seen cleaning bricks in Strasburg in 1946. Occasionally there was a small shop that had opened in the basement apartment of a ruin, and there were some blocks of houses which hadn't been touched by war. We arrived in Celle by five that afternoon. We removed our bicycles from the lockup and rode back to the barracks. Oma was happy to see us and had a stew waiting for us. I was both apprehensive and excited about going to Hannover. I didn't care to be a baker, but I was excited about going to a city. As soon as Oma found out that I was going to be a baker's apprentice, she started talking up the bakery business. Sure enough, she even had a relative who had been a successful baker in the past.

On our last day of school, we were more subdued than normal, and we sat down at our usual positions knowing it would be for the last time. Our homeroom teacher entered and said a few words, and after an hour we went home. There was no ceremony; no names were read out loud, no certificates presented. We were finished. I found the ending of our schooling to be abrupt, as if the state were embarrassed and glad to be rid of us, the war children. The following day, Saturday, the girls had planned a party for us and our teachers. They arranged the tables in one classroom into a U, with the school principal, Herr Soffner, sitting at the head table. The girls had baked cakes and fancy *Torten*, and served real coffee. We ate cake, drank coffee, and smiled at each other. The girls had composed a short poem about each one of us and ceremoniously read them to embarrassed laughter and genuine applause. I was surprised at their talent. School was over for us. We were on our own. Why didn't I feel prepared? There was so much more for me to learn, I thought, and yet school, one of the anchors of my life for three years, was now a thing of the past.

My friend Arnim Krüger found an apprenticeship in Switzerland as a butcher. I was a little envious of him for going to Switzerland, although not for becoming a butcher. Others in my class went into training with the post office, at various businesses in Fassberg, and in villages in the surrounding area. Eberhard Gundlach, whose father had started a nursery and flower shop in Fassberg after the war, got the best apprenticeship, I thought, learning to be a nurseryman under his father's watchful eye. Eventually he'd take over his father's business and one day would be his own boss. That appealed to me, the thought of being my own boss. Soon I would be off to Hannover to become a baker. I went to a shop in Celle and bought the traditional baker's uniforms I was required to wear—black-and-white checkered pants, a short white jacket, and a white hat to cover my hair.

I arrived in Hannover late in the afternoon on April 30, 1950. The Krampes seemed less cordial than when we had first met. They were all business, treating me as if I were their property. At seven that evening, Frau Krampe's sister, Emma, called me into the kitchen, where she had prepared a plate of salami and liverwurst sandwiches. After I had eaten, Emma suggested that I go to bed, because two in the morning would come before I knew it. Two in the morning? I had never gotten up at two in the morning unless I was running from Russians or needed to hide in the cellar from a bombing raid. I remembered that Herr Krampe had mentioned the early hours when we first met. I went to my room, brushed my teeth, and went to bed. At two in the morning precisely a hand shook my shoulder. I bolted out of bed.

"Get up," said Herr Krampe in a stern voice. "It's time to go to work." I dressed quickly in my new baker's uniform. There was no breakfast and no time to wash up. Herr Krampe and I went straight down to the bakery. I followed him around as he started the ovens and went about measuring flour and other ingredients into different bowls of enormous size. By the time the others arrived at four, the starter dough had been divided up, and the men began to mix dough for bread and rolls. Then the heavy slabs of dough were pushed to the center of the tables, and, with two people on each side of the tables, the cutting and rolling of bread and breakfast rolls began. I watched closely and was soon directed to grab a dough knife to imitate their actions.

Baker's Apprentice

The morning progressed as Herr Krampe had described it on my initial visit. Right now I was a handyman and ran to and fro taking and bringing things. After the dough was processed, Herr Krampe gave me an extra chunk he had held back and told me to stand at the table and practice cutting and rolling dough. I practiced for half an hour and still wasn't getting even close to the way it was supposed to be done. Herr Krampe wasn't pleased with my lack of instantaneous progress. Even when I thought I had a perfect dough ball, he disapproved of it.

"Are you stupid?" he yelled at me. "This is so easy! Any donkey can learn this in a few minutes just by watching." Obviously I couldn't. I wasn't a donkey either, I thought resentfully. Five hours later, at seven o'clock that morning, Emma came into the bakery and called for me to come outside.

"Your food is on the table in the shop on the other side," she whispered into my ear. I followed her into the sales room. A tiny table with a single chair stood near the counter, there for customers who wanted to enjoy a piece of *Torte* or cake in the store. Emma gestured for me to sit. "Eat," she whispered, "you need to be out of here by seven-thirty. That's when the store opens for business." I was hungry. I ate all seven of the delicious, fresh-from-the-oven breakfast rolls laden with salami and smoked ham.

By twelve o'clock noon, the baking was done, and the master baker, who lived upstairs on the second floor above the bakery, waved his hand at us in a cheerful gesture of *auf Wiedersehen* and left the rest of us to continue. He had worked eight hours and not a minute longer. By one o'clock, the journeyman baker had also left after completing the starter dough for the following day. He had worked nine hours and not a minute more. It was up to the second-year apprentice and me to clean the bakery. The second-year apprentice stayed until two o'clock and then gave me directions on how to finish the job. He had worked ten hours. I finished by four o'clock that afternoon, just as Herr Krampe had predicted I would, fourteen hours after I had walked down the stairs from the apartment above. I was starting to go upstairs to my room when Emma grabbed me by the arm and ushered me into the sales room. There, on the table, stood another plate of sandwiches and a bottle of mineral water.

"Your evening meal," she announced. As I ate, Herr Krampe entered the room with a man whom he introduced as my union representative. In his presence, Herr Krampe and I signed the contract. I noticed that the contract called for me to receive room and board and pocket money of four marks each month the first year, six marks the second year, and eight marks the third and final year. A cola at a stand in the *Stadtpark* cost one mark and fifty pfennig. The representative from the *Gewerkschaft* accompanied me upstairs to look at my room. He looked around briefly and then indicated that he had seen enough. We went back downstairs where Herr Krampe sat waiting, the contract before him. Satisfied that everything was as it should be, the *Gewerkschaft* man initialed the contract and bade Herr Krampe a *Guten Abend*. Evidently I didn't exist for him anymore since he didn't speak to me as he left. Herr Krampe cleared his throat loudly and then, looking at the floor, said, "Oh, I had to move your room temporarily next door. Get your things from upstairs and let me take you over."

I was puzzled, but too tired to question him. As far as I remembered, next door was a bombed-out ruin. I gathered my few belongings from what ostensibly had been my room and followed Herr Krampe into the yard. He walked me through the gaping hole of what had once been a door to the bombed-out apartment house. The hallway was strewn with debris. On the right I could see a new door; it led into a damp room which smelled of wet plaster. Since there were no stairs, I had to step up high to enter the room. One window looked onto the courtyard; I hadn't noticed before that a window had been installed in the otherwise totally ruined building. The walls were still wet from the grey plaster that couldn't have been applied more than a day before. The flooring consisted of raw pine boards. A bed, a small wooden table with one chair, and a dresser furnished the desolate room. To one side stood a washbasin with a cold-water faucet, a small mirror above it. A single lightbulb hung from the ceiling, barely illuminating the room. I was aghast.

"This is only temporary," Herr Krampe said. "We are having some work done next door. That's why I had to have this room fixed up for you. There is a shower in the bakery downstairs which you can use. Be ready by two o'clock tomorrow morning." He turned abruptly and left me standing in the middle of my room. I felt mentally crushed and physically exhausted. I wanted to run away, but there was no place to run to, and I was too tired anyway. My situation had changed so rapidly. I felt taken advantage of. My room was what I imagined a prison cell would be like. I had lived in nicer conditions in the barracks. At least there the walls were painted, I had a stove to heat the room, and curtains hung at the windows. I washed up as best I could under the cold-water faucet. When I went next door to take a shower, I found the door locked. I returned to my room, set my alarm for one forty-five, and went to bed. It was six o'clock in the evening, still daylight outside for several more hours.

The next morning my room was even damper and colder, and I shivered as I put on my uniform. I ran next door as fast as I could to get into the warmth of the bakery. The routines were the same as the day before. Day after day I rose in the damp, freezing room, facing five hours of work without food. Only two meals a day were provided, not the three promised, and always rolls or sandwiches. At least there were lots of them, and Emma made sure that they were amply filled with tasty liverwurst, salami, and ham. Emma sent my dirty uniforms to a laundry, so at least I didn't have to wash them myself, as I had feared. By the first Saturday after my arrival, I was totally exhausted and happy just to have a little time to myself. I knew I would never have the opportunity to visit a library or a museum or to enjoy Hannover in the ways I had imagined before I had come. I would spend most of my life in the basement and in the damp room of the bombed-out apartment house. It promised to be a long three years.

Frau Krampe, who tended to the shop next to the bakery, had a pronounced overbite which made it seem as if she were perpetually smiling. I learned quickly that such was not the case. She was a bitter and bossy woman who used the often uncovered stump of her right arm as a grisly pointer to emphasize her orders to me. She was a cold person, seemingly preoccupied with her lost arm. If Frau Krampe was aloof, Herr Krampe was just the opposite, constantly breathing down my neck. Every move I made was under his stern scrutiny, and every action I took received a withering critique. I was never fast enough, strong enough, quick enough, or alert enough for him. He yelled and screamed at me constantly, to the point where I began to fear his tirades. The only place I could hide to get away from him was the toilet. So I went to the toilet as often as I could. He soon caught on and timed me. If I wasn't out of the toilet in five minutes, he knocked on the door and shouted for me to get out.

In addition to my seven o'clock half-hour breakfast, I received a half-hour break at noon. I usually left the basement and went outside if it wasn't raining. Being in the basement day in and day out was depressing. I had no idea what was going on outside the bakery, in Germany or in the rest of the world. I missed the fresh air, the forest, the birds and small animals of the heath. Emma was always nice, giving me huge portions of food. Sometimes

I received leftovers from their Sunday dinners in lieu of sandwiches, a pleasant change. Emma always remained near me when I ate, and after a while I felt that perhaps she wanted more than just to feed me. On weekends, Emma and I were always alone in the basement shop, and I became uncomfortable with her hovering around me. I avoided looking at her and just concentrated on my food, trying hard to finish as quickly as I could.

The master baker who lived upstairs was married to a nice-looking young woman. He had been a journeyman in Herr Krampe's bakery before he had taken his master's examination. Occasionally he joked about Emma. "Ja, when I was still a bachelor," he boasted, "I took Emma out a few times. She wasn't bad in bed. Then she wanted me to marry her"—he laughed loudly—"and naturally I couldn't do that. Just imagine me being in the Krampe family. Can you imagine that?" No one answered. Instead everyone laughed, because they knew he was referring to bossy Herr Krampe and haughty Frau Krampe. "I like my beautiful girl, fellows. And when I go upstairs and you are still working down here like slaves, you know what I am doing, don't you?" He raised his eyebrows meaningfully and grinned from ear to ear. The other two bakers laughed. I wasn't sure I knew what he was talking about, but I smiled anyway.

"Poor Emma," he continued, pounding a slab of bread dough while he was speaking. "Someday someone will come along for her, too. Or maybe she'll be an old maid. Ja, she will probably be an old maid." He laughed loudly, seeming very amused by his monologue. "She is definitely the old maid type," he concluded with authority, and again broke into laughter. I liked all three of the bakers—the master baker, the journeyman, and the senior apprentice. They made me feel like a person instead of a servant, and each one was helpful.

Herr Krampe came into the bakery early in the morning like everybody else. By ten he had usually left to go to the downtown store. When he was gone, the men joked and talked about many different things. The time seemed to go faster with their constant chatter. We were relaxed in Herr Krampe's absence, and we still got our jobs done. They tried to help me develop the necessary skills to expertly form dough balls for bread and rolls, and showed me how to cut off just enough dough for a loaf of bread from the daily practice chunk lying in the middle of the table.

"It's just a matter of experience," the master baker said one day. The others nodded their heads in agreement. "We had to learn these things, too, just like you. Don't worry about it, it will all come in time. Krampe is a hard man. Don't let him get to you." On Saturdays we baked only enough bread and rolls so as to be sold out by noon; that was when the downtown store closed. I spent much of my time on Saturdays cleaning. I normally finished by two o'clock and had the rest of the afternoon to myself.

Trudy, a fifteen-year-old girl, came on Saturdays to clean the small sales area, the landing, and the concrete stairs leading to the basement. She worked as a maid cleaning the Krampes' apartment during the week, and I rarely saw her then. I helped her clean the stairs. She was a slim girl, nice looking. Whenever I worked near her I felt different. Although I was fifteen and had been exposed to sex in various forms for the past several years, I was totally ignorant about nearly all aspects of it. No one had ever spoken to me on the subject. I hadn't even read a dirty book. I knew about venereal disease. That scared me. I also was aware of the fires burning in my body, but I understood them no better than I understood girls. My ignorance of sex combined with my misconceptions served to make me wary of girls. In spite of the environments I had lived in since 1945, I was an innocent boy who felt at a loss as to how to deal with his nascent manhood. Still, Trudy drew me to her like a magnet.

One Saturday, Trudy and I were cleaning the landing and the concrete stairs, each of us with our own water bucket, rags, and brushes. We bent over with our backs to each other. I put a rag down behind me, and, when reaching back to retrieve it, I accidently touched her between the legs. I pulled my hand back quickly once I realized that I was touching her. I stood up, shocked by what I had done, and apologized. She continued to work as if nothing had happened. My face felt hot in embarrassment. Although I considered asking her to go walking in the park or to a movie on Saturday afternoons, I never found the courage. I couldn't get the words out. Maybe she would laugh at me, I thought. Every Saturday I promised myself that I would talk to her and ask her to go with me for a walk in the park and share a cola. My mouth simply wouldn't move. We never went for that walk and never shared that cola.

A war had broken out in Korea. I wasn't sure exactly where Korea was, other than that it was on the other side of the world, somewhere near Japan or maybe Manchuria. The fellows in the bakery talked about the war and speculated as to whether the Americans could save themselves, because the North Koreans supposedly had them and the South Korean army running for their lives straight to the end of the Korean peninsula. Then what? I was interested in their discussion, because it was the first I had known of the Americans being in a war again, and maybe they were being beaten by some small country I had never even heard of. Wasn't it only yesterday that I had seen the mighty American army, which had just beaten the German Wehrmacht in a long and bloody war? Where was that American army? Where did that powerful air force go, with its thousands of planes that bombed Germany into rubble? I was living in a building right then that had been destroyed by the English or the Americans. I couldn't understand how such a mighty army and air force would no longer be capable of defending itself. I found it shocking, and I said so to my colleagues.

"No, it's not shocking," the master cake baker said in response to my comment, having come into our room from the back and listened to our conversation. "The Amis are getting what they deserve. Now they know what it feels like to be on the run like we were. It'll do them good to get some of their own medicine." He laughed in a self-satisfied way, leaving our conversation as quickly as he had entered it.

"I don't think it's good for us if the Americans are beaten," I said to the others in the room. "They just saved us from the Russians last year when the Russians wanted to starve Berlin. If it weren't for the Americans, the Russians would have taken Berlin without firing a shot. Then we would have been next. The English are too weak to stand up to them." I felt angry about what the cake baker had said. To my surprise, the others agreed with me. I couldn't get it out of my mind that the Americans were in trouble. I just couldn't believe that all the military strength that I had witnessed not long ago had disappeared.

I received a letter from Mutti asking me if I could come to visit her and Leo. I was surprised when Herr Krampe agreed to let me go for one week, starting September 29. I couldn't wait for the day to arrive. On my bicycle every morning, I delivered freshly baked rolls to two hotels. One of them was near the train station. From the hotel entrance, I could see the trains come and go, and I watched them with hungry eyes. Every day I lingered for a minute or so to watch the trains speed over a bridge and see carefree passengers lean out of windows as the trains picked up speed. I wanted to be one of those passengers so badly that I almost felt I could will myself aboard.

Then some news came over the radio that was almost as exciting as the thought of going to visit my mother. The Americans, who were fighting to hang on to Korea in a pocket called Pusan, had made an amphibious landing behind enemy lines at Inchon, near Seoul, Korea's capital. The North Koreans were taken by surprise. In the bakery that day, we talked about the new turn of events and agreed it was what we had expected from the Americans. The Communist North Koreans would be on the run now. But the cake baker wagged his finger at us and said, "Not so fast, not so fast, my boys; just wait and see."

"Wait and see what?" I shouted at him. "The Americans are winning. I always knew they had a powerful army. I saw them in 1945. The tanks rolled all night long past our barn. They have a huge and powerful army."

"Not anymore," said the cake baker. "Armies cost money, and the tanks you heard in 1945 have long since been melted down to make automobiles and frying pans. The Americans don't have a large army anymore, believe me." I didn't know what to say.

"Well," I ventured defensively, "I want the Americans to win." The cake man left with a smile. I thought I knew what he was hoping for. I didn't know why.

On September 29, I took the train to Munich. I was finally one of the passengers going somewhere, not just a bakery delivery boy watching the trains departing the Hannover station. My spirits were high. I couldn't wait to see Mutti and Leo again. Germany slid past me as I watched from the train window. I had never really seen the country in its entirety. All I knew well was the east, Berlin, the poor north, and the Lüneburg Heath.

Actually, that wasn't quite right. Mutti had taken me to Munich for a week to visit a girlfriend of hers in the early summer of 1941. I was six. Then I remembered the day when I started school that year, and had to laugh at how afraid I was. Mutti had left me sitting behind a desk. I was desperately holding on to my *Schultüte* as if it were my life raft. I thought she was abandoning me, leaving me with that strange woman, my teacher. The teacher had come over and put her hand on my head and said, "Everything will be all right, little boy." I remembered the calming touch of her hand. When it was all over, on the way home, I had stuffed myself with cookies and candies from my *Schultüte* until my stomach hurt.

The motion of the train felt comforting. I pushed myself back into my corner seat and looked out the window. The countryside was bathed in gentle early autumn colors of old greens and fresh yellows and golds. The train entered the *Mittelgebirge*. I looked down into deep valleys from high arching bridges. Mists rose from storybook streams and forests below, and the train entered tunnels as black as night, suddenly reemerging into the soft and tentative sunlight of early autumn. As the train rolled through Kassel, Würzburg, and Nürnberg, cities with storied names and colorful histories, my spirits were dampened by the endless sea of ruins, the brutal scars left behind by that evil war. Germany's cities were too severely damaged to be able to arise again so soon after such a catastrophe. An article I had once read in the *Hamburger Abendblatt*, the weekly newspaper Opa Samuel took, speculated that it would take fifty years to rebuild Germany. Fifty years? Nearly a lifetime. I hoped that the writer of the article was wrong.

As we passed through the ruins of Germany's cities, I was overcome by the magnitude of the disaster that had befallen my country. Seeing the savaged towns glide by me was unnerving; it brought back the horror of those days and nights. An involuntary shudder ran through me. So many people killed. So much destruction. What was worth all that pain? I had asked my father, Opa Samuel, teachers, and others that question. No one ever gave me an answer. I pressed my nose against the window and stared from my comfortable compartment at row upon row of burned-out buildings, at street after street without one human being in sight, at remnants of walls staring back at me with hollow eyes which once had been the windows and doors to someone's happiness. Maybe the cities could be rebuilt, even if it took fifty years. But who was going to repair the pain I felt inside? Who would take away the faces of the dead I saw at night in my dreams? How long would that take? I stared down into my lap, fearing that perhaps someone in the compartment had seen the tear running down my face. No one had.

In Munich I changed to one of the incredibly slow local trains to Fürstenfeldbruck. Mutti and Leo were waiting for me at the station. I saw them before I got off the train. Leo, in his new blue United States Air Force uniform, stood out. In Fassberg, Leo was still wearing his brown army uniform; now the American air force uniform was blue. They greeted me warmly. I hugged Mutti for a long time, and Leo gave me one of his bear hugs. Both smelled of cigarette smoke. Almost every adult and teenager in Germany smoked. I still had no interest in smoking, nor did I have the money for cigarettes even if I had wanted to. We walked down the hill from the train station along a tree-lined dirt path that took us through open fields and finally into a residential area of town. I saw no war damage in

Fürstenfeldbruck. We walked past bakeries, butcher shops, a shoe store, and a dry goods store. Finally, at the end of the road, at the top of a rise, stood a high-gabled house with plaster walls.

"That's it!" Mutti exclaimed. "That's where we live, Schillerstrasse 26." Leo took my cardboard suitcase and carried it up the steps. The front door opened just as we got to it, and there stood an older woman. She reminded me of my Oma Grapentin, with her greying hair pulled back in a bun and her dark clothing. "Frau Buck," my mother said, "this is my son, Wolfgang." I shook Frau Buck's hand.

"Your mother has spoken of you often, and I am glad to finally meet you," Frau Buck said. "Come on in. It is getting cold outside."

I felt an immediate liking for Frau Buck and her Bavarian dialect. We entered the foyer, and Frau Buck closed the door behind us. Mutti proceeded through an inner door to an interior corridor with Leo and me trailing behind. "This is our room," she said, opening the door to a room that served as their bedroom, living room, and dining room. Frau Buck had gone into her kitchen. We three squeezed into the little room, and Mutti closed the door.

"Take off your coat, Wolfgang, and make yourself at home." Their room had a bed, a nightstand, a *Schrank*, a round table, two chairs, and a lamp. There wasn't room for much more. They felt they were lucky to have found a room in a nice house with such pleasant landlords. Herr Buck was a shoe-maker who spent much of the day in his shop in town. The Bucks' son, who had been in the German army during the war and stationed in Greece, had married a Greek girl, and both of them lived in the house, too. "A full house," Mutti explained, "but everyone gets along." Against one wall of the room stood a couch where I was to sleep.

One day during the week, Leo took me to lunch at the Sergeants' Club in town, an old mansion that had been requisitioned by the American army. The dining room tables were covered with white tablecloths, and on each was a vase of freshly cut flowers, as well as an arrangement of small bottles. Leo helped me with the menu. I chose mock turtle soup, which sounded exciting, and an American hamburger, recommended by Leo. When the soup came, I asked Leo if any of the bottles on the table were for use with soups.

Leo took a small, thin, round bottle with a reddish liquid in it and said, "A little of this will make your soup more interesting." I wasn't sure what "interesting" meant, so I took the bottle, shook it mightily, and poured a torrent of the red stuff into the soup. "Oh, no," Leo groaned, putting his hands over his face. "Too much, Wolfgang. We have to send the soup back."

"No, no," I protested. "I'll eat it." Leo looked at me dubiously and said, "Okay."

I took my first spoonful of soup and knew immediately what Leo had meant by "interesting." I ate the soup, even though my mouth felt like it had just caught on fire. I picked up the offending bottle and translated its name for Leo into German—"*Heisse Sosse von Louisiana.*" We both laughed, and I drank lots of water.

On Saturday night, Leo and Mutti took me to the Noncommissioned Officers' Club at the Fürstenfeldbruck Air Base. A band played fast American music. I especially liked the Glenn Miller tunes. After dinner I built up enough courage to dance with one of the women at our table who had asked me if I would like to try it. I had never danced before in my life. She smiled, took me out on the floor, firmly grasped my waist and my left hand, and steered me around. I soon caught on to the rhythm of the melody, and I thought I was dancing. I was having such a good time that I danced with every woman at our table, including my mother. The women seemed to enjoy teaching me the intricacies of the dances, and they thought I was hilarious to watch. Their laughter gave me added encouragement. I kept on dancing until finally I had to go to the rest room.

When I came out of the men's room, a soldier in the old brown army uniform with his right arm in a plaster cast barred my way and wouldn't let me pass. He spoke in English, and I couldn't understand what he was saying. He kept pushing me with his plaster cast toward a fire exit. I tried to edge around him, and he shoved me back roughly, talking all the time. His eyes reflected hate, and his breath was thick with alcohol. As the soldier was about to open the emergency exit and shove me outside, one of Leo's friends from our table came looking for me. I called to him for help. I told him in German that the soldier wouldn't let me return to our table. He spoke to the soldier, who then moved away on unsteady legs. Later Leo told me that the soldier was just a young boy whose brother had been killed in the war in Germany. "He thinks he hates Germans. He was going to throw you out because you are a German. He was also drunk."

Halfway through my stay, Mutti asked me if I would accompany her to the United States once she and Leo were married. "I really don't want to go if you won't come along, Wolfgang. I would be too alone without you. Ingrid won't come, I've already spoken to her. She wants to stay with her father."

"Of course I will go with you," I replied. I had never considered the possibility, but accompanying my mother if she was going to America seemed only natural. I had always lived with her. There was no other option.

"Well, then," she continued, "we will have you see a doctor while you are here. Your papers need to be submitted along with ours for visas to enter the United States." She seemed relieved. Then she pulled a picture out from amongst some papers and held it out for me to look at. "What do you think?"

The picture showed several children, a young woman, and an older-looking man, Leo's age perhaps, deeply tanned as if he worked outside, a half-smoked cigarette hanging from his mouth. They were standing in front of what looked like the basement to a house, but there was no house on top, only a flat roof of tar paper. "I don't know what to think," I replied, after studying the strange picture. "Who are these people?"

"Leo's brother," she said, her voice unsteady. "His wife and their three children. She is pregnant again. Look at that house! That's not a house. I won't live in anything like that. I don't know if I want to go to America." Her eyes reflected her feelings, showing emotions I had never seen in her before—fear and indecision. Now I understood why she wanted me to see the picture and why she would not go to America without me.

"Mutti," I said, taking hold of her hands, "you are marrying Leo, not his brother. You don't have to live like that. Once you get to America, you will make your own life with Leo, and you will have your own house. I can see from the picture that they are poor people. So what?" Mutti still looked troubled.

"But America is so far away, and maybe I can't come back to Germany, ever."

"When I grow up," I told her, "and I make my own money, I will buy you a ticket back to Germany any time you want to go. That's a promise. Let's forget this picture and put it away. Surely America is much more beautiful than what you see here on this photograph. We will love it there. Just wait and see." I looked at her with my own excitement surely showing in my eyes. She sighed, put her arms around me, and laid her head on my shoulder.

Baker's Apprentice

"I don't know what I would do without you, Wolfgang. I am glad you are coming." With that, our conversation on the subject ended. She had decided. When Leo came home that evening, she told him that I had agreed to accompany them to the United States. Leo reached across the table, took my hand, and shook it. He was a generous person, totally unselfish. I had never met anyone quite like him.

"I will make an appointment for Wolfgang at the base hospital," Leo said. "I hope I can get one before he leaves."

The sign over the main entrance to the hospital read 36TH MEDICAL GROUP, FURSTENFELDBRUCK AIR FORCE BASE. Inside, Leo did the talking while I followed him around. I sat in the examining room for a moment, and then an American nurse took me by the hand to a windowless room. She motioned for me to remove my shirt. *"Hemd aus ziehen,"* she said, and laughed loudly at the sound of her German. I removed my shirt, and she pressed my chest against a glass plate. The X-ray plate felt cold as she took the picture. Later the nurse showed me the negative, and I could see my ribs inside my body. Then she took blood from my arm, and had me leave a urine sample. An American doctor in an officer's uniform covered loosely by a white coat listened to my lungs and heart while asking several questions which I didn't understand. Leo gave him the answers he wanted to hear. We were finished. It didn't seem like there was much to the examination.

When Sunday came, Mutti and Leo walked me to the station early in the morning. I watched the same beautiful countryside glide past that I had seen a week earlier, only in reverse order. The bombed cities with their ruined houses and churches stood unchanged. Near some of the train stations I noticed new construction. Wooden scaffolding clung to the exterior of some bombed-out ruins. Something new was about to arise from the ashes of our awful past. It was a start, even if it would take fifty years to finish.

Chapter 22

LOOKING WEST

Soon after my return from Fürstenfeldbruck, I received a letter from Mutti informing me that their papers were in order and that she and Leo could marry at any time. They had set the date for October 14, 1950. If I could come for the wedding it would make them very happy, she wrote. I was fearful of Herr Krampe's response to my request for additional time off. I mustered my courage and approached him that noon. He didn't like my request for another week off, but he didn't yell at me. I was ecstatic to be going. Everything seemed to be looking up. Very soon I would be leaving for America, the land of my dreams. I didn't say anything to my coworkers, but if they had looked closely they surely could have read the excitement in my eyes.

Whenever Herr Krampe was not in the bakery, Korea was a continuing topic of discussion. The Americans had chased the North Koreans back across the thirty-eighth parallel. The cake baker who had seemed so gleeful over the Americans' misfortunes earlier in the year kept to himself and didn't get involved in our discussions. Occasionally I stuck my head into his room to give him a status report on the progress of the Americans. All he ever said was, "Just wait; just wait." I decided this was a case of sour grapes. He was probably the sort of person who was happy when bad things happened to others.

On Thursday, October 12, I again took the train from Hannover to Munich and then on to Fürstenfeldbruck. When I arrived, only Leo awaited me on the station platform. Mutti was probably busy, I thought, preparing things for the wedding and the reception they would surely have afterwards at the NCO Club. As I got off the train and approached Leo, I perceived that something wasn't right. He was smoking in quick, short puffs, uncharacteristic of a man who enjoyed smoking his cigarettes slowly and deliberately. He had a frown on his face, which usually wore a smile. When he saw me approaching, his expression lightened, but he was still serious, and his characteristic smile did not appear. Discarding his cigarette, he shook my hand vigorously.

"Wolfgang, dear Wolfgang," he said, "it's wonderful to see you again." With that, he grabbed my suitcase, and I followed him out of the station. "Your mother can't be here today," he said in a tense tone of voice, as we walked down the familiar, tree-lined lane toward town. Not waiting for any questions from me, he continued, "Soon after she wrote you she had to go into the hospital. She was carrying our baby and something went wrong. She started bleeding and had a fever and they were forced to operate on her."

"Is Mutti all right?" I asked Leo in broken English and German.

"Yes, she is doing well, and the doctors think we can get married on Saturday. It will have to be in the hospital. I already talked to the German *Standesamt* and to my chaplain and everything is set, as long as Hedy's health does not deteriorate." I was pleased to hear that Mutti was feeling well enough to go through with the ceremony, although I was sorry she and Leo couldn't have the kind of wedding they had planned. As we walked beside each other in silence, I recalled an earlier conversation I had had with my mother when she asked my opinion about her having another baby. It was not to be, after all.

Frau Buck, as friendly as ever, greeted me at the door. Herr Buck, sitting in the kitchen, gave me a hearty *"Grüss Gott,"* as I passed by. When I opened the door to Mutti and Leo's room, there was a surprise waiting for me—Ingrid. Leo's smile returned to his face. He had kept this little secret, and now that he saw how delighted I was to see my sister again, he freely shared in our joy. I hugged him. Leo had become more like a father to me than my own father. Ingrid had arrived earlier in the day and already visited Mutti at the hospital.

"Mutti looks just fine," Ingrid said.

Although it was actually the city and county hospital, being in the Catholic region of Germany it seemed like a Catholic hospital to me. Many of the nurses were nuns. Schedules were strictly adhered to, including visiting hours and morning, afternoon, and evening prayers. On Saturday, Mutti's room was decorated with plants and flowers sent by friends. The German marriage ceremony was performed first in the presence of doctors and nurses. Only one other couple was allowed to be present in addition to Ingrid and me. They were friends of Mutti's and Leo's and served as witnesses. Next the American chaplain performed his ceremony, and Mutti and Leo were finally married, under both German and American law. After cake and coffee, none for Mutti, of course, the sisters ushered us out of the room.

"She needs her rest," they said, with smiles on their faces but with firmness in their hands and voices. "You may return tomorrow." Leo went back to work, even though it was his wedding day. Ingrid and I went to the Post Hotel to celebrate with a Coca-Cola, a luxury at DM 1.50 for a small bottle. As I sipped the precious liquid, I decided that, while it was all right for Leo to buy Coca-Cola, for Ingrid and me it was still unaffordable. Ingrid and I departed on Monday.

Herr Krampe was pleased to see me return so soon, and within a day it seemed as if I had never gone anywhere. In my absence, Herr Krampe had a cast-iron stove installed in my damp room in the ruin, which meant that I was going to stay there for the winter. Herr Krampe had no intention of moving me back into the house where I had slept the first night after my arrival.

Pyongyang, the capital city of North Korea, was captured by the Americans on Thursday, October 19. I couldn't help myself—I rushed into the cake baker's workroom as soon as I heard the news and in a solemn voice made the announcement to him. I felt vindicated by my American army. I knew it was the best army in the world. The North Koreans must have had luck and the element of surprise back in June. I felt vindicated about the way my Americans were progressing.

I had been going to my twice-monthly trade school classes since August and generally found them to be dull. I had thought that in school I would learn the theory of my craft, but the first year proved to be merely a general curriculum for all apprentices. In our biweekly afternoon sessions we covered basic mathematics, social issues, and German. The teacher much preferred talking about his wartime experiences. Nevertheless, I was pleased to be able

Looking West

to leave the bakery at eleven o'clock in the morning on class days. I didn't really care what my instructor said or did. He couldn't upset me. Having half a day off was what was important to me.

During one period, our class discussion turned to the subject of America. One of the apprentices maintained that in America—and he insisted that he had heard this from reliable sources—everyone had a helicopter. "You know," he said, "those airplanes without wings." No one challenged him. I was speechless when I heard such ignorance expressed in a classroom. I kept quiet as one apprentice after another chimed in about how easy life was in America. I knew Leo and his soldier friends lived a good life here in Germany, but they, too, worked for a living. Leo's family didn't have a helicopter, I knew that. In the picture Mutti had shown me of Leo's brother, Raymond, and his family, Raymond looked like a poor factory worker, like someone who worked hard with his hands. I'll find out for myself soon enough, I thought. I was not going to America with crazy ideas like that in my head. I was going to be an immigrant, just like those I read about in my books. I knew I would have to work hard to achieve anything. One thing, though, I knew for sure. America was a land without war and without burned cities. There had to be opportunities for young people.

When class was over that day, I rode my bike back to the bakery in deep thought about what I might find on the other side of the Atlantic Ocean. I realized that most of what I knew about America consisted of old, romantic descriptions of a land and a people which had changed long ago. What was America really like? A country able to build huge armies of tanks and great fleets of four-engined bombers and transport planes had to be a place of great opportunity. It just had to be.

My life had quickly fallen back into the familiar routine of work and sleep, work and sleep, day in and day out, interrupted only briefly by my twice-monthly attendance of trade school classes and the brief few hours off on Saturday afternoons and on Sundays. If the weather was nice on Saturday or Sunday, I went to the city lake and rode my bike around its perimeter. Or I went to the Amerika Haus near the Krampes' store in the center of town and tried to learn more about present-day America. I didn't find much useful information at the Amerika Haus. It was a building with spacious rooms filled with huge pictures of workers in automated factories and endless landscapes of deserts and fields of grain. The few books I found were mostly

Looking West

picture books, and I got the uneasy feeling that they contained propaganda rather than any truth about this land that was such an enigma to me.

Across from the Amerika Haus was a park filled with flimsy stands selling lemonade, hot *Würstchen* and *Brötchen*, trinkets, cigarettes, cigars, newspapers, and a myriad other things on, behind, or below the counters. I wandered among the stands and soon discovered that their real reason for being there had to do with the black market. To my great surprise, the black market was still thriving. I recognized the familiar behavior of the black marketeer, and I wondered what it was they were trading. I wore my American army pants and sweater. Soon a thin man, smoking a cigarette in short, hurried puffs, approached me, and, pointing at my pants, asked if I could get him American army uniforms like what I was wearing. "I'll give you a good price for them. You won't regret it," he said.

"I just wear these things because I don't have anything else," I told him truthfully. "I wouldn't know where I could get clothes like this." He wasn't shaken off that easily.

"Look here," he said, thrusting out his left arm. I saw the tattoo. A number. "You can trust me," he mumbled in a low voice. "I was at Bergen-Belsen. Many of us here came from there. Come back and see me if you decide that you have something to sell. I am always here at this shack." He stuck his cigarette back into his mouth and leaned with one arm on the counter and stared at me. People stood talking and bartering. I felt like I needed more air, as though my shirt collar was too tight and my sweater too warm. I felt like I couldn't breathe. I had to get out of there.

"Yes," I replied to the man as I hurried to leave, "if I ever have anything I will come and see you." I unchained my bicycle from the bike stand and rode off toward the lake. I slowly settled down as I rode my bike through Hannover. The experience with the black marketeer had been unexpected and unsettling. I wasn't sure what it was that had upset me so. The black market? No. I was used to that. Was it the fact that the man had a number on his arm, indicating that he had survived a concentration camp? Yes, that was what had upset me. I had never seen a concentration camp. I had heard of them from many people since the war ended, but I didn't want to believe what Germans had done to other Germans simply because they were of the Jewish faith.

I remembered the empty shops in Strasburg and the desecrated Jewish cemetery. I recalled how in Sagan, in late 1944, the teacher had given me an *Ahnentafel* to fill out because my last name was Samuel. The *Ahnentafel* required me to list my ancestors back for four generations, including their places and dates of birth, the dates of their deaths, and their religious beliefs. The teacher had asked me for the *Tafel* several times. I put her off each time by telling her I had sent it to my father in France to be filled out by him since I did not know the answers to the questions. I never returned the *Ahnentafel* to the teacher, because in January of 1945 we fled to Berlin. It all came back.

A sense of outrage and guilt swept over me as if I were personally responsible for the evil that had happened in Germany. I felt intense hostility toward those who had caused so much pain and suffering in people whose only crime had been that they were Jewish and not Catholic or Protestant. I felt shame—deep, personal shame, as if somehow I were covered with dirt that would never wash off. I had not felt like this before in my life. I had always been proud to be a German boy. Suddenly I was ashamed of my heritage, of belonging to a people of wanton murderers. And yet, the people I knew—my grandparents, my parents, my friends and classmates and their parents—were regular people. Who were the people who had done these awful things? Where were they now? How would I know them if I met them? Unanswered questions, bitterness about an evil war that had done so much harm to my people, and feelings of personal guilt mixed together. As a young boy, I felt violated by my elders. How could they have done this to us children?

The wind blew through my hair as I rode around the city lake not looking at anyone or anything, not really aware of where I was riding. I had nothing to do with this heinous crime, and yet I felt wounded. I felt a deep sense of personal responsibility. I knew I had to push these feelings away from myself. I had to forget, just as I tried to forget other ugly things. I had to move on with my life and leave the past behind. But the past of my people, I thought, clung to me like an odor. I was afraid that it would never fade away. I returned to my cold, damp room and went to bed. I couldn't go to sleep for a long time.

As the month of November came to an end, stories of Korea were again in the papers. This time the talk was about the Chinese coming into the war. The cake baker joined our speculative discussions again. "Just wait," he would say, shaking his finger at us, and particularly at me. "You just wait; the time will come." And then the time he was apparently talking about came. Shortly after the Chinese attacked across the Yalu River, the American army was again in retreat. This time I chose to ignore the cake baker and his prophesies of doom. I admitted to myself that I didn't understand what was happening in Korea. I hardly knew where the place was, much less anything about its climate and topography. Still, I decided that my American army would somehow do the right thing, and prevail.

On Monday, November 27, I received a letter from Mutti instructing me to come to Fürstenfeldbruck not later than December 5. We had an appointment at the American consulate in Munich on the sixth. This time I would not return to Hannover. I was sorry to leave my baker friends. Herr Krampe I wouldn't miss much; he only looked at me as cheap labor. Maybe in America I could go to school again, I thought. That was what I wanted to do most. To learn more. That night I went to sleep with my blanket pulled over my head and with a vision of Leo's hometown. It was a town called Denver, and was nestled at the foot of the Rocky Mountains. Since that was where Leo was from, I imagined that we would be going there. I just knew Colorado was beautiful, and I couldn't wait to go.

I rose as usual at fifteen minutes before two in the morning. This time I felt excited, because I knew my ordeal in Herr Krampe's bakery was about to end. I decided to tell him the news about my leaving after most of the baking was done, at ten o'clock, when he usually left for the downtown store. When the time came, I was suddenly afraid. I knew that there was nothing he could do. But I was afraid of him screaming at me for breaking my contract. Punctually at ten, Herr Krampe took off his white apron, washed his hands under the cold-water tap across from the ovens, and wiped his hands on the towel hanging next to the sink. He proceeded to exit the bakery.

"Herr Krampe, please," I said, and I was surprised at how firm and strong my voice sounded, as if it had come from someone else, "could I have a minute of your time?" He was halfway to the door when he stopped in apparent surprise.

"Yes," he replied, "but be quick about it." I followed him out the door.

"*Ja?*" he asked.

"I received a letter from my mother yesterday," I said, looking him straight in the eyes. "She wants me to be in Munich by the sixth of December. We need to be at the American consulate to get our visas for America."

Herr Krampe looked at me calmly and then said, "I am not surprised. I expected something like that, though not quite so soon. So, you will leave here on the fifth of December, *Ja?*"

"*Ja,* Herr Krampe," I replied, relieved that the feared outburst had not occurred.

"Then let's get back to work," he said, almost kindly, as he turned to go. It felt as if a heavy weight had been lifted off my shoulders when the conversation ended. On the first Saturday in December, after I had completed my chores, I caught the train for Celle and then the narrow gauge to Trauen to say *auf Wiedersehen* to my dear grandparents Samuel. I couldn't leave Germany without seeing them and receiving their blessings for my long journey ahead. When I arrived at the Trauen station, I jumped off the train before it came to a full stop and ran all the way to the barracks. Both Oma and Opa Samuel were there.

Oma was puttering around the stove, while Opa was stacking wood. I kissed her on the cheek and hugged her, knowing that she would give me a scolding for ruffling her apron and her dress. Opa wore his old ski hat. His blue eyes smiled when he saw me; his cold pipe was clamped between his teeth. I hugged him and gave him a kiss on his stubbled cheek.

"My dear boy," Opa said through his teeth, never taking the pipe out of his mouth. His love for me was cradled in those few words. I smiled, looking at this brave, kind, and generous old man. He wore a blue, long-sleeved shirt, buttoned all the way to the top of his neck. He had probably learned to do it that way in the kaiser's army and had never buttoned his shirts any other way since. He had on his old, grey tweed jacket, with all three buttons buttoned, and his old grey pants, which showed no evidence of a crease ever having been there and which bulged at the knees from his frequent kneeling when he fetched wood from the barn. I had to turn away from these two wonderful people to keep them from seeing my emotions welling up in my eyes. Opa had noticed anyway.

"Tell me now, my boy, what brings you here today?" he said, pushing a chair in my direction. I sat down as he wanted me to. He always liked calling me "my boy." That was his way of telling me he loved me. I liked being called "my boy" by him; I would miss hearing him call me that. Oma stood watching from near the stove. "We are happy to see you so soon again," Opa continued, "but we are both surprised at the suddenness of your visit. Is it something good that brings you here?"

"Yes, Opa," I replied softly, trying hard to keep my voice from breaking,

"I am going to America." I shouldn't have had to choose between my mother and my dear grandparents, but life had put me in this position.

"Oh, my dear God," Oma said, starting to cry, "I will never see my dear Wolfgang again. First his father wanted to go to America. Now his son is leaving us." The tears ran down her hollow cheeks, and she bravely tried to wipe them away. I leapt off my chair and put my arms around her. This time she didn't protest when I pulled her close to me. She just let me hold her.

"No, Oma, I will be back to see both of you again many times. You are my dearest grandparents, and I can't imagine not seeing you again. Don't worry. I'll be back. At least I don't have to be a baker anymore," I said, trying to make light of the situation. Oma smiled through her tears.

Opa and I left the kitchen and walked to the barn, where we looked after the chickens. Another pig grunted in its stall, and I boxed him in the head and rubbed his back with a brush. He stood still and let me do it. Opa filled his basket with wood, and I carried it as we walked back together. I couldn't take my eyes off Opa's beard-stubbled face. That evening Oma, Opa, and I sat together in the kitchen after dinner, Opa at the end of the table smoking his pipe, I near the center with my chair turned toward him. Oma sat in her special chair, which she had pulled between the two of us. She listened to Opa and me talk about days long gone, days in Schlawe, times that seemed like only yesterday, or at most the day before. Oma leaned forward on her cane, its handle encircled by her swollen arthritic fingers. Around her head she wore a simple black cotton scarf, and a few strands of her salt-and-pepper hair hung down her pretty, smooth cheeks. She listened to us talk about those bygone days, and I could see in her watery eyes that she was back in Schlawe, in her beloved house and garden, remembering a little boy who was now leaving her forever, she believed, for a strange land called America.

It was late when I went to sleep in the old hospital bed. Oma was still puttering around near the stove, trying to grasp what was happening with her grandson. Before I left the next morning, Opa slipped me some money. "Go buy yourself something," he said with a cracking voice, and he patted me on the back. Then he went out to the barn. Oma prepared two salami sandwiches for my trip back to Hannover.

"Will you say *auf Wiedersehen* to my father for me?" I asked Oma, as she was busy fixing my sandwiches.

"Yes, of course, I will," she replied. "He doesn't come home regularly anymore from Munster. When I see him I will tell him that you came to say *auf Wiedersehen* to him." She handed me my sandwiches, carefully wrapped in wax paper. Then she said in a surprisingly firm voice, "Go now, my dear boy. May God bless you on your long journey. Write soon."

She walked out front with me, stopping at the corner of the barracks to watch me walk down the familiar path to the station. She held her cane in her right hand and leaned forward slightly as she waved *auf Wiedersehen* with her left. She waved until I was at the station. As the train pulled away from the platform, I saw her lonely figure still standing next to the barracks, resting on her walking stick. She raised her arm for a final wave. I was back in Hannover by early afternoon.

On Monday, December 4, 1950, I said *auf Wiedersehen* to my friends in the bakery. They told me that as soon as they had found out that my mother had married an American, they had known I wouldn't be staying much longer. I listened to what they had to say and smiled back at them. To my surprise, the cake baker came out of his room, wiping his hands ceremoniously on his white apron, which was smudged with flour and remnants of pastry dough. He took my right hand and shook it vigorously.

"I wish you much luck, my young friend," he said, looking me in the eyes. "And I hope that you will remember us now and then. Write us a letter and tell us about what you find in that America you love so much. We would like to know what it really is like over there. Have a good trip. And don't worry"—he turned back toward his room—"*your* American army in Korea will do just fine." I was surprised and taken aback by the sincerity of his comments. I thought that I had probably misjudged him; maybe he knew more about armies and war than I had thought. Maybe he had not always been a cake baker.

"*Auf Wiedersehen*," I said, as he passed through the door into his world of cakes and pastries. He didn't hear me anymore. The few possessions I had fit into my old cardboard suitcase. I packed Tuesday evening after work, and the next morning Herr Krampe took me to the train station in his odd-looking three-wheeled delivery truck. He shook my hand and wished me a good trip. Before I left that morning, Emma had fed me an extra-large plate of sandwiches. For a moment, her eyes had seemed watery. Then she grabbed my hand and said, "*Auf Wiedersehen und eine gute Reise nach Amerika.*" She then ran off to ready her wares to take to the downtown store.

Looking West

Frau Krampe had been her usual cool self, shaking my left hand with hers, smiling her built-in smile.

When Herr Krampe's truck had disappeared from view, I grasped my suitcase, straightened up, and resolutely walked toward the station. I am free, I said to myself out loud over and over again as I approached the station—I am free. I bought my one-way ticket to Fürstenfeldbruck and boarded the fast train that would take me as far as Munich. It was a nice December day. As the train carried me south the length of Germany, I felt as if I were traveling into a dream world. I was no longer a baker's apprentice. Over there in America a new life awaited me, new opportunities; maybe I could even go to school again. Over there was hope. I wondered if my feelings were similar to those of the thousands of German emigrants who had gone before me as they struck out for the New World. Surely they felt the same exhilaration that hope brought, the exhilaration of new opportunities imagined. Yes, they must have felt just as I did at that moment.

Since I had no chance to write Mutti about my arrival, I wasn't surprised to find no one waiting for me at the station. Fürstenfeldbruck was cold, and there was snow on the ground. I wore my new brown overcoat, the one I had bought in Hannover with the money Opa had given me. The coat was a size too large because that was all I could find, but it was warm, which was what really mattered. I could feel the spring in my steps as I took the familiar path to Frau Buck's house. When I knocked on the door, Frau Buck opened it and greeted me in her usual friendly manner. I shook her hand and followed her inside. I knocked on Mutti's door. Leo let me in. Both of their faces lit up when they saw me. I was welcome. I was finally home again. My mother, Leo, and I, we were a family.

Early the next morning, December 6, the three of us went to catch the train for Munich. We spent much time in the consulate, sitting on old, hard, wooden benches in dark waiting rooms. We filled out papers and had our pictures taken. I was ushered into a doctor's office—by myself. I sat there for a while on a chair by his desk until he entered the room. He looked down at the floor and said nothing as he walked toward me. Then, in German, he said, still not looking at me, "Please drop your pants and let me look at you." His German was perfect, without a trace of accent. His request shocked me into inaction. Perhaps I hadn't understood him correctly. I remained seated without moving a muscle or saying anything, hoping I had misunderstood him.

"Please get up," he repeated matter-of-factly, without any expression on his face, "and do drop your pants, including your underpants." This time I got up slowly, undid my belt, and unbuttoned the fly of my pants. Then, looking at him for encouragement but receiving none, I pulled down first my pants, dropping them on the floor, then my underpants. I stood there more embarrassed than I could recall ever having been in my entire life. The doctor approached and touched my genitals. He examined my penis with some care. Then he said, "I am finished, you may put your pants on again." I did as I was told. He washed his hands, went to his office door, and opened it. I left the room; Mutti went in next. I sat quietly next to Leo on the wooden bench in the waiting room. My English wasn't good enough to permit me to ask Leo any questions about what had just happened.

We went downstairs to a cafeteria for soup and sandwiches. I finally found a moment during lunch to tell Mutti about what had happened in the doctor's office. "Oh," she said with a laugh, putting her arm around my shoulders and pulling me toward her, "that can be embarrassing for a young boy. The doctor was only checking to see if you had venereal disease. He checked me, too. We are both fine."

We were issued a passport that afternoon with visas allowing us to enter the United States of America. I still couldn't believe it was happening; it had to be a dream. The passport had taken almost a year for Mutti and Leo to obtain. The booklet was colored an ugly frog green, and on the front, in gold capital letters in English, French, and German it read TEMPORARY TRAVEL DOCUMENT IN LIEU OF PASSPORT FOR GERMAN NATIONALS. I ran my fingers over the visas, which had been impressed on the page with a metal stamp. Imprinted in the paper was the eagle of the United States and the words "Consulate General of the United States of America, Munich, Germany." My mother's immigration visa number was 794, a low number, I thought. Written next to it was the word "nonquota." My number was 20,488, and it was annotated "quota." I didn't know what quota or nonquota meant, and I didn't care. With this document in my hand, I knew that now we could travel to the United States of America.

I had thought we would be leaving within days. That didn't happen. For some reason Leo had not yet received his travel orders. The month of December passed. On Christmas it started to snow in earnest, and Fürstenfeldbruck and the surrounding fields and forests were covered with a thick blanket of beautiful, fluffy white snow. The countryside looked like a picture postcard. I liked the natural beauty of Bavaria. Except for Munich, there was little destruction, in contrast to the north, where almost every town of any size seemed to have been bombed at one time or another or to have suffered from the fury of ground combat during the last weeks of war. In Bavaria it was easy to forget all that had happened—the war, the barracks, the hunger, the cold and the years of degradation.

On January 10, Leo came home with a beaming face and a sheaf of papers in his hands. He had his travel orders sending him and his new family to Bremerhaven on January 20 for subsequent movement by ship to the United States. That was what his written orders said. I read and reread that sentence several times, liking the sound of it. On Saturday, January 20, we said *auf Wiedersehen* to the Bucks. They had become close friends of Mutti's and Leo's. We took the slow train from Fürstenfeldbruck to Munich, where we changed to a waiting troop train to take us overnight to Bremerhaven. We were assigned a private compartment, just for the three of us, and beds in a sleeper car. At four o'clock in the afternoon, the train pulled out of the station. Since it was still light outside, I watched the damaged city glide by from my window in the dining car. I had never traveled in such luxury before, eating in a dining car with a waiter taking our orders.

After dinner we returned to our compartment. The creaking coach, the whoosh of the wind, the occasional hooting of the engine's whistle, and the clickety-clack of the wheels were soothing sounds. It was a train similar to the one we had taken from Sagan in January 1945 to escape to Berlin. This time there were no Russian tanks threatening or bombs being dropped or antiaircraft shrapnel bouncing off the roof of the car. I felt more secure than I had for the past six years of my life. I fell into a totally relaxing sleep without dreaming of anything. When I woke, I was stretched out alone on the upholstered bench of our compartment. The train was moving slowly, and it was dark outside. I looked up at the dim ceiling light, feeling an incredible sense of happiness. I closed my eyes again and went back to sleep.

We arrived in Bremerhaven early the next morning. At the station we were met by American army buses and, along with many other families, driven to a hotel in an army compound. There we were assigned two nicely furnished hotel rooms. Because I was fifteen years old, I had a room to myself, including my own bathroom. I threw myself on the bed and stretched out my arms and legs, for once totally unconstrained and happy. We ate our meals in a dining room for transiting families. We had a permanent table assigned where we ate breakfast, lunch, and dinner. Dinner was served by a friendly German waiter in a white coat who always carried a white linen towel over his left arm.

"Where are you going to?" he asked Mutti that first evening.

"Colorado," she replied.

"You will never want to leave Colorado once you get there," the waiter said to my great surprise. "It is such a beautiful land. I was there for over two years as a prisoner of war in a camp south of Denver, near Colorado Springs. I enjoyed every day of my imprisonment. Wait and see. You will just love it in Colorado." That certainly was encouraging news, and I smiled at Mutti. Maybe now she wouldn't worry anymore about Leo's brother and the way he and his family appeared to live in that basement house.

Our ship was the USS *Goethals*, a liberty ship sailing between the United States and Europe as a troop transport. We boarded on Wednesday, January 24, 1951, and were assigned a cabin amidship with other American families returning to the United States. Our area was roped off and had "off limits" signs posted for the troops who were quartered in the belly of the *Goethals*. I had never been on a ship before. Now I was going to cross a stormy ocean in the middle of winter. Once we had settled into our cabin, I excused myself from Mutti and Leo and went outside, over to the side rail to watch the troops coming on board. Hundreds of soldiers carrying duffel bags over their shoulders were boarding the ship. They stood patiently in two long lines, inching their way up narrow gangways into the belly of the ship. When all were on board, the gangways were unhooked and stowed on the dock. Then the dock became quiet.

It was late afternoon, and the sky was overcast with a low-lying blanket of grey clouds stretching from horizon to horizon, which was typical for north Germany this time of year. A light breeze blew off the water. I pulled my new overcoat tighter around myself. On the other side of the ship two tugs were pushing. I perceived that we were moving. There was a rumble within the ship; I could feel the engines through the wooden deck planks under my feet. On the pier below, several people were watching the ship pull away. One figure, a man, stood apart from the rest. He waved his right arm in a slow *auf Wiedersehen*. I looked around but saw no one else on deck. Only I was standing at the rail. I wondered who the man was waving to. I decided to wave back at him. Then he just stood there watching the ship pull away from the dock. The man wore an overcoat like my father's and a hat with the brim pulled toward his face, the way my father always wore his hat. Could it be my father? I couldn't tell. I was too high up and the ship was too far away from the dock. Maybe he had come to say *auf Wiedersehen* in his own way. He would do that. He had come to the Russian zone to get us in 1946. I looked again, and still there was no one else to be seen on deck. Mutti and Leo were in our cabin. I would stay on deck, I decided, until I couldn't see Germany anymore.

As the USS *Goethals* proceeded out to sea, the docks receded slowly; soon only a thin shoreline remained visible. I looked back at Germany, my country. I felt sadness. I was only fifteen years old, and I had never really had the opportunity to get to know the land of my ancestors. Now I was leaving. Only six years earlier I had been a happy boy living in a small, unimportant town in the east of Germany. Then suddenly the war was upon us. I lost my home, and my family broke apart. We became refugees, unwanted strangers in our own land. Everyone in my family lost their homes and possessions, their houses and farms were either destroyed or taken away. My grandfather Grapentin was beaten to death. My aunt and cousin were raped by Russian soldiers, and then Mutti's sister died of disease. My own mother was raped and shot, and had to sell her body to keep me and my sister alive. What was it my family had done to deserve such awful punishment? My grandmother Samuel appeared before my eyes, the way I remembered her when she stood near the barracks, waving at me as I walked toward the train station in Trauen. It was I, her grandson, who was going where her son had once wanted to go. This time she couldn't stop it, nor did she want to. *Amerika*, as she called it, was her family's destiny after all.

I tried hard to keep the shoreline in sight. It suddenly disappeared; only water and sea gulls floating across the horizon remained. The ship stopped briefly to discharge the pilot, who clambered down the side on a rope ladder and jumped into a pitching motorboat that had come to take him back to Bremerhaven. Then the USS *Goethals* strained mightily and moved swiftly into the lead-grey waters of the North Sea. The wind was cold, and I pulled my coat around my body. I stayed at the ship's railing until dark, until I could see no more and could only feel the movement of the ship as it headed out to sea, to the northwest. Tomorrow I would come back up on deck, I decided as I turned toward our cabin, to stand at the railing and look to the west. To look for my new country.

EPILOGUE

Oma and Opa Samuel did build a house again—not only one, but two, in a village called Elmpt, up against the Dutch-German border. The second, larger house my grandfather built for my father, Willi, and his second wife. Willi continued to work for the British at Royal Air Force station Brüggen, near Elmpt, until his retirement in 1977. He had two sons with his second wife, who divorced him for transgressions similar to those he had indulged in while married to my mother, Hedy. His third marriage also ended in divorce. Willi lived to be eighty-seven years old and is buried in the Elmpt cemetery alongside his parents, both of whom also attained the age of eighty-seven.

Hedy and Leo settled in Denver, Colorado, and in time built their dream house with a view of their beloved mountains. In the mornings, from her breakfast room, Hedy could watch the sun rise over the Great Plains. Then, in the evenings, she and Leo could watch it set behind the majestic, snow-capped peaks of the Rocky Mountains or see jets rising into the darkening sky from Stapleton Airport. From the time we came to this country in 1951 until her death, my mother and I never once spoke of the days of horror we had left behind. Leo loved Hedy deeply until the day he died, from lung cancer, at the young age of sixty-one. Hedy, who never came to terms with Leo's death, died of heart failure in 1986 at age seventy-two. They are both buried at Logan National Cemetery in Denver.

I will never forget Leo, a proud American soldier, lighting his cigarette and saying to a young German boy in tattered clothes, "My name is Leo Ferguson—call me Leo, please." That is my first clear memory of a man who changed my life forever and whom I loved without reservation. Hedy, my mother, who became my hero and friend, was a woman of boundless courage. She rose to the difficult challenges fate thrust upon her. *I will never forget Hedy*, a lone woman standing by the side of a rain-slicked, cobblestone road in April 1945, dressed in her finery, pleading with German troops fleeing a pursuing Russian army to save her small family.

As for me—my young mind had been deeply impressed by the men who flew airplanes, whether they were Ju-52s, B-17s or C-54 Skymasters. From my youngest days of watching airplanes pass overhead, I wanted to be one of those flyers. On the back of an old picture taken of me in 1943, when I was eight, my mother wrote, "He likes airplanes." So I did. In the summer of 1951, having been in the United States for only a few weeks and still groping to learn the language of my new country, I purchased a set of gold lieutenant bars in a pawnshop in Denver. The gold bars served as a goal, and I did what it took to earn them. I served in the United States Air Force for thirty years, first as an enlisted man and then as an officer, retiring in the grade of colonel in 1985. During the Cold War, I flew against the Soviet Union as an electronic warfare officer in RB-47H reconnaissance aircraft with the 55th Strategic Reconnaissance Wing. Every mission I flew against my former nemesis was a secret thrill; the more dangerous it was, the better I liked it. During the Vietnam War, I flew with the 355th Tactical Fighter Wing out of Takhli Royal Thai Air Force Base in Thailand, supporting F-105 fighters and B-52 strategic bombers in their raids on targets in Laos and North Vietnam. That war gave me none of the thrill I had felt as a young lieutenant and captain. I saw my brave friends die, their lives expended for no purpose. For me, as for many Americans of my generation, Vietnam was a heart-wrenching experience.

Education was something I had thirsted for as a boy subsisting in the ruins of my former country, Germany. My new country gave me all the education I could have dreamed of. Six months after my arrival in New York in February 1951, I entered East High School in Denver, graduating with my class in 1953. That was only possible through the generous help given me by dedicated teachers at the Emily Griffith Opportunity School in Denver, who diligently prepared me to enter East High that fall, as a high school junior. I eventually earned a B.S. degree from the University of Colorado and an M.B.A. from Arizona State University, and I spent a year as an Air Force Research Associate at the Center for International Studies at the Massachusetts Institute of Technology. As a U.S. Air Force exchange officer from 1973 to 1975, I attended the *Führungsakademie der Bundeswehr*, their leadership academy, in Hamburg, Germany, an institution whose lineage goes back to Scharnhorst and the *Kriegsakademie* in Berlin. One of its early students was a Prussian officer by the name of Klausewitz. Finally, in 1981, I attended the National War College at Fort Lesley J. McNair in Washington D.C., a college with as proud a history as the *Führungsakademie* and its predecessor, but one that was much more successful in training its officers to defend freedom and democracy.

After retirement from the air force in 1985, I worked for eight years as a program manager for E-Systems, now a division of Raytheon Corporation, until I retired again to devote my life to family and to writing. It may interest the reader to know that my son, Charles, who as a child accompanied me on many of my assignments in the United States and Germany, chose to follow in my footsteps. He, too, entered the air force, in 1985, and I had the privilege of swearing him in as a second lieutenant at Ohio State University. Charles went on to fly the A-10 Warthog from bases in England, Germany, Kuwait, and Italy. His last European assignment was the 52nd Tactical Fighter Wing at Spangdahlem Air Base, Germany, the same wing I had flown with when I was assigned there in the early 1970s. Charles now flies the A-10 with the Connecticut Air National Guard and is a pilot with United Airlines.

In the end what I remember most from this journey along my road of life are the people who held out a helping hand, and by doing so gave me life to live.

Epilogue